# Truth and Veridicality in Grammar and Thought

*Mood, Modality, and Propositional Attitudes*

ANASTASIA GIANNAKIDOU
& ALDA MARI

THE UNIVERSITY OF CHICAGO PRESS     CHICAGO AND LONDON

The University of Chicago Press, Chicago 60637
The University of Chicago Press, Ltd., London
© 2021 by The University of Chicago

All rights reserved. No part of this book may be used or reproduced in any manner whatsoever without written permission, except in the case of brief quotations in critical articles and reviews. For more information, contact the University of Chicago Press, 1427 E. 60th St., Chicago, IL 60637.

Published 2021

Printed in the United States of America
30 29 28 27 26 25 24 23 22 21     1 2 3 4 5

ISBN-13: 978-0-226-76320-0 (cloth)
ISBN-13: 978-0-226-76334-7 (paper)
ISBN-13: 978-0-226-76348-4 (e-book)
DOI: https://doi.org/10.7208/chicago/9780226763484.001.0001

Library of Congress Cataloging-in-Publication Data

Names: Giannakidou, Anastasia, author. | Mari, Alda, author.
Title: Truth and veridicality in grammar and thought : mood, modality, and propositional attitudes / Anastasia Giannakidou, Alda Mari.
Description: Chicago : University of Chicago Press, 2021. | Includes bibliographical references and index.
Identifiers: LCCN 2020037056 | ISBN 9780226763200 (cloth) | ISBN 9780226763347 (paperback) | ISBN 9780226763484 (ebook)
Subjects: LCSH: Truth. | Language and languages—Philosophy. | Sociolinguistics.
Classification: LCC BC171 .G45 2021 | DDC 401—dc23
LC record available at https://lccn.loc.gov/2020037056

TO OUR CHILDREN
*NICHOLAS* AND *ARIADNE*
*GIACOMO* AND *FLAVIO*

Ἁπλοῦς ὁ μῦθος τῆς ἀληθείας ἔφυ.
The language of truth is uncomplicated.
– Euripides

# Contents

Acknowledgments   xiii

Abbreviations   xvii

CHAPTER 1.   Truth, Veridicality, and Grammatical Mood   1
    1.1  What This Book Is About   1
    1.2  Truth and Veridicality   3
    1.3  Mood Selection in Complement Clauses: The Basic Pattern   10
        1.3.1  Mood Selection Patterns in Romance and Greek   11
        1.3.2  Attitudes and Modal Verbs: Strict Patterns   16
        1.3.3  Modal Expressions as *Antiknowledge* Markers   22
    1.4  Mood Flexibility   24
        1.4.1  Subjunctive of Negation   24
        1.4.2  Mood Choice in Relative Clauses   25
        1.4.3  Subjunctive in Questions   27
        1.4.4  Mood Shift in Italian Complement Clauses   28
        1.4.5  Doxastic Verbs in Portuguese   30
        1.4.6  Hopes, Promises, and Persuasions   32
        1.4.7  Verbs of Saying   33
        1.4.8  Factive Verbs   35
        1.4.9  Memory and Perception Verbs   37
    1.5  What Regulates Mood Choice?   39
        1.5.1  The Indicative: Veridicality and Commitment   39
        1.5.2  Our Thesis for the Subjunctive: Nonveridical Stance   43
    1.6  Road Map   46

CHAPTER 2. Modalization, Nonveridicality, and Commitment   51
2.1 Veridical Commitment   51
2.2 The Framework: Objective and Subjective Veridicality   56
  2.2.1 Objective (Non)veridicality, Semantic Tense   56
  2.2.2 Subjective Veridicality   57
  2.2.3 Subjective Nonveridicality   64
2.3 Modal Operators and the Subjunctive: Possibility   66
2.4 Epistemic Necessity: Nonveridicality with Bias   71
  2.4.1 MUST Is Incompatible with Knowledge   72
  2.4.2 MUST: Ideal and Non-Ideal Worlds   79
  2.4.3 Positive Bias of Necessity Modals   82
  2.4.4 Summing Up: (Non)veridicality, Bias, and Weakened Commitment   86
2.5 Necessity Modals and Positive Polarity   89
  2.5.1 Modal Spread   90
  2.5.2 MUST, the Adverb, and Negation   94
  2.5.3 Possibility and Nonveridical Equilibrium   99
  2.5.4 Manipulations of O by the Adverbs   101
2.6 Conclusion: Nonveridicality, Modalization, and Bias   104

CHAPTER 3. Mood and Tense in Complement Clauses   107
3.1 Greek Subjunctive in Main and Embedded Clauses   107
3.2 Morphological and Semantic Tenses in Greek   112
3.3 The Semantic NONPAST: Future Orientation   118
3.4 The Subjunctive and NONPAST   124
3.5 Subjunctive with a Lower PAST   128
3.6 Syntax-Semantics of Tense and Mood in Italian   131
  3.6.1 From Greek to Italian   131
  3.6.2 Mood and T in Complement Clauses   136
3.7 Temporal Constraints Imposed by the Selecting Verb   138
  3.7.1 Indicative Selecting Verbs: No NONPAST   138
  3.7.2 Subjunctive Verbs: NONPAST   141
3.8 Conclusions   144

CHAPTER 4. Solipsistic and Suppositional Belief   147
4.1 Veridical Belief and Doxastic Commitment   148
4.2 Solipsistic Doxastic Commitment: The Indicative   154

        4.2.1 Attitudes of Certainty, Opinion, Awareness, and
              Memory   154
        4.2.2 Attitudes of Thought and Opinion   158
        4.2.3 Dream and Fiction Attitudes   160
    4.3 Suppositional Belief and the Subjunctive   163
        4.3.1 Solipsistic and Suppositional Belief: Italian   165
        4.3.2 Nonveridical Epistemic Space with Suppositional
              Belief   166
        4.3.3 Summary: Typology of Doxastic Attitudes and
              Mood   171
    4.4 More Flexible Doxastics: Memory, Semblance,
        Perception   173
        4.4.1 Mood Flexibility with Memory Verbs   173
        4.4.2 Semblance Verbs   175
        4.4.3 Perception Verbs   178
        4.4.4 Summary: Doxastic Verbs, Modals, and the
              Subjunctive   181
    4.5 The Update Functions of Mood Morphemes   183
    4.6 Conclusions   188

CHAPTER 5. Bouletic Attitudes: Volition, Hope, Promising, and
           Persuasion   191
    5.1 Introduction   192
    5.2 WANT: Bouletic Commitment, Antifactivity   194
        5.2.1 Against Bouletic Preference as Subjunctive Trigger
              with WANT   197
        5.2.2 A New Semantics for WANT   200
    5.3 Hoping   204
    5.4 Promising   208
    5.5 Attitudes of Persuasion   211
    5.6 Verbs of Assertion   216
    5.7 The (Non)veridicality Theory of Mood Selection   220

CHAPTER 6. Ability Modals, Temporality, and Implicatives   225
    6.1 Core Patterns of Ability Modals and Implicatives   226
        6.1.1 Ability and Action   228
        6.1.2 Implicatives   231
    6.2 Ability Modality   234
        6.2.1 Some Background Notions   235

        6.2.2 ABLE and MUST: The Structure of the Ability Modal Base   236
        6.2.3 Zero Tense, Obligatory Control   240
    6.3 The Actuality Entailment: Previous Accounts   243
        6.3.1 Identification of Events across Worlds   246
        6.3.2 Action Dependent Abilities   249
        6.3.3 Actualistic Present Perfect   251
    6.4 New Account: Actualizing ABLE Is Scoping below PAST   252
        6.4.1 ABLE under PAST   252
        6.4.2 No Entailments When the Modal Is Not Agentive and Abilitative   255
        6.4.3 The Nonveridicality of the Modal with the Entailment   258
    6.5 Implicative Verbs and the Choice of Infinitive, Subjunctive   260
        6.5.1 The Puzzle from the Perspective of Greek and Italian   260
        6.5.2 Veridicality of Aspectual Operators: Actualization of an Event   264
        6.5.3 No Actualization with TRY   266
        6.5.4 MANAGE, *un*-TRY, and the Subjunctive   268
    6.6 Conclusions   270

CHAPTER 7. **Propositional Attitudes of Emotion: Gradability and Nonveridicality**   273
    7.1 Introduction: The Puzzles of Emotion Attitudes   274
    7.2 The Veridical Presupposition of Emotive Attitudes   281
    7.3 Gradability, Emotiveness, and Nonveridicality   285
        7.3.1 The Presupposition of Nonveridicality of the Emotive Space   285
        7.3.2 The Assertion of Emotives   288
    7.4 Attitudes of Awareness   289
    7.5 Presuppositional Indicative Complementizer *pu*   292
        7.5.1 Updates of Mood Morphemes and Their Sensitivity to (Non)veridicality Connected   293
        7.5.2 Knowledge, Memory, and Perception   295
    7.6 Attitudes of Fear   300
        7.6.1 Three Empirical Patterns   300
        7.6.2 The Semantics and Pragmatics of Fear   304
    7.7 Conclusions   308

CHAPTER 8. Epilogue: Truth and Veridicality in Grammar and Thought   309
    8.1 What We Found   309
    8.2 Veridical and Nonveridical Stance   310
    8.3 Mood Choice   312
    8.4 What Mood Flexibility Tells Us   314
    8.5 Anchoring, (Non)veridicality, and Informativity   316

References   321

Index   337

# Acknowledgments

This book is the result of an intellectual journey that started in 2012 when we met in Paris. We were, at the time, independently working on two related topics: the future tense, and actuality entailments of ability modals. It immediately became apparent that we were tracking the same phenomenon of nonveridicality and the role it played in the meaning of the future and modality in general. The impetus for our theory of epistemic modality comes from those initial discoveries, and in the years since we made it our mission to uncover how similar modality expressions and propositional attitudes are. In this book, we present an integrated and comprehensive framework where modals have counterparts in the attitudinal domain, and where mood is also a type of modality as well as a diagnostic for nonveridicality.

No great accomplishment is a singular act, and ours is no exception. We have been fortunate to have supportive colleagues that accompanied us in this intellectual journey. With their curious, knowledgeable and sometimes critical insights, our commentators have contributed to the growth of our theory, and for this we are extremely thankful. Anastasia spent several months at Institut Jean Nicod and taught there in 2013; Alda spent two years in Chicago to closely work on the project, from 2014 to 2016. During those times, we benefited from numerous discussions with colleagues and friends such as Claire Beyssade, Bridget Copley, Francis Corblin, Paul Egré, Salvador Mascareñas, François Recanati, Benjamin Spector (Paris), and Fabrizio Cariani, Katerina Chatzopoulou, Itamar Francez, Chris Kennedy, Jason Merchant, Patrick Muñoz, Sofia Sklaviadis, Eleni Staraki, and Malte Willer (Chicago). A special thanks from Alda to all the Chicagoans for making her feel at home, and likewise from Anastasia to the Paris crowd.

Parts of this material have also been presented at different stages of development in numerous colloquia, workshops, and conferences across the planet. We are very grateful to the audiences in Lisbon, Berlin, Thessaloniki, Brussels, Konstanz, Amsterdam, Northwestern University, Pisa, Neuchâtel, Geneva, Oslo, Caen, Paris-8, and Athens Georgia. In 2015 we cotaught a first version of our theory of modality in Barcelona at the ESSLLI summer school. Anastasia taught this material again in 2017 at the LOT summer school at the University of Leiden, and at a summer school at the University of Geneva in 2019. Many thanks in particular to Laura Baranzini, Kathryn Bove, David Blunier, Marion Carel, Elena Castroviejo-Miro, Pillar Chammoro, Ivano Ciardelli, Regine Eckardt, Hasmik Jivanian, Jack Hoeksema, Michail Kissine, Manfred Krifka, Pierre Larrivée, Sven Lauer, Ora Matushanski, Jacques Moeschler, Maribel Romero, Louis de Saussure, Henriette de Swart, Rui Marques, Andreas Trotzke, Hedde Zeijlstra. We are particularly thankful to Juan Uriagereka for following up with intriguing syntactic insights of our theory which we hope to pursue in future work.

Anastasia would like to thank Savvas Tsochatizidis for the invitation to give a seminar at the University of Thessaloniki in the spring of 2017 where the initial stages of the attitude material were presented. It was a fantastic experience to be able to discuss the Greek data in a class filled with native speakers of Greek, with vivid intuitions and great responses. Many thanks to Savvas, as well as Tasos Tsangalidis, for their comments and suggestions and their hospitality.

A special thanks to our dear friend and colleague Paul Portner, who has read carefully previous versions of our material and has offered generously his comments and sharp input that helped us push forward and expand the scope of our analysis.

We also both enjoyed interacting with Mingya Liu, who visited Chicago for several months in 2018 during which many key aspects of our theory were developed. We are very thankful to Thomas Grano for carefully reading parts of this manuscript and offering insights and challenges that helped us improve especially our analysis of volitional attitudes in chapter 5. We would also like to express our gratitude to Natalia Pavlou who worked efficiently and happily on the bibliography and helped us enormously with this time consuming task.

Last but not least, we want to thank the readers of the manuscript for the University of Chicago Press for their positive reception of our ideas and their most helpful comments and suggestions. We are also thankful to

Alan Thomas, Tamara Ghattas, and the editorial team at the University of Chicago Press for their diligent work in producing this book. A note of gratitude to Marta Steele for her assistance with the index.

This journey was not just intellectual, but also personal. A friendship was born in 2012, and has been growing deeper in all these years—for which we are grateful to one another. At the same time, through various Skype (yes, that was the pre-Zoom world!) conversations and full days of writing, we knew that we could dive deep and free into our thinking only because we could rely on the caring love of our husbands Jason and Pascal: wizard syntactician and enchanting probabilist respectively, superbly smart and patient to support us intellectually but also daily for the smaller, yet equally essential, things.

Finally, above anything else, we want to thank our amazing and wise children: Nicholas Demetrios and Ariadne, Giacomo and Flavio. *Without their light and smile, nothing.* This book is dedicated to them, with our love and gratitude for giving us the precious gift of being their sometimes distracted but always adoring mothers.

# List of Abbreviations in the Glosses

| | |
|---|---|
| AUX | auxiliary |
| COND | conditional |
| FCI | free choice item |
| FUT | future |
| GERUND | gerund |
| IMPF | imperfective |
| IND | indicative |
| MOD | modal |
| NONPAST | nonpast |
| NPI | negative polarity item |
| OPT | optative |
| PAST | past |
| PART | participle |
| PERF | perfect |
| PFV | perfective |
| PL | plural |
| PRES | present |
| PROG | progressive |
| PROSP | prospective |
| SG | singular |
| SUBJ | subjunctive |

CHAPTER ONE

# Truth, Veridicality, and the Problem of Grammatical Mood

This book is about how the concepts of truth, knowledge, and, broadly speaking, belief are reflected and codified in the grammar of natural languages. Does language directly access the world (what is true), or does it do so via semantic representations of the world categories?

The question of truth has a venerable historical pedigree, a long intellectual history that originates, in the Western world, in classical Greek thought. Aristotle pioneered what can be understood as the modern *empiricist* view, namely that we can apply the fundamental principles of logic, systematic observation, and analysis to identify the truth in natural things and explain causes, i.e., why things occur. Plato's idealism holds that observation of the natural world might actually be misleading; only philosophical contemplation can lead to truth. They both agree that truth lies at the foundation of what it means to think and analyze. Contemporary formal semantics and philosophy of language are *truth conditional*, which means that they continue in this tradition.

## 1.1 What This Book Is About

Since analytical contemplation is mediated by language, an additional layer of issues arises about language, specifically about whether and how language mediates to express thinking about the world. Natural languages vary in the vocabulary, form, and grammatical categories they realize; yet in addressing the question of language and thought, most Continental philosophy overlooks this striking variation and almost exclusively focuses on English. This focus affects negatively the set of data deemed relevant for analysis, and in effect diminishes, not to say dismisses, the role of linguistic diversity in revealing aspects of the logic needed in order to handle accurately and successfully the central questions of truth and knowledge.

In this book, we will explore the interaction between truth, knowledge, and *veridicality* as they interact in the grammatical phenomenon of mood choice (subjunctive, indicative) in European languages. Our main illustrators will be Standard Modern Greek and the Romance language family, with specific emphasis on Italian and French. Mood choice is a multidimensional phenomenon, as we shall see, involving interactions between syntax, semantics, and pragmatics; and raises a number of issues that are literally invisible if we pay attention only to English simply because Modern English lacks the morphological category of mood in embedded clauses. Despite this absence, terms such as "subjunctive" and "indicative" continue to be routinely used by philosophers, e.g., in the discussion of English conditionals, often misleading us to think that we are dealing with a mood phenomenon. (We are not. Indicative and subjunctive conditionals are really about tense.)

On the other hand, mood has been studied by traditional grammarians as a mainly morphosyntactic phenomenon, and in this tradition very little attention is paid to the semantics of propositional attitude verbs which are responsible for regulating mood choice. Traditional analyses are mostly interested in taxonomies and labeling of the verbal classes, with reference to *realis* and *irrealis* to cover the semantics of modal verbs (*must, may, can* etc.) and propositional attitude verbs (such as *know, believe, remember, want, persuade* and the like). The intuition is that somehow the indicative signals that the sentence is *true (realis)*, whereas the subjunctive signals that the sentence is *untrue (irrealis)*, thus implying that language directly accesses reality. This, however, as we will show, is an unwarranted assumption. Language, it will turn out, mostly encodes *subjective* representations of truth and reality construed by linguistic agents, i.e., the speaker or the subject of the attitude verb. In forming these representations, linguistic agents build *veridicality stances*, i.e., subjective judgments toward the propositional content of sentences. Crucially, we will argue, it is veridicality stances that regulate, for the most part, mood choice. We must admit, then, that language accesses reality mostly indirectly via subjective veridicality, and not directly via objective truth.

The semantics of modal expressions and propositional attitude verbs is a privileged landscape within which to observe how systematic the formation of the veridicality judgement is in the grammar of human language. Speakers rely on their own conceptualization of reality, through language, in the attempt to structure possibilities according to their knowledge, beliefs, memories, expectations, desires, and priorities. Across modal verbs, adverbs, and propositional attitude verbs, language reveals that humans anchor reality not only to truth but to their own subjective understanding of truth. Contrary to given wisdom, we will offer a unified perspective on linguistic modality and propositional attitude verbs by showing that they are quite similar. They differ in what kind of linguistic anchor they have—the speaker for modality expressions, but the attitude subject for propositional attitudes—but the logic of, and constraints in, reasoning with modals and attitudes are essentially the same.

An important aspect, often overlooked, is the interaction between the attitude and modal meaning with the tense of the embedded complement. Because of emphasis on English, research has tended to focus on the finiteness distinction, i.e., the *that* versus *to* contrast. We will see that studying only this contrast prevents us from understanding that the actual culprit of many apparent meaning shifts in propositional attitudes is the tense of the complement. We will distinguish between veridical tense (the past and present) and nonveridical tense which is what we will call *nonpast*. We will show that this simple dichotomy helps substantially in uncovering dimensions in the meaning of the embedding attitudes—and it determines fully the kinds of readings speakers extract with modal verbs and attitudes.

Let us start by laying out an intuitive understanding of the foundational ideas of truth and veridicality. This will allow us to ease into the phenomenon of mood, which will be our window into the study of how linguistic categories mediate in the construction of truth.[1]

## 1.2 Truth and Veridicality

Since its central role in classical Greek thinking, truth has been essential in the study of linguistic meaning and has also been the foundation of axiomatization in modern scientific thought. Aristotle gives a well-known definition of truth in his *Metaphysics* (1011b25): "To say of what is that it

---

[1]. In referring to attitude verbs, modal verbs and auxiliaries, and the meaning family independent of specific language, we will use upper case, italics for expressions in a specific language, and roman for English translations.

is not, or of what is not that it is, is false, while to say of what is that it is, and of what is not that it is not, is true." Very similar formulations can be found in Plato (Cratylus 385b2, Sophist 263b).

The Aristotelian truth serves as the foundation for the modern approach to truth—advocated by Russell, Moore, and Tarski in the early 20th century—known as the *correspondence theory* of truth. Truth consists in a direct relation of a sentence to reality: the sentence *Snow is white* is true if and only if snow is white. This well-motivated understanding is central to natural language semantics, and is associated with metaphysical realism that acknowledges *objective* truth. Objective truth correlates with *fact* but also with *time*: simple positive present and past sentences such as *Ariadne arrived in Paris last night, Ariadne is eating breakfast right now*, are true or false objectively, which means that the sentences, if true, denote facts of the world. Future sentences, on the other hand, such as *Ariadne will go to Paris next week* are objectively false at the time of utterance (since they have not happened yet), but could or must be true—depending on the strength of prediction—at a future time.

In addition to the present/past versus future distinction, consider the contrast between an unmodalized and a modalized sentence:

(1) a. It rained in Chicago (yesterday).
    b. It is raining in Chicago.
    c. It may be raining in Chicago.
    d. It must be raining in Chicago.

Only the present and past sentences can be understood as factual. The modal sentences, even the one with *must*, do not make reference to actual facts. They do not entail that it is raining.

In formal logic, a sentence $S$ is true iff the valuation function $V$ assigns to the proposition $p$ that $S$ denotes the value true. Veridicality is therefore defined as the semantic property of linguistic expressions, or more generally functions $F$, that are truth-bearing. Following Zwarts (1995) and Giannakidou (1994, 1998, 1999, 2013b), a function $F$ that takes a proposition $p$ as its argument is veridical if $Fp$ entails that $p$ is true, and nonveridical if it doesn't entail that:

(2) Veridicality: A function $F$ is veridical iff $Fp$ entails $p$.

(3) Nonveridicality: A function $F$ is nonveridical iff $Fp$ does not entail $p$.

Thus, a function $F$ is veridical if it is truth entailing, and nonveridical if it is not truth entailing. Past and present tense and adverbials, for instance, denote veridical functions: *It rained in Chicago (yesterday)* entails that it rained in Chicago. Modal expressions, on the other hand, denote nonveridical functions: *It may be raining in Chicago* and *It must be raining in Chicago* do not entail that it is raining. Veridicality is objective in both cases, and depends on whether the adjacent $p$ is a fact of the world, in which case $F$ is veridical, or not, in which case $F$ is nonveridical. Veridical functions are in this view factual or, as they are sometimes called, *factive*. Veridicality, therefore, understood in reference to truth, is the formal counterpart of the traditional *realis* that we mentioned earlier.

Veridicality has also been understood in relation to the existence of entities in the world (Montague 1969). Montague characterized direct perception verbs such as *see* as veridical because *I see a unicorn* entails that a unicorn exists. Giannakidou (2013a) establishes a connection between truth and existence in her study of mood choice in relative clauses. Labels such as "veridicity" (Karttunen 2005) and "veracity" have also been used to refer to veridicality as a property that relates to truth. The term "veridicality" has been used also in psychology and cognitive science, somewhat more broadly, but still anchored to the real, external world. In cognitive science, for instance, "veridicality" refers to the degree to which an internal representation of the world accurately reflects the external world. In psychology, "veridical perception" is the direct perception of stimuli as they exist.

Linguistic agents do not simply assign true or false to sentences, but engage in a more complex *judgment* about the veridicality of sentences. They appear to form subjective stances toward the propositional content. Paul Grice in his classic paper *Logic and Conversation* established Quality as one of the foundational principles of cooperative conversation: rational cooperative interlocutors continuously make assumptions about each other's beliefs and intentions, i.e., about what each believes, knows, or expects to be true. In making these assumptions, interlocutors form judgments about veridicality and intentions that include one's mental states of knowing, believing, remembering, and the like.

A major goal in this book will be to unpack under what conditions a linguistic agent chooses to use a modal or a propositional attitude verb, and what mood choice reveals about the attitude and the modal meaning. To start with, consider verbs of belief:

(4) Ariadne believes that Milan is the capital of Italy.

That Milan is the capital of Italy is objectively false; however, the speaker can use this sentence to report Ariadne's contested belief, and in Greek, the speaker would have to use the indicative mood, designated below by the mood particle *oti*, which in Greek surfaces as a complementizer element (equivalent to *that*). The Greek subjunctive particle *na* is, crucially, excluded:

(5) I    Ariadne pistevi              oti/*na       to  Milano ine i
    the Ariadne believe.PRES.3sg that.IND/SUBJ the Milan  is   the
    protevousa tis       Italias.
    capital      the.GEN Italy.GEN
    Ariadne believes that Milan is the capital of Italy.

The fact that indicative and not subjunctive is used to convey this obviously false belief indicates that, despite what the speaker knows to be the case, when it comes to mood selection, grammar forces Ariadne to lay claim to the veridicality of her belief, and forces the speaker to follow suit, *regardless* of relation to actual truth.[2] The selection of indicative with belief and doxastic verbs is observed not just in Greek but seems to be the rule in most Romance languages (with the exception of Italian, which we discuss extensively in the book, and also some varieties of Portuguese and Spanish).

Indicative extends further to other fictional classes such as attitudes of dream, imagination, and deception:

(6) I    Ariadnie onireftike   oti/*na       to  Milano ine i
    the Ariadne  dreamt.3sg that.IND/SUBJ the Milan  is   the
    protevousa tis       Italias.
    capital      the.GEN Italy.GEN
    Ariadne dreamed that Milan is the capital of Italy.

(7) I    Ariadne ksejelastike/       fantastike    oti/*na        to
    the Ariadne was.deceived.3sg/ imagined.3sg that.IND/SUBJ the
    Milano ine i    protevousa tis         Italias.
    Milan  is   the capital       the.GEN Italy.GEN
    Ariadne was deceived/imagined that Milan is the capital of Italy.

---

2. See also Morency and de Saussure (2008), who argue that whether a speaker commits to a content embedded as a report is entirely pragmatic.

The use of indicative in fictional contexts and with doxastic verbs to convey objectively false beliefs forces us to distinguish truth—as a matter of fact—from the subjective construct of veridicality judgment, where truth is assessed relative to the internal cognitive states of linguistic agents. The need to appeal to "relative truth" for mood choice has long been acknowledged since McCawley's (1981) and Farkas' (1985, 1992) work in the eighties and early nineties. Building on these pioneering works, Giannakidou (1994, 1997, 1999, 2009) used the expressions *relativized veridicality* and *individual anchor* to refer to the speaker or the attitude holder, i.e., the subject of the main sentence, as the two main anchors.[3]

Embedded sentences of attitude reports, we will argue in this book, create subcontexts that are by default anchored to the attitude holder, since it is this individual's attitude that is being reported. With the exception of factive and what we will define here as *antifactive* attitudes (corresponding to the desiderative meaning of WANT), doxastic verbs such as the English *believe* and Greek *pistevo* are not objectively but subjectively veridical: the attitude holder is committed to the truth of the embedded sentence. The speaker might know the sentence to be actually false, but this is, apparently, irrelevant for indicative mood. The indicative, therefore, depends not on objective veridicality, but on *subjective* veridicality, built as a representation of the world by the attitude holder.

Subjective veridicality, as we just said, is very naturally understood as the speaker's *commitment* to the truth of $p$, irrespective of what actually holds in the world. When the world becomes relevant for mood choice, as we will show, it does so only via knowledge.

Before we move further into the the problem of mood choice, we want to give the reader an idea of how far-reaching the notion of veridicality, in both its forms, is for the study of grammar. Another linguistic dependency where we see the relevance of veridicality is the distribution of polarity items such as negative polarity items (NPIs) and free choice items (FCIs). Both phenomena have been discussed extensively in previous work (Giannakidou 1994, 1997, 1998, 2001, 2011), we will therefore

---

3. Other individuals might also have opinions about the truth of sentences, e.g., the hearer or multiple hearers in the audience. What the hearer knows plays an indirect role in truth assessment, mostly in terms of what the speaker assumes to be part of the common ground, i.e., the knowledge shared among conversation participants. Common knowledge does not seem to affect the choice of indicative mood, but we will discuss its role when relevant.

not expand on details here. But it is important to show the connection because we will see that crucial aspects of the polarity vocabulary will be used in our analysis of mood, and for good reasons.

NPIs and FCIs, like mood morphemes, are limited distribution expressions. They appear in nonveridical contexts only. Veridical past and present sentences block NPIs and FCIs. We give here examples with the English word *any*, which has both NPI and FCI uses:[4]

(8) a. Did Ariadne eat any cookies?
    b. Any student can solve this problem.
    c. Ariadne didn't eat any cookies.
    d. Ariadne will eat any cookies.
    e. Any complains must be addressed to the manager.

(9) a. *Ariadne ate any cookies.
    b. *Ariadne is eating any cookies right now.
    c. *Ariadne believes that she ate any cookies.

As we see, *any* is excluded from the veridical past and present sentences, as well as from the subjectively veridical BELIEVE sentence. NPIs and FCIs, instead, require the presence of higher nonveridical operators such as modal verbs, the future, negation, and the question operator. These are all not-truth entailing in the objective as well as in the subjective sense, as we will show. Negation, importantly, can be understood as the logical strengthening of objective nonveridicality from *not entailing p* to *entailing not p*. Following Giannakidou (1998), we call this *antiveridicality*:

(10) Antiveridicality: A function $F$ is antiveridical iff $Fp$ entails $\neg p$.

It is obvious that antiveridicality is a subcase of nonveridicality, since if $Fp$ entails $\neg p$, it also does not entail $p$. Polarity items appear in the scope of nonveridical and antiveridical functions $F$, and, following standard practice, the dependency of NPIs is stated as a scope condition in terms of *licensing*:

---

4. Languages tend to distinguish empirically between NPIs and FCIs, and both appear in the contexts above (see extensive typological data in Haspelmath (1997) and Giannakidou (2001, 2011) for an overview.

(11) *Nonveridicality thesis for NPIs/FCIs* (Giannakidou 1994, 1997, 1998; Zwarts 1995):
An expression $F$ licenses NPIs and FCIs in its scope iff $F$ is nonveridical.

Licensing is a relation between a higher element, i.e., negation, the question operator, or a modal, which is called the "licencer" in the literature, and which has a semantic property that is needed for the "licensee" (i.e., the NPI and FCI) to appear. Licensing has been proposed as a condition on the semantics of the licenser: if an expression $F$ is nonveridical, $F$ will be able to license NPIs or FCIs. It can also be understood as a condition on the licensee: when we see an NPI or an FCI, we know that the context is nonveridical because it is in the scope of a nonveridical operator $F$. Giannakidou (1997) schematizes the concept of licensing as follows:

(12) NPI Licensing (Giannakidou 1997):
$R(\beta, \alpha)$; where R is the scope relation, $\alpha$ is the polarity item, and $\beta$ is a negative or nonveridical expression which serves as the licenser.

Licensing requires that the NPI $\alpha$ be in the scope of $\beta$. R is a scope relation, and as such it is both a semantic relation—a matching relation of semantic and morphological features (Giannakidou 1997, Zeijlstra 2004)—and a syntactic relation, specifically c-command (as it appears in various NPIs in Greek, Romance NPIs, and in many other languages).[5] Nonveridicality allows unification of negative and nonnegative polarity contexts as a natural class, something that no previous theory of polarity could afford.

There is much to be gained by the generalization that negation, nonveridicality, and modality form a natural class. It takes little attention to notice that the semantically driven syntactic dependency of NPIs is similar to the problem of restricted mood distribution that we will tackle. We will argue, in fact, echoing earlier formulations (Giannakidou 1997, 1998, 2009; Quer 2001, 2009, and references therein) that the two phenomena are closely related, and that the mood morphemes are subject to licensing by nonveridicality in a way similar to NPIs.

Let us now focus on the empirical puzzles of mood.

---

5. Individual distributions of various NPI and FCI paradigms can of course differ, but NPIs and FCIs will always be in the scope of nonveridical operators.

## 1.3 Mood Selection in Complement Clauses: The Basic Pattern

Mood selection is the case where a propositional attitude verb embeds a complement that needs to appear in a particular grammatical form, traditionally called mood. Mood is a morphological category. Indicative, subjunctive, and imperative are all grammatical moods.

While the imperative is selected in main clauses and occurs in all European languages, whether a language grammaticalizes mood distinctions in embedded clauses and to what extent is subject to crosslinguistic variation. Greek, Italian, Spanish, Catalan, Serbian, Romanian, and French systematically distinguish mood in embedded clauses (i.e. complement, adjunct, and relative clauses), but English doesn't.

English does have a form that traditional grammar labels "subjunctive", but its use is limited, and it is almost never obligatory. We find it in clauses after verbs such as *require, wish*, and in the conditional protasis (see Portner 1997, 2018 for recent discussion). Crucially, the so-called subjunctive form is identical to a past or bare infinitive.

(13) a. The Dean requires that we be/are on time.
b. I wish you were here.
c. If I were rich I would buy a boat.
d. Eat your vegetables!

What is labeled as "subjunctive" is not a designated grammatical form specific to this category; the same can be said for the English imperative, as can be seen. Morphologically, we see past tense and a bare infinitive; and while the imperative does have certain properties that grant it the status of independent mood (see Potsdam 1997 for syntactic arguments), it does not appear in embedded nonquotative contexts. The English "subjunctive", furthermore, is quite limited to a handful of verbs, and it is not obligatory. We do not, in other words, find a systematic and productive pattern of subjunctive vs. indicative choice in embedding in English. It is therefore accurate to say that English lacks productive mood choice in embedded sentences; instead, English distinguishes between finiteness (*that*) and nonfiniteness (*to, -ing*) in complements, a correlation that we will discuss in this book.

Greek, Latin, and its descendent Romance languages, on the other hand, employ the grammatical category of mood in a number of productive patterns with propositional attitude verbs—but also with adjunct clauses, specifically those meaning BEFORE and WITHOUT:[6]

(14) Prin na/*oti vreksi, as pame spiti.
before that.SUBJ/IND rain.3sg, OPT go.1pl home
Before it rains, let's go home.

(15) Andiamo a casa prima che piova.
go.IMP.1pl to home before that rain.SUBJ.3sg
Let's go home before it rains.

(16) Ekane tin metafrasi xoris na/*oti xrisimpopiisi
did.3sg the translation without that.SUBJ/IND use.3sg
leksiko.
dictionary
He did the translation without using a dictionary.

The mood pattern is systematic, as we see: the indicative particles cannot be used, the connectives meaning BEFORE and WITHOUT are therefore said to *select* subjunctive complements.

### 1.3.1 Mood Selection Patterns in Romance and Greek

Regarding the subjunctive versus indicative contrast in complement clauses, observe the basic contrast, now in French and Italian:

(17) a. Marc sait que le printemps est/ *soit arrivé
Marc knows that the spring be.IND.3sg/ SUBJ.3sg arrived
Marc knows that spring has arrived.
b. Marc veut que le printemps soit/*est long.
Marc wants that the spring be.SUBJ.3sg/IND.3sg long.
Marc wants spring to be long
c. Le printemps est/*soit arrivé.
The spring be.IND.3sg/SUBJ.3sg arrived
The spring has arrived.

---

[6]. In the book, we will employ uppercase letters to designate the abstract meaning of actual words: BEFORE, e.g., is the abstract meaning of temporal connectives such as English *before*, Greek *prin*, and Italian *prima*. Lowercase italics will always refer to the actual words in the various languages, as we said earlier.

(18) a. Marco sa    che la  primavera è/*sia           arrivata
       Marco knows that the spring   be.IND.3sg/SUBJ.3sg arrived.
       Marc knows that spring has arrived.
    b. Marco vuole che la  primavera sia/*è           lunga.
       Marco wants that the spring   be.SUBJ.3sg/IND.3sg long
       Marc wants spring to be long.

The verb of knowledge *savoir* (*know*) is said to select the indicative, but the volitional verb *vouloir* (*want*) selects the subjunctive. The indicative is the default mood of unembedded sentences, as indicated. This is a typical pattern in all European languages; and in the cases above, the mood morphemes are in complementary distribution, i.e., one mood excludes the other.[7]

In French and most Romance languages the mood exponent appears on the verb, like tense and aspect. This was also the case in Ancient Greek. In contrast, mood can be realized outside the verbal form in the subordinating particle, i.e., the complementizer. The mood contrast in contemporary Greek is of that kind, as we mentioned already. All dialects of Greek have mood particles (*oti, na*), from Pontic Greek (spoken at the region of Pontos on the Black Sea), to Cypriot Greek (Sitaridou 2014; Pavlou 2018; and references therein), to Griko, i.e., the Greek dialect spoken in Southern Italy (Lekakou and Quer 2016). Balkan languages including Romanian exhibit similar particle subjunctives (Farkas 1985; Rivero, 1994; Terzi, 1997; Giannakidou 1998, 2009, 2011, 2016; Roussou 2009, Bulatovic 2008; Todorovic 2012; among others).

Modern Greek has four mood particles that precede the tensed verb: three indicatives *oti, pos, pu*, and the subjunctive particle *na*, which appear with modals. The difference between *oti* and *pos* is stylistic, so we will not

---

[7] Though the indicative-subjunctive pattern has been most extensively described in Indo-European languages, it is by no means restricted to these. It appears in many of the world's languages, including Native American languages (see a recent article by Matthewson 2010 for Salish, and Wiltschko 2016). The contrast between subjunctive and indicative also correlates with evidentiality, especially in languages that have only one indirect evidential morpheme (Murray 2016; Smirnova 2013).

make much of it here. The difference with *pu*, however, is important: *pu* appears to be used with factive complements only, as is illustrated below with an emotive factive verb.

(19) O  Pavlos kseri          oti/pos/pu/*na           efije    i
     the Paul  know.PRES.3sg that.oti.IND/pu.IND/SUBJ left.3sg the
     Roxani.
     Roxani
     Paul knows that Roxanne left.

(20) O  Pavlos lipate          pu/*oti/*na              efije
     the Paul  be-sad.PRES.3sg that.pu.IND/*oti.IND/SUBJ left-3sg
     i    Roxani.
     the Roxani
     Paul regrets that Roxanne left.

(21) O  Pavlos pistevi         oti/pos/*na       efije  i   Roxani.
     the Paul  knowPRES.3sg that.IND/SUBJ left.3sg the Roxani
     Paul knows that Roxanne left.

(22) Thelo     na/*oti        kerdisi           o  Janis.
     want.1sg that.SUBJ/IND win.NONPAST.3sg the John
     I want John to win.

(23) Prepi/bori        na/*oti        kerdisi           o  Janis.
     must.3sg/may3.sg that.SUBJ/IND win.NONPAST.3sg the John
     John must win./John may win.

*Pu* is also the complementizer used to introduce relative clauses, as we will see later, and in this case it might co-occur with *na*.

There is, in addition, an optative particle *as* used in main clauses only. The optative gets a wish-like, soft invitation interpretation. The subjunctive is also used in main clauses and gets a similar reading:

(24) As/Na     fiji/                  efevge             o  Janis!
     OPT/SUBJ leave.NONPAST.3sg leave.IMPRF.3sg the John
     Let John leave! / I wish John had left!

(25) Thelo na/*as fiji o Janis.
    want.1sg that.SUBJ/OPT leave.NONPAST.3sg the John
    I want John to leave.

In contrast to the subjunctive, however, as we see, the optative cannot embed. These main clause uses are associated with non-assertive illocutionary force, and we will come back to this point.

Mood choice has been a central issue in semantics, both formal and descriptive. Since this book is not a historical overview, and because a lot of the history on the topic has been addressed in previous works—including Portner's (2018) recent rather comprehensive survey—we will not attempt a general overview here (see also earlier overview discussions in Farkas 1982, 2003; Villalta 2008; Quer 2009; also Portner and Rubinstein 2012; Smirnova, 2012; Giannakidou 1994, 1998, 1999, 2009, 2011, 2016 specifically for Greek; Marques 2004, 2010 for Brazilian and European Portuguese; Mari 2016a, 2017a, b for Italian; Quer 1998, 2001, for Catalan and Spanish; Sarigul 2015 for Turkish; Baunaz 2015 for French; Abraham 2020 for German).

Often a distinction is made between verbal mood and sentential mood (Portner 2009), with sentential mood referring to the imperative which contributes non-assertive illocutionary force. However, Greek allows us to see that such a distinction is not essential, as the mood exponent in embedding appears on the C head without any change in illocutionary force. Certainly for embedding illocutionary force appears irrelevant.

One of the recurring characterizations of the subjunctive mood is that it is *dependent*, as opposed to the indicative which is said to be independent, and is the mood par excellence of unembedded assertions. As Giannakidou (2009: 1883) notes: "A corollary of this distinction renders the subjunctive usable only in complement clauses of verbs that share a particular semantic characteristic, and which select the subjunctive. In its strong form, the dependency thesis is not mere selection by a higher predicate, but claims that the subjunctive is *triggered* by certain semantic properties of the embedding context, pretty much the way polarity items (PIs) are triggered by their licensers; the subjunctive can thus be viewed as a PI of some kind."

Mood choice and polarity phenomena, as we noted before, are indeed similar in being syntactic dependencies that are motivated semantically. As with NPIs, the distributions of mood morphemes are constrained and regulated by semantic properties of the higher structure. In both cases, the semantic property that plays the key role is (non)veridicality. The connection is further observed below, where we see that polarity item licensing happens in subjunctive clauses, but not in indicative ones, an observation first made in Giannakidou (1994):

(26) *O Pavlos pistevi oti idhe kanenan/ opjondhipote.
 the Paul believe.3sg that.IND saw.3sg NPI/FCI
 *Paul believes that he saw anybody.

(27) *Kseri oti agorasa kanena/opjodhipote aftokinito.
 know.3sg that.IND bought.1sg NPI/FCI car
 *He knows that I bought any car.

(28) I Ariadne tha ithele na milisi me
 the Ariadne would like.3sg that.SUBJ talk.1sg with
 opjondhipote/kanenan fititi.
 FC/NPI student
 Ariadne would like to talk to any student.

(29) I Ariadne bori na milise me
 the Ariadne can that.SUBJ talked.3sg with
 opjondhipote/kanenan fititi.
 FC/NPI student
 Ariadne might have talked to any student.

We see here that NPIs and FCIs are blocked in the indicative complements but are allowed in subjunctive complements. Notice also that the contrast holds in English too, and correlates with the *that* vs. *to* difference. NPIs, FCIs, and the subjunctive appear to depend on the presence of a higher expression to "license" them.

Some basic questions arise at this initial stage. Why would a language exhibit dependencies such as mood and polarity? Why would Greek, French and Italian employ mood in complements and adjuncts, whereas English doesn't? Similar questions arise with other verbal categories such as tense and agreement. Why would one language mark tense or agreement whereas another one would not? What is gained by having tense and agreement?

We will investigate closely a number of propositional attitude meanings and show that the mood patterns are instrumental in uncovering dimensions in the meaning that necessitate the subjective constructs of the veridical and nonveridical stances mentioned earlier. Mood marking, in our theory, emerges as a grammaticalization of subjective (non)veridicality, pretty much the way tense is a grammatical reflex of the notion of time, and agreement a grammatical reflex of the notion of person.

*1.3.2 Attitudes and Modal Verbs: Strict Patterns*

We talk about "strict" selection when the mood is fixed and cannot vary. Flexible patterns, on the other hand, are observed when mood can be variable. Let us summarize the strict patterns. In Greek and Italian we observe the following:

(30) Indicative selecting verbs in Greek:
   a. fiction verbs: *onirevome* (dream), *fandazome* (imagine)
   b. doxastic verbs: *pistevo* (believe), *nomizo* (think), *theoro* (consider), *vrisko* (find), *katalaveno* (understand)
   c. epistemic and emotive verbs: *ksero, gnorizo* (know), *metaniono* (regret), *xairome* (be glad)
   d. assertives: *leo* (say), *dhiavazo* (read), *isxirizome* (claim), *dilono* (declare, assert)
   e. memory verbs: *thimame* (remember)
   f. perception verbs: *vlepo* (see), *akouo* (hear)

(31) Indicative selecting verbs in Italian: *sapere* (know)

In Italian, the only verb that strictly selects the indicative is *sapere* (know). Because Italian mood is considerably more flexible, it will be discussed in the next section as *mood shift*.

Here is the list of verb classes that select subjunctive in Greek and Italian:

(32) Subjunctive selecting verbs in Greek:
   a. volitionals: *thelo* (want), *epithimo* (desire)
   b. modal verbs: *prepi* (must), *bori* (may)

c. *try* verbs: *prospatho* (try), *dhokimazo* (attempt)
d. directive, future oriented verbs: *protino* (suggest), *simvulevo* (advise)
e. implicatives: *kataferno* (manage)
f. permissives: *apagorevo* (forbid)

(33) Subjunctive selecting verbs in Italian:
a. volitionals: *volere* (want)
b. directives: *ordinare* (order)
c. modal verbs: *essere possibile, necessario* (be possible, necessary)
d. permissives: *impedire* (forbid)

The two languages are very similar in the subjunctive taking classes, as we see. Implicatives in Italian select the infinitive because of obligatory control, and will be considered as part of the subjunctive class in our analysis. Modern Greek lacks the infinitive, and all complementation is finite.

Here are some Greek examples from the indicative class, recalled from earlier discussion:

(34) O Nicholas kseri oti/*na efije i Ariadne.
 the Nicholas knows.3sg that.IND/SUBJ left.3sg the Ariadne
 Nicholas knows that Ariadne left.

(35) O Nicholas onireftike/ nomize oti/*na efije i
 the Nicholas dreamt.3sg /thought.3sg that.IND/SUBJ left-3sg the
 Ariadne.
 Ariadne
 Nicholas dreamt/thought that Ariadne left.

(36) O Nicholas theori oti/*na to Milano ine i
 the Nicholas consider.3sg that.IND/SUBJ the Milan is the
 protevousa tis Italias.
 capital of Italy
 Nicholas considers Milan to be the capital of Italy.

*Nomizo* (think), *pistevo* (believe), *onirevome* (dream), *theoro* (consider) are all doxastic and take *oti, pos* complements. It seems to be a robust generalization that, in Greek, epistemic and doxastic attitude verbs pattern on a par in selecting indicative. The doxastic verbs appear to be *solipsistic*, in that they are strictly anchored to the attitude holder's doxastic space, ignoring what is in the common ground and lacking entirely factual commitments.

While indicative verbs are epistemic, doxastic, or variants thereof, the subjunctive classes, on the other hand, include modal verbs (deontic and epistemic modals), verbs of volition, implicatives, and generally propositional attitude verbs with future orientation. This group of verbs appears often with the tense NONPAST, which is also used with the future particle and enables forward shifting in time. Notice below the case of WANT:

(37) I    Ariadne theli       na         grapsi/*egrapse
     the Ariadne want.3sg that.SUBJ write.NONPAST.3sg/PAST.3sg
     to   gramma
     the letter.
     Ariadne wants to write the letter.

(38) Maria vuole che Susanna sia           contenta.
     Mary wants that Susan    be.SUBJ.3sg happy
     Mary wants that Susan be happy.

(39) *Maria vuole che Susanna sia               stata contenta.
     Mary wants that Susan    be.SUBJ.PAST.3sg been happy
     *Mary wants that Susan had been happy.

We find strong correlations between the tense of the complement and the semantics of the higher attitude verb, and elaborate on it later. Tense constraints are imposed by the attitude, and it is not uncommon, as we shall see, to find meaning changes along the temporal or mood shifts.

Epistemic modal verbs, on the other hand, allow combinations with all tenses. Greek has two modal verbs: a possibility modal *bori*, and a necessity modal *prepi* (see Staraki 2013, 2017 for recent extensive discussions on the Greek modals; and for the interaction with tense, Mari and Martin 2007, 2009; Giannakidou 2009, 2011, 2012; Mari 2015a, 2016b; Giannakidou and Mari 2016a,b, 2018a):[8]

---

[8]. While in Standard Modern Greek, *na* clauses can have temporal independence, some dialects (specifically Griko) is said to feature only NONPAST. Lekakou and Quer (2016) take this to suggest that there is specialization of morphology in Griko for the marking of subjunctive on the verb. We will not explore the dialects of Greek here, but it should be noted that

(40)  Prepi na/*oti        vrehi.
      must that.SUBJ/IND rain.3sg
      It must be raining.

(41)  Bori na/*oti         vrehi.
      may  that.SUBJ/IND rain.3sg
      It may be raining.

(42)  Prepi na/*oti        evrekse.
      must that.SUBJ/IND rain.PAST.3sg
      It must have rained.

(43)  Bori na/*oti         evrekse.
      may  that.SUBJ/IND rain.PAST.3sg
      It may have rained.

The non-past form creates a prediction or an interpretation as a deontic statement:

(44)  Prepi na/*oti        vreksi.
      must that.SUBJ/IND rain.NONPAST.3sg
      For all I know, it must rain (in the future).
      Given what is needed, it has to rain (in the future).

Deontic readings arise only with NONPAST. Hence we have a dependency of deontic modality to this temporal form—a dependency that doesn't exist for epistemic modals. It is these kinds of correlations that we find to be crucial in meaning shifts in chap. 3, 5, and 6. As can be seen in the examples above, both modal verbs require the subjunctive, but, in addition, the epistemic reading is compatible with all tenses. The type of modality doesn't seem to matter for mood choice: the above sentences are epistemic, but deontic, teleological (Portner 2009) and ability modals also require subjunctive:

given that mood affects potentially two syntactic positions (Giannakidou 2009), grammaticalization paths may be unstable (Chatzopoulou 2012, 2019). The semantic generalizations for the verb classes, on the other hand, seem to be pretty solid.

(45) Prepi na/*oti       fas                 olo to  fagito sou!
    must that.SUBJ/IND eat.NONPAST.2sg all the food yours
    You must eat all your food!

(46) Ja na         perasis      ston epomeno giro,  *prepi*
    for that.SUBJ pass.on.2sg to.the next    round, must
    na/*oti        apandisis              tris   erotisis.
    that.SUBJ/IND answer.NONPAST.2sg three questions
    In order to pass on to the next round (of the game), you must answer three questions.

(47) Boris na/*oti      klisis             tin porta.
    may SUBJ/IND close.NONPAST.2sg the door
    You may close the door.

The past tense is excluded with deontic modality (unless generic, see Mari 2015a, 2016b):

(48) Prepi na      efage        olo to  fagito tou.
    must that.SUBJ eat.PAST.3sg all the food his
    #He must eat all his food!
    He must have eaten all his food.

With past tense, we shift to an epistemic reading. This means that the lower tense can trigger a shift in the modal base: from epistemic to circumstantial (which is the one employed with deontics). Such a shift, we show in chapter 5, is observed also with propositional attitudes, specifically the ones of persuasion and assertion, and this again suggests that modals and attitudes are much closer in meaning than was previously thought.

In Italian, modal verbs are strict subjunctive selectors, as in Greek. The modal *essere possibile* allows past, but necessity modal *essere necessario* only allows future orientation, with a prominent deontic reading (and a parasitic epistemic one, given the uncertainty of the future).

(49) È            possibile/*necessario che sia            venuto.
    be.PRES.3sg possible/necessary    that be.SUBJ.3sg come
    It is possible that he has come.

(50) È         possibile/necessario che venga.
     be.PRES.3sg possible/necessary that come.SUBJ.3sg
     It is possible/necessary that he will come.

To summarize the mood patterns, what becomes clear by looking at the morphological exponents of mood in Greek and Romance is that mood affects two positions in the embedded clause: the verb (Latin, Romance languages, Ancient Greek), and the subordinator C (Modern Greek, Balkan languages, including Romanian which is a Romance language). The subordinating C can be thought to do some work related to updating with the information coming from the embedded clause. Since we have embedding, the C position can be understood as introducing a local context, and the mood morpheme as giving instructions on how to anchor the embedded proposition to the local context, as we argue later:

(51)

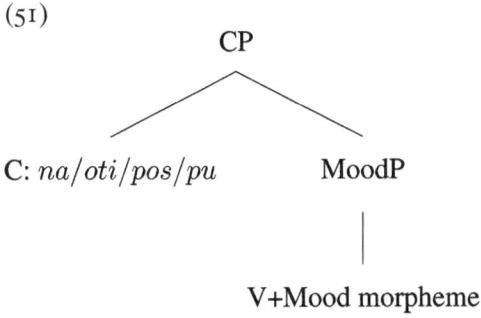

One can think of the contrast between indicative and the subjunctive particles in Greek as *that* vs. *to* complements in English, bearing also in mind that in Modern Greek all complementation is finite (the language lacks infinitives).[9] One must ask the question of how to extend our analysis of Greek and Italian moods to a language that lacks systematic mood distinctions such as English. Baunaz (2015) in some recent work on French argues for three different subordinators *que* even though French does not mark mood in this position. French, however, does mark mood; in a language like English, which lacks mood in embedded clauses,

---

9. Giannakidou (2016) further argues that the emotive C *pu* contains expressive meaning. Chatzopoulou (2019) does away with the MoodP and replaces it with a Nonveridicality Phrase based on arguments from the diachrony of Greek.

it is possible to transfer our view presented in chapter 4 about update functions of mood morphemes to the complementizers *that* and *to*.

### 1.3.3 *Modal Expressions as* Antiknowledge *Markers*

The study of modality has its roots in the Aristotelian *Categories*, and since then theoreticians across different frameworks have developed numerous theories of what modals are and do. In the linguistic formal semantic tradition, Kratzer (1977, 1981, 1990) and Portner (2009) developped theories based on possible worlds, enriching the systems of modal logic stemming from Lewis and Kripke's work by adding ordering sources besides modal bases. We adopt the Kratzer/Portner framework of modality here and aim to build a richer system based on our recent work (Giannakidou and Mari 2016a, b, 2018a, b).

Modals, possibility as well as necessity, we will argue, are *antiknowledge markers*: they indicate that the speaker is in a nonveridical state, specifically that she lacks knowledge of *p*. When the speaker does have knowledge of *p*, she is in a veridical state that precludes the use of a modal expression, as illustrated in the well-known cases below:

(52) Context: I am looking through the window and see that it is raining.
  a. #It may be raining.
  b. #Bori na vrehi.
   may that.SUBJ rain
  c. #Può piovere.
   may.3sg rain
  d. #It must be raining.
  e. #Prepi na vrehi.
   must that.SUBJ rain
  f. #Deve piovere.
   must.3sg rain

If I see the rain, I know that it is raining, and knowledge is veridical: if *I know p*, then *p* is a fact. If I see the rain, I am in a veridical state of mind, and modals are incompatible with the state of knowledge. In choosing to use a modal when I have knowledge of the prejacent sentence, I am saying something weaker than what I know, violating Gricean Quantity (which requires that I say as much as I know). In Giannakidou and Mari (2016a, b), we used the continuation "but I am not entirely sure" as a diagnostic for the absence of knowledge (in Italian, the observation is first found noted in Bertinetto 1979; Mari 2009, 2010a; Giannakidou 1998, 1999, Giannakidou and Mari 2012b). Consider:

(53) Deve essere a casa, ma non sono totalmente sicuro.
 must.PRES.3sg be at home, but not be.PRES.3sg entirely sure
 He must be home, but I am not entirely sure.

Observe the contrast with the bare positive assertion and the knowledge predicate which do not accept such continuation:

(54) a. #He is at home but I am not entirely sure.
 b. #I know he is at home but I am not entirely sure.

Lassiter (2016) offers numerous attested examples where *must* is followed by "I don't know for sure", and similar expressions challenging knowledge, belief, or remembering of *p*:

(55) This is a very early, very correct Mustang that has been in a private collection for a long time. . . . The speedo[meter] shows 38,000 miles and *it must be 138,000, but I don't know for sure*.

(56) *I don't know for sure*, sweetie, but she *must have been* very depressed. A person doesn't do something like that lightly.

(57) It must have been a Tuesday (but I don't know for sure), I can't remember.

(58) I have an injected TB42 turbo and don't like the current setup. There is an extra injector located in the piping from the throttle body . . . *Must be an old DTS diesel setup but I'm not certain*. Why would they have added this extra injector?

These examples support the conclusion that all modals, including MUST, do not entail knowledge of *p* (see also Goodhue 2018). The modal verbs, then, are antiknowledge markers and convey uncertainty. We will identify uncertainty with the concept *nonveridicality* in our work. Modal verbs and propositional attitudes that select the subjunctive are all nonveridical, as it will be established.

## 1.4 Mood Flexibility

Let us move on now to mood flexibility. In many cases, the speaker has a choice between indicative and subjunctive, and the phenomenon is also known as mood *shift* (Quer 2009). It is both interesting (because mood reveals meaning layers) and challenging (because mood shift can reflect a change in the meaning of the higher verb that can pass by as ambiguity).

There are many well documented cases studied under the label of *optional subjunctive* (Giannakidou 2016):

(59) Optional subjunctive:
  a. Subjunctive triggered by negation in the complement of an otherwise indicative selecting verb (Quer 1998, 2001, 2009 for overview, Giannakidou 1995);
  b. In relative clauses to convey uncertainty of existence (see Farkas 1985; Quer 1998; Giannakidou 1998, 2013a for recent discussion);
  c. In free relatives, adding the dimension of free choice (Quer 1998, 2001; Marques 2010; Giannakidou and Cheng 2006);
  d. Epistemic subjunctive in questions, equivalent to an epistemic modal of possibility (Rocci 2007; Giannakidou 2016)

In these cases, the speaker uses one mood or another for a reason. Giannakidou (2016) argues that in optional cases the subjunctive performs an *evaluation*, which is an epistemic modal dimension.

### 1.4.1 Subjunctive of Negation

Consider first the subjunctive after negation with doxastic verbs. This is a phenomenon attested in many Romance languages and in Greek:

(60) Dhen pistevo    na    erthi    o Janis.
    not  believe.1sg that.SUBJ come.NONPAST.3sg the John
    I don't believe that John will come.

(61) Dhen pistevo    na    irthe   o Janis.
    not  believe.1sg that.SUBJ came.3sg the John
    I don't believe that John come.

The doxastic verb *pistevo* (believe) selects indicative, as we saw earlier, but with negation the subjunctive becomes possible. Notice that subjunctive, as in the case of epistemic modals, is compatible with both past and nonpast, and the nonpast has a future-oriented reading. As Giannakidou (1995, 2016) notes, in Greek mood shift depends crucially on first person singular. A third person subject is unable to shift to subjunctive with negation:

(62) *I  Ariadne dhen pistevi    na    erthi    o
    the Ariadne not  believe.3sg that.SUBJ come.NONPAST.3sg the
    Janis.
    John
    Ariadne doesn't believe that John will come.

(63) *I  Ariadne dhen pistevi    na    irthe   o Janis.
    the Ariadne not  believe.3sg that.SUBJ came.3sg the John
    Ariadne doesn't believe that John came.

Romance languages are less constrained (Giorgi and Pianesi 1996, Quer 2009, Mari 2016a), though the degree of flexibility varies. In Greek, when the individual anchor is not the speaker, the lexical subcategorization of the doxastic verb remains robust, i.e., selecting indicative.

## 1.4.2 Mood Choice in Relative Clauses

Consider now the subjunctive in relative clauses:[10]

---

10. *Pu* is also the relativizer "who", "what", "that" used in relative clauses. The two uses, i.e, that of a subordinator in complement clauses and a relativizer, have hardly been linked in the literature with the exception of Roberts and Roussou (2003) who argue that the relativizer *pu* contains a D layer, it is therefore a kind of definite. Such analysis would be compatible with the idea that *pu* is sensitive to presupposed veridicality that will propose in this book, and Roussou and Roberts also make the connection to veridicality.

(64) Theloume na       proslavoume      mia gramatea [pu
    want.1pl    that.SUBJ hire.NONPAST.1pl a    secretary that
    na       gnorizi    japonezika].
    that.SUBJ know.3sg Japanese
    We want to hire a secretary that knows Japanese. But it is hard to
    find one, and we are not sure if we will be successful.
    #Her name is Jane Smith.

(65) Theloume na       proslavoume      mia gramatea [pu
    want.1pl    that.SUBJ hire.NONPAST.1pl a    secretary that
    gnorizi    japonezika.]
    know.3sg Japanese
    We want to hire a secretary that knows Japanese. Her name is Jane
    Smith.
    (#But it is hard to find one, and we are not sure if we will be
    successful.)'

Here we see that the subjunctive *na* can be licensed in a relative clause headed by *pu*. Farkas (1985) studied the phenomenon in Romanian and called the subjunctive in relative clauses "intensional". Giannakidou (1997, 1998, 2013a) analyzed the phenomenon in Greek, arguing that the subjunctive has an epistemic anti-specificity effect. When a subjunctive is used, the indefinite nominal receives a *de dicto*, narrow-scope reading: we do not have a particular secretary in mind, and there are worlds *w* where we find a secretary that speaks Japanese, but we do not know if the actual world is such a world. The subjunctive statement says: there are doxastic alternatives *w* such that there is a secretary in *w* and she speaks Japanese. But there are also doxastic alternatives *w'* where there is no such secretary, and it may turn out that the real world is one of those. So, we don't know, at the time of utterance, if there exists in the real world a secretary who speaks Japanese that we can hire. Because we don't know that, the continuation *Her name is Jane Smith*, as indicated, is not permitted.

The indicative version, on the other hand, has a *de re*, wide-scope or specific interpretation, and it is about the specific person Jane Smith who we want to hire. As Giannakidou (1997, 1998, 2013a) emphasized, the narrow scope produces an antispecific reading of the indefinite nominal, while the wide scope of indicative produces specific de re readings. The effect of the mood choice in relative clauses is therefore epistemic and depends on whether the speaker knows that there exists a specific value to the indefinite or not. If a specific value is known to the speaker, indicative will be chosen. The subjunctive will be chosen when the speaker is uncertain about the value.

### 1.4.3 Subjunctive in Questions

Now consider the case discussed by Giannakidou (2016), where the subjunctive is licensed in questions. In this case, it is argued, the subjunctive contributes an epistemic possibility modal:

(66) Ti na theli?
What that.SUBJ want-3sg
What might he want?

(67) Na tou arese to fagito?
that.SUBJ he.GEN liked-3sg the food
Might it be the case that he liked the food?

Rouchota (1994) called subjunctive in questions "dubitative." As indicated, the subjunctive behaves as if it contains a possibility epistemic modal *might*. Similar use of the subjunctive exists in Statimcets (Matthewson 2010). Importantly, these questions are "weaker" than without subjunctive: they are open-ended, reflective, and may not seek an answer at all. They are questions that one can posit to oneself; Giannakidou and Mari 2019 call them therefore *reflective*. Giannakidou argues that the subjunctive in the question is akin to a possibility modal, as indicated also in the translations. Notice that epistemic MUST is notoriously bad in questions (see Papafragou 2000, 2006, Hacquard and Wellwood 2012 for discussion and data):

(68) a. #What must he want?
b. #Must he be here already?

German so-called modal particles are reported to have similar reflective use in questions (the example is from Zimmermann 2011 with his translation):

(69) Hat Hans wohl Maria eingeladen?
has Hans PRT Mary invited
What do you reckon: Has Hans invited Mary?

Zimmerman says: "The question above is not about whether or not Hans has invited Mary, but by using *wohl* the speaker indicates her awareness that the addressee may not be fully committed to her answer." (Zimmermann 2011, p. 2020). This idea resonates with our characterization of the subjunctive question as reflective.

Let us now move to mood choice in complement clauses.

### 1.4.4 Mood Shift in Italian Complement Clauses

Italian features mood shift for most of the classes where Greek selects the indicative (see Mari, 2016a).

(70) Mood shift in Italian:
   a. emotive factives: *essere contento, sorpreso* (be happy, be surprised) mostly subjunctive, allow indicative (71)
   b. doxastic (non-factive): *credere, pensare, trovare* (believe, think, find) mostly subjunctive, allow indicative (72)
   c. certainty: *essere certo* (be certain) mostly indicative, allow subjunctive (73)
   d. consciousness: *essere cosciente* (be aware) mood shift (74)
   e. pure assertives: *dire* (say) mostly indicative, allow subjunctive (75)
   f. verbs of denial: *negare* (deny) mood shift (76)
   g. fiction verbs: *immaginare, sognare* (imagine, dream) mood shift (77)
   h. memory verbs: *ricordare/ricordarsi* (remember) mood shift (78)

(71) Sono contenta che sia/è venuto.
 am happy that be.SUBJ.3sg/IND.3sg come
 I am happy that he has come.

(72) Credo che sia/è bella.
 believe.1sg that be.SUBJ/IND cute
 I believe that she is cute.

(73) Sono sicura che sia/è bella.
 am certain that be.SUBJ/IND cute
 I am certain that she is cute.

(74) Sono cosciente che sia/è bella.
    am  aware  that be.SUBJ/IND cute
    I am aware that she is cute.

(75) La gente dice che sia/è bella.
    the people say that be.SUBJ/IND cute
    People say that she is cute.

(76) Maria nega che sia/è bella.
    mary denies that be.SUBJ/IND cute
    Mary denies that is cute.

(77) Maria immagina che Laura sia/è bella.
    mary imagines that Laura be.SUBJ/IND cute
    Mary imagines that Laura is cute.

(78) Maria ricorda che Laura sia/è bella.
    mary remembers that Laura be.SUBJ/IND cute
    Mary remembers that Laura is cute.

Apparent flexible mood within a language is challenging for almost all analyses of mood as it targets the very idea of selection. To deal with the varying patterns, most accounts (our own earlier works included) would have to say in some way or other that the verb is ambiguous or polysemous, and that the meaning changes depending on the mood chosen.

The Italian data have never been systematically addressed in the literature, and since the pioneering work of Giorgi and Pianesi (1996) very little progress has been made to explain the flexibility that this language allows. Generally speaking, Italian can be described as a language that "favors" the subjunctive, but the indicative is also allowed. The overwhelming flexibility needs a principled and unified explanation—and we will offer such an analysis in this book. Our idea will be that the Italian belief verbs are the counterpart in the domain of attitudes of the epistemic MUST. The Italian subjunctive therefore offers a strong argument that attitudes and modals are a natural class semantically.

Following Mari (2016a), we will argue that with subjunctive belief in Italian there is no doxastic uncertainty. Instead, we will propose that a fundamental difference is to be tracked between knowledge and *doxa*. As Mari writes:

> Non-factive epistemic predicates allow us to see a systematic polysemy between what we call an expressive-belief (featuring only a doxastic dimension) and an inquisitive-belief (featuring both a doxastic and an epistemic dimension conveying doxastic certainty (in the assertion) and epistemic uncertainty (in the presupposition)). (Mari 2016a: 61).

We will therefore distinguish two layers. First, belief, or *doxa*, can be pure, and in this case we have indicative and commitment of the believer without regard of knowledge. This is the case of the Greek belief that we described earlier. But belief can be weakened when it is contrasted with knowledge. This distinction will play a central role in our theory, and we will show that it in fact generalizes across a number of doxastic attitudes, including memory, imagination, perception, and fiction attitudes. We will call the stronger construals of belief *solipsistic* and the latter *suppositional*. Solipsistic doxastics will select the indicative, and suppositional doxastics select the subjunctive. Italian, Portuguese, and Yucatec Spanish (as recent work by Bove 2020 has shown) doxastic verbs are underspecified lexically as to which way they are construed.[11]

Based on the proposal that the trigger for subjunctive with belief is a presupposition of epistemic uncertainty—which is a presupposition of nonveridicality, in our terms—we will propose a unified view of mood flexibility, which cuts across languages to an extent that has been only rarely considered before.[12] Crucially, the epistemic effect of the subjunctive shows that the category "preference" is not relevant. In our earlier examples with such verbs, the subjunctive indicates conjectural stance and is thus correlated with supposition and not preference.

### 1.4.5 Doxastic Verbs in Portuguese

Italian is not alone among Romance languages in allowing both moods with doxastic verbs. Marques (2010) notes that in Portuguese, belief and

---

11. Note that, unlike Mari (2016a), we will not consider the verbs polysemous, but argue that the notion corresponding to the predicate can have different values that can be instantiated in different languages, and which are responsible for intra - and crosslinguistic variation. Some mood variation in Germanic (Icelandic, Konjuktiv I in German) can be understood as part of this pattern too.

12. See Farkas (2003) for a theory of mood choice with multiple layers; note, however, that Farkas cannot achieve full coverage and does not explain subjunctive with Italian belief.

assumption verbs may also allow the subjunctive. Here are examples from Marques, discussed in Giannakidou (2016):

(79) Acredito que a Maria está doente.
believe-1sg that the Maria is.IND.3sg ill
I believe that Maria is ill.

(80) Acredito que a Maria esteja doente.
believe.1sg that the Maria is.SUBJ.3sg ill
I believe that Maria is ill.

Marques says that the selection of one or another mood is related to the "degree of belief" being expressed: the indicative signals a high degree of belief, and the subjunctive a lower degree. According to Marques, "the concept of veridicality accounts for this case of mood variation. With the indicative, the inference follows that the relevant proposition is true (according to the subject of the main clause), contrary to what happens if the subjunctive is selected." (Marques 2010, p. 145). The same idea is also present in Homer (2008) who identifies subjunctive with belief as a cancelable inference of uncertainty.

Giannakidou (2016) comments on that by saying that when the speaker choses to utter the subjunctive version, she is making a point to distinguish between what she believes and what she knows for sure. "When she choses the indicative version, the speaker is content with the belief ("higher degree of certainty"), but when she chooses the subjunctive, she seems to be aware that she her belief might not be justified as knowledge. The speaker, in the subjunctive version, has some uncertainty in her epistemic state and her commitment to *Maria is ill* is weaker, i.e. she allows for the possibility of not *p*." (Giannakidou 2016: 173).

The commitment weakening of the subjunctive is observed in English too, when we add a modal verb in the embedded clause:

(81) a. I believe that Maria might be sick.
b. I believe that Maria is sick.

We see therefore that the effect of the subjunctive is equivalent to using a modal (indeed, of possiblity). This is a key observation supporting Giannakidou's (2016) view that the subjucntive itself, when chosen, is equivalent to a possibility modal.

Let us now give a brief overview of the other verb classes that feature mood flexibility.

*1.4.6 Hopes, Promises, and Persuasions*

There are some other interesting verb classes that allow both moods crosslinguistically. Consider verbs of the HOPE class which allow both moods in Greek and Italian, with past, future and present:

(82) a. Elpizo      na         kerdisi/kerdise          o   Janis.
        hope.1sg that.SUBJ win.NONPAST/PAST.3sg the John
        I hope for John to win/to have won.
     b. Spero        che Gianni abbia         vinto/vinca.
        Hope.1sg.PRES that John have.SUBJ.3sg won/win.SUBJ.3sg
        I hope that John has won.

(83) a. Elpizo    oti      kerdise o  Janis.
        hope.1sg that.IND won.3sg the John
        I hope that John won.
     b. Elpizo    oti      tha kerdisi         o  Janis.
        hope.1sg that.IND FUT win.NONPAST.3sg the John
        I hope that John will win.
     c. Spero       che il Milan vincerà/ha          vinto.
        Hope.PRES.1sg that the Milan win.FUT.IND.3sg/has won
        I hope that Milan will win/has won.

Equivalents of *hope* are also flexible in other languages (see e.g. a recent discussion of French in Portner and Rubinstein 2012; Anand and Hacquard 2013).

The verb meaning PROMISE behaves similarly. Notice the exact parallel with *promise to* and *promise that*.

(84) a. I   Ariadne iposxethike      na           fiji                     noris.
        the Ariadne promised.3sg that.SUBJ leave.NONPAST.3sg early
        Ariadne promised to leave early.
     b. I   Ariadne iposxethike     oti       tha fiji
        the Ariadne promised.3sg that.IND FUT leave.NONPAST.3sg
        noris.
        early
        Ariadne promised that she left early.

Only the *oti* version counts as a true performative, according to Giannakidou (1997). The *na* version does not convey the commitment of the speaker to carry out the action indicated by the *oti* clause. Past tense is excluded with the *oti* clause because of the nature of promise which is about action to be performed in the future:

(85) #I Ariadne iposxethike oti efije noris.
 the Ariadne promised.3sg that.IND left.PAST.3sg early
 Ariadne promised that she left early.

The verb meaning PERSUADE *pitho* behaves in a parallel way:

(86) a. I Ariadne epise ton Nikola na
 the Ariadne persuaded.3sg the Nicholas that.SUBJ
 fijoun noris.
 leave.NONPAST/PAST.3pl early
 Ariadne persuaded/convinced Nicholas (for them) to leave early.
 b. I Ariadne epise ton Nichola oti i idea tou
 the Ariadne persuaded.3sg the Nicholas that.IND the idea his
 ine kali.
 is.PRES.3sg good
 Ariadne persuaded/convinced Nicholas that his idea is good.

Notice the alteration in English between *persuade/convince to* (equivalent to *na*), and *persuade/convince that* (equivalent to *oti*). The English difference is discussed in a recent paper by Grano (2018). *Pitho na* means convince to act, but *pitho oti* means to make someone believe the complement proposition. This difference is brought about in Greek by the mood, in English by the *to* vs. *that* choice.

It is important to also note that both mood patterns, just like with *to* vs. *that*, feel canonical and unmarked. This holds for all HOPE, PROMISE and PERSUADE. The choice of *na* and the ensuing nonpast correlates with action or thought of the future.

### 1.4.7 Verbs of Saying

Here, mood choice correlates with different lexical choice of verb in English. Observe the verbs *leo*, and *arnoume* (examples from Giannakidou 2016, and Giannakidou and Staraki 2013):

(87) a. O  Janis lei   oti        efijan  noris.
       the John says that.IND left.3pl early
       John says that they left early.
   b. O  Janis lei   na         figoun   noris.
       the John says that.SUBJ leave.3pl early
       John *wants* them to leave early.

(88) a. O  Janis arnithike oti        efijan  noris.
       the John denied    that.IND left.3pl early
       John *denied* that they left early.
   b. O  Janis arnithike na         fiji       noris.
       the John says      that.SUBJ leave.3sg early
       John *refused* to leave early.

Lei (says) with the *oti* complement has the expected reporting meaning, but with the *na* complement it acquires a volitional meaning, and we translate it as *wants*. Likewise, with subjunctive *na*, arnithike means *refused* but with indicative *oti* it means *denied*.

Verbs of assertion are also flexible in Italian, with the subjunctive version enabling a reportative interpretation. The subjunctive here in Italian is related to the use of reportative subjunctive in Latin (which is not observed in Ancient or Modern Greek).

(89) La gente  dice che sia/è       bella.
     the people say  that be.SUBJ/IND cute
     People say that she is cute.

Verbs of denial are also flexible in Italian. Descriptively, with the indicative the matter is settled in the common ground, whereas with the subjunctive it is not (see Mari, 2016a).

(90) Maria nega   che Laura sia/è       bella.
     Mary  denies that Laura be.SUBJ/IND cute
     Mary denies that Laura is cute.

We will show how our framework accommodates this difference in interpretation.

### 1.4.8 Factive Verbs

Recall that Greek marks the complement of an emotive factive verb with *pu*. With imperfective aspect, however, *na* is also allowed:

(91) a. O Janis xarike pu episkeftike ti
 the John was-happy.PERF.3sg that.IND visited.PRF.3sg his
 jaja tu.
 grandmother
 John was happy that he visited his grandmother.
 b. O Janis xerete na episkeptete ti
 the John is-happy.IMPERF.3sg that.SUBJ visit.IMPERF3sg the
 jaja tu (ala dystyxos tora teleftea dhen
 grandmother his but unfortunately now lately not
 prolaveni).
 find.time.IMPERF.3sg
 John is happy to visit his grandmother (but unfortunately he doesn't find time to do that lately).

Of the two sentences, only the *pu* one is factive: John visited his grandmother (hence that John visited his grandmother is true), and that fact made John happy. Notice the perfective in both the higher and the lower verb. The *na* version, on the other hand, contains imperfective on both forms, and this renders the sentence nonfactive, as can be seen in the continuation. Similar mood shifts with emotives are observed in many Romance languages (see Quer 2001, 2009 for recent overviews).

With emotive factives, we will ultimately establish a distinction between three types of languages:

(92) (i) Languages that require subjunctive (Spanish, French);
 (ii) Languages that allow both subjunctive and indicative (Brazilian Portuguese, Catalan, Turkish; to a lesser extent, Italian);
 (iii) Languages where emotives select indicative (Greek, Hungarian, Romanian, Bulgarian); the emotive complement may be distinguished in some other way as in Greek.

Note the rigidity in French and the flexibility (although with a strong preference for subjunctive) in Italian.

(93) Je suis contente qu'il    soit/*est              venu.
     I am happy     that-he be.SUBJ.3sg/IND.3sg come
     I am happy that he has come.

(94) Sono contenta che    sia/è        venuto.
     I        am    happy that-he be.SUBJ.3sg/IND.3sg come
     I am happy that he has come.

Mood choice can also produce change in meaning with the verb *ksero* (know), becoming equivalent to a *how-to* complement in English (see Varlokosta 1994; Giannakidou 2011):

(95) O Janis kseri       na         kolibai.
     the John knows.3sg that.SUBJ swim.IMPRF.3sg
     John knows how to swim.

Finally, the verb *ksero* 'know' may also combine with *pu*:

(96) O Pavlos kseri      pu/oti/*na          efije  i Roxani
     the Paul   knows.3sg that.IND/IND/SUBJ left.3sg the Roxani
     Paul knows that Roxanne left.

The compatibility of KNOW with *pu* should not be a surprise if, as we said, the generalization is that *pu* is the factive complementizer, selected by verbs whose complements denote facts. Crucially, *pu* can't be used in the following context where the speaker doesn't know *p*. Consider a context where we ask the question: How much did that book cost?

(97) Ksero      *pu/oti            kostise  25 dollaria.
     know.1sg that.IND-pu/IND-oti cost-3sg 25 dollars
     I know that it cost $25.

In this context of seeking information, the person asking the question does not know how much the book costs. Hence that the book cost 25 dollars is not part of the common ground, and *pu* cannot be used. We will suggest that *pu* is a presuppositional complementizer. With indicatives, then, Greek seems to distinguish between the assertion of veridicality (indicative *oti*) and the presupposition of it (*pu*).

Finally, we note that, when embedding a question, *sapere* also allows the subjunctive.

(98) Sai      dov'è              la macchina?
     know.2sg where-be.IND.3sg the car
     Do you know where is the car?

(99) Sai      dove sia          la macchina?
     know.2sg where be.SUBJ.3sg the car
     Do you know where is the car?

This is a case where, just as with negation, a higher nonveridical operator (question) triggers the subjunctive. The embedding, crucially, creates nonveridicality: *? KNOW p* does not entail or presuppose *p*.

### 1.4.9 Memory and Perception Verbs

Verbs of perception such as *vlepo* (see) and *akouo* (hear) take *oti* complements when they combine with past:

(100) O   Nicholas idhe     oti/*pu/*na                    efije    i
      the Nicholas saw.3sg that.IND-oti/IND-pu/SUBJ left.3sg the
      Ariadne.
      Ariadne
      Nicholas saw that Ariadne left.

(101) O   Nicholas akouse    oti/*pu/*na                    efije    i
      the Nicholas heard.3sg that.IND-oti/IND-pu/SUBJ left.3sg the
      Ariadne.
      Ariadne
      Nicholas heard that Ariadne left.

(102) O   Nicholas thimate       oti/*na              ekleise  tin
      the Nicholas remember.3sg that.IND/that.SUBJ closed.3sg. the
      porta.
      door
      Nicholas remembered that he closed the door.

But when these verbs combine with the present tense (imperfective nonpast, Giannakidou 2014), *na* can be used:

(103) O Nicholas idhe tin Ariadne *oti/*pu/na
the Nicholas saw.3sg the Ariadne that.IND-oti/IND-pu/SUBJ
kleini tin porta, alla dhen ine sigouros.
close.PRES.3sg the door, but not is sure
Nicholas saw Ariadne closing the door (but he is not entirely sure).

(104) O Nicholas thimate na kleini tin porta,
the Nicholas remember.3sg that.SUBJ close.PRES.3sg the door,
alla dhen ine sigouros.
but not is sure
Nicholas remembered closing the door, but he is not entirely sure.

The *na* version is compatible with a context where Nicholas is not fully sure about his memory or vision; he has some doubt. The *oti* clause is incompatible with such context:

(105) #O Nicholas thimate oti eklise tin porta, alla
the Nicholas remember.3sg that.IND closed.3sg the door, but
dhen ine sigouros
not is sure.
#Nicholas remembered that he closed the door, but he is not entirely sure.

Note the exact parallel with the English -*ing* clause. The *that* vs. *ing* difference is reflected in Greek with the *oti* vs. *na* distinction.

Memory verbs, finally, can also take a *pu* complement. In this case, just as we saw with *ksero* (know), *pu* will be blocked if the speaker doesn't already know *p*. Consider again the context that raises the question: How much did that book cost?

(106) Thimame *pu/oti kostise 25 dollaria.
remember.1sg that cost-3sg 25 dollars
I remember that it cost $25 dollars.

In this context, the person asking the question does not know how much the book costs. Hence that the book cost 25 dollars is not known in the common ground. In this case, *pu* cannot be used. This suggests again that *pu* requires that *p* to be part of the common ground.

(107) Thimame      pu/oti   to vivlio kostise  25 dollaria.
      remember.1sg that.IND the book cost-3sg 25 dollars
      I remember that the book cost 25 dollars.

In this case, memory corresponds to common knowledge.

Unsurprisingly, memory verbs are also flexible in Italian, where the subjunctive introduces a suppositional layer, as we will extensively explain in the rest of this book.

(108) Maria ricorda    che Laura sia/è         bella.
      Mary  remembers that Laura be.SUBJ/IND cute
      Mary remembers that Laura is cute.

We discuss the patterns of memory and perception along with the other doxastics in chapter 4. We also include in that chapter discussion of semblance predicates (*seem, appear*), which are not strictly speaking attitudinal, but share key similarities with perception verbs.

Having taken a taste of all this variation, let us proceed now to ask one of the central questions in this book: what regulates mood choice?

## 1.5 What Regulates Mood Choice?

### 1.5.1 The Indicative: Veridicality and Commitment

The regulating factor for mood choice cannot be direct access to truth—since doxastic, dream, and fiction verbs in Greek and most Romance take indicative complements. Recall:

(109) O   Nicholas nomizi        oti/*na          to Milano ine i
      the Nicholas thinks.3sg that.IND/SUBJ the Milan  is the
      protevousa tis Italias.
      capital    of Italy
      Nicholas thinks Milan is the capital of Italy.

(110) O   Nicholas theori          oti/*na          to Milano ine i
      the Nicholas considers.3sg that.IND/SUBJ the Milan  is the
      protevousa tis Italias.
      capital    of Italy
      Nicholas considers Milan to be the capital of Italy.

The striking thing here is that even with an obviously false sentence the indicative is required. It therefore seems to be a robust generalization that indicative selecting attitude verbs do not care about objective truth or factuality.

In previous works (Giannakidou 1994, 1997, 1998, 2009, 2011, 2013b, 2016), Giannakidou argues that the indicative, rather, signals subjective veridical commitment of the attitude subject. What is subjective veridical commitment? Such commitment relies on an information state M. Let us define the state M first:

(111) Information state of an individual anchor $i$ (Giannakidou 2013b):
An information state $M(i)$ is a set of worlds associated with an individual $i$ representing worlds compatible with what $i$ knows or believes.

$M(i)$ is the private space of $i$'s thoughts, belief, and knowledge; it is actually much richer than that, as we shall see. $M(i)$ can include also one's perceptions, expectations, memories, tastes, etc., and these different sets of worlds are determined specifically by the lexical meaning. These subjective private spaces are reminiscent of Kratzer's *modal bases* for modal verbs, and are key to understanding how linguistic agents make assessments about truth. The idea is that such modal bases can always be formed, and truth assessment is relative to these subjective spaces. This relativization, Giannakidou argues, holds for *all* sentences.[13]

Consider a basic sentence with no modal and no embedding. In this case, the relevant linguistic agent $i$ is the speaker, and M(speaker) is the information space determining veridicality:

(112) Efije   i    Ariadne.
      left.3sg the Ariadne
      Ariadne left.

---

13. Recent work shows these subjective spaces to be important in extracting truth assessment from texts; de Marneffe et al. (2012) say that "unadorned" declaratives like *Ariadne left* convey firm speaker commitment, whereas qualified variants with modal verbs or embedded sentences 'imbue the sentence with uncertainty' (de Marneffe et al. 2012: 102). Trnavac and Taboada (2012), in a recent study, examine the interactions between nonveridicality and evaluative structure in corpora, and conclude that a nonveridical device "tampers with the evaluative content of utterances, with the result of weakening the evaluation." (Trnavac and Taboada: 2012: 316)

This sentence is true if and only if all the worlds in M(speaker) are worlds in which Ariadne left. This is a veridical information state:

(113) Veridical information state:
An information state M($i$) is veridical about $p$ iff:
$\forall w'[w' \in M(i) \rightarrow w' \in \{w'' \mid p(w'')\}]$.

A veridical state conveys absolute certainty of the agent that the sentence is true. It is *homogenous*, therefore entails $p$. In Gricean terms, a cooperative speaker, in uttering the sentence *Ariadne left*, follows Quality (Be truthful), and this means that she is in a veridical state, i.e., to her knowledge, the sentence is true:

(114) $[\![$Ariadne left$]\!]^{M(speaker)} = 1$ iff
$\forall w'[w' \in M(speaker) \rightarrow w' \in \{w'' \mid $ Ariadne $w''\}]$

The requirement for a veridical state holds irrespective of mood, as can be seen, and is a prerequisite for assertion:

(115) Veridical information state as a prerequisite for assertion:
A sentence $S$ is assertable if and only if the speaker is in a veridical state about the proposition $p$ denoted by $S$.

The veridical state is the foundation for the speaker's, or an individual anchor's *commitment* to a sentence, and we discuss it further in chapter 2. Now, suffice it to note that the indicative can be understood as by default associated with the veridical state. Because veridicality is a prerequisite for assertion, continuations such as *I don't believe it* give rise to Moore effects (Giannakidou and Mari 2016c):

(116) Efije    i    Ariadne, #ala dhen to pistevo.
left.3sg the Ariadne, but   not   it believe.1sg
#Ariadne left but I don't believe it.

In order to utter "*Ariadne left*", the speaker must be in a veridical state of knowing or believing that Ariadne left; the negative continuation ascribes contradictory beliefs to the same individual. At the foundation of Moore paradoxical effects, therefore, lies the need to posit veridicality as a precondition on the assertability of sentences (as we argued in Giannakidou and Mari (2016c)).

In embedding, M(speaker) is still relevant, as is the Stalnakerian common ground C, i.e., the set of mutually known propositions or commitments. But the crucial anchor now will be the attitude holder which is the grammatical subject of the attitude verb, and mood will be anchored to M(subject), suggesting tight locality of individual anchoring. Consider first a verb of knowledge. The complement of knowledge is a fact because knowledge is justified true belief:

(117)  O  Nicholas kseri      oti/*na            efije    i    Ariadne.
       the Nicholas knows.3sg that.IND/SUBJ left.3sg the Ariadne
       Nicholas knows that Ariadne left.

(118) [[Nicholas kseri /know $p$]] will be defined iff the actual world $w$ is a $p$ world. (factivity)
If defined, [[Nicholas kseri oti $p$]] is true in $w$ with respect to M(*Nicholas*) iff:
$\forall w'[w' \in M(Nicholas) \to w' \in \{w'' \mid p(w'')\}]$

KNOW thus combines a factual (objectively veridical) presupposition (that the actual world $w$ is a $p$ world) with a veridical assertion: the information state of the subject, M(Nicholas), is homogeneous, i.e., all worlds are $p$ worlds. Importantly, the verb of knowledge does not *assert* that Ariadne left; hence the choice of indicative does not depend on assertion (as argued in Farkas 2003). Rather, it depends on veridicality.

Unlike knowledge, belief lacks the presupposition of factivity, or any presupposition whatsoever; but it has a truth condition similar to knowledge in that it involves a veridical, homogenous, information state:

(119)  O  Nicholas pistevi    oti/*na            efije    i    Ariadne.
       the Nicholas believe.3sg that.IND/SUBJ left.3sg the Ariadne
       Nicholas believes that Ariadne left.

Whether Ariadne actually left or not is irrelevant for Nicholas' beliefs. Also irrelevant is whether the speaker shares the belief. For the sentence to be true, it is simply enough if *Ariadne left* is a proposition believed by the attitude subject Nicholas. Following the classical Hintikka treatment of belief (Hintikka 1962), then, the truth condition for a doxastic attitude verb such as *believe* and its equivalents also involves a homogenous veridical state:

(120) ⟦Nicholas pistevi/believe *p*⟧ is true in *w* with respect to M(*Nicholas*) iff:
$\forall w'[w' \in M(Nicholas) \to w' \in \{w''| p(w'')\}]$

We discuss in chapter 4 the veridicality properties of other doxastic spaces, and offer more insights into the nature of the veridical states and solipsistic belief they impose.

We can then take the following generalization as the starting point for the indicative:

(121) Indicative mood and veridicality:
The indicative will be licensed in the complement of a propositional attitude that is veridical objectively (i.e., factive) or subjectively.

The illusion of indicative being sensitive to assertion (Farkas 2003) is due to the fact that subjective veridicality is a prerequisite of assertion. The homogeneity of subjective veridicality allows us to say that an individual anchor is committed to a sentence, as we noted here, and we explore the tight relation between veridicality and commitment in chapter 2 where we develop our formal system.

### 1.5.2 Our Thesis for the Subjunctive: Nonveridical Stance

While the indicative seemed relatively easy to handle, when it comes to the subjunctive, generalizations might, as first glance, seem elusive, and the literature indeed sometimes appears pessimistic about finding a unifying property (e.g., Witschko 2016). It is said correctly that the subjunctive cannot be simply identified with a single label such as "epistemic modality" or "bouletic modality", since the subjunctive is used with both epistemic and dynamic modals. And the fact that the subjunctive behaves like a modal itself, as we saw, adds to the complexity.

Efforts to unify the licensing factors of the subjunctive have been made under the concepts of *preference* or gradability (as in Villalta 2008 for the Spanish subjunctive). Such efforts are bound to fail because they overlook the fact that the subjunctive, as we showed, is licensed by attitude verbs with doxastic meaning. Recall also that both epistemic and deontic modals select the subjunctive in Greek, and that the subjunctive has epistemic contribution in relative clauses and with questions in Greek and Romance languages. Finally, we noted that the subjunctive is used in adjunct clauses with BEFORE and WITHOUT, clearly lacking a preference component.

Portner (2018) presents a rather comprehensive survey of subjunctive theories (see also earlier overview discussions in Quer 2009, also Portner and Rubinstein 2012; Smirnova, 2012; Giannakidou 2009, 2011; Marques 2004, 2010 for Brazilian and European Portuguese; Giorgi and Pianesi, 1996; Mari 2016a, 2017a, b for Italian; Sarigul 2015 for Turkish; Baunaz 2015 for French). Often a distinction is made between verbal mood and sentential mood (Portner 2009), with sentential mood referring to illocutionary force. However, Greek allows us to see that such a distinction is not essential, as we said earlier, as mood exponents appear on the sentential C level.

The association of mood with illocutionary forces is an illusion. While in main sentences a classification based on illocutionary act may indeed seem possible—e.g., the indicative comes with assertive force, the subjunctive and imperative have directive forces—the generalization clearly breaks down in embedding: the embedded indicative is not an assertion of the sentence it introduces, i.e., it does not add that sentence to the common ground. The embedded subjunctive, likewise, is not a wish or command. And the imperative cannot be embedded. The same holds for adjunct clauses: BEFORE and WITHOUT clauses select the subjunctive, but they are in no way non-assertions. An association of subjunctive mood with non-assertive illocutionary force would therefore fail spectacularly in sentence embedding.

In recent work, we have pursued individually and jointly a view of mood as having an "epistemic substratum", as Giannakidou (2013a) puts it, and that subjective veridicality and nonveridicality are the key properties regulating mood distribution in complement clauses (an idea going back as early as Giannakidou 1994). Building on these previous works, we will offer a quite expansive program in this book.

In a nutshell, we will argue that at a deep level of interpretation, the presence of a nonveridical state is the key to understanding both modality and the subjunctive mood itself. The subjunctive, embedded and unembedded, is a signal of subjective nonveridicality which is an *epistemically weaker* belief than the Hintikka belief we described earlier. The subjunctive sentence is epistemically weaker than the indicative one because the individual anchor is not committed to the truth of the complement but rather expresses a nonveridical *stance*. What does that mean? It means that the speaker's information space allows uncertainty, i.e., it contains both $p$ and $\neg p$ worlds:

(122) Epistemic weakening (Giannakidou 2014, 2016, Giannakidou and Mari 2016c):
Epistemic weakening is the creation of a nonveridical information state.

(123) Nonveridical information state (Giannakidou 2013):
An information state $M(i)$ is nonveridical about $p$ iff $M(i)$ contains both $p$ and $\neg p$ worlds. A nonveridical $M(i)$ does not entail $p$.

In contrast to the veridical states that entail $p$, nonveridical states have $p$ and $\neg p$ as open possibilities and do not allow entailment to $p$. The modal bases of modals, as we will show in chapter 2, are nonveridical states, and modal verbs select uniformly the subjunctive as we saw here. Our main thesis for the subjunctive will therefore be the following:

(124) Subjunctive mood expresses nonveridical stance:
The subjunctive signals the presence of a nonveridical information state.

Modal verbs and propositional attitudes that are evaluated with nonveridical states follow, as we will propose more concretely later, the *Nonveridicality Axiom* (Giannakidou and Mari 2016c, 2018). The Nonveridicality Axiom, crucially, manifests itself as a presupposition of nonveridicality in the lexical entries, introducing uncertainty and therefore weakened commitment.

In sum, the subjunctive versus indicative distinction reflects not only the grammaticalization of the distinction between a veridical and a nonveridical state of mind, but also the difference between what an attitude asserts and what it presupposes. Mood flexibility with attitude verbs indicates that the verb can be construed with or without the nonveridical presuppositional layer (Mari, 2016b).

## 1.6 Road Map

Let us give now a brief outline of what we will do in each chapter.

In chapter 2, we build the formal framework of our theory, centering around the notions of veridicality, nonveridicality, commitment, epistemic weakening, and the new concept of *bias* that we will define for necessity modals such as MUST. Bias gives the illusion of commitment, but a biased modal base is still nonveridical, i.e., it does not entail $p$. We use modality as the illustrating grounds for our theory. As we said here, the presence of a nonveridical epistemic modal base renders all modals nonveridical — and the presence of such a nonveridical epistemic state is the regulating factor for the subjunctive. If a lexical entry contains a nonveridical epistemic space M, it will be able to license the subjunctive. In the rest of the book, this simple idea will be able to explain a vast set of data concerning various classes of propositional attitudes and their mood choice properties.

In chapter 3, we discuss the correlation between mood and embedded tense. We show that there is a strong correlation between attitude meaning and the temporal properties of the embedded complement — and explaining mood and lexical shifts requires that we have a solid understanding of the tense system. The present and past are veridical, but the nonpast is nonveridical, we will argue. The nonpast is the tense of future orientation, and it is the dependent tense that we find with future-oriented subjunctives. This is also the tense of the bare infinitive in English, we will argue. In languages lacking productive morphological mood, the verbal correlate of mood is tense. We will offer an explicit syntax-semantics of tenses in Greek and Italian that will explain also the common observation about anaphoric tense in the subjunctive.

In chapter 4, we offer a detailed analysis of the mood choice with doxastic attitude verbs in Greek and Italian. We use the label "doxastic" to refer to verbs that express attitudes of belief, thought, consciousness, consideration, dream, imagination, fiction, and memory. These attitudes are also sometimes referred to as "cognitive". As it has become clear already, there are two main patterns: (a) doxastic verbs strictly select the indicative, which is the pattern observed in Greek and the bulk of European languages, and (b) doxastic verbs can flexibly allow both moods, with repercussions in meaning, as is illustrated in Italian and Portuguese. We develop in this chapter our notion of epistemic and doxastic commitment of an anchor to the truth of $p$.

There are, we will see, two ways of conceptualizing doxastic attitudes: (a) as purely subjective, veridical, solipsistic attitudes with Hintikka-style truth conditions, that do not engage with factuality and knowledge, or (b) as *doxa*, i.e. nonveridical *suppositional* states that engage with factuality and knowledge. Italian verbs are underspecified lexically and can be construed either way, thus explaining why they are compatible with both indicative and subjunctive. Greek doxastic verbs, by contrast, are lexically specified as solipsistic beliefs and select only the indicative. Doxa is sensitive to the unsettledness of $p$ in the epistemic space of the attitude holder. By carefully distinguishing knowledge and doxa, we will argue that, just as Greek, Italian belief is strong doxa-wise but it is weak epistemic-wise.

Significantly, the flexibility in mood choice does not necessitate imposing ambiguity in the lexical entries of propositional attitude verbs. It rather shows that doxastic propositional attitudes exhibit the variability that we see typically with modals in being able to pick different modal bases. Presuppositional doxastics take two modal bases as arguments: a veridical doxastic one (assertion) and a nonveridical epistemic one (presupposition). Acknowledging flexible propositional attitude meaning offers a new way of understanding attitudinal meaning.

In chapter 4, finally, we discuss the pragmatic function of mood, which is to anchor the complement proposition to the local information state. Mood is local to the anchor and its subjective information space. We distinguish between *assertive* indicative *oti*, which adds $p$ to M, and *presuppositional* indicative *pu* which requires that $p$ already be present in the subjective space of the subject or the common ground. The subjunctive never adds the complement proposition to the subjective space or the common ground. The fact that Greek lexicalizes an assertive and a nonassertive indicative gives further support to our idea that the indicative mood is not isomorphic to assertability.

In chapter 5, we discuss "classically" subjunctive verbs such as verbs of volition and desire. We argue that the truth conditions of these predicates require the notion of *bouletic commitment*, as the counterpart of doxastic commitment in the realm of doxastics. Like pure belief which can be construed solipsistically, some volitional verbs (such as those meaning PROMISE and PERSUADE) are also construed as solipsistic desires and can be defined on variants of bouletic models. When construed solipsistically, volitional attitudes select indicative as expected.

HOPE can also be construed as having a nonveridical presupposition, in addition to the bouletic commitment. In this case, it will select the subjunctive. The suppositional and assertive layers are also featured by WANT, but WANT selects the subjunctive strictly in all languages we know and is never compatible with indicative. Why is that? We propose that WANT is the equivalent of MUST in the realm of volition, i.e., it conveys only bias toward $p$ in the bouletic space, not bouletic commitment (as HOPE does). In addition, WANT appears to have an *antiveridical* presupposition that $p$ is believed by $i$ to *not* be true at the time of utterance. This antiveridical presupposition produces *antifactivity*. Antifactivity characterizes *all* nonindicative moods such as the optative and imperative.

The emerging landscape of desiderative predicates shows a parallelism between doxastic and bouletic verbs. Our semantics for pure volition is novel and includes no preference. It is therefore quite different from the preference-based semantics proposed in earlier works (including our own).

In chapter 6, we discuss implicative and ability predicates, both selecting the subjunctive. We explain why the subjunctive and infinitive are chosen with ability modals and implicative verbs in Greek and Italian (and Romance languages in general). The selection of the subjunctive is expected with ability modals since, as modals, they obey the Nonveridicality Axiom. We propose a new analysis of ability modality by treating the modal ABLE as the dispositional counterpart of epistemic MUST, entailing action to $p$ only in the Ideal worlds. Implicatives such as MANAGE, on the other hand, appear to pose a challenge for the subjunctive because they appear to entail that $p$ is true. We offer an analysis of MANAGE as presupposing that a volitional agent $i$ tried to bring about $p$, without in fact entailing actualization of $p$. This presupposition alone suffices to license the subjunctive.

Under certain circumstances, ability modals do allow entailment to $p$, i.e., the entailment that the ability was actualized and led to $p$. This is often labeled in the literature "actuality entailment". The actuality entailment renders the prejacent true at a pasttime, and depends crucially—we newly argue—on ABLE being embedded under past. We offer a thorough analysis of this phenomenon consistent with the fact that the choice of subjunctive mood and the nonveridical analysis of ability are not affected. We also show that the actuality entailment does not arise with epistemic modals because these never scope under tense. In our analysis, implicative operators and ability modals in the veridical reading are not equivalent, contrary to popular claims in the literature. The ability modal is a modal operator that lacks entirely the presupposition of trying that MANAGE has, but MANAGE is an aspectual operator taking the eventuality as its argument, and does not convey modality or propositional attitude in any obvious sense.

In chapter 7, we consider the mood patterns observed with propositional attitudes of emotion which include (a) attitudes known as emotive such as, e.g., the English *be happy, regret, be surprised, be angry*, (b) attitudes that we label "epistemic emotives", such as the English *be aware, remember*, and attitudes of fear known also as *verba timendi* such as, e.g., the English *fear, be afraid*. Emotion attitudes utilize verbs and adjectives that are gradable. In dealing with emotion attitudes we articulate a precise new semantics for emotion which capitalizes on their subjective and scalar nature. We propose a morphism between emotion scales and worlds which renders the emotive space nonveridical, thus sanctioning the subjunctive. Emotive predicates also have a presupposition of subjective veridicality or factivity, which is responsible for licensing the Greek presuppositional complementizer *pu*. Languages that lack this complementizer typically resort to the subjunctive because of the nonveridical semantics of emotion. Emotion predicates will come with lexical entries that are akin to the mixed veridicality patterns of modals, bouletic attitudes, and suppositional doxastics. Verbs of awareness can also be construed as containing emotive scales, and in this case they select subjunctive, as expected. This is the case of Italian. Again as expected, Greek grammaticalizes awareness as a knowledge predicate.

We distinguish, finally, three kinds of fear attitudes: *fear to, fear that, fear lest*. Fear is not a monolithic emotion in our framework. We offer a new semantics for fear predicates which accounts for the variation in the mood patterns observed without appeal to expressive content.

Our work in this book brings together different levels of analysis—philosophical, semantic, syntactic, and pragmatic—in order to develop a comprehensive theory of how (non)veridicality is reflected in the grammatical behavior of propositional attitudes and modal expressions in language. We use mood choice in sentence complementation as a diagnostics for the rich and flexible semantics of modal verbs and propositional attitudes, and we develop a compositional and fully transparent analysis of various propositional attitude meanings and their interaction with tense. Our semantics has implications for other languages too, including, of course, English. We conclude with some discussion of crosslinguistic implications of our theory in chapter 8.

CHAPTER TWO

# Modalization, Nonveridicality, and Commitment

In this chapter, we build the formal framework of our theory, centering on the notions of veridicality, nonveridicality, commitment, epistemic weakening, and bias. We put these to work in the analysis of modalization. As we alluded to in the opening chapter, the presence of a nonveridical epistemic modal base renders all modals nonveridical—and the presence of such a modal base is the regulating factor for the subjunctive. The subjunctive is used when an individual anchor $i$ does not know that $p$ is true. Epistemic modals are prototypical *antiknowledge* markers. This simple idea will guide our analysis of the semantics of propositional attitudes and their mood choice properties in the following chapters.

We will uncover a number of layers in the structure of modal operators, including a layer of metaevaluation function whose realization is a modal adverb. The notions of commitment and epistemic weakening are shown to also have implications for informativity: veridical commitment conveys maximum informativity, i.e., $p$ is added to the common ground. But epistemically weaker sentences such as those with modal operators and nonindicatives in general are less informative about $p$, and do not add $p$ to the common ground.

## 2.1 Veridical Commitment

The speaker has a chance to engage with truth by choosing to use a sentence without modality in the simple past or present tense, or by using a modal expression, e.g., a modal verb:

(1) a. It is raining.
    b. It rained.
    c. It must be raining.
    d. It may be raining.

We call the sentence without a modal a "bare sentence". The assertion of a bare sentence, if the speaker is co-operative, requires that the speaker follows Gricean Quality, i.e., she is truthful and knows, or has grounds to believe, that it is raining or that it rained. By uttering the sentence "It is raining", the speaker wants to share her knowledge with her audience. Sharing the knowledge means that the speaker intends $p$ to be added to the common ground and become public knowledge. Upon adding $p$ to the common ground, a listener might object if they know otherwise, e.g., if they just came back from outside and it is no longer raining. But insofar as the speaker is concerned, and *given what she knows at the time of utterance*, it is true that it is raining. When the speaker has this knowledge, we say that the speaker is in a veridical state regarding the proposition *It is raining*. Being in a veridical state means that the speaker is fully committed to the proposition *It is raining*.

Likewise, when the speaker asserts a negative sentence, she is committed to the truth of $\neg p$:

(2) It is not raining.

In this case, the speaker knows or believes that it is not raining; by asserting the sentence we assume that she is fully committed to $\neg p$, and proposes to add $\neg p$ to the common ground. The unmodalized negative assertion is epistemically stronger than the assertion of a modal sentence: $\neg p$ is known by the speaker, whereas the modal sentence implies that the speaker is uncertain and considers both $p$ and $\neg p$ possible. In the case of $\neg p$ we can talk about negative commitment, or commitment to the falsity of $p$, and $\neg p$ is added to the common ground.

When the speaker decides to use an epistemic modal, she does so because she cannot be committed to $p$—neither positively nor negatively:

(3) It may/must/might/could be raining.

Depending on whether a possibility or a necessity modal is used, the speaker may have some or many reasons to believe that the prejacent sentence could be true; but she is still in a state of uncertainty. By embedding a proposition $p$ under a modal, therefore, the speaker signals that she cannot be fully committed to $p$, i.e., her epistemic commitment is *weaker* than knowledge of $p$. She still has some commitment to *It is raining* because she is not denying it, but the speaker is not committed enough to add $p$ to the common ground.

As we see, there are two options: one is to use a possibility modal $\Diamond p$ (*It may be raining*), in which case the speaker is merely raising (or, not excluding) the possibility of $p$. The commitment in this case is pretty weak, and we will call it *trivial*. If the speaker chooses to use a necessity modal, on the other hand, the commitment is stronger: the speaker has grounds to consider the prejacent *It is raining* likely or probable. Yet she still has some uncertainty, and might be aware that she doesn't have all the facts. With a necessity modal, we will argue, the speaker is at best *biased* toward $p$, but she is not fully committed to it.

When we think of this weakened commitment with modals, it is helpful to also consider questions. Modalized assertions and questions are similar, according to Giannakidou (2013b),[1] who called modal assertions *inquisitive*, just like questions. Questions and modals are also similar in licensing NPIs. In this, they contrast with past or present veridical assertions, which block these items.[2] Recall:

(4) a. Did Ariadne eat any cookies?
    b. At the party, Ariadne may/can talk to anybody.
    c. Any student can solve this problem.

(5) a. *Ariadne ate any cookies.
    b. *Ariadne is eating any cookies right now.
    c. *Ariadne ate any cookies.

From the perspective of the NPI-licensing diagnostic, it is clear that modals and questions pattern on a par and contrast with bare positive assertions. Recall also that NPIs appear in subjunctive classes of modal verbs, as illustrated below with the two modal verbs of Greek, but not

---

1. For more ongoing work on questions and modality, see Giannakidou and Mari (2019).
2. Following standard practice, we take the English present progressive to be the semantic present, or PRES; see Giannakidou (2014) and references therein and more discussion in chap. 3.

in indicative clauses with epistemic or doxastic attitudes and positive assertions:

(6) *O Pavlos pistevi oti idhe kanenan/opjondhipote.
    the Paul believe.3sg that.IND saw.3sg NPI/FCI
    *Paul believes that he saw anybody.

(7) *Kseri oti agorasa kanena/opjodhipote aftokinito.
    know.3sg that.IND bought.1sg NPI/FCI car
    *He knows that I bought any car.

(8) I Ariadne prepi na milise me
    the Ariadne MUST.3sg that.SUBJ talked.3sg with
    opjondhipote/kanenan fititi.
    FCI/NPI student
    Ariadne would like to talk to any student.

(9) I Ariadne bori na milise me opjondhipote/kanenan
    the Ariadne can that.SUBJ talked.3sg with FCI/NPI
    fititi.
    student
    Ariadne might have talked to any student.

(10) *I Ariadne milise me opjondhipote/kanenan fititi.
     the Ariadne talked.3sg with FCI/NPI student
     *Ariadne talked to any student. [3]

Giannakidou (2013b) argues that nonbiased information-seeking questions and possibility modals convey the state of *nonveridical equilibrium*. The inquisitiveness approach to questions defines questions as being of zero informativity (Ciardelli et al. 2013), and nonveridical equilibrium is the way to capture this generalization, as we will further explore here.

In recent work (Giannakidou 2014, 2016, Giannakidou and Mari 2016c, 2018), we proposed the gradient concept of "commitment strength," and veridicality forms the basis for commitment. When the speaker knows $p$ or believes it to be true, she is in a veridical state and therefore *fully* committed to $p$. We will call this state of full commitment veridical commitment:

[3]. The negative assertion does allow NPIs: *Ariadne didn't talk to any student.*

(11) Scale of veridical commitment (Giannakidou and Mari 2016c):
$<p, \text{MUST } p, \text{MIGHT } p>$;
where $i$ is the speaker, $p$ conveys veridical commitment of $i$ to $p$; MUST $p$ conveys *partial* commitment of $i$ to $p$, and MIGHT $p$ conveys *trivial* commitment of $i$ to $p$.

The criterion for commitment is (non)veridicality: knowledge and belief denote veridical states. A veridical state epistemically commits $i$ to $p$; MUST $p$, and MIGHT $p$, on the other hand, reveal nonveridical states and weakened (or, reduced) commitment. MUST $p$ is stronger than MIGHT $p$ because it entails partial commitment (in Ideal worlds, as we shall argue here), and this creates positive bias toward $p$. Positive bias is weaker than knowledge or belief of $p$. Trivial commitment, finally, is simply raising the possibility of $p$. In all cases, veridical commitment is a state, an attitude towards truth, and in no way implies action. Veridical comittment is entirely dissociated from commitment to act.

In terms of informativity, commitment entails the following:

(12) Veridical Commitment and informativity (Giannakidou and Mari 2016c):
$<p \gg \text{MUST } p \gg \text{MIGHT } p>$; where "$\gg$" means "informationally stronger than"
Nonmodalized $p$ (speaker knows $p$, $p$ added to the common ground) $\gg$
MUST $p$ (speaker does not know $p$, but is biased toward $p$) $\gg$
POSSIBLY $p$ (speaker does not know $p$, and there is nonveridical equilibrium)

Only the veridical, committed assertion of $p$ adds $p$ to the common ground. Introducing a modal does not add $p$ to the common ground, hence MODAL $p$ is informationally weaker than $p$. Bias toward $p$, in turn, is informationally stronger than nonveridical equilibrium but still does not add $p$ to the common ground.

In the discussion to follow, we will develop an explicit formal theory of modalization that uses the concepts above in order to explain both the semantic properties of modals as well as their mood patterns.

## 2.2 The Framework: Objective and Subjective Veridicality

*2.2.1 Objective (Non)veridicality, Semantic Tense*

In objective extensional semantics, sentences are assigned a truth value by a valuation function. Veridicality in this case is "objective", it is about what expressions entail, irrespective of what agents believe (Zwarts 1995; Giannakidou 1994, 1997, 1998, 1999, 2013):

(13) Objective veridicality:
 (i) A propositional function $F$ is veridical iff $Fp \rightarrow p$ is logically valid.
 (ii) $F$ is nonveridical iff $Fp \not\rightarrow p$.
 (iii) $F$ is antiveridical iff $Fp \rightarrow \neg p$.

Objective veridicality is a property of truth-entailing expressions. A factive verb such as *know* entails (in fact: presupposes) that its complement is true; it is therefore objectively veridical. *Know* is veridical because *know* $(p)$ entails that $p$ is true. But *believe, want* are not veridical:

(14) I know that Nicholas brought dessert.

(15) Anastasia believes that Nicholas brought dessert.

*Believe* is not objectively veridical because if *Anastasia believes that p* is true, $p$ may or may not be true.

Temporal operators such as the present (PRES) or the past (PAST), expressed by tenses or adverbials, are objectively veridical. Consider:

(16) a. Yesterday, Nicholas brought dessert.
 b. Right now, Nicholas is washing the dishes.

(17) Veridicality of temporal operators:
 Let $F$ be temporal function, $t$ an instant or an interval.
 $F$ is veridical iff $Fp$ at a time $t$ entails that $p$ is true at a (contextually given) time $t' \leq t$; otherwise $F$ is nonveridical. (Giannakidou 2002: 23)

PAST and the adverb *yesterday* are veridical because (PAST/*yesterday* (p)) at the time of utterrence $t_u$ entail that p was true at a time $t' \leq t$. Likewise, PRES and *right now* are veridical because (PRES/*right now* (p)) at $t_u$ entail that p is true at $t_u$. The future (FUT), however, is nonveridical because (FUT (p)) at $t_u$ does not entail that p is true at $t_u$ or a time $t' \leq t$. Temporal veridicality is thus objective veridicality anchored to $t_u$; the criterion is whether there is a time prior to $t_u$, or $t_u$ itself, where p is true, and this excludes the future from the veridical realm.

Modal verbs, crucially, appear to "remove" the veridicality of the tensed sentence:

(18) a. Nicholas might/must be sleeping now.
 b. Nicholas might/must have slept earlier.

(19) a. MUST (PRES/PAST (p)) does not entail that p is true at a time $t' \leq t$.
 b. MAY (PRES/PAST (p)) does not entail that p is true at a time $t' \leq t$.

We discuss the interactions of modals with tense later. For now, simply note that modal verbs are veridicality blockers: the veridicality entailment just noted under present or past is lost in the scope of a modal. This holds for epistemic modal verbs— which are thus to be distinguished from aleithic necessity modals, which indeed validate the principle T that guarantees veridicality. Epistemic necessity does not validate this principle (see Giannakidou 1998, 1999; and Portner 2009).

Modals introduce epistemic uncertainty, indicating that the speaker is taking a *nonveridical stance* toward the proposition. Let us unpack this.

### 2.2.2 Subjective Veridicality

Speakers and hearers form judgments about the truth of statements based on what they know, expect, or believe (Giannakidou 1994, 1998, 1999, 2009, 2013; Harris and Potts 2010; de Marneffe et al. 2012; Mari 2015c on perspectival generics). That such relativization is needed becomes visible when a modal expression is used; but it is intuitively clear that every sentence is interpreted against prior knowledge or experience. Harris and

Potts 2010 express this very clearly in their assertion that "all sentences are perspectival."

When speakers make assertions or ask questions or assess statements of others, they make veridicality judgments that are not *ex nihilo*, but rather based on their own body of information, evidence, and overall perspective. The veridicality judgement is more complex than truth assignment: it depends on what speakers know or believe to be true, on general assumptions they make about what is being said, their overall beliefs and experiences, and on how they extract information, evidence, and overall data from context (see especially Giannakidou 1998, 2013; Mari 2003, 2005; Giannakidou and Mari 2016c; de Marneffe et al. 2012 confirm this complexity with corpus data).[4]

Generally speaking, then, we must talk about objective and relative veridicality for all sentences. Objective veridicality depends on what is true or not in the world, it corresponds to truth; but in the formation of relative veridicality judgements, an individual anchors the propositional content to their own informational spaces, sometimes without regard to truth (as is the case of pure belief or imagination).[5] For unembedded sentences, the individual anchor is always the speaker. For embedded sentences, the speaker still has an opinion, but for mood choice it is the subject of the attitude that matters, as we said and showed in earlier work. Individual anchoring of truth should be seen on a par with other kinds of anchoring of propositional content, i.e., temporal anchoring, event anchoring (e.g., Hacquard 2006, 2010), or *Now*-anchoring, as we discuss further in chapter 3.

Notice that we do not talk about relative truth but relative *veridicality*. Truth is objective and independent of individual anchors—it can therefore not be relativized. Rather, it is the veridicality judgement that is relative because it relies on the formation of subjective information states of various kinds. Expressions such as "my truth" and "your truth", which are sometimes used carelessly, can only be understood as shorthands for *i*'s veridicality judgement or *i*'s perspective on truth, not as referencing truth itself.

---

4. The relation between assertion and belief is complex and currently under close scrutiny (see Lauer 2013; Krifka 2015; Mari 2017a, b). We will take up this question in chapter 4.

5. With sentences containing predicates of personal taste (Lasersohn 2005; Stephenson 2007) veridicality is determined not by knowledge but by taste or experience, and the individual anchor is called the *judge*. The judge is just one case of anchor in our theory.

Giannakidou (1994, 1997) was the first to offer a system of relativization of veridicality. She used the term "models of evaluation" and the letter M to refer to the subjective private information states of individual anchors. Giannakidou (1999: 45) calls these models epistemic states, and Giannakidou 2013 uses the term 'information state'. The models M are sets of worlds, relative to the individual anchor $i$, corresponding to what $i$ believes, knows, dreams, imagines, remembers, wants and the like, depending on the lexical meaning of the propositional attitude verb. We will use the term "information states", and continue to use M following Giannakidou's work. The basic definition is as follows:

(20) Information state of an individual anchor $i$:
An information state $M(i)$ is a set of worlds associated with an individual $i$ representing worlds compatible with what $i$ knows or believes in the context of utterance.

We can think of $M(i)$ broadly as a private space encompassing $i$'s worldview. It is a nontrivial, nonsingleton set that encompasses $i$'s beliefs and knowledge about the world (as well as memories, perceptions, desires, expectations, etc.). M is the body of what counts as "evidence", in other words, that $i$ constructs to form a veridicaility judgment about a sentence. M can encompass also idelogy, political or religious beliefs and the like (though we will not study how these influence the judgment here). Another way of thinking about these information states is as mental states. As our analysis develops in this book, we will see that there are many kinds of states that are relevant for propositional attitudes, including states such as memory, perception, awareness, and emotion.

Given $M(i)$, we can now identify (non)veridicality subjectively, relative to M as follows:

(21) Subjective Veridicality:
(i.) A function $F$ that takes a proposition $p$ as its argument is veridical with respect to an individual anchor $i$ and an information state $M(i)$ iff $Fp$ entails $p$ in $M(i)$.
(ii.) $Fp$ entails $p$ in $M(i)$ iff $\forall w'[w' \in M(i) \to w' \in \{w'' \mid p(w'')\}]$.

Subjective, or relative, veridicality is entailment within M. It reflects total endorsement of $p$ by $i$, and imposes homogeneity of the entire $M(i)$.

This is crucial. When all worlds in M(i) are p worlds, M(i) is a veridical state, and p is entailed in M(i).

(22) Veridical information state:
An information state M(i) is veridical about p iff it is homogeneous:
$\forall w'[w' \in M(i) \rightarrow w' \in \{w'' \mid p(w'')\}]$.

From the definition of subjective veridicality we can now derive epistemic commitment as a property that characterizes the individual anchor when she knows p to be true:

(23) Epistemic commitment of i to a proposition p:
An individual anchor i is epistemically committed to p iff M(i) contains worlds compatible with what i knows, and M(i) is veridical, i.e., if M(i) entails p.

In other words, an individual anchor i is epistemically committed to p if i knows p. The veridical commitment state conveys settledness of p in the space of knowledge M. Things that are known are settled. In chap. 4, we will distinguish epistemic from doxastic commitment which is commitment based on belief (and variants thereof). Doxastic commitment is subjectively veridical since it does not rely on knowledge. In the most intuitive sense, anchors commit based on both knowledge and beliefs.

The requirement for a veridical state which forms the basis for commitment can now be understood as a prerequisite for assertion:

(24) Veridical commitment as a prerequisite for assertion:
A sentence S is assertable by the speaker i if and only if M(i) is veridical, i.e., if M(i) entails p; where p is the denotation of S.

The above means that the speaker i can assert a sentence S only if i is veridically committed to its proposition p. For example:

(25) *Flavio is a doctor* is assertable by speaker i iff
$\forall w'[w' \in M(i) \rightarrow w' \in \{w'' \mid doctor(Flavio)(w'')\}]$.

The cooperative assertion of an unmodalized unembedded positive sentence relies on the speaker's belief or knowledge of p.

If the sentence is negative, in a parallel manner, assertability relies on the speaker's commitment to $\neg p$:

(26)  *Giacomo is not a doctor* is assertable by speaker $i$ if and only if
$\forall w'[w' \in M(i) \rightarrow w' \in \{w'' \mid \neg doctor(Giacomo)(w'')\}]$.

Again we have entailment in M: all worlds in $M(i)$ are $\neg p$ worlds. We can therefore say that the assertion of unmodalized sentences, positive or negative, requires homogeneous states of commitment of $i$ to $p$ or its negation $\neg p$. In the case of negation, we talk about commitment to $\neg p$:

(27)  Epistemic commitment of $i$ to a $\neg p$ (Subjective Antiveridicality):
An individual anchor $i$ is committed to $\neg p$ iff $M(i)$ contains worlds compatible with what $i$ knows and $M(i)$ entails $\neg p$.

Commitment to $\neg p$ is subjective antiveridicality. Objective antiveridicality, recall, is the property of entailing $\neg p$ irrespective of M:

(28)  Objective antiveridicality:
A function $F$ is antiveridical iff $Fp$ entails $\neg p$.

At this point, it is useful to relate veridicality and antiveridicality to *epistemic settledness*:

(29)  Epistemic settledness in $M(i)$:
(i.) $M(i)$ is epistemically settled about $\phi$, where $\phi$ is $p$ or $\neg p$, iff $\forall w'[w' \in M(i) \rightarrow w' \in \{w'' \mid \phi(w'')\}]$.
(ii.) $M(i)$ is positively settled iff $\forall w'[w' \in M(i) \rightarrow w' \in \{w'' \mid p(w'')\}]$.
(iii.) $M(i)$ is negatively settled iff $\forall w'[w' \in M(i) \rightarrow w' \in \{w'' \mid \neg p(w'')\}]$.

The notion of epistemic settledness is useful in order to understand the implications of veridicality and homogeneity for entailment: when all worlds are $p$ worlds, the epistemic state is positively settled and entails $p$; when all worlds are $\neg p$ worlds, the epistemic state is negatively settled and entails $\neg p$. When $M(i)$ entails $p$, we can say that $M(i)$ supports

$p$ (a term that we used in earlier work). When M($i$) entails ¬$p$, M($i$) supports ¬$p$. When M($i$) supports $p$, we will say again that $i$ is epistemically committed to $p$; when M($i$) entails ¬$p$, $i$ is said to be committed to ¬$p$. Commitment to ¬$p$ is rejection of $p$. Asserting $p$ and rejecting $p$ both reveal homogeneous, settled commitment states.

We now want to discuss factivity. Verbs of knowledge such as *know, ksero, gnorizo, sapere* and their equivalents (KNOW) have the following truth condition:

(30)  〚Nicholas kseri /know $p$〛 will be defined iff the actual world $w$ is a $p$ world. If defined,
〚Nicholas kseri oti $p$〛 is true in $w$ iff:
$\forall w'[w' \in M(Nicholas) \to w' \in \{w'' \mid p(w'')\}]$, and
$\forall w'[w' \in M(speaker) \to w' \in \{w'' \mid p(w'')\}]$

KNOW is objectively veridical since its complement is a fact, i.e., true in the actual world $w$, hence KNOW $p$ entails $p$ in $w$. At the same time, KNOW reflects *common*, i.e., shared knowledge between speaker and subject, which means that it entails $p$ in M(Nicholas) as well as M(speaker). KNOW is therefore both objectively and subjectively veridical. Giannakidou (1998, 1999) calls KNOW for this reason *strongly veridical*.

Factivity emerges as an objective veridicality presupposition:

(31)  Factivity as a presupposition of objective veridicality:
A propositional function $F$ is factive iff $Fp$ presupposes that $p$ is actually true.

In other words, an objectively veridical F can simply entail $p$ (like past tense or *yesterday*), or presuppose it like KNOW, in which case F is factive.

Subjective veridicality, of course, does not entail factivity or objective veridicality. For instance, *Nicholas believes that Ariadne is a doctor* reflects a veridical epistemic state (with respect to Nicholas = $i$ and Nicholas's belief state = Dox($i$)), but the sentence *Ariadne is a doctor* can be objectively false, i.e., Nicholas might have a false belief:

(32)  〚Nicholas believes that $p$〛 is true in the world of the utterance context $w$ iff:
$\forall w'[w' \in \text{Dox}(Nicholas) \to w' \in \{w'' \mid p(w'')\}]$

Here we are using Dox to refer specifically to a doxastic state. The truth condition of *believe* does not entail actual truth. However, (32) renders *believe* subjectively veridical, because the whole M(*Nicholas*) entails *p*. As we shall see in this book, other nonfactive verbs denoting private spaces such as *dream, imagine* are subjectively veridical because they denote variants of Dox that entail *p* in them, without entailing actual truth.

Subjective veridicality, then, and not objective truth or veridicality is the prerequisite property for the licensing of the indicative mood. This is why verbs of belief and knowledge both select the indicative. Our thesis will be the following, as can be recalled from chapter 1:

(33) Indicative mood and veridicality:
The indicative will be licensed in the complement of a propositional attitude that is veridical (objectively or subjectively).

Verbs of negative assertion, which we briefly mentioned in chapter 1, are also veridical and select the indicative:

(34) O  Nicholas arnithike  oti/*na        i    Ariadne ton
 the Nicholas denied.3sg that.IND/SUBJ the Ariadne him
 voithise
 helped.3sg.
 Nicholas denied that Ariadne helped him.

DENY *p* does not entail *p*; but it express commitment to ¬*p*, and it therefore selects indicative:

(35) 〚Nicholas denied that *p*〛 is true in the world of the utterance context *w* iff:
$\forall w'[w' \in M(Nicholas) \to w' \in \{w'' \mid \neg p(w'')\}]$

In other words, if *i* denies that *p*, then *i* knows or believes ¬*p* to be true. Hence, entailment and homogeneity in M explains why we get indicative with even negative assertives.

Let us move on now to define subjective nonveridicality, which is the defining property of modalization, and the licensing property of the subjunctive mood.

## 2.2.3 Subjective Nonveridicality

Nonveridicality is a property of epistemic and doxastic (broadly construed) uncertainty. Uncertainty functions F do not imply that $i$ knows or believes $p$ to be true. In this case, $i$ cannot be fully committed to $p$; rather, $i$ is undecided, or as we said earlier, she is only *weakly* committed, which means partially or trivially (with possibility) committed. With a subjectively nonveridical function, therefore, M($i$) does not entail $p$. We define subjective veridicality as follows:

(36) Subjective nonveridicality:
A function $F$ that takes a proposition $p$ as its argument is subjectively nonveridical with respect to an individual anchor $i$ and an epistemic state M($i$) iff F$p$ does not entail $p$, i.e., iff $\exists w'[w' \in M(i) \land w' \in \{w'' \mid p(w'')\}]$ & $\exists w'''[w''' \in M(i) \land w''' \in \{w'''' \mid \neg p(w'''')\}]$.

A subjectively veridical function creates a space where both $p$ and $\neg p$ are open possibilities. The nonveridical state is partitioned:

(37) Nonveridical epistemic state:
An epistemic state M($i$) is nonveridical about $p$ iff M($i$) contains both $p$ and $\neg p$ worlds.

Nonveridical epistemic states M($i$) are nonhomogenous, containing both $p$ and $\neg p$ worlds. They are therefore epistemically unsettled, not entailing $p$. A nonveridical state expresses weaker commitment to $p$ than a veridical state, which is full commitment (homogeneity).

Modal functions, as we will show in this chapter, are nonveridical functions. Inquisitive spaces such as questions also denote nonveridical epistemic states, as we said (see also Giannakidou 2013b). We will move on to examine the nonveridicality of modal expressions next, but before we do that let us summarize below the typology of modal spaces (sets of worlds) that we just talked about:

(38) Veridicality of modal spaces and veridical commitment:

   a. A *veridical* modal space is fully committed:
   $\forall w'[w' \in M(i) \rightarrow w' \in \{w'' \mid p(w'')\}]$.
   (For short, in the lexical entries: $\forall w' \in M(i) : p(w')$).

b. An *antiveridical* modal space is fully committed:
∀w'[w' ∈ M(i) → w' ∈ {w'' | ¬p(w'')}].
(For short, in the lexical entries: ∀w' ∈ M(i) : ¬p(w')).
c. A *nonveridical* modal space is weakly committed:
∃w'[w' ∈ M(i) ∧ w' ∈ {w'' | p(w'')}] & ∃w'''[w''' ∈ M(i) ∧ w''' ∈ {w'''' | ¬p(w'''')}].
(For short, in the lexical entries: ∃w' ∈ M(i) : p(w') & ∃w'' ∈ M(i) : ¬p(w''))

A nonveridical space is thus epistemically weaker than the veridical space or antiveridical space which entail the prejacent proposition $p$ or $\neg p$. The nonveridical M conveys weakened commitment of $i$ to $p$. We say that the commitment is weakened, and not that there is no commitment, because the possibility of $p$ still conveys commitment albeit *trivial*, as we characterized it.

In terms of informative content, a homogeneous veridical or antiveridical state corresponds to a move by $i$ to add the $p$ or $\neg p$ to the common ground (or to private grounds, as we show in chap. 4). Following Giannakidou (2013), we call this "full informativity". Positive and negative bare assertions are fully informative in that they allow addition of the prejacent to the common ground:

(39) Fact. Homogeneity and informativity:
Homogeneous (veridical and antiveridical) information states are fully informative.

Homogeneous states contrast with nonveridical states which are partitioned ($p$ and $\neg p$) thus preventing addition of $p$ to the common ground. Nonindicative assertions—assertions with modals, questions, optatives, imperatives—all convey nonveridical states and therefore do not add $p$ to the common ground.

We are now going to show that modal verbs as a natural class, no matter how "strong" they might initially give the impression to be, are epistemically weaker than the unmodalized assertions because their modal bases denote nonveridical states. By having such modal bases, modal operators do not entail knowledge or belief of $p$. When a speaker uses a modal, in other words, she does so because she wants to signal that she does not have knowledge or belief of $p$ and can therefore not be committed to it.

The subjunctive, we argue, will be licensed in precisely this situation; it is, in other words, the mood of nonveridicality and uncertainty.

## 2.3 Modal Operators and the Subjunctive: Possibility

The notions of possibility and necessity are already at the core of the Aristotelian *Categories*. Contemporary possible world semantics and modal logics build systems based on Kripke's (1972) and Lewis's (1973) pioneering works. Our base framework here will be Kratzer's (1977, 1981, 1990) and Portner's (2009) theory of linguistic, that is, nonaleithic modality. Aleithic modality, from the Greek word *aletheia* (truth), refers to purely logical necessity or possibility which is unrestricted, in contrast to linguistic modalities that are restricted by modal bases and ordering sources. In the Kratzerian theory, modal verbs are restricted quantifiers that take modal bases and ordering sources as arguments, determining to a large extent what kind of modality we have—i.e., epistemic, deontic, teleological, ability, bouletic, dynamic—as well as particular flavors of modality (e.g., *must, should, ought*). Portner (2009) offers a very clear and comprehensive introduction to Kratzer's theory and refines it in many ways; we refer the reader to that excellent work for a detailed presentation of the framework of linguistic modality.

In recent work (Giannakidou 1998, 1999, 2013b; Mari 2015a, 2016b; and Giannakidou and Mari 2012a, b, 2013, 2016c), we added the *Nonveridicality Axiom* to the theory of linguistic modality. The Nonveridicality Axiom says that nonaleithic modal expressions require their modal bases to be nonveridical, i.e., they must contain $p$ and $\neg p$ worlds.[6] Modal verbs and adverbs are signals that the speaker does not know $p$ to be true and can therefore not commit to it. Epistemic modals, of course, are also objectively nonveridical as was shown earlier, since no version of MODAL $p$ entails $p$. Modals are uncertainty operators.

By "modals", we intend to refer to expressions that denote the necessity or possibility operators of modal logic, regardless of grammatical

---

6. Beaver and Frazee (2016) follow suit and adopt nonveridicality as a defining property of modality, and Condoravdi (2002) posits a similar "diversity" condition for modal bases. Aleithic necessity, as we said earlier, is veridical since it is unrestricted universal quantification in all worlds.

category. Modals thus can be verbs, adverbs, adjectives, tenses, and particles:

(40) a. Flavio *may/must/might/should* be at home. (modal verbs)
b. Flavio is *probably/maybe/perhaps* at home. (modal adverbs)
c. It is *possible/probable* that Flavio is at home. (modal adjectives)

Notice that modals can be ambiguous: *Flavio must/should be at home* can be epistemic or deontic (or teleological, or other fine-grained distinctions one wishes to make). The key factor for the apparent ambiguity is the modal base the modal verb has as its argument: with an epistemic base we get epistemic modality, with a deontic base we get deontic modality. Kratzer discusses this meaning flexibility at length and proposes that it is not ambiguity but underspecification of the modal base. *Flavio might be at home*, on the other hand, is not flexible but strictly epistemic, hence we need to allow for modals such as *might* which lexically select their modal base. In our theory of propositional attitudes, we find, likewise, flexible and nonflexible attitudes—and we will argue, like Kratzer, for underspecification rather than ambiguity. The relation between modal verbs and propositional attitudes is, as we shall see, strikingly close.

The future modals and tenses are also epistemic necessity operators, just like MUST, we have argued in Giannakidou and Mari (2018b).

(41) a. O Janis tha erthi spiti.
the John FUT come.NONPAST.3sg home
(Greek modal future particle)
John will come home.
b. Gianni arriverà domani. (Italian modal tense)
John arrive.FUT.3sg tomorrow
John will arrive tomorrow.

In the discussion below, when we use MUST we refer to the future modal too.

The epistemic subjunctive used with questions in Greek (recall the data from chapter 1) is a possibility modal in the semantics (Giannakidou 2016). Modals come in different shapes (particles, tenses, or verbs), and modal flavors, as we said. A classic distinction is between epistemic and deontic modality, but Portner talks about *priority* modality to include teleological, bouletic, and ability modality. In this chapter, we focus mainly on epistemic modals, but we will discuss the deontic, priority modality and ability in chapter 6.

Modal verbs as a class, it must be recalled, require the subjunctive:

(42) a. Prepi na/*oti vrehi.
       must that.SUBJ/IND rain.3sg
       It must be raining.
    b. Bori na/*oti vrehi.
       may that.SUBJ/IND rain.3sg
       It may be raining.
    c. Prepi na/*oti evrekse.
       must that.SUBJ/IND rain.PAST.3sg
       It must have rained.
    d. Bori na/*oti evrekse.
       may that.SUBJ/IND rain.PAST.3sg
       It may have rained.

The infinitive is allowed in Italian but is impossible in Greek. Greek has two modal verbs—a possibility modal *bori*, and a necessity modal *prepi*. Staraki (2013, 2017) offers extensive discussions on the Greek modals, including further interactions with tenses (see also Giannakidou 2012; Giannakidou and Mari 2016c, 2018b). As can be seen in the examples above, both modals require the subjunctive. The type of modality also doesn't seem to matter: the above sentences are epistemic, but deontic modals also require subjunctive:

(43) Prepi na/*oti fas olo to fagito sou!
     must that.SUBJ/*IND eat.2sg all the food yours
     You must eat all your food!

(44) Ja na perasis ston epomeno giro, prepi
     for SUBJ. pass.on.2sg to.the next round, must
     na/*oti apandisis tris erotisis.
     that.SUBJ/IND answer.2sg three questions
     In order to pass on to the next round (of the game), you must answer three questions.

(45) Boris na/*oti klisis tin porta.
     must that.SUBJ/IND close.2sg the door
     You may close the door.

Deontic modality requires the subjunctive, as we see, even when used for rules, definitions, etc. In Italian, subjunctive is also the choice, along with infinitive. Modal verbs never select the indicative.

Every modal has an epistemic modal base as its argument, which we will designate as M($i$). In our framework, M($i$) is the set of propositions known by the speaker $i$ at $t_u$ (the utterance time) and $w_0$ is the world of evaluation, by default the actual world:

(46) M($i$)($t_u$)($w_0$) = $\lambda w'$($w'$ is compatible with what is known by the speaker $i$ in $w_0$ at $t_u$)[7]

Epistemic modality is, therefore, by default 'subjective' (Lyons 1977), and knowledge changes with time. Epistemic modality is parametric to knowledge at $t_u$, as is often acknowledged in the literature (see Portner 2009; Hacquard 2006, 2010, Giannakidou and Mari 2016c).

When a speaker chooses to modalize, she chooses to take a nonveridical stance. If she knows the prejacent proposition $p$ to be true, it is odd to modalize. The modal base, therefore, is a nonveridical space and contains both $p$ and $\neg p$ worlds and does not entail $p$. Following Giannakidou and Mari (2016c, 2018b), we formulate nonveridicality as a precondition on modalities in the form of the axiom below:

(47) Nonveridicality Axiom of modal expressions (MODAL):
MODAL (M)($p$) can be defined if and only if the modal base M is nonveridical, i.e., M contains both $p$ and $\neg p$ worlds.

The modal base is therefore a weakened commitment space, with $p$ and $\neg p$ being open possibilities. Nonaleithic modals (possibility and necessity, epistemic, deontic, bouletic, etc) obey this principle, and therefore come with partitioned, unsettled modal bases.[8] Unmodalized assertions express full commitment and are therefore stronger than modalized sentences.

---

[7] Our notation M($i$) corresponds to the Kratzerian notation using set intersection $\cap f_{epistemic}(w_0, i, t_u)$, where this returns the set of worlds compatible with what is known in $w_0$ by $i$. It is also clear that modality, in our framework, is always subjective, allowing also for cases where $i$ is a collective individual or group of people to capture what others would call objective modality.

[8]. There are two exceptions to the axiom, and both result in trivialization of modality. The first case is the actuality entailment of ability modals, where the modal is trivialized (see Mari 2017c and our discussion in chap. 6). The second case is aleithic modality, as in *1 + 1 must*

In agreement with the common analysis of epistemic possibility, we take it that epistemic possibility modals are existential quantifiers and that they lack ordering sources.[9] The absence of ordering sources with epistemic possibility renders $p$ and $\neg p$ equal possibilities revealing that the assessor is in a state of *nonveridical equilibrium* which Giannakidou 2013b calls "true" uncertainty (see also Giannakidou and Mari 2016c, 2018b):

(48) Nonveridical equilibrium (Giannakidou 2013b):
An information state M is in nonveridical equilibrium iff M is partitioned into $p$ and $\neg p$, and there is no bias toward $p$ or $\neg p$.

Nonveridical equilibrium conveys the weakest commitment in merely not excluding the possibility of $p$. Possibility modals and unbiased polar questions (*Did Ariadne win the race?*) are in nonveridical equilibrium, in a state of balanced indecision where both $p$ and its negation are equally plausible options, and $i$ has no reason to prefer one over the other (see Kang and Yoon 2018 for some more discussion of the concept of equilibrium as it applies to certain question particles in Korean). Giannakidou (2013b) argues that "inquisitive" and "nonveridical" describe the same state of possibility and questions.

The bare truth condition of epistemic possibility is the following, considering also the explicit contribution of tense and focussing on the present and past cases. We use MIGHT as an umbrella for epistemic possibility modals:

(49) $[\![\text{MIGHT (PRES }(p))]\!]^{M,i,S}$ is true iff $\exists w' \in M(i) : p(w', t_u)$

(50) $[\![\text{MIGHT (PAST }(p))]\!]^{M,i,S}$ is true iff $\exists w' \in M(i) \exists t' \prec t_u : p(w', t')$

These conditions will be enriched later, but we give them here as base truth conditions. By choosing a possibility modal, the speaker $i$ conveys

---

*equal 2.* Giannakidou and Mari (2016c) distinguish this aleithic *must* from the epistemic use —thus maintaining nonveridicality and so-called "weakness" of epistemic MUST (Karttunen 1972). With both aleithic modality and actuality entailment, the distinction between modal and non modal statement is lost. We offer more discussion on this point in chap. 6.

9. Deontic possibility modals are claimed to use a circumstantial modal base and a deontic ordering source (Portner 2009).

*trivial commitment*. Recall, indeed, that as a modal, MIGHT is nonveridical, hence the modal base contains $p$ and $\neg p$ worlds. The inference that all worlds are $p$ worlds cannot thus arise. Nonveridical equilibrium and the ensuing trivial commitment come with very low informativity about $p$, again comparable to that of information-seeking questions.

Before moving on, and given that all modals select the subjunctive, it seems reasonable to formulate the following licensing condition of the subjunctive:

(51) Licensing condition of subjunctive mood:
An expression $F$ licenses the subjunctive mood in its scope iff $F$ is non-veridical.[10]

We propose this condition as a sufficiency condition (on the semantics of the licenser, i.e. the modal verb). The possibility modal is nonveridical, it can therefore license the subjunctive mood.

## 2.4 Epistemic Necessity: Nonveridicality with Bias

We move on now to epistemic necessity modals. This class includes modal verbs meaning MUST, SHOULD, as well as the future modal and morphemes (FUT). We will use upper-case MUST to refer to such expressions jointly, and we refer to Giannakidou and Mari (2018a) for detailed arguments that FUT expressions are epistemic necessity modals. Necessity modals obey the Nonveridicality Axiom, but now the modal base favors the worlds where $p$ is true. We will call this "positive bias" toward $p$ and we will propose a theory of how exactly that happens (building on Giannakidou and Mari 2013, 2016c, 2018a, b).

In his seminal work, Kartunnen (1972) claims that English *must* is "weak". Recall that just like the possibility modal, Greek and Italian select the subjunctive. From the perspective of mood licensing, therefore, one could never be led to believe that MUST is anything but weak. We start by offering evidence that MUST expressions are not compatible with knowledge of $p$. In making this argument, we will refute Kartunnen's thesis that

---

10. We will make clear later on that $F$ must be nonveridical in one of the meaning dimensions, which include the presupposition.

the weakness of *must* has to do with a requirement that evidence be indirect. It is not directness or indirectness that matter but whether there is knowledge or not of *p*. If *i* knows *p*, *i* is in a veridical state, and in this case MUST cannot be used. After we establish this, we discuss the property of positive bias.

### 2.4.1 MUST Is Incompatible with Knowledge

Kartunnen (1972) held that the weakness of MUST is intimately related to the weakness of the source of information: when the speaker has indirect evidence that the prejacent is true, she uses MUST to signal that she is uncertain. Giannakidou and Mari (2016c) argued that the epistemic weakening is not due to the fact that knowledge is indirect but to the fact that knowledge is *partial*. Von Fintel and Gillies (2010: 361) also challenge Kartunnen: "Weakness and indirectness are not two sides of a single coin at all. They are just different." Their claim is that the epistemic modal *must* presupposes indirect evidence, but it is nevertheless "strong." We have addressed von Fintel and Gillies in earlier work and consider here only what appears to be their strongest argument, which concerns deductive contexts.[11]

Let us proceed to offer arguments showing that it is not indirect evidence that sanctions MUST but lack of knowledge. Direct visual perception contexts are famously cited as evidence for need of indirect evidence:

(52) Context: *i* is standing in front of the window and sees the rain.
    a. #It must be raining.
    b. #Tha vrehi.
       FUT rain
    c. #Piovera.
       rain-FUT.3sg
    d. # Prepi na vrehi.
       must that.SUBJ rain
    e. #Dovrà piovere.
       Must.FUT.3sg rain

---

11. See also discussion in Papafragou (2000, 2006).

MUST is infelicitous here because, Kartunnen's argument goes, it requires indirect evidence but if I see the rain, the evidence is direct. Yet, if I see the rain, I *know* that it is raining, and knowledge, as we said, is veridical. It seems thus likely that MUST is excluded not because the evidence must be indirect, as Karttunen argued, but because evidence is a reliable path to knowledge. It can be concluded from the paradigm above that MUST is incompatible with knowledge of *p*.

Giannakidou and Mari (2016c) note that MUST statements can be continued by "but I am not entirely sure" (as first noted in Bertinetto 1979; Mari 2009, Giannakidou and Mari 2012b):

(53) Deve essere a casa, ma non sono totalmente
 Must.PRES.3sg be at home, but not be.PRES.1sg entirely
 sicuro.
 sure
 He must be home, but I am not entirely sure.

Veridical assertions do not accept such continuation:

(54) a. #He is at home but I am not entirely sure.
 b. #I know he is at home but I am not entirely sure.

For English, Lassiter (2016) offers a plethora of attested examples where *must* is modified with "I don't know for sure", and similar expressions challenging knowledge of *p*:

(55) a. This is a very early, very correct Mustang that has been in a private collection for a long time. . . . The speedo[meter] shows 38,000 miles and *it must be 138,000, but I don't know for sure.*
 b. *I don't know for sure*, sweetie, but she *must have been* very depressed. A person doesn't do something like that lightly.
 c. It must have been a Tuesday (but I don't know for sure), I can't remember.
 d. I have an injected TB42 turbo and don't like the current setup. There is an extra injector located in the piping from the throttle body . . . *Must be an old DTS diesel setup but I'm not certain.* Why would they have added this extra injector?

These examples support the conclusion that MUST does not entail knowledge of *p* by the speaker *i*. MUST, rather, allows inference to *p* based on a number of premises and potential gaps (see also recent discussion in Goodhue 2018).

Giannakidou and Mari (2016c) offer new arguments against indirectness. We summarize two arguments here and add two more. Consider, first, the contrast between the veridical context we presented before where I see the rain, and the following case (56), where I only see a wet umbrella.

(56) Context: I see a wet umbrella.
    a. It must be raining.
    b. Tha/Prepi na    vrehi. (Greek)
       FUT/Must that.SUBJ rain.
    c. Deve star piovendo. (Italian)
       must be   rain.GER.
    d. Pioverà.
       rain.FUT.3sg
    e. Deve star piovendo, ma non sono sicura.
       must be   rain.GER, but not am  certain
       It must be raining, but I am not certain.
    f. Deve probabilmente star piovendo.
       must probably   be rain.GER
       It must probably be raining.

In this context, I see a wet umbrella, but I don't see the rain, therefore I do not *know* that it is raining. The wet umbrella is an indication, and can support "It is raining" in a subset of M. But M can contain also worlds in which the umbrella got wet in some other way—and these worlds could be considered by me more likely, for instance in a context when I left the house this morning the weather was sunny and the forecast predicted no rain. Continuation with "I am not sure" is allowed here, as we see.

Auditory perception is compatible with MUST, but hearing is just as direct as seeing (Willett, 1988):

(57) Context: I am in a room with no windows, but I hear sounds of rain on the roof.

a. It must be raining.
b. Tha vrehi.
   FUT rain.
c. Pioverà.
   rain.FUT.3sg.
d. Tha prepi na        vrexi
   FUT must that.SUBJ rain.

If I only hear something that sounds like rain, I do not know that it is raining. I only have the sound of something that could be rain. The stimulus is direct, but inadequate for knowledge. What I hear might be caused by something other than the rain. Auditory perception is nonveridical (as we will discuss further in chap. 5), while visual perception is veridical; recall that the first discussions of veridicality in linguistics come from Montague's (1969) analysis of the verb *see* as veridical. Overall, perceptions can of course be deceiving, and just because something *looks like* or *sounds like* it has the property P doesn't mean that it does. Semblance verbs—as will be shown in chap. 4—can be construed as nonveridical. (Semblance, like belief, it turns out, can be construed as commitment as well as supposition in which case it is contrasted with knowledge.)

Now consider the case where I see, but my vision is not clear. In this case, I can use MUST:

(58)  Context: I am looking through the window, and it is foggy and dark. I don't fully trust what I am seeing:

   a. Prepi na        vrexi.   (Greek MUST)
      must that.SUBJ rain.3sg
      It must be raining.
   b. Tha vrexi.   (Greek, epistemic future, equivalent to MUST)
      FUT rain.3sg
      It must be raining.

Clearly, then, MUST does not depend on direct perception but on how reliable I take the sensory information to be in establishing knowledge. If my vision is unclear and it's foggy, I do not trust my senses fully as a source for knowledge; I can therefore not be committed to "It is raining". von Fintel and Gillies and Karttunen cannot predict the contrast between this example with improved MUST and the classical one that motivated the indirectness argument. In both cases perception is direct.

As an additional argument, consider the following case, reproducing an example from Smirnova (2013). Here we see a contrast between MUST and the Bulgarian indirect evidential which is fine in the reportative context.

(59) Reportative context: you and your sister were out of touch for a couple of years. Today she calls you on the phone to catch up. She tells you that her daughter Maria plays the piano. Later, you tell your husband:

   a. Maria svirela   na piano.
      Maria play.EV on piano  (Smirnova 2013: 2)
   b. #I   Maria tha/prepi na   pezi piano.
      The Maria must      play the  piano.
   c. #Maria deve           suonare il   piano.
      Maria must.PRES.3sg play       the piano
   d. Mary must play the piano.

MUST is blocked here because the speaker has knowledge of *p* provided by her sister's utterance. Most of the knowledge we acquire, in fact, comes from hearing and reading sources that we trust. If the speaker trusts the source of the report *Maria plays the piano*, i.e., her sister, and has no reason to doubt her, then upon hearing the information that Maria plays the piano, the speaker knows that Maria plays the piano. This is a classical veridical exchange, and MUST is ruled out. This example, therefore, clearly shows that it is not indirect evidence that matters but knowledge. If one has knowledge of *p*, even if this knowledge is indirect, one cannot use a modal, not even MUST.

In other words, the apparent evidential indirectness effect of MUST is due to the fact that with modals we have reasoning with epistemic uncertainty. But the inadequacy of indirectness is deeper than this. It is indeed possible to show that the same evidence can lead to two different types of statements—bare veridical assertion indicating knowledge, or a MUST statement—depending on the epistemic state of the speaker (see also Goodhue 2018). Consider a context where I am preparing dinner and ask my son to switch off the oven when the timer rings. I know that what is in the oven is all we will eat, but my son doesn't:

(60) Context: the oven timer rings.
Mom: Dinner is ready.
Son: Dinner must be ready.

Since my son does not know what his mom has in mind, it would be infelicitous for him to utter *Dinner is ready*. The bare assertion is instead felicitous when uttered by the mom, as she has the dinner plan in mind. Here, direct evidence does not block MUST: the MUST sentence, uttered by the son, is felicitous because his knowledge state is that of only partial knowledge. Note that here the son has direct evidence (the timer ringing), but he still lacks knowledge; hence lack of knowledge is compatible with direct evidence, as in the case of the foggy window.

Conversely, as indicated in the earlier reported conversation example, indirectness does not always trigger MUST. We will use again an example modeled after Smirnova (2013). You and your sister were out of touch for a couple of years. Today you visit her for the first time. As she shows you around her apartment, you see that there is a piano. Later, you tell your husband:

(61) a. I Maria tha pezi/prepi na pezi piano.
      the Maria FUT play/must SUBJ play piano
   b. Maria deve suonare il piano.
      Maria must.PRES.3sg play the piano
   c. Maria must play the piano.

Here we have a piano, but we don't actually see Maria playing it, and there is no report that she does. The speaker, knowing her sister and her husband do not play the piano, infers that their daughter Maria plays the piano. Again, it is not a matter of indirectness but of knowing. Another way to state this is that MUST relies on an inference where several conclusions are possible, only some but not all supporting $p$.

In Giannakidou and Mari (2016c), we summarized our conclusions in the following:

(62) Evidential component of Universal Epistemic Modals (UEMs): *partial* knowledge

   a. UEMs can only effectively weaken a proposition $p$ if the speaker's knowledge that supports $p$ is not complete.

b. Complete knowledge is knowledge of all the relevant facts for *p*. More technically, it is a set of propositions that *entails p*.
c. All other knowledge is partial.

The generalizations that we establish for MUST are very relevant for the discussion of evidentiality, especially in languages that have indirect evidential morphemes but do not mark direct perception (e.g. Native American languages such as Cheyenne (Murray 2016) and Turkish, Bulgarian (Smirnova 2013)). The direct evidential is typically an unmarked past or present, and the marked form is the so-called indirect evidential, which indicates that the source of information is not first-hand knowledge of the speaker. The indirect evidential—like MUST in English, Greek and Italian—is a nonveridical marker that marks the reduced commitment of the speaker to *p*. Direct perception and reliable reports, on the other hand, as we discussed, entail full knowledge, veridical commitment.

Before we explore further the technical part of our analysis, we want to consider an argument for "strong" *must* put forth by von Fintel and Gillies (2010). The argument comes from deductive contexts. Consider:

(63)   The ball is either in A, B, or C. It is neither in A nor in B. It must be in C.

In this case, MUST indeed entails that the speaker knows *p*. But is this truly epistemic MUST? Giannakidou and Mari (2016c) claim that MUST in this case is not epistemic but aleithic. How do we know? Aleithic MUST, we want to suggest, can be distinguished from epistemic MUST by means of focus. Aleithic MUST can bear focus, but epistemic MUST cannot. Consider how odd it is to focus *must* in an inferential context:

(64)   Context: I see a wet umbrella.
       # It MUST be raining.
       # PREPI na vrexi.

(65)   The ball is either in A, B, or C.
       a. The ball is neither in A nor in B. It MUST be in C.
       b. Dhen ine sto A oute sto B, ara PREPI na ine sto C.
       c. La palla è in A o in B. Non è nè in A, nè in B. DEVE essere in C.

The von Fintel and Gillies example, then, involves an aleithic use of MUST which obeys veridicality and is therefore indeed strong—but has no bearing on the discussion of epistemic MUST.

### 2.4.2 MUST: Ideal and Non-Ideal Worlds

Epistemic MUST, and specifically Italian *dovere* (see also Giorgi and Pianesi 1997; Portner 2009) and Greek *prepi*, associates with an epistemic modal base M($i$) which is the set of propositions known by the speaker $i$ at $t_u$ (the utterance time). Again, $w_0$ is the world of evaluation, by default the actual world. The modal base set is most likely not infinite, but there is a domain restriction applying:

(66)  M($i$)($t_u$)($w_0$) = $\lambda w'(w'$ is compatible with what is known by the speaker $i$ in $w_0$ at $t_u$)

The epistemic modality is, as we said earlier, "subjective", and knowledge changes with time. Epistemic modality is therefore parametric to knowledge at $t_u$, as is often acknowledged in the literature (see extended discussion in Portner 2009 and references therein). We also assume that the domain of M($i$) is restricted and possibly finite, following the usual assumption of domain restriction with quantifiers.

Given what the speaker knows, the modal base of epistemic MUST is nonveridical, i.e., it does not entail $p$ and contains both $p$ and $\neg p$ worlds. To derive the truth conditions of MUST we assume with the literature (see, e.g., Portner 2009) that MUST uses a set of propositions $S$ which describe shared stereotypical/normalcy conditions. Such conditions have most notably been discussed in relation to genericity (see Asher and Morreau 1995), progressives (Dowty 1979; Landman 1992; Portner 1998), but appear also as *inertia* (Dowty 1979), stereotypicality (Portner 2009), and reasonability (Landman *ibid.*, Portner 1998; Mari 2014; see also discussion in Mari, Beyssade and Del Prete 2013). They are rationality conditions that apply well beyond epistemic modality to linguistic categories that appeal to inferencing and causal reasoning more broadly.[12]

---

12. Stereotypicality appears related to the concept of stereotype studied in social psychology. In psychology, however, stereotypes tend to be beliefs about people's attributes relying on social norms, whereas in modality stereotypicality is about expectations of outcomes based

The Kratzer/Portner semantics posits an ordering source *Best* which ranks worlds according to how close they are to the stereotypical ideal. Our account encodes that the modal base is partitioned into stereotypical and nonstereotypical worlds, but we dissociate stereotypicality from ranking. This allows us to capture possibility modals as undergoing the initial partition between stereotypical and nonstereotypical worlds without ordering. Ranking in our system is done via a metaevaluation which ranks the two sets of worlds produced by the initial partition.

In the epistemic modal base $M(i)(t_u)(w_0)$, we define $Ideal_S$ as a function over $M(i)(t_u)(w_0)$, still in the spirit of Portner (2009). The output $Ideal_S$ is a subset of $M(i)(t_u)(w_0)$:

(67) $Ideal_S (M(i)(t_u)(w_0)) = \{w' \in M(i)(t_u)(w_0) : \forall q \in S(w' \in q)\}$

So defined, $Ideal_S$ delivers the worlds in the epistemic modal base, a subset of $M(i)$, in which all the propositions in $S$ are true. $S$ is a set of propositions that corresponds to common ground norms.[13] The set $Ideal_S$ is also parametric to time. Unless otherwise stated, we consider that $Ideal_S$ is determined at the actual world and at the utterance time (this will be indeed always the case in the remainder of this book). As we can see, there is no ranking.

The overall modal structure looks like this:

(68)
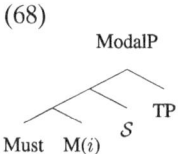

This structure has the following basic truth condition requiring that $p$ is true in the Ideal set of $M(i)$. Tense comes from below (a semantic present or past; see Giannakidou and Mari 2018a for discussion of tense); recall

---

on what is expected *under normal circumstances*. Stereotypically therefore functions as a constraint for rational outcomes and is not about building categories.

13. Since only those worlds are considered in which *all* the propositions in $S$ are true, the function $Ideal_S$ determines a cut-off point.

that $t_u$ is the utterance time. From now on, we assume that, unless otherwise stated, $M(i)$ is projected at the time of utterance in the actual world. Given a set $Ideal_S$ and the utterance time $t_u$,

(69) (Provisory lexical entry)
$[\![prepi/devere/must\ (PAST\ (p))]\!]^{M,i,S}$ is defined only if $M(i)$ is nonveridical and is partitioned into $Ideal_S$ and $\neg Ideal_S$ worlds. If defined,
$[\![prepi/devere/must\ (PAST\ (p))]\!]^{M,i,S} = 1$ iff $\forall w' \in Ideal_S : \exists t' \prec t_u : p(w', t')$

(70) (Provisory lexical entry)
$[\![prepi/devere/must\ (PRES\ (p))]\!]^{M,i,S}$ is defined only if $M(i)$ is nonveridical and is partitioned into $Ideal_S$ and $\neg Ideal_S$ worlds. If defined,
$[\![prepi/devere/must\ (PRES\ (p))]\!]^{M,i,S} = 1$ iff $\forall w' \in Ideal_S : p(w', t_u)$

Echoing Giannakidou and Mari (2016c) and Knobe and Szabo (2013), we can think of $Ideal_S$ as the "inner" domain of MUST, and $M(i)$ as the "outer" domain. The outer domain is a nonveridical epistemic space that does not as a whole support $p$; but the $Ideal_S$ space is veridical: all worlds are $p$ worlds. In other words, MUST is nonveridical with respect to M but veridical with respect to $Ideal_S$. It is, in other words, both weak and strong. This accounts for why we say that MUST expresses partial commitment: it expresses commitment to $p$ in the $Ideal_S$ subset of $M(i)$. This makes it stronger than MIGHT and grants MUST *mixed* veridicality status. Because of the nonveridical $M(i)$, MUST satisfies the licensing condition for the subjunctive we posited, and this explains why the complement appears in the subjunctive.

The partition between Ideal and Non-Ideal worlds is not based on ranking of the worlds (as in Portner or Kratzer), but, as we show next, the two sets are indeed ranked by a metaevaluation function. This additional step produces, we argue, positive bias.

### 2.4.3 Positive Bias of Necessity Modals

We will now derive positive bias following the analysis in Giannakidou and Mari (2018b). As we just said, the partition between Ideal and Non-Ideal worlds is not based on ranking; rather, the two sets, i.e., Ideal$_S$ and ¬Ideal$_S$, are ranked according to an ordering source $\mathcal{O}$. It is not uncommon to assume secondary ordering sources (von Fintel and Iatridou 2008; Rubinstein 2014; Portner and Rubinstein 2016); but given that our initial partitioning into Ideal$_S$ and non-Ideal$_S$ worlds does not depend on ranking, $\mathcal{O}$ is not a secondary ordering. It is the primary ordering source, a metaevaluation that compares Ideal$_S$ to its complement in M($i$).

In everyday life, we constantly evaluate whether the actual world follows stereotypical rules. What counts as normal or reasonable outcome depends on one's knowledge and experience, and human agents make use of expectations relying on knowledge and experience when they reason. Normalcy and reasonability manifest themselves as domain restriction with quantifiers, or ignoring exceptions with generic statements, to mention just two well-known examples. Of course, actual outcomes do not always conform to what is expected under normalcy conditions, and the expectation of not conforming to what it is "normal" determines often our uncertainty (besides not having complete knowledge). We propose the metaevaluation $\mathcal{O}$ as a way to capture the speaker's confidence in normalcy effects. $\mathcal{O}$ contains those propositions that allow $i$ to evaluate the relative ranking of stereotypical as better possibilities than nonstereotypical worlds.

Consider the case of John who is invited to a party. He is leaving from Place de la Sorbonne and needs to reach the Louvre. We know that he takes the metro. We also know that usually the metro works well in Paris. Ideal$_S$ creates a partition is M($i$) in which John arrives on time (these are worlds in which the metro worked well) and worlds in which he does not arrive on time (these are worlds in which the metro breaks down). Now, how likely are the worlds in which John arrives on time in comparison with those in which he does not? Usually, we believe, they are very likely, one of the propositions in $\mathcal{O}$ being "I trust the metro system more than the car." Stated otherwise, stereotypicality triggers high confidence in, thus more commitment to, one's conclusion, and this seems to be something basic about the way humans draw conclusions inductively. One will have a tendency to rank the stereotypical worlds as more reliable than the nonstereotypical ones. In this case one would probably utter something like (71-a) or even (71-b).

(71) a. John must be at the Louvre.
b. John must definitely be at the Louvre.

Notice here the co-occurrence of MUST with the adverb *definitely*—an apparent "redundancy", which we revisit in section 6. Higher ranking of stereotypical worlds over nonstereotypical ones is an intuitive inclination of rational human reasoning which is centered around relevance: when we think, we devalue or exclude nonstereotypical cases as nonrelevant, and the general tendency to domain restrict seems to be part of that process.

Sometimes one can evaluate the situation in a different manner. Based on one's pessimistic personal inclinations, or convinced that public transportation is not as reliable as expected, one can draw a different conclusion. $\mathcal{O}$ will be different in this case, including "I do not trust the metro system." In this case, in a language like Italian, one would probably utter something like the following sentence, where MUST combines with a possibility modal:

(72) Deve forse essere al Louvre.
must maybe be at the Louvre
He must be at the Louvre.

This combination is perfect in Italian, and illustrates that while the dependency between stereotypicality and $\mathcal{O}$ reveals trust in the normalcy conditions, the dependency can be fragile because $\mathcal{O}$ is subjective and may not rely on shared rules like the initial $\text{Ideal}_S$ partition. Cases like the above show that $\mathcal{O}$ is a negotiable (Rubinstein 2014; Portner and Rubinstein 2016) meta-evaluation of how confident $i$ is about $\text{Ideal}_S$ being a better possibility than $\neg\text{Ideal}_S$. In this sense, $\mathcal{O}$ can change as more arguments are added in the conversation.

Importantly, languages differ in the negotiability of the metaevaluation. Languages like Greek disallow occurrence of MUST with a possibility adverb.

(73) Prepei malon na ine giatros.
must probably that.SUBJ be.3sg doctor
He must probably be a doctor.

(74) #Prepei isos    na       ine    giatros.
     must  maybe that.SUBJ be.3sg doctor
     He must perhaps be a doctor.

Greek appears to be more rigid that Italian or English—though it is conceivable that Greek patterns may change over time. (A corpus study could shed light). Importantly, lexical items encode whether $\mathcal{O}$ is empty or not, that it is to say, whether stereotypicality triggers ordering or not. MUST, we claim, lexically encodes a default preference for a nonempty $\mathcal{O}$, but epistemic possibility tends to encode an empty $\mathcal{O}$.

Let us now consider further how bias is produced. In our semantics, MUST quantifies universally over the Ideal$_S$ worlds. In the specific case of the positive assertion, all Ideal$_S$ worlds are $p$ worlds. $\mathcal{O}$, in addition, reveals $i$'s confidence toward the prejacent; it does so indirectly by determining an ordering between the Ideal$_S$ worlds where the prejacent is true and ¬Ideal$_S$ worlds. With universal epistemic modals, $\mathcal{O}$ ranks Ideal$_S$ worlds as better possibilities (in the sense of Kratzer's work) than ¬Ideal$_S$ worlds. We encode this below as *positive bias*:

(75) Positive bias of epistemic necessity modals:
     Ideal$_S$ is a better possibility than ¬Ideal$_S$, relative to M($i$) and $\mathcal{O}$.

According to (75), there is no ¬Ideal$_S$ world in M($i$) which is not outranked by an Ideal$_S$ world. And since, by the truth condition of MUST, all Ideal worlds are worlds in which the prejacent is true, $\mathcal{O}$ is responsible not just for positive bias toward Ideal$_S$, but also toward the prejacent itself. Crucially, (75) states that worlds that are compatible with what the speaker knows in the actual world $w_0$ (recall that M($i$) is projected from the actual world) are Ideal thus better ranked. This means that, according to the speaker, the actual world is more likely to be a world where the prejacent is true.

We can now build on the connection between weak necessity and better possibility (see Portner 2009: 70), so we restate (75) as in (76).

(76) Positive bias of epistemic necessity modals (weak necessity):
     Ideal$_S$ is weak necessity with respect to ¬Ideal$_S$, relative to M($i$) and $\mathcal{O}$.

As we noted earlier, authors have generally acknowledged a need to discriminate between the two options in the modal base with necessity modals (e.g. Rubinstein 2014, Portner and Rubinstein 2016). Our own implementation proceeds in two steps, determining a partition based on stereotypicality and then evaluating the relative ranking of the two subsets. And recall again that the preference for Ideal$_S$ relies on a (potentially fragile) connection between stereotypicality and confidence of $i$ that the actual world behaves in a stereotypical way.

Existential modals, as we said, are in nonveridical equilibrium which we defined as follows:

(77) Nonveridical equilibrium (Giannakidou 2013b):
An information state M is in nonveridical equilibrium iff M is partitioned into $p$ and $\neg p$, and there is no bias toward $p$ or $\neg p$.

Nonveridical equilibrium, as can be recalled, conveys the weakest stance to $p$ in merely not excluding the possibility of $p$, which means that the $p$ or $\neg p$ worlds are not evaluated further. Epistemic possibility modals are generally taken to not have ordering sources (although there is variation across types of existential modals; see discussion in Portner 2009). We can thus identify nonveridical equilibrium with an empty $\mathcal{O}$. Section 5 offers more discussion, and in section 6.2, we see that the default preference can sometimes be overwritten.

Since Ideal$_S$ is the set of worlds in which the prejacent is true, in ranking the Ideal$_S$ worlds as higher than the $\neg$Ideal$_S$, $\mathcal{O}$ reveals $i$'s confidence that the prejacent is true. Recall that MUST does not convey full commitment: its modal base is nonveridical. However, it conveys partial commitment, and the set Ideal$_S$ in which the prejacent is true is ranked as higher by $\mathcal{O}$. In order to successfully convey partial commitment toward the prejacent, the Ideal$_S$ set must be homogeneous and contain only those worlds in which the prejacent is true. Indeed, if the Ideal$_S$ set were not homogeneous, the sentence would convey that the speaker is equally committed toward the prejacent and its negation and the sentence would become uninformative about the speaker's stance toward the prejacent.

This leads us to formulate the following:

(78) Homogeneity constraint on Ideal$_S$:
$\mathcal{O}$ requires that Ideal$_S$ be homogeneous as far as the prejacent of MUST is concerned.

So, $\mathcal{O}$ requires that, by the time it is computed, all Ideal$_S$ worlds are $p$ worlds or that all Ideal$_S$ are $\neg p$ worlds. This constraint is not merely a stipulation. As just said, if the Ideal$_S$ set contains both $p$ and $\neg p$ worlds, this would reveal partial commitment toward both the prejacent and its negation. This situation of triviality is to be avoided, and, as the reader can foresee (and shown further in section 6), it also proves instrumental when we consider the effect of negation.

It is important to note that when $S$ is non-empty, the bias will be necessarily positive, and the reader can already anticipate that, in virtue of using $\mathcal{O}$, the necessity modal will not be able to express negative bias.

### 2.4.4 Summing Up: (Non)veridicality, Bias, and Weakened Commitment

At this point, it is helpful to go back to the ground issues about veridicality and commitment, and show how the key pieces of the analysis we unfolded come together. The driving idea has been that veridicality and nonveridicality are the criteria for commitment.

Following the literature, we adopted an analysis of epistemic possibility modals as existential quantifiers lacking ordering sources (as opposed to deontic possibility modals which, as we mentioned earlier, may use a circumstantial modal base and a deontic ordering source, Portner 2009). The absence of ordering sources with epistemic possibility renders $p$ and $\neg p$ equal possibilities, revealing that the assessor is in a state of *nonveridical equilibrium*, see 77.

Nonveridical equilibrium conveys the weakest commitment in merely not excluding the possibility of $p$. Possibility modals and unbiased polar questions (*Did Ariadne win the race?*) are in nonveridical equilibrium, in a state of balanced epistemic indecision where both $p$ and its negation are equally plausible options and $i$ has no reason to prefer one over the other. Giannakidou (2013b) argues that "inquisitive" and 'nonveridical' describe the same state of possibility and questions.

Epistemic necessity, on the other hand, while being nonveridical, is stronger than mere possibility in that it conveys bias toward $p$. Our analysis of epistemic necessity involves three ingredients: (a) a nonveridical modal base $M(i)$, (b) a partition of $M(i)$ into Ideal$_S$ and a $\neg$Ideal$_S$ subsets, relying on stereotypical assumptions, and (c) a metaevaluation $\mathcal{O}$, relying on rationality, producing bias toward $p$ by ranking the Ideal$_S$ worlds as better possibilities than $\neg$Ideal$_S$ worlds in $M(i)$ (positive bias). The preference for higher ranking of Ideal$_S$ is lexically specified, and MUST and

MIGHT differ in their lexical preferences: both use $\mathcal{S}$, but higher ranking of Ideal$_\mathcal{S}$ is only a feature of MUST. This analysis explains why MUST gives off the impression of strength while it remains weak in not entailing $p$ in the nonveridical modal base.

We can now rank modals along a scale of veridical commitment and contrast them with the bare sentence which implies a veridical state of knowledge or belief of $p$. The bare sentence expresses the highest, i.e., veridical commitment of $i$. Modal verbs express only weakened commitment to $p$, as we said. Weakened commitment means that the modal base M is nonveridical. MUST expresses partial commitment and is therefore stronger than mere possibility which expresses nonveridical equilibrium and trivial commitment. Recall from our earlier discussion:

(79) Veridicality, nonveridicality and *weakened* commitment:
   a. A *veridical* modal space is fully committed:
      $\forall w'[w' \in M(i) \rightarrow w' \in \{w'' \mid \phi(w'')\}]$.
   b. A *nonveridical* modal space is weakly committed:
      $\exists w'[w' \in M(i) \land w' \in \{w'' \mid p(w'')\}]$ & $\exists w'''[w''' \in M(i) \land w''' \in \{w'''' \mid \neg p(w'''')\}]$.

A nonveridical space is partitioned and still allows the possiblity of not $p$; it is, therefore epistemically weaker than the homogeneous veridical space which entails $p$. Nonveridicality, by creating a partition, creates epistemic weakening as we have noted numerous times also in our previous work.

Looking now into the contrast between MUST $p$ and MIGHT $p$, these too can be ranked: MUST $p$ is stronger than MIGHT $p$ because it supports $p$ in the Ideal worlds, whereas MIGHT is in nonveridical equilibrium.

(80) Scale of veridical commitment (Giannakidou and Mari 2016c):
   <$p$, MUST $p$, MIGHT $p$>; where
   (i.) the veridical $p$ conveys the strongest *full* commitment of $i$ to $p$; biased MUST $p$ conveys *partial* commitment, and nonveridical equilibrium MIGHT $p$ conveys *trivial* commitment; and
   (ii.) Order is from strongest to weakest.

The categories of equilibrium and bias are central to defining two types of modality, we have been arguing—and are better descriptors than anything else we know of what counts as "strong" and "weak" within modality. The key piece is that within the epistemically weakened nonveridical space, individuals can take a weaker (possibility) or a stronger (necessity) position; but the stronger position is at best bias, and never veridical commitment to the prejacent. The correlation between veridicality, nonveridicality, and commitment is not exclusive to modals, of course. We offer it as a tool for the understanding and analysis of various other structures that involve subjective truth assessment. In recent work, Liu (2019) proposes the concept of *elastic veridicality* in her analysis of conditional sentences, inspired by the gradient analysis of (non)veridicality and commitment we outlined. We think of *elastic veridicality* as a promising development.

The degree of commitment, finally, correlates also with how informative the sentence is. As we said earlier, a veridical state expresses maximal informativity, a biased state of MUST expresses medium informativity, and equilibrium conveys minimal informativity:

(81)  Commitment and informativity (Giannakidou and Mari 2016c):
$<p \gg \text{MUST } p \gg \text{MIGHT } p>$; where "$\gg$" means "informationally stronger than"
Non-modalized $p$ (speaker knows $p$, $p$ added to the common ground) $\gg$
MUST $p$ (speaker does not know $p$, but is biased toward $p$) $\gg$
POSSIBLY $p$ (speaker does not know $p$, and there is nonveridical equilibrium).

Only the veridical assertion of $p$ adds $p$ to the common ground. Introducing a modal does not add $p$ to the common ground, hence MODAL $p$ is not just epistemically weaker, but also informationally weaker. Bias toward $p$ is informationally stronger than nonveridical equilibrium but still does not add $p$ to the common ground.

Having clarified these core conceptual connections, we can move on now to explore the interaction of modal verbs and adverbs, and the related property of positive polarity of MUST modals.

## 2.5 Necessity Modals and Positive Polarity

In this section, we will consider the co-occurrence of modal verbs with modal adverbs and argue that the latter are the realization of $\mathcal{O}$. The modal structure is as follows:

(82)
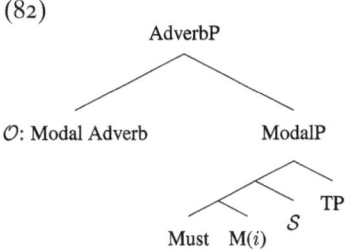

We propose that, by default, there is a covert adverb meaning "probably":

(83) $[\![\emptyset]\!]^{\mathcal{O},M,i,\mathcal{S}} = \lambda q.$ Ideal$_\mathcal{S}$ is a weak necessity with respect to $\neg$Ideal$_\mathcal{S}$ relative to $M(i)$ and $\mathcal{O}$ & $q$

The complete lexical entry for MUST is thus the following:

(84) $[\![\emptyset \text{ MUST (PRES } (p))]\!]^{\mathcal{O},M,i,\mathcal{S}}$ is defined only if the modal base $M(i)$ is nonveridical and it is partitioned into Ideal$_\mathcal{S}$ and $\neg$Ideal$_\mathcal{S}$ worlds. If defined,
$[\![\emptyset \text{ MUST (PRES } (p))]\!]^{\mathcal{O},M,i,\mathcal{S}} = 1$ iff: Ideal$_\mathcal{S}$ is a weak necessity with respect to $\neg$Ideal$_\mathcal{S}$ relative to $M(i)$ and $\mathcal{O}$ & $\forall w' \in$ Ideal$_\mathcal{S}$ : $p(w', t_u)$

In Giannakidou and Mari (2018b), we motivated the above structure which we called *modal spread*, rather than "concord" or "agreement". The analysis we are about to present also derives the positive polarity behavior of necessity modals, and the lack of polarity sensitivity of possibility modals.

*2.5.1 Modal Spread*

Modal spread refers to examples such as the following:

(85) a. John must probably/certainly be sleeping.
 b. John may possibly be a doctor.

Here *must* and *may* co-occur with the adverbs *probably/certainly* and *possibly* respectively. Lyons (1977) talks about "harmony" in these cases—the idea being that there is a concord running through the clause which results in the double realization of a single modality (Lyons 1977: 808; see also Willer 2013), and this makes us think of other cases of concord such as negative concord, person, or gender agreement. This observation, namely that there is one modality in these cases, is found in most of the analyses of the phenomenon (Geurts and Huitink 2006; Huitink 2012, 2014; Grosz 2010, Iatridou and Zeijlstra 2013, *a contrario* Anand and Brasoveanu 2010). Syntactically, if we admit one modality in these cases, we are saying that there is no embedding of one modal operator to the other, and the two work together to produce a single modal structure. This situation is distinct from true embeddings:

(86) It may turn out that Ariadne must give her speech this afternoon.

This is a genuine case of *must* embedded under *may*; notice also the clause boundary (*that*), and the different modal flavors (the higher modal is epistemic, but the lower *must* has a deontic flavor). Embedding can also happen within one clause, of course, as in *Ariadne may have to give her speech this afternoon*.

What is the semantic contribution of the adverb in modal spread? In more philosophical works it has been claimed that "iterating epistemic possibility operators adds no value in the semantics" (Yalcin 2007: 994), or "embedding an epistemic modal under another epistemic modal does not in general have any interesting semantic effects" (Willer 2013: 12). These statements reveal a concord-like perspective where some of multiple morphological exponents of modality are semantically vacuous (just like, e.g., multiple exponents of negation in negative concord). Huitink (2012) and Moss (2015), on the other hand, argue that the multiple exponents of modality have a semantic role, and Huitink in particular argues that the adverb lexicalizes the ordering source of the modal. Our analysis is similar in acknowledging that the adverb has a semantic role, and we will rely on our idea of the metaevaluation function.

In understanding modal spread, it must also be acknowledged that we are not always dealing with concord, and this fact by itself serves as an argument that the use of the adverb is contentful. As we briefly mentioned earlier, modal verbs and adverbs with apparently opposing forces can co-occur with a single modality reading, as (87) shows for Italian *dovere* (must) co-occurring with *forse* (maybe). And, though marginally, we also find some attested examples of the combination of epistemic *must* with *maybe* in English (see discussion in Lassiter 2016).

(87) Le luci   sono accese.      Gianni deve forse   essere a  casa.
 the lights are  switched-on. Gianni must maybe be      at home
 The lights are on. John must (#maybe) be at home.

Below is an attested example (see also Cui 2015 for a corpus study of modal concord). The discussion is about an archeological reconstruction of the town Castel Nuovo, near Naples.

(88)  Il vaso, che costituisce uno dei premi guadagnati dagli atleti negli agoni panatenaici di Atene, **deve forse** fare parte del corredo di una sepoltura ubicata non lontano dall'area di Castel Nuovo.
 The jar, which constitutes one of the prizes earned by the athletes in the pan-athenians olympics of Athens, must maybe belong to the kid of a burial located not far from the area of Castel Nuovo.[14]

Sentences like these have, to our knowledge, rarely been discussed in the literature (see some comments in Moss 2015), and every theory of modal concord would claim that they do not have a single modality reading. We will argue here, however, that they do have a single reading, and this is why we use the neutral term "modal spread" instead of "concord" (or "harmony"). Huitink (2012) states that conditions on the adverbs "really can only be decided on a case to case basis" (Huitink 2012: 30), but we aspire to show that there are general principles that delimit the set of possible interactions.

---

14. Source:   http://www.comune.napoli.it/flex/cm/pages/ServeBLOB.php/L/IT/IDPagina/1425/UT/systemPrint

Apparent harmonic uses seem to be pervasive in Greek and Italian:

(89) a. Prepi malon/oposdhipote na    ine    giatros.
        must probably/definitely that.SUBJ be.3sg doctor
        He must probably/definitely be a doctor.
     b. Deve           probabilmente/sicuramente essere un dottore.
        must.PRES.3sg probably/certainly          be   a doctor
        He must probably/definitely be a doctor.

(90) a. Prepi malon/oposhipote na    efije    noris.
        must probably/definitely that.SUBJ left.3sg early
        He must have probably/definitely left early.
     b. Deve           probabilmente/sicuramente essere partito
        must.PRES.3sg probably/certainly          be    left
        presto.
        early
        He must have probably/definitely left early.

We see here the modal adverbs *malon probabilmente* (probably), *oposdhopote/certamente* (definitely), etc. co-occur with the necessity modals *prepi/dovere/must*. In Greek and Italian, modal spread is very common and unmarked. We offered combinations with present and past tenses, to illustrate that the phenomenon is tense independent. We find the co-occurrence also with the future, see (91) (Bertinetto 1979; Mari 2009, 2010; Giannakidou 2012; Giannakidou and Mari 2012a, 2013):

(91) a. Arriverà      certamente/probabilmente alle 4.
        arrive.FUT.3sg certainly/probably       at  4
        John will definitely/probably arrive at 4.
     b. O Janis tha erthi       sigoura/malon    stis 4.
        the John FUT come.3sg certainly/probably at  4 pm
        John will definitely/probably arrive at 4.

In Greek strong adverbs cannot co-occur with possibility *bori/may/might*. In Italian and English, on the other hand, weak modals can co-occur with strong adverbs just as strong modals can co-occur with weak adverbs:

(92) a. *Bori malon/oposdhipote na        efije    noris.
         may probably/definitely that.SUBJ left.3sg early
     b. Può           probabilmente    essere partito presto.
        can.PRES.3sg probably/certainly be    left    early
        He may have probably/definitely left early.

(93) a. *Bori malon    na        ine     giatros.
         may probably that.SUBJ be.3sg doctor
     b. Può           probabilmente    essere un dottore.
        may.PRES.3sg probably/certainly be    a doctor
        He may probably be a doctor.

In Italian, the co-occurence of existential modality with a strong adverb is not rare. In (94), we can be certain that the existential modal is epistemic insofar as it embeds a stative meaning which cannot be coerced into an eventive giving rise to the abilitative or circumstantial interpretation of *potere* (*might*). We also see in the second sentence ("no matter how the facts were settled") that the truth is not established and that the first sentence is described as expressing a conjecture. In this attested example, *potere* (might) combines with *probabilmente* (probably). Notice a similar combination in English:

(94)   ... e a questa circostanza **può probabilmente** essere dovuto il fatto che egli fosse arrivato al nono compleanno. Comunque stessero le cose, in ogni modo, era il suo nono compleanno.
       ... and the fact that he reached his ninth birthday might probably be due to these circumstances. No matter how the facts where settled, in any case, it was his ninth birthday.[15]

---

15. Source: https://books.google.fr/books?isbn=8804536829

(95) In some cases, however, the psychosis **might definitely** be due to anxieties and conflicts associated with the pregnancy.[16]

On the other hand, the possibility adverb is grammatical with possibility modals in Greek, Italian, and English.

(96) a. Bori isos      na           efije   noris.
       may maybe that.SUBJ left.3sg early
    b. Può         forse   essere partito presto.
       can.3sg.pres maybe be    left      early
       He may have possibly left early.

(97) a. Bori isos      na           ine    giatros.
       may maybe that.SUBJ be.3sg doctor
    b. Può         forse   essere un dottore.
       can.3sg.pres maybe be    a  doctor
       He may possibly be a doctor.

We can summarize the facts above in the following three generalizations:

1. Modal matching appears to be the general case, attested in all three languages (Greek, Italian, English), as well as Dutch (Geurts and Huitink 2006; Huitink 2012, 2014), and German (Grosz 2012).
2. Modal spread also allows nonmatching. It appears to be a more restricted option, a fact that needs to be explained.
3. Languages are subject to variation with respect to whether they allow non-matching (Italian does, but Greek doesn't; English shows some of the flexibility of Italian).

Let us now consider the interaction with negation.

### 2.5.2 *MUST, the Adverb, and Negation*

The interaction of modal verbs with negation has recently received a lot of attention (Iatridou and Zeijlstra 2013; Rubinstein, 2014; Homer 2015;

---

16. Source: https://books.google.com/books?id=c6JPyfOBZYIC&pg=PA74&lpg=PA74&dq=%22might+definitely%22&source=bl&ots=LXLgsQVXTj&sig=S5u9MCjN4HwRHnfYTs_yQOSbL9Y&hl=fr&sa=X&ved=0ahUKEwjp-4Xm36XVAhUJh1QKHWPFCVA4ChDoAQg5MAQ#v=onepage&q=%22might%20definitely%22&f=false

Zeijlstra 2017). A common observation is that necessity modals such as *must* scope above negation, but possibility modals scope below:

(98) a. Ariadne must not be a doctor. (= It must be the case that Ariadne is not a doctor.)
b. Ariadne must not eat meat. (Ariadne is a vegetarian.)

(99) a. Ariadne cannot be a doctor.
b. Ariadne cannot talk to Dean.

(100) a. Ariadne doesn't have to be a doctor (to apply for this job).
b. Ariadne doesn't need to spend a lot of money (for Jason's birthday gift).

The English modal *must*, in both epistemic and deontic use, is interpreted with scope above negation. *Can*, on the other hand, takes scope inside negation, on a par with modals such as *have to, need*. These scope constraints are reminiscent of polarity, and van der Wouden (1994) already proposed that *need* is a negative polarity item (NPI), identifying similar NPI modals in Dutch (*hoeven*) and German (*brauchen*). If the necessity *need* is an NPI, then its counterpart *must* must be a *positive* polarity item (PPI), since it escapes the scope of negation.

This basic polarity contrast in English has been reproduced in a number of languages, and though the data are not always exactly parallel (in part depending on what the actual modal verb system is in each language), the general tendency is that a necessity modal which is not an NPI will tend to scope above negation. Below are the relevant data from Greek and Italian:

(101) a. Gianni deve essere malato.
John must be ill
John must be ill.
b. Gianni non deve essere malato. MUST > NEG
John not must be ill
John must not be ill.

(102) a. I Ariadne dhen prepi na einai eggyos. MUST > NEG
the Ariadne not must that.SUBJ be pregnant
Ariadne must not be pregnant (based on what I know).
b. I Ariadne dhen xreiazete na ine eggyos NEG > MUST
the Ariadne not need.3sg that.SUBJ be pregnant
Ariadne need not be pregnant (to be eligible for this leave).

The question is how we can explain this behavior. Does it follow from the semantics we have given thus far? Our answer is positive. Observe below the truth conditions for MUST (we only consider here the PRES option for simplicity), which contains the default adverbs PROBABLY:

(103) $[\![\text{PROBABLY MUST (PRES }(p))]\!]^{\mathcal{O},M,i,\mathcal{S}}$ is defined only if the modal base $M(i)$ is nonveridical and it is partitioned into $\text{Ideal}_\mathcal{S}$ and $\neg\text{Ideal}_\mathcal{S}$ worlds. If defined,
$[\![\text{PROBABLY MUST (PRES }(p))]\!]^{\mathcal{O},M,i,\mathcal{S}} = 1$ iff: $\text{Ideal}_\mathcal{S}$ is a weak necessity with respect to $\neg\text{Ideal}_\mathcal{S}$ relative to $M(i)$ and $\mathcal{O}$ & $\forall w' \in \text{Ideal}_\mathcal{S} : p(w', t_u)$.

MUST presupposes a nonveridical modal base and a nonempty $\mathcal{O}$ which are parameters of evaluation; it then universally quantifies over the $\text{Ideal}_\mathcal{S}$ worlds. When we add negation, we have the following:

(104) a. Malon    dhen prepi na        ine      giatros.
probably not   must that.SUBJ be.pres doctor
b. Probabilmente non deve essere un dottore.
probably       not must be      a doctor
He must not be a doctor.

(105) $[\![\text{PROBABLY MUST NOT (PRES }(p))]\!]^{\mathcal{O},M,i,\mathcal{S}}$ is defined only if the modal base $M(i)$ is nonveridical and it is partitioned into $\text{Ideal}_\mathcal{S}$ and $\neg\text{Ideal}_\mathcal{S}$ worlds. If defined,
$[\![\text{PROBABLY MUST NOT (PRES }(p))]\!]^{\mathcal{O},M,i,\mathcal{S}} = 1$ iff: $\text{Ideal}_\mathcal{S}$ is a weak necessity with respect to $\neg\text{Ideal}_\mathcal{S}$ relative to $M(i)$ and $\mathcal{O}$ & $\forall w' \in \text{Ideal}_\mathcal{S} : \neg p(w', t_u)$.

The adverb ranking, which remains intact along with the nonveridicality presupposition, will again rank as higher the Ideal$_S$ worlds than the ¬Ideal$_S$ ones. Only now the Ideal worlds will be ¬$p$ worlds.

In Greek and Italian negation is preverbal and appears directly preceding the modal verb (Zanuttini 1992; Giannakidou 1998):

(106)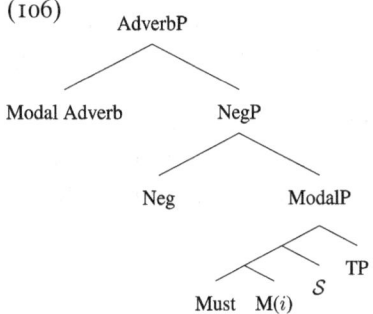

The adverb appears above negation and can never intervene between negation and the modal:

(107) a. *Dhen malon prepi.
         not  probably must
      b. *Non probabilmente deve.
          not  probably      must

We observe the same distributions for the existential.

(108) a. Isos  dhen bori.
         maybe not  can
      b. Forse non può.
         maybe not can

(109) a. *Dhen isos  bori.
          not  maybe can
      b. *Non forse può.
          not maybe can

Hence the adverb must be above the negation syntactically. Crucially, the adverb can never appear lower than negation, even in English, as we noted in section 1, repeated here:

(110)  #Ariadne must not probably/definitely be at home.

Only a metalinguistic negation reading is acceptable here, which is irrelevant. In other words, scoping of modal adverbs under negation seems to be generally prohibited in languages. In English, *must* precedes negation (*must not*) anyway, and the constraint on the adverb not scoping low also holds (110).

Now, what would it mean for the structure to be interpreted with negation scoping between the adverb and the modal verb as given in the apparent surface structure of 106? The corresponding truth conditions would be as in (111):

(111)  $[\![\text{PROBABLY NOT MUST (PRES } (p))]\!]^{\mathcal{O},M,i,\mathcal{S}}$ is defined only if the modal base M($i$) is nonveridical and it is partitioned into Ideal$_\mathcal{S}$ and ¬Ideal$_\mathcal{S}$ worlds. If defined,
$[\![\text{PROBABLY NOT MUST (PRES } (p))]\!]^{\mathcal{O},M,i,\mathcal{S}} = 1$ iff: Ideal$_\mathcal{S}$ is a weak necessity with respect to ¬Ideal$_\mathcal{S}$ relative to M($i$) and $\mathcal{O}$ & ¬∀$w'$ ∈ Ideal$_\mathcal{S}$ : $p(w', t_u)$

The default adverb retains the content that Ideal$_\mathcal{S}$ is a weak necessity relative to $\mathcal{O}$, but Ideal$_\mathcal{S}$ now is targeted by negation and can be nonhomogeneous. This means that the homogeneity constraint on Ideal$_\mathcal{S}$ is not satisfied (recall the constraint in 78), and this produces infelicity. There is no infelicity when negation is interpreted below the modal.

Notably, the low scope of negation is not a stipulation but a consequence of the analysis we offered. Recall that in the ranking of the Ideal$_\mathcal{S}$ worlds with respect to ¬Ideal$_\mathcal{S}$, $\mathcal{O}$ is intended to capture $i$'s confidence in the truthfulness of the prejacent. In order to successfully establish this comparison between Ideal$_\mathcal{S}$ and ¬Ideal$_\mathcal{S}$ worlds and express confidence toward the prejacent, Ideal$_\mathcal{S}$ needs to be homogeneous insofar as the prejacent is concerned. $\mathcal{O}$ cannot produce a well-formed ranking if the Ideal$_\mathcal{S}$ set is itself partitioned, as this implies confidence in both $p$ and ¬$p$ worlds. The sentence would become uninformative about the speaker's stance toward $p$. Hence, the positive polarity property of MUST is derived as a result of its semantics that includes the ranking of Ideal$_S$ worlds as better possibilities than ¬Ideal$_S$ worlds, which itself forces homogeneity on the Ideal$_S$ set.

As regards NPI-universals like *need, hoeven, xreiazete* (which are typically deontic), our theory would have to say that they have an empty $\mathcal{O}$. That would be a lexical feature of them which sets them apart from epistemic PPI universals. The two necessity modals would thus differ by lexical properties.

### 2.5.3 Possibility and Nonveridical Equilibrium

Our analysis of epistemic possibility modals treats them as existential quantifiers lacking ordering sources. The absence of ordering sources renders $p$ and ¬$p$ equal possibilities, revealing that the assessor is in a state of indecision or, as we said, true uncertainty. We call this *nonveridical equilibrium*, and rephrase it in the following way:

(112) Nonveridical equilibrium and metaevaluation:
A partitioned space M($i$) is in nonveridical equilibrium if the metaevaluation ordering $\mathcal{O}$ is empty.

Nonveridical equilibrium implies that Ideal$_S$ and ¬Ideal$_S$ are not compared to one another; $p$ and ¬$p$ are equal possibilities, neither is privileged over the other. This is what characterizes typically possibility modals, at least the epistemic ones. Recall that, in addition to possibility modals, neutral nonbiased polar questions are also in nonveridical equilibrium. We take equilibrium to be the default for epistemic possibility—though this may be subject to variation.

We assume, as before, that a silent adverb, this time MAYBE, hosts the default preference for equilibrium of *bori/potere/might*:

(113) $[\![\emptyset \text{MIGHT (PRES } (p))]\!]^{\mathcal{O},M,i,S}$ is defined only if M($i$) is nonveridical and partitioned into Ideal$_S$ and ¬Ideal$_S$ worlds. If defined,
$[\![\emptyset \text{MIGHT (PRES } (p))]\!]^{\mathcal{O},M,i,S} = 1$ iff $\mathcal{O}$ is empty & $\exists w' \in M(i)$ : $p(w', t_u)$

(114)   $[\![\emptyset \text{MIGHT (PAST }(p))]\!]^{\mathcal{O},M,i,\mathcal{S}}$ is defined only if $M(i)$ is non-veridical and is partitioned into Ideal$_\mathcal{S}$ and ¬Ideal$_\mathcal{S}$ worlds. If defined,
$[\![\emptyset \text{MIGHT (PAST }(p))]\!]^{\mathcal{O},M,i,\mathcal{S}} = 1$ iff $\mathcal{O}$ is empty & $\exists w' \in M(i)\, \exists t' \prec t_u : p(w', t')$

The covert adverb adds the presupposition that $\mathcal{O}$ is empty. The existential quantifier operates on the entire modal base $M(i)$ and not on one of the subsets created by $\mathcal{S}$ (and Ideal$_\mathcal{S}$ in particular). This amounts to stating that the quantifier is unrestricted, i.e, blind to stereotypicality conditions (as is typical for existential quantifiers also in the nominal domain). Note also that there might be $p$ worlds which are not in the set Ideal$_\mathcal{S}$. Stereotypicality conditions, however, as we will show, might in some cases trigger a nonempty $\mathcal{O}$ for possibility in some languages.

Just as the presence of stereotypicality conditions with universal modals triggers positive bias (i.e., higher ranking of the Ideal$_\mathcal{S}$ over non-Ideal$_\mathcal{S}$), the absence of stereotypicality conditions with existential modal does not produce any ranking. In virtue of this, the most straightforward combination which we find in all languages is MAYBE + MIGHT.

(115)   a. Bori isos      na            efije    noris.
           may maybe that.SUBJ left.3sg early
        b. Può            forse    essere partito presto.
           can.PRES.3sg maybe be     left       early
           He may have possibly left early.

(116)   a. Bori isos      na            ine      giatros.
           may maybe that.SUBJ be.3sg doctor
        b. Può            forse    essere un dottore.
           can.PRES.3sg maybe be     a    doctor
           He may possibly be a doctor.

When we add MAYBE (*possibly, maybe, perhaps*, and their crosslinguistic equivalents) we obtain 117-118. The combination maintains the default, which now is nonveridical equilibrium. With possibility modals, MAYBE has no effect on the equilibrium, since it does not provide ranking. For any proposition $p$ and the utterance time $t_u$,

(117)  ⟦MAYBE MIGHT (PRES $(p)$)⟧$^{\mathcal{O},M,i,S}$ is defined only if M($i$) is nonveridical and is partitioned into Ideal$_S$ and ¬Ideal$_S$ worlds. If defined,
⟦MAYBE MIGHT (PRES $(p)$)⟧$^{\mathcal{O},M,i,S}$ = 1 iff $\mathcal{O}$ is empty & $\exists w' \in$ M($i$) : $p(w', t_u)$

(118)  ⟦MAYBE MIGHT (PAST $(p)$)⟧$^{\mathcal{O},M,i,S}$ is defined only if M($i$) is nonveridical and is partitioned into Ideal$_S$ and ¬Ideal$_S$ worlds. If defined,
⟦MAYBE MIGHT (PAST $(p)$)⟧$^{\mathcal{O},M,i,S}$ = 1 iff $\mathcal{O}$ is empty & $\exists w' \in$ M($i$) $\exists t' \prec t_u$ : $p(w', t')$

Possibility modals are not forced to scope above negation; nonveridical equilibrium is compatible with both scopes. Empirically, possibility modals tend to scope below negation crosslinguistically. In *John cannot be at home*, the possibility is denied that John is at home.

The reason for this preference, we want to suggest, seems to be that low scope with negation appears to be the general case with all kinds of existentials: *Ariadne didn't see any student / a student / one student* all scope below negation. If this is a general tendency of existential quantifiers, possibility modals simply follow this systemic pattern. (There do appear to be PPI existentials like *some*—*Ariadne didn't see SOME student*—but note that this use is marked; Giannakidou 2011). It is an open question whether PPI possibility modals can be found in languages. Our analysis predicts, in any case, both scopes.

### 2.5.4 *Manipulations of O by the Adverbs*

We have up to here built our theory on the assumption that the adverbs are in harmony with the modal verbs. Researchers, as we said earlier, indeed talk about "harmony" or "modal concord."[17] Yet some languages allow combinations of opposing forces. We did note earlier that Italian and English are more flexible than Greek, and here we will consider some more cases.

---

17. On a different analysis of the adverbs as contributing at a not-at-issue level, see Mayol and Castroviejo (2013) and Giannakidou and Mari (2017). See Giannakidou and Mari (2018a) for a criticism.

Let us begin with MUST. All languages allow strengthening of the bias from 'probably' to 'definitely'. In this case, the bias of weak necessity is strengthened to necessity:

(119) a. Prepi malon/oposdhipote na ine giatros.
      must probably/definitely that.SUBJ be.3sg doctor
      He must probably/definitely be a doctor.
   b. Deve probabilmente/sicuramente essere un dottore.
      must probably/certainly be a doctor
      He must probably/definitely be a doctor.

(120) $[\![\text{DEFINITELY MUST (PRES }(p))]\!]^{\mathcal{O},M,i,\mathcal{S}}$ is defined only if the modal base M(*i*) is nonveridical and it is partitioned into Ideal$_\mathcal{S}$ and ¬Ideal$_\mathcal{S}$ worlds. If defined,
$[\![\text{DEFINITELY MUST (PRES }(p))]\!]^{\mathcal{O},M,i,\mathcal{S}} = 1$ iff: Ideal$_\mathcal{S}$ is a necessity with respect to ¬Ideal$_\mathcal{S}$ relative to M(*i*) and $\mathcal{O}$ & $\forall w' \in$ Ideal$_\mathcal{S} : p(w', t_u)$

This combination reveals that the speaker is very highly biased toward *p*. Note, however that, no matter how strong the bias is, it remains a commitment within a subset in the modal base, and it is not equivalent to knowledge of *p*.

Consider now opposing forces for the adverb and the modal verb in Italian and English. Here we see the combination of MUST and a weak adverb.

(121) Il vaso, che costituisce uno dei premi guadagnati dagli atleti negli agoni panatenaici di Atene, **deve forse** fare parte del corredo di una sepoltura ubicata non lontano dall'area di Castel Nuovo.
The jar, which constitutes one of the prizes earned by the athletes in the pan-athenians olympics of Athens, must maybe belong to the kid of a burial located not far from the area of Castel Nuovo.[18,]

(122) So there **must perhaps** be some glitch somewhere along the line or something that makes this happen. I am sure is a cache or technical glitchup.[19]

---

18. Source: http://www.comune.napoli.it/flex/cm/pages/ServeBLOB.php/L/IT/IDPagina/1425/UT/systemPrint
19. Source: https://www.blackhatworld.com/seo/. We thank Paul Portner for pointing this out.

Recall that opposing forces are impossible in Greek.

(123)  #**Prepi isos** na ine giatros.
         must maybe that.SUBJ be.3sg doctor
         He must probably/definitely be a doctor.

In Italian and English, then, the adverb can be used to *weaken* the default bias. We get the following interpretations:

(124)  $[\![\text{MAYBE MUST (PAST } (p))]\!]^{\mathcal{O},M,i,S}$ is defined only if $M(i)$ is nonveridical and is partitioned into Ideal$_S$ and ¬Ideal$_S$ worlds. If defined,
$[\![\text{MAYBE MUST (PAST } (p))]\!]^{\mathcal{O},M,i,S} = 1$ iff $\mathcal{O}$ is empty & $\forall w' \in \text{Ideal}_S \; \exists t' \prec t_u : p(w',t')$

The manipulation is that now, because O is empty, there is no ranking of the Ideal$_S$ worlds over the ¬Ideal$_S$ ones. This is, then, a weaker MUST than the one with PROBABLY, and the effect is due entirely to the manipulation by the adverb. When a weak adverb combines with a strong modal, the bias of the modal is weakened, reduced to no ranking.

Conversely, Italian and English allow strengthening the default with existential epistemic modals. Once again, Greek is a strict language that forbids this combination.

(125)  ... e a questa circostanza **può probabilmente** essere dovuto il fatto che egli fosse arrivato al nono compleanno. Comunque stessero le cose, in ogni modo, era il suo nono compleanno.
       ... and the fact that he reached his ninth birthday might probably be due to these circumstances. No matter how the facts where settled, in any case, it was his ninth birthday.[20]

(126)  In some cases, however, the psychosis **might definitely** be due to anxieties and conflicts associated with the pregnancy.[21]

---

20. Source: https://books.google.fr/books?isbn=8804536829
21. Source: https://books.google.com/books?id=c6JPyfOBZYIC&pg=PA74&lpg=PA74& dq=%22might+definitely%22&source=bl&ots=LXLgsQVXTj&sig=S5u9MCjN4HwRHnfYTs _yQOSbL9Y&hl=fr&sa=X&ved=0ahUKEwjp-4Xm36XVAhUJh1QKHWPFCVA4ChDoAQ g5MAQ#v=onepage&q=%22might%20definitely%22&f=false

(127) #Bori malon na ine giatros.
   may probably that.SUBJ be.3sg doctor

(128) ⟦PROBABLY MIGHT (PAST (p))⟧$^{\mathcal{O},M,i,\mathcal{S}}$ is defined only if M($i$) is nonveridical and is partitioned into Ideal$_\mathcal{S}$ and ¬Ideal$_\mathcal{S}$ worlds. If defined, ⟦PROBABLY MIGHT (PAST (p))⟧$^{\mathcal{O},M,i,\mathcal{S}}$ = 1 iff Ideal$_\mathcal{S}$ is a weak necessity with respect to ¬Ideal$_\mathcal{S}$ relative to M($i$) and $\mathcal{O}$ & $\exists w' \in M(i)\, \exists t' \prec t_u : p(w', t')$

The adverb PROBABLY ranks now the Ideal$_\mathcal{S}$ set over the ¬Ideal$_\mathcal{S}$ set, but quantification is over M($i$). This creates a strengthened MIGHT, combining the expected hesitation of the speaker about the truthfulness of $p$ (given that a possibility modal is used) with an ordering of the $p$ possibility as better. This is a strengthening that overrides the equilibrium. For this reason, such uses are generally discouraged, but as we see are not impossible. As a general tendency, the combinations of different forces will be dispreferred because they go against the natural inclinations of the modals and the adverbs. But as we showed, manipulations are possible—a fact that supports our idea that ranking is independent of the modal verb itself.

Note, finally, that the partition between $p$ and ¬$p$ worlds in the modal base and the partition between Ideal$_\mathcal{S}$ and ¬Ideal$_\mathcal{S}$ worlds are orthogonal. The ¬Ideal$_\mathcal{S}$ sets are ranked as higher, however, it is not guaranteed that quantification happens over the worlds in the Ideal$_\mathcal{S}$ set.

## 2.6 Conclusion: Nonveridicality, Modalization, and Bias

In this chapter, we developed a theory for modalization where the logical properties of veridicality and nonveridicality serve as the foundation for modeling the commitment of individual anchors $i$ to the truth of a proposition $p$. We made the following central distinctions:

1. When the speaker $i$ makes the choice to use a modal expression, she decides to take a nonveridical stance toward a proposition. A nonveridical stance means that $i$ cannot be fully committed to $p$ because $i$ lacks evidence to support knowledge of $p$. We proposed the *Nonveridicality Axiom*, i.e., a presupposition that the modal bases allow both $p$ and ¬$p$ worlds as open possibilities. Nonveridicality imbues the modal base with uncertainty.

2. Veridicality and nonveridicality characterize information states of individual anchors that are homogenous (veridical) or nonhomogeneous (nonveridical). The veridical state is the basis for full commitment, and a prerequisite for assertion.
3. Possibility modals express *nonveridical equilibrium*: $p$ and $\neg p$ are equal options in the modal base, and the speaker has no reason to prefer one over the other. Questions are also in nonveridical equilibrium (and this is why possibility modals, but not necessity ones, are good in questions, see more details in Giannakidou and Mari 2019).
4. The illusion of strength with necessity modals comes from the fact that necessity modals come with nonempty metaevaluation $\mathcal{O}$, which produces *positive bias*, namely that the Ideal worlds are better possibilities than the non-Ideal ones.
5. The categories of equilibrium and bias are central to defining two types of modality, and are better descriptors of what counts as "strong" and "weak" within modality. Within the nonveridical stance, individuals can take a weaker (possibility) or a stronger (necessity) position; but the stronger position is at best bias and never veridical commitment to the prejacent.
6. The use of subjunctive with modal verbs supports the generalization that the subjunctive is sensitive to the nonveridical presupposition.

The correlation between veridicality, nonveridicality, and commitment is not exclusive to modals, of course. We offer it as a tool for the understanding and analysis of various other structures that involve subjective truth assessment. We will demonstrate how this system works and how far it can reach in the rest of this book.

CHAPTER THREE

# Mood and Tense in Complement Clauses

Having presented our formal framework for modalization, our goal in this chapter is to move on to propositional attitudes and offer a thorough analysis of the interaction between mood, and tense morphemes in complement clauses. There is a three-way correlation between the higher propositional attitude verb, the mood exponent, and the embedded tense. The choice of mood correlates not with finiteness but with a choice of embedded tense: the indicative complement, specifically, is incompatible with NONPAST, but the subjunctive of volitional and directive verbs requires it. NONPAST, and not the subjunctive or future, is responsible for future orientation, and we articulate explicit syntax-semantics compositions to illustrate how the embedded tenses are derived in Greek and Italian.

The tense of future orientation is the NONPAST (Giannakidou 2009; Giannakidou and Mari 2016c, 2018a), and it is the dependent tense that we find with future-oriented subjunctive clauses. Key to understanding the dependent property of NONPAST is the fact that this tense needs to be anchored to the utterance time. We propose a *Now*-anchoring rule that is operative also in the bare infinitive in English. Our claim will be further that in languages lacking productive morphological mood, the verbal correlate of mood is tense. The apparent finiteness distinction in English and other Germanic languages distorts this correlation.

## 3.1 Greek Subjunctive in Main and Embedded Clauses

Typologically, we find morphological distinctions such as indicative, subjunctive, optative, imperative, conditional mood; of these, only the former two appear in complement clauses. Greek, recall, has imperative, as well as an optative particle *as*, both only appearing in main clauses. The subjunctive particle *na* also appears in main clauses:

(1) a. Na/ As fiji/ efevge o Janis.
 SUBJ/ OPT leave.NONPAST.3sg/ PAST.3sg the John
 John may go/Let John go.
 John could have left.
 b. Thelo na/*as fiji o Janis.
 want that.SUBJ/OPT leave.NONPAST.3sg the John
 John may go/Let John go.

(2) a. Fige Jani!
 leave.imperative.2sg John
 John, go!
 b.*Thelo fige Jani!
 want.1sg leave.imperative.2sg John
 *I want John, go!

In main clauses, the subjunctive *na* appears equivalent to *as* and the imperative in producing nonassertions such as permissions, requests, or wishes. We can think of the main clause subjunctives as "hybrid" imperatives. It is often assumed that, as in the case of the imperatives, there is an illocutionary force operator in C in main clauses. The subjunctive particle *na* can be argued to move to this position (Giannakidou 2009), again as has been argued for the imperative morpheme (Rivero and Terzi 1994; Giannakidou 1997, 1998). One can also hypothesize that the subjunctive remains in Mood phrase and that it behaves as a possibility modal—a position that receives support from the fact that *na* itself appears with other illocutionary forces, e.g., in questions, as we have mentioned in chapter 1. In this case, recall, the subjunctive is equivalent to a possibility modal:

(3) Pjos na kerdise?
 who that.SUBJ win.PERF.PAST.3sg
 Who might have won?

Here we have a question, and the presence of the subjunctive particle does not turn the question into a command or a wish. It must then be understood that *na* does not have illocutionary force of its own, but appears in the scope of other nonassertive forces. If *na* is a polarity item in need to appear in the scope of a nonveridical operator, then we have an explanation for why the force is nonassertive: assertion relies on the veridical state which is a prerequisite for it — but all other illocutionary forces rely on nonveridical states.

We schematize this discussion below:

(4)

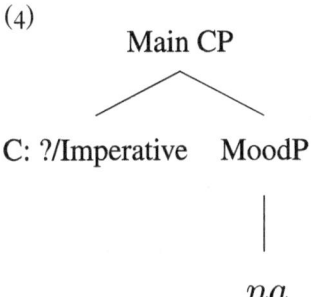

In a main *na* permission or request, we can either assume that there is a covert imperative operator in C, or that *na* denotes a deontic modal. The hybrid imperative cases are interesting as they allow a modal analysis of what appears to have an imperative force, therefore supporting approaches to imperatives such as Kaufmann (2012) who treats the imperative itself as a deontic modal (of necessity). Unlike Kaufmann, the default force of deontic *na* appears to be possibility, as can be seen in questions. *Na* also appears with modal adverbs of possibility but not necessity (Giannakidou 2012, 2016c):

(5) a. Isos    na          efije            o Janis.
       maybe that.SUBJ leave.PAST.3sg the John
       Maybe John left.
    b.*Mallon  na          efije            o Janis.
       probably that.SUBJ leave.PAST.3sg the John
       *Probably John might have left.

*Na* is therefore a possibility modal, as Giannakidou has argued. And in that use, it combines with both past and nonpast:

(6) $[\![\text{Na}_{main}\ (\text{PRES}\ (p))]\!]^{M,i,S}$ is true iff
$\exists w'[w' \in M(i) \wedge w' \in \{w'' \mid p(w'', t_u)\}]$
(For short, we will write $\exists w' \in M(i) : p(w', t_u)$).

(7) $[\![\text{Na}_{main}\ (\text{PAST}\ (p))]\!]^{M,i,S}$ is true iff
$\exists w' \exists t'[w' \in M(i) \wedge t' \prec t_u \wedge w' \in \{w'' \mid p(w'', t')\}]$
(For short, we will write $\exists w' \in M(i) \exists t' \prec t_u : p(w', t')$).

In the context of our theory in chap. 2, the subjunctive *na* indeed appears to be the modal head, with the modal adverb of possibility appearing in the meta-evaluation position $\mathcal{O}$. A necessity adverb is at odds with *na* because in Greek we only have agreement patterns, i.e., the modality needs to be matched, as we illustrated in chapter 2. Hence, though a particle, the Greek subjunctive behaves on a par with a modal verb in main clauses. Crucially, when co-occurring with modal adverbs, Greek *na* cannot be argued to be higher than Mood, obviously. In embedded clauses, on the other hand, *na* has a life as a subordinator, and for this reason it is often characterized as a complementizer.

The syntactic characterization of the Greek mood particles in embedded clauses has been the subject of intense study since the early 90s. The main question has been: are the Greek particles Mood exponents or complementizers? Clearly, *na* is the realization of Mood heading MoodP; we follow Philippaki-Warburton 1994, 1998; Philippaki-Warburton and Veloudis 1984; Tsimpli 1990; Giannakidou 1998, 2009).[1]

Another approach claims that *na* is a complementizer C (Agouraki 1991; Tsoulas 1993; and Roussou 2000, who uses an extended C-domain in the spirit of Rizzi 1997). Giannakidou (2009) offers detailed discussion of both approaches and concludes that *na* is a Mood head that moves to C in embedded clauses because it is also a subordinator, hence the tree looks as follows:

---

1. Or, as Chatzopoulou 2019 argues, NonveridicalityP. Chatzopoulou replaces MoodP with the Nonveridicality projection to account for this intermediate position between C and T that hosts historically various nonveridical particles including the conditional *an*. Greek appears to make extensive use of this intermediate position and encodes nonveridicality quite systematically.

(8)

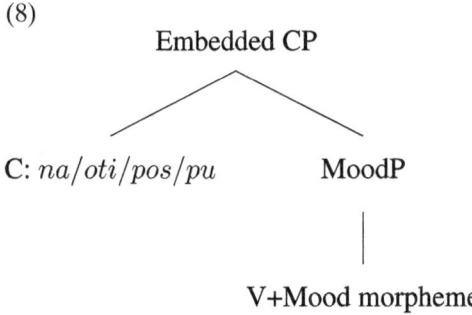

In other words, in embedded clauses, the mood particles—both subjunctive and indicative—are subordinators, and this explains why in embedding there is no meaning contribution. *Na* is thus both a modal, in main clauses, and a subordinator in embedded clauses; *oti*, on the other hand, is only a subordinator (like *that*) and cannot be used in main clauses. The same holds for *pu*. Main clause particles such as the optative are illocutionary force operators and cannot appear as subordinators.

Here we will take the above structure as the point of departure for both Greek and Italian. Giannakidou (1998, 2009) considers also cases where *na* appears under an actual subordinator, e.g., in relative clauses as mentioned in chapter 1, with temporal connectives (*prin na, xoris na, before, without*), and in purpose clauses:

(9)  I    Ariadne irthe       gia na         mas di.
     the Ariadne came.3sg for that.SUBJ us  see.3sg
     Ariadne came in order to see us.

When *na* appears with complementizers it seems reasonable to treat it as composing with these; *na* is, after all, a clitic. For Italian, we can adopt Bauanaz's (2015) and Todorovich's (2012) position that, despite the fact that we have no lexically distinct complementizers, these are nevertheless different: a subjunctive *que* that appears with nonpast, and an indicative one that appears with present and past. In these analyses, the subjunctive correlates with tense, in a way that we will make precise below. In the main clause, as we said, *na* itself functions as an epistemic modal, but in embedding there is no evidence that it adds modality to the embedded clause.

What becomes immediately clear by looking at the morphological exponents of mood in Greek and Romance languages is that mood affects three positions in the embedded clause: the Mood/verb (Latin, Romance languages, Ancient Greek), the subordinator C (Modern Greek, Balkan languages, including Romanian which is a Romance language), and the embedded tense. Following Giannakidou (2009, 2016), we will show that in Greek there is a strong correlation: the subjunctive combines typically with a nonpast and has future orientation, whereas the indicative is freer, i.e., it combines with past and present or with future. Yet the nonpast is never compatible with the indicative in Greek and Italian.

Let us proceed now to examine in more detail the correlation between mood and embedded tense. In doing so, we will revisit some of the selection patterns and identify the main propositional attitude classes that are relevant for mood choice. In order to understand the role of tense, we give first some necessary background on tense and aspect in Greek.

## 3.2 Morphological and Semantic Tenses in Greek

Tense and aspect are always reflected morphologically on the Greek verb. The grammars (Holton et al. 2007, Tzevelekou et al. 2012) describe the morphological opposition between past and nonpast, and the aspectual distinction is perfective vs. imperfective. The morphological combinations create three semantic tenses (Giannakidou 2009, 2014): a present (PRES), a past (PAST), and a NONPAST, which is the tense used for prediction and future orientation. In our discussion in this book, the uppercase names of tenses will refer to the semantic tenses, and the lowercase to the morphological forms.

We start with the morphological nonpasts. Consider first the imperfective nonpast.

(10)  graf-         -o.          (imperfective nonpast: PRES)
      write.IMPFV NONPAST.1sg
      I am writing (right now).
      I write (generally).

The morphological imperfective nonpast is semantically the present tense (PRES) in Greek (Giannakidou 2014), comparable to English present progressive. The Greek form also has a generic, habitual reading because of imperfective aspect. The combination of these two readings is very common with imperfective forms crosslinguistically.

The perfective nonpast is a dependent form, *ungrammatical* by itself as indicated. It cannot occur on its own; it needs the subjunctive, future, optative, conditional and other modal particles to be grammatical.

(11) *grap- s-    o                  (perfective nonpast: *on its own)
     write- PERF NONPAST.1sg.

The perfective nonpast has no English equivalent, and it is in fact quite rare to find grammatical perfective nonpasts in languages (Giorgi and Pianesi 1996). Romance languages do not exhibit a morphological perfective nonpast; they only retain the aspectual distinction in the past paradigm. Holton et al. (1997) and Giannakidou (2009) call this form the *verbal dependent*. This is the form used for prediction and future orientation:

(12)   Tha/As/Na         grapsi                    to grama avrio
       FUT/OPT/SUBJ write.PERF.NONPAST.3sg the letter tomorrow.
       She will write the letter tomorrow.
       Let her write the letter tomorrow.

We analyze this form as a semantic NONPAST in the next subsection. NONPAST is also the tense of the infinitive, as we illustrate with Italian. We also claim that this is the tense of the infinitive in English. In Russian and other Slavic languages morphological perfective nonpasts are able to future-shift on their own, unlike the Greek form (see, e.g., Bulatovic 2002 for Serbian). This suggests to us that these forms lexicalize as semantic futures and not NONPAST.

The past is marked typically in Greek with the presence of the augment *e-*, and we have again two options, perfective and imperfective. The imperfective past is the equivalent of the preterite in Romance languages. The preterite is a combination of a semantic past plus habitual or progressive aspect, both typical readings with this morphological form:

(13)   e-    graf-       a. (Greek imperfective past)
       PAST write.IMPFV 1sg
       I used to write.
       I was writing.

The perfective past, on the other hand, is called the *aorist* and denotes a single (usually completed) event in the past. It is interpreted as a default simple past in English:

(14)  e-    grap- s-    a.  (Greek perfective past (aorist))
      PAST write- PERF 1sg
      I wrote.

This form is a simple semantic PAST. Giannakidou (2004) offers discussion of why this form is not telic but tends to be interpreted as telic—as a form of implicature, perhaps, since the perfective past instead of the imperfective is used.

For future, Greek has the modal particle *tha* that we are by now familiar with. Italian has a future tense. They both combine with all of the above tenses. Notice first the combinations of FUT with the PRES (imperfective nonpast in Greek, gerund plus stative in Italian):

(15)  a. I    Ariadne tha   troi                        tora.
         the Ariadne FUT eat.IMPF.NONPAST.3sg now
         Ariadne must be eating now.
      b. Giacomo ora  starà          mangiando.
         Giacomo now be.FUT.3sg eat.GER
         Giacomo must be eating now.

As shown above, FUT plus PRES does not have a predictive reading and is equivalent to an epistemic MUST modal statement. In Italian, as we discussed in Giannakidou and Mari (2018a), Aktionsart plays the role that aspect plays in Greek. (The role of Aktionsart in connection with modal interpretation has been studied across languages and categories; see Condoravdi 2002; Laca 2008; Copley 2009; Mari 2015a, b, 2018a). Combinations of FUT with a lower PAST (an aorist in Greek) also receive epistemic nonpredictive readings:

(16) a. I   Ariadne tha   itan         arrosti xthes.
        the Ariadne FUT be.PAST.3sg ill   yesterday
        Ariadne must/#will have been ill yesterday.
    b. Giovanni sarà        stato malato ieri.
        Giovanni be.FUT.3sg been ill      yesterday.
        Giovanni must/#will have been ill yesterday.

(17) a. I   Ariadne tha   efige                xthes.
        the Ariadne FUT leave.PERF.PAST.3sg yesterday
        Ariadne must have left yesterday.
    b. Gianni avrà         parlato ieri.
        Gianni have.FUT.3sg spoken yesterday
        Gianni must/ #will have spoken yesterday.

Pietrandrea (2005), Mari (2009), and Giannakidou and Mari (2018a) call these "epistemic futures". (Note that English *will* does not combine with the past; for differences between Greek/Italian FUT and *will* see Mari, 2015b,2018; Giannakidou and Mari 2018b. French future is similar to *will*; see Mari, 2015b, 2018).[2] These uses, crucially, are quite common and do not feel in any way marked or exceptional. The readings are equivalent to the combinations of MUST with exactly the same tense combinations:

(18) a. I   Ariadne prepei na     itan         arrosti xthes.
        the Ariadne must  that.SUBJ be.PAST.3sg ill     yesterday
        Ariadne must have been ill yesterday.
    b. Giovanni deve        essere stato malato ieri.
        Giovanni be.FUT.3sg be    been ill    yesterday.
        Giovanni must/#will have been ill yesterday.

(19) a. I   Ariadne prepi na     efige                xthes.
        the Ariadne must  that.SUBJ leave.PERF.PAST.3sg yesterday
        Ariadne must have left yesterday.

---

2. See Tasmowski and Dendale (1998); Dendale (2001); de Saussure and Morency (2011) on the differences between French MUST and FUT.

b. Gianni avrà         parlato ieri.
   Gianni have.FUT.3sg spoken yesterday
   Gianni must/ #will have spoken yesterday.

For the sake of completeness, consider that with PAST, we do not obtain a future of a past reading in either language (Giannakidou and Mari 2018a). To obtain a future of a past, Italian uses the conditional (Mari 2015d), and Greek the imperfective past (Giannakidou 2012: 21):

(20)  Gianni sarebbe        arrivato più   tardi.
      Gianni be.COND.3sg    arrived   more late
      Gianni would arrive later.

(21)  I   Ariadne tha  efevge                argotera.
      the Ariadne FUT  leave.IMPF.PAST.3sg   later
      Ariadne would leave later.

*Tha* plus imperfective past is argued to be the Greek equivalent to conditional mood (Iatridou 2000; Giannakidou 2012), a position that we adopt here.

Before we move on, let us remind the reader that the NONPAST is the tense used in embedded subjunctive clauses:

(22)  Thelo     na     ftasi                          noris o   Janis.
      I-want    that.SUBJ arrive.PERF.NONPAST.3sg     early the John
      I want John to arrive early.

(23)  Bori      na     ftasi                          noris o   Janis.
      maybe     that.SUBJ arrive.PERF.NONPAST.3sg     early the John
      John might arrive early.

As can be seen, temporal reference shifts to the future with this form. On the other hand, NONPAST never occurs with indicative:

(24)  *Pistevo/ksero         oti      ftasi                         noris o
      I-believe/know         that.IND arrive.PERF.NONPAST.3sg       early the
      Janis.
      John
      ?? I believe John to arrive early. / *I know John to arrive early.

(25) *Xarika      pu       ftasi                        noris o   Janis.
     was.glad.3sg that.IND arrive.PERF.NONPAST.3sg early the John
     *I am glad John to arrive early.

As can be seen, NONPAST is also not acceptable with English factive verbs. We have a robust correlation between NONPAST and the subjunctive, on the one hand, and the indicative and PAST, PRES on the other.

Recall that the PRES and PAST are the veridical tenses:

(26) Veridicality of temporal operators:
Let $F$ be temporal function, $t$ an instant or an interval.
$F$ is veridical iff $Fp$ at a time $t$ entails that $p$ is true at a (contextually given) time $t' \leq t$; otherwise $F$ is nonveridical. (Giannakidou 2002: 23)

PAST/*yesterday* are veridical because (PAST/*yesterday* ($p$)) at $t_u$ entails that $p$ was true at a time $t' \leq t$. Likewise, PRES/*right now* is veridical because (PRES/*right now* ($p$)) at $t_u$ entails that $p$ is true at $t_u$. The future (FUT) and NONPAST, however, are nonveridical because FUT/*tomorrow* ($p$)) at $t_u$ does not entail that $p$ is true at $t_u$ or a time $t' \leq t$; likewise, as we will see next, for the NONPAST. Temporal veridicality is objective veridicality anchored to $t_u$, and we discuss next the centrality of $t_u$ in the interpretation of NONPAST.

As in our earlier work, we will assume that the morphological tense and aspect combinations map onto semantic tenses PRES (imperfective nonpast), PAST (perfective past) and NONPAST (perfective nonpast), designated with uppercase. The imperfective past is a compositional combination of PAST and PROGRESSIVE or GEN (Giannakidou 2009). The syntax we adopt for particles, mood and tense, following Giannakidou (2009), is the following:

(27)     Modal Particle (MOD) P

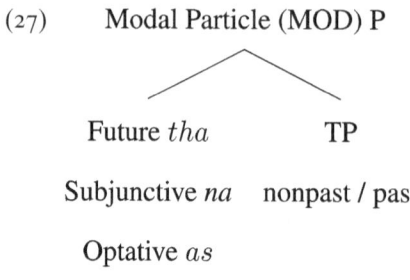

Future *tha*        TP

Subjunctive *na*   nonpast / past

Optative *as*

The modal and temporal information are dissociated in the Greek clause. The tensed verb appears in T. Modal particles are MOD heads above TP in what we now call Modal particle P (equivalent to Chatzopolou's 2019 NonveridicalityP, and ealrier MoodP).[3] We assume that the differentiation of tense and modality is true also for Italian and holds perhaps even universally. In any case, the transparency of modality and tense in the Greek clause allows us to see the clear contribution of each component, and the interaction between mood/modal particle and tense.

## 3.3 The Semantic NONPAST: Future Orientation

In Greek, the modal particle is separated from the tense system as we saw, and appears above the tensed verb (TP). The first key observation is that the indicative particles are incompatible with NONPAST. Recall:

(28)  Thelo    na         kerdisi              o  Janis.
      want.1sg that.SUBJ  win.NONPAST.3sg the John
      I want John to win.

(29)  *O   Pavlos kseri     oti        kerdisi           i  Roxani.
       the Paul   knows-3sg that.IND   win.NONPAST.3sg the Roxani
       Paul knows that Roxanne left.

---

3. Similar patterns are found in typologically unrelated languages such as Gitksan, with prospective aspect under a modal (Matthewson 2012), and Hindi (Kush 2011), where the mood is also dissociated from tense.

(30) *O Pavlos lipate pu kerdisi i Roxani.
 the Paul is-sad-3sg that.IND win.NONPAST.3sg the Roxani
 Paul regrets that Roxanne left.

The incompatibility of NONPAST with the indicative particles suggests a matching relation between mood and embedded tense in terms of (non)veridicality: the past and present tenses are veridical, but NONPAST is nonveridical. This correlation appears also in noncomplement clauses, as shown below with the temporal connective BEFORE *prin*:

(31) O Nicholas irthe prin (na)
 the Nicholas came.3sg before (that.SUBJ)
 figi o Janis.
 leave.PERF.NONPAST.3sg the John
 Nicholas came before John left.

(32) *O Nicholas irthe prin efige o Janis.
 the Nicholas came.3sg before leave.PERF.PAST.3sg the John
 Nicholas came before John left.

Giannakidou and Zwarts (1999) were the first to discuss this basic property of Greek BEFORE in selecting the perfective nonpast (NONPAST) as well as, optionally, the subjunctive (see also Xherija 2016 for more recent discussion and corroborating data from Albanian). Given that the *prin* (before) clause is nonveridical (Sanchez-Vanencia et al. 1993) and denotes a relative future with respect to the main clause, NONPAST generalizes as a nonveridical tense. NONPAST is also used with the conditional *an* and the temporal *otan* (when), always producing future orientation (see Giannakidou 2009 for details):

(33) An figi o Janis, tha
 if leave.PERF.NONPAST.3sg the John, FUT
 figoume ki emeis.
 leave.PERF.NONPAST.1pl and we
 If John leaves, we will leave too.

(34) Otan figi                o   Janis, tha
    when leave.PERF.NONPAST.3sg the John, FUT
    figoume            ki   emeis.
    leave.PERF.NONPAST.1pl and we
    When John leaves, we will leave too.

(35) Otan efige   o   Janis, figame ki   emeis.
    when left.3sg the John, left.1pl and we
    When John left, we left too.

The perfective nonpast is a semantic NONPAST and is responsible for the prospective orientation consistently in all cases. Giannakidou 2009 defines *semantic* NONPAST as follows:

(36) Morphological perfective nonpast in Greek denotes NONPAST: (Giannakidou 2009)
    $[\![\text{NONPAST}]\!] = \lambda P \lambda t \lambda w (P(t, \infty)(w))$

(Following standard practice, we use "(" in the left interval to show that $t$ is excluded from the interval, hence $P$ will be true at a time later than $t$). NONPAST introduces a prospective interval, like Abusch's (2004) WOLL, a work Giannakidou draws on; but unlike WOLL and other morphological nonpasts that can forward shift by default, the left boundary $t$ of the Greek NONPAST is a *dependent* NPI variable in need of binding. Giannakidou argues that the NONPAST is a temporal *polarity item* and needs to be licensed. Licensing here means that $t$ must be identified with $t_u$. The distinctive property of Greek is that $t_u$ (or, $n$, for Now in Giannakidou and Abusch's original formulations), needs to be introduced in the syntax. The modal particles occupy the higher structure, and because they all have $t_u$ as a parameter of evaluation (as we saw modal operators do in chap. 2), they satisfy the licensing requirement and supply $t_u$.[4]

Licensing of NONPAST requires anchoring to $t_u$, and, following Giannakidou and Mari (2018a), we will call this *Now*-anchoring. How is *Now*-anchoring done? There are two possible implementations. One way

---

4. Giannakidou (2009) claims that the particles *denote* $t_u$, thus rendering them temporal operators. In Giannakidou and Mari (2018a), we modified that analysis and argued that $t_u$ is introduced syntactically in Greek in the higher structure by default. It is this formulation that we rely on here.

is to say that the modal particle actually adds $t_u$ in the syntax, as suggested by Giannakidou (2009). If we take that view, then we must concede that $t_u$ is added also by the other particles that appear in MOD, namely the subjunctive and the optative, as well as IF, BEFORE, WHEN as we mentioned earlier. But if we say that, we end up saying that the modal particles and the connectives *as a class* all denote $t_u$. Such a claim is not adequately justified. Consider also that, when combining with PAST, $t_u$ would be redundant, and we would have to somehow cancel it (which is what Giannakidou 2009 does).

Alternatively, *Now*-anchoring can be seen as a substitution rule for free variables. This was the spirit of Abusch's (2004: 39) rule for WOLL: "In the substitution operator, $t$ is a bound variable that corresponds to the tense argument of WILL. For a top-level occurrence of WILL, the effect is to substitute $(n, \infty)$ for $n$." It is this implementation that we will pursue here, and posit the following rule:

(37) *Now*-anchoring rule, triggered at MOD:
Substitute any free variables $t$ in TP with $t_u$.

This rule will be triggered only if there are free variables in TP, and it will not apply to lower PAST, for instance, as we will show soon. The rule will enable the free variable $t$ of NONPAST to be identified with $t_u$. As a result, the interval provided by NONPAST will then be anchored to $t_u$, which is what we want. The advantage of having this rule is that it allows us to keep the semantics of modality clear of time—and it avoids the undesirable positions that all modal particles introduce $t_u$, and that $t_u$ is dually present both as a parameter of evaluation *and* an argument of FUT. Introducing $t_u$ appears to be a property of the higher structure therefore positing the *Now*-anchoring rule seems to be the better option.

The analysis for the future sentence (38) is provided below (following Giannakidou and Mari 2018a):

(38) O Janis tha kerdisi.
the John FUT win.PERF.NONPAST.3sg
John will win.

(39)

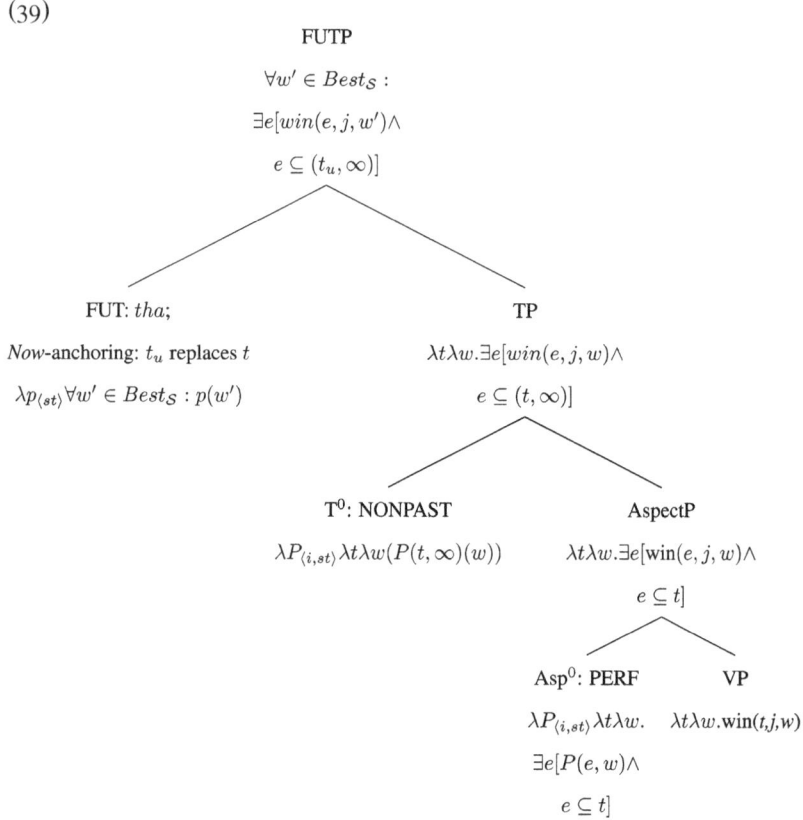

Meaning is represented explicitly at LF, and semantic composition is limited to function application, variable binding, and type raising. Starting from the bottom, perfective aspect applies, yielding a statement that there is a winning event. Following Giannakidou (2009), PERF and NONPAST are modifiers:[5] their input is a property P, and give back the same property with the addition of the event argument and replacement of $t$ by $(t, \infty)$. PERF introduces the event argument and existentially closes it (as in Giannakidou 2002 also Hacquard 2009). This event has to be located at $t$, which itself must be placed within the interval provided by NONPAST. At TP, the $t$ variable remains unbound. At FUT, the *Now*-anchoring rule applies, resulting in identifying the $t$ provided by NONPAST with $t_u$. The

---

[5]. The same analysis might apply to Russian, which also constructs future meaning from the combination of PERF and NONPAST. We thank a reviewer for this comment.

interval at FUTP is set to $(t_u, \infty)$. The modal meaning can be thus properly computed.

Our analysis of nonpast embedded under FUT is very similar to the idea of a prospective marker under FUT, found in recent literature in Kush (2011) and Matthewson (2012) for Gitksan, which actually has an overt prospective aspect marker *dim*:

(40) da'akxw[-i]-'y      dim     ayee=hl     bax-'y      (Gitksan)
     circ.poss[-tra]-1sg.II PROSP go.fast=CN run-1sg.II
     I can run fast.

We want to make clear that Greek does not have a prospective aspect, but a morphological and semantic NONPAST. Kush (2011), further, studies the Hindi modal particle *gaa*, which, like FUT, shows a flexibility between epistemic and predictive readings. The future reading arises with the bare verb (no tense or aspect) 41, and the epistemic with perfective (past) (42-a) or progressive aspect (42-b) (examples and glosses from Kush 2011 ex. (5)-(6a)-(6b)):

(41) ve        bacce        do din=mẽ aa-ẽ-gee.
     dem.3pl child.m.pl two day=in come.SUBJ.PL.MOD.m.pl
     Those children will come in two days.

(42) a. ve       log     ab$^h$i=tak pahũc$^h$-ee
        dem.3pl people now=by arrive.PFV.PL
        hõ-Ø-gee.
        AUX.SUBJ.PL.MOD.m.pl
        They must have arrived by now.
     b. ve       log     ab$^h$i naac            rah-ee
        dem.3pl people now dance.PROG.m.pl aux.SUBJ.MOD.m.pl.
        hõ-Ø-gee.
        They must be dancing now.

Kush analyzes *gaa* as a modal operator but posits metaphysical modality for the future reading. Future/metaphysical modal base arises with no tense in Kush's account, and the epistemic reading relies on aspect: "from the ungrammaticality of auxiliaries in Future constructions we can conclude that Tense is absent." (Kush 2011: 417).

Given the Greek system we outlined above, we cannot say that tense is absent with morphological nonpast. Morphologically, nonpast is a tense in

Greek. So, when FUT selects a perfective nonpast, it selects a tense/aspect combination, which is assigned the denotation of NONPAST. At the same time, the non-predictive epistemic reading in Greek and Italian rely on PAST and PRES, and this creates a parallel with Hindi; but, unlike Kush (2011) and Giannakidou and Mari (2013), we do not claim that there is a shift in modal base, as FUT uniformly quantifies over epistemic alternatives in our account. Overall, and this is worth emphasizing, looking at Kush (2011) and also Matthewson (2012), we find that modality and tense/aspect are dissociated, and the modal particle scopes above tense/aspect. Therefore the data from Greek, Italian, Gitksan, and Hindi jointly suggest that future modals at least in these languages are not mixed modal-temporal operators (*pace* Condoravdi 2002).

## 3.4 The Subjunctive and NONPAST

The derivation with the subjunctive will proceed in similar steps. Consider first the main subjunctive. Here is the derivation from Giannakidou (2009:63):

(43)

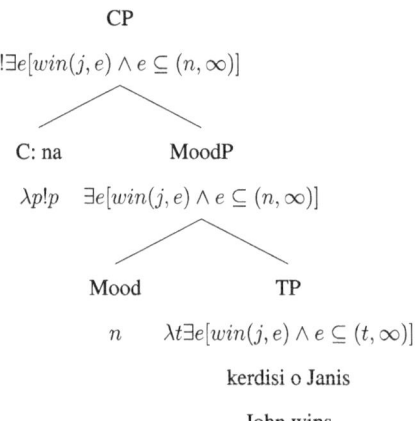

In current terms, we can actually assume, as we suggested at the beginning, that *na* is a bouletic or teleological possibility modal:

(44) $[\![\text{na (NONPAST }(p))]\!]^{M,i,S}$ is true iff $\exists w' \in M(i) : \exists e[win(j,e,w') \wedge e \subseteq (n,\infty)]$; where $M(i)$ is set of worlds corresponding to what is desired or permitted or set as a goal.

*Now*-anchoring will be triggered at MOD (Mood), just as with FUT in the case of the future particle. In the present work, we want to keep the analysis unified, and there is no necessity for illocutionary force in the embedded CP.

Consider now the epistemic case:

(45) O Janis isos na kerdisi.
    the John maybe that.SUBJ win.PERF.NONPAST.3sg
    John might win.

(46) Pjos na kerdise (araje)?
    who that.SUBJ win.PERF.PAST.3sg question particle
    Who might have won?

In the question, there is arguably a question operator; with the adverb, the structure is as below. The subjunctive and the adverb would enter a modal spread relation, as outlined in chapter 2; we omit the details here and spell out the modality on the higher, adverbial layer. The two denote one single modality.

(47)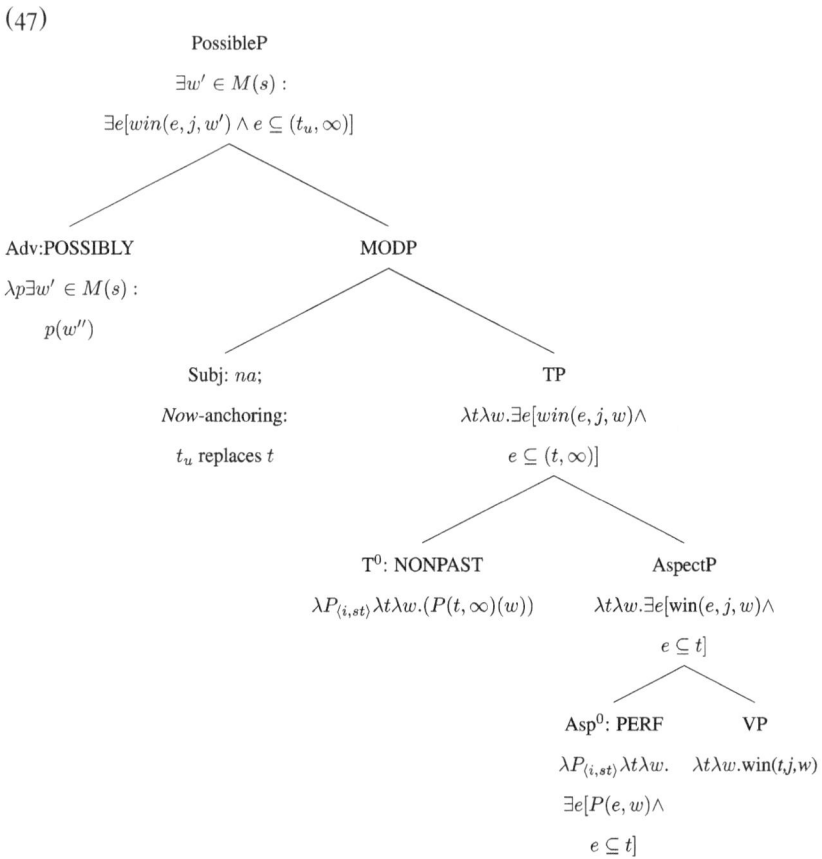

When it comes to complement clauses, it is important to remember that there is neither illocutionary force nor modality by *na* itself. Again $t_u$ is introduced by the Mood head, which is hosting *na*; but *na* moves to C in embedded clauses as a subordinator. Embedding now identifies the left $t$ of the NONPAST with the time of the higher verb, which can be present or past (or even future). If the attitude verb is in the present tense, $t$ of the NONPAST will be identified with $t_u$, as in the unembedded clauses. If we have a past tense attitude verb, the complement now will denote an event to be located at the time $t$ through infinity, but now $t$ is in the past, just like the attitude verb:

(48) Ithela na kerdisi o Janis.
wanted.1sg that.SUBJ win.PERF.NONPAST.3sg the John
I wanted John to win.

(49) Volevo         che Gianni vincesse.
    want.IMPF.1sg that John win.IMPF.SUBJ.3sg
    I wanted John to win.

A common observation for the embedded subjunctive tense (see Ambar (2016) for recent discussion) is that it is anaphoric. Anaphoric means dependent on the attitude tense. With the past tense *ithela/volevo* (wanted), the top T contributes a time *t* prior to now, a past. We get a reading where I wanted in the past that there be an event of John's winning that is not in the past, but in the interval that starts at my wanting time and looks forward, to times possible prior or after $t_u$:

(50)

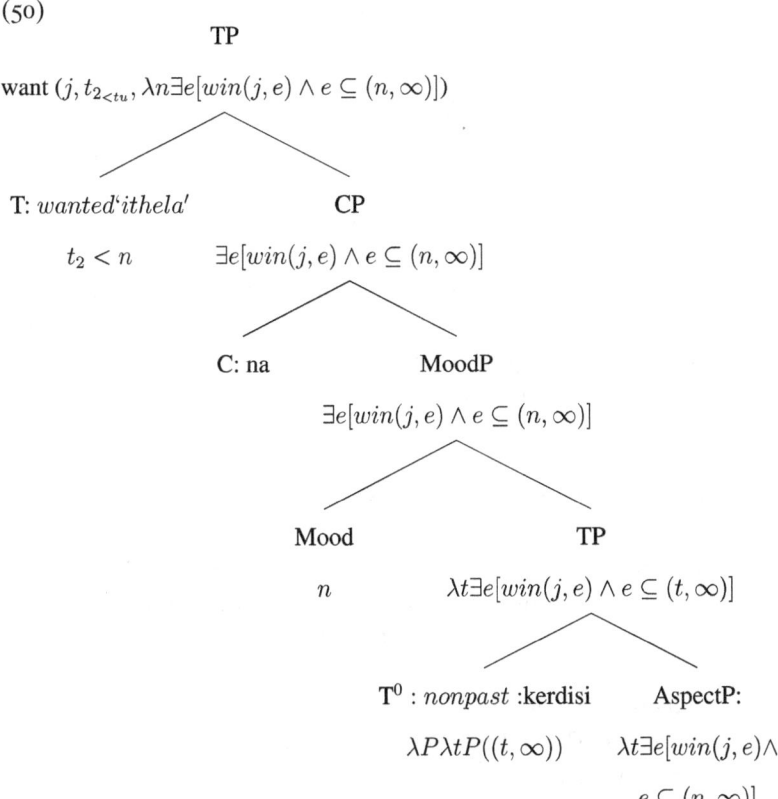

When *na* is a subordinator, there is no modality of its own, since it leaves the Mood phrase. My desire in this reading is expressed in the following paraphrase: the time $t_2$ of my wanting is located in the past, and the time $t$ of John's winning is located in the future interval that starts at $t_2$.

(51)  $want(j, t_u, \lambda n \exists e[win(j, e) \wedge e \subseteq (t_u, \infty)])$

That interval, then, would be the one that starts at the internal now of the attitude (which can be identified with $t_2$) and moves forward to include the actual utterance time and times after that. Hence, when embedded, the lambda-bound *n* of *na* cannot refer to the utterance time but to the relative *n* of the attitude. If the attitude, on the other hand, is anchored to the present, the interval will be $[t_u, \infty)$, thus identical to the main occurrence of subjunctive.

Hence, the embedded interpretation of nonpast with *na* follows compositionally from the meaning of NONPAST and *Now*-anchoring. The tense anaphoricity is a temporal dependency between the time of the higher attitude and the time of the complement and is enabled by the NONPAST, which can be identified with $t_u$ or a time prior to it if the attitude needs it.

To sum up: the Mood position triggers the *Now*-anchoring rule; *na* as a subordinator moves to C and has no modal meaning. The temporal information comes from nonpast just as with the FUT. The inherent modality on *na* surfaces only in main clauses and it can be deontic or epistemic.

## 3.5 Subjunctive with a Lower PAST

Let us now provide the analysis for modal particle with PAST. We illustrate first with FUT as the simple case without embedding. We distinguish a morphological perfective and a past layer.

(52)  O Janis tha kerdise.
      the John FUT win.PERF.NONPAST.3sg
      John must have won.

Here, the embedded time is a PAST which is deictic and denotes the anteriority relation with respect to $t_u$: $t' \prec t_u$. The *Now*-anchoring rule does not apply since there are no free variables.

(53)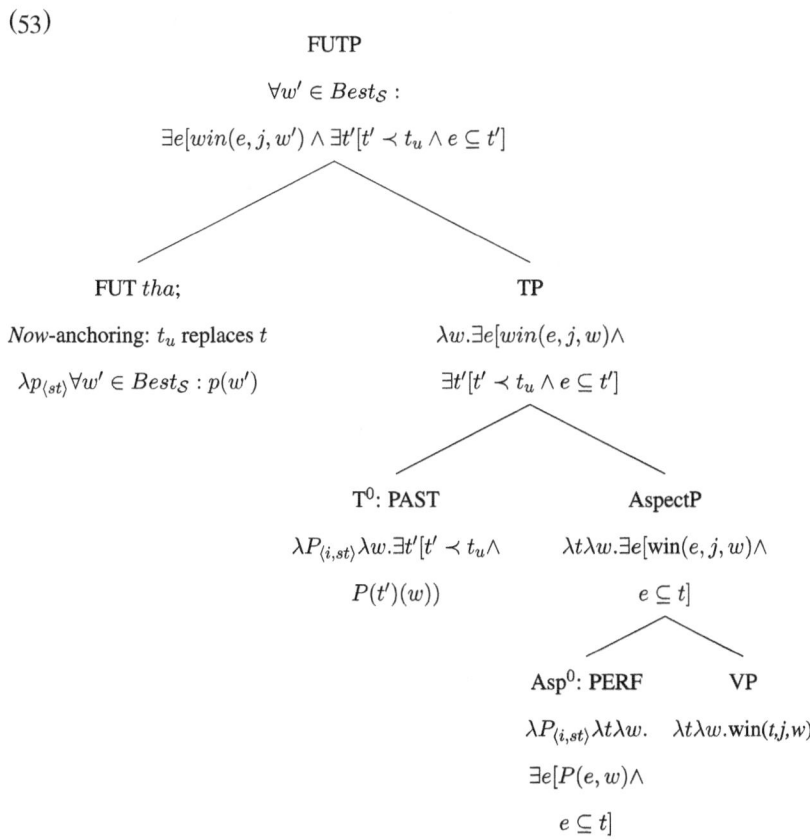

FUT thus does not provide tense. With a lower NONPAST we get future orientation and a prediction, but with a lower PAST, the FUT sentence is equivalent to a MUST sentence with embedded PAST. The temporal information, in both cases, comes from the tense below FUT. Incidentally, PAST is also possible under the Dutch and German futures:

(54) Hij zal wel slecht geslapen hebben!
he FUT.3sg particle bad slept have
He must have slept really bad! (Giannakidou and Mari 2018a)

(55) Ich habe meinem Freund letzte Woche einen Brief geschrieben; er *wird* ihn sicher schon bekommen haben.
I wrote a letter to my friend last week; he must surely have already received it. (Lederer 1969: 98, ex. 584).

Morphologically, a present perfect appears in Dutch and German, just as in English *must have slept*, and not a simple past **must slept*. This can be taken to show, in agreement with what we said earlier, that the default tense of the infinitive is NONPAST. This, as Giannakidou and Mari (2018a) suggest, necessitates the use of a NONPAST auxiliary resulting in the apparent present perfect.[6] Greek, on the other hand, lacks infinitives and the modal embeds a tensed clause which can be a simple past or a nonpast. The sentences above, in any case, show that a future morpheme can combine with lower PAST, and when this happens the predictive reading disappears. The future reading requires a lower NONPAST.

(56) O Janis isos na kerdise.
the John maybe that.SUBJ win.PERF.PAST.3sg.
John must have won.

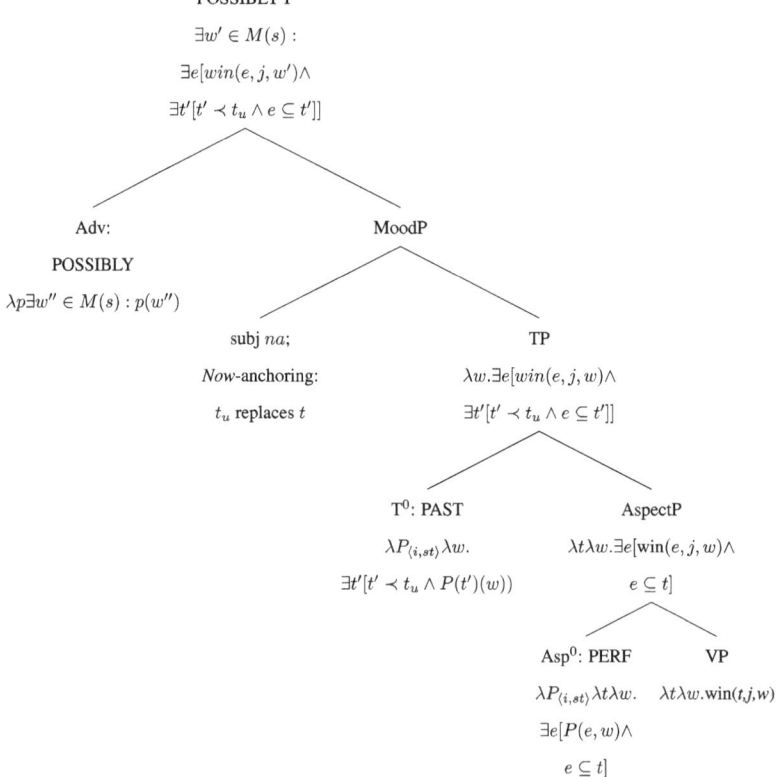

---

[6]. McCawley 1988 notes that in nonfinite contexts, past tense and the perfect are equivalent; for recent discussion see Arregi and Klecha (2015).

In the embedded *na* clause, the lower past interval is anchored to the attitude time, as in the previous case with past.

(57) Elpizo    na              efije       o  Janis.
     hope.1sg  that.SUBJj      left.3sg    the John
     I hope that John left.

## 3.6 Syntax-Semantics of Tense and Mood in Italian

We now extend this analysis to Italian, by using the modal future to maintain the parallelism.

### 3.6.1 From Greek to Italian

In Italian, *futuro* appears on the verb (58-b), like present (58-a) and simple past (58-c).

(58) a. Arriv- a.
        arrive PRES.3sg
        He arrive any moment soon.
     b. Arriv- erà.
        arrive FUT.3sg
        He will arrive.
     c. Arriv- ò.
        arrive SIMPLE.PAST.3sg
        He arrived.

We propose that abstractly the structure is similar to Greek, with FUT being expressed higher than TP. The order of application of the semantic functions is the same as in Greek—and it is merely a morphological fact that future is a Tense, and must therefore stay within the V-form in Italian. In Greek, FUT is a particle and stays outside the V. In other words, in Italian there is a mismatch between the function of *futuro* (modal) and its status as a verbal category. The same, by the way, holds for subjunctive, which in Italian, unlike Greek, also appears on V.

The main difference between Italian and Greek is that, in Italian, Aktionsart determines the aspectual information—since in Italian there is no grammatical aspectual distinction. We note with previous literature (and most notably Bertinetto 1979) that, in Italian, the eventive/stative distinction plays a role, just as in a variety of other languages (see Cipria and Roberts 2000; Condoravdi 2002; Copley 2002; Laca 2008; Mari, 2015a, b, Frana and Menendez-Benito 2019). With eventive predicates embedded under present (59-b) or future (60-b), the time of evaluation of the prejacent is forward-shifted—unlike with stative predicates (59-a) and (60-a). Such data can be replicated for English, and extend beyond present and future (e.g., see Copley 2009).

(59) a. Gianni è         malato. (stative, present reading)
         John    be.PRES.3sg ill
         John is ill.
     b. Gianni arriva.         (eventive, future reading)
        Gianni arrive.PRES.3sg
        John will arrive immediately.

(60) a. Gianni sarà        malato. (stative, present epistemic reading)
        John    be.FUT.3sg ill
        John must be ill.
     b. Gianni arriverà.       (eventive, predictive reading)
        John    arrive.FUT.3sg
        Gianni will arrive.

Condoravdi (2002) notes the same pattern for modals (see (61)) and proposes an account that relies on aspectual differences between statives and eventives, from which it follows that the time of evaluation of the prejacent is forward-shifted only with eventive ones.[7]

(61) a. John might be ill. (stative, present orientation)
     b. John might become ill. (eventive, future orientation)

---

[7] When the prejacent is stative (and the time of evaluation is not forward-shifted), the modal has an epistemic interpretation. According to Condoravdi (2002) the modal has a metaphysical interpretation in (61-a).

According to Condoravdi (2002) the modal itself bears the temporal information and provides a forward-shifting interval. We cannot adopt this view here, since forward-shifting with eventives is independent of modal embedding; see (59-b). Our proposal builds on a parallelism between grammatical and lexical aspect, according to which lexical statives are standardly imperfective, whereas eventives are perfective unless they are marked by a progressive verb form (see Smith 1991; Boogaart and Trnavac 2011). In this line of thought, lexical eventives provide aspectual information—perfectivity—and perfectivity, in absence of PAST, triggers futurity (NONPAST, $\lambda P \lambda t \lambda w(P(t, \infty)(w))$). Aspect is thus contributed in the VP.

Note that, just as in Greek morphological perfectivity combines with either nonpast or past to produce PERF, NONPAST, and PERF PAST in Italian lexical perfectivity is also compatible with PAST or NONPAST leading to PERF PAST and PERF NONPAST, as is the case here to produce the predictive reading.[8]

Above the VP, the derivation in Italian is parallel to the one in Greek. We see that, by being parametric to the time of utterance, FUT provides *Now*-anchoring in Italian as well.[9] Consider (62).

(62) Flavio vincerà.
 Flavio win.FUT.3sg
 Flavio will win.

---

8. As often noted, forward-shifting is observed with statives too, e.g., as in *Domani sarà malato'* (Tomorrow he will be ill), see Giannakidou and Mari (2018a) for details.

9. Why in nonpast environments the perfective triggers futurity has been the object of much study— but there is no final answer (Copley 2009; Mari 2015a; Boogaart and Trnavac 2011). Here we tend to align with Boogaart and Trnavac (2011) who espouse the classical view from Comrie (1976): "a perfective verb form instead presents a situation, "from the outside", as a completed whole, thus including both its starting point and endpoint." Perfectivity thus establishes a distance between the boundaries of the event and the perspectival point, which in the case of future is $t_u$. For this reason perfectivity can combine with past or nonpast, but does not provide PRES.

(63)

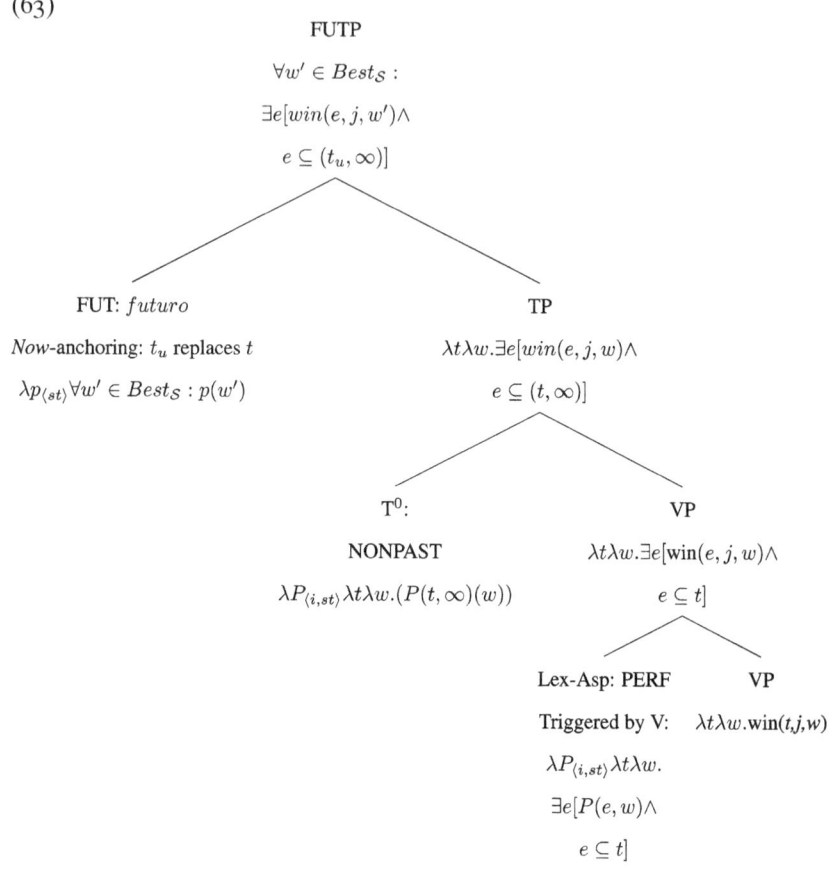

As for the so called "anterior future'" in Italian we observe what follows.

(64) Gianni sarà andato al cinema ieri.
John be.FUT.3sg gone to-the theatre yesterday
John must have gone to the theatre, yesterday.

Recall that the corresponding sentence in Greek is a simple past, i.e., past perfective, in Greek. In Italian, FUT is in complementary distribution with a variety of auxiliaries bearing different tenses (65), thus entering apparent Perfect constructions (see de Swart 2007).

(65) è,fu,sarà andato.
be.PRES,SIMPLE-PAST.FUT gone

We decompose the perfect component as a combination of PAST and PERF, as in Greek. PERF provides the temporal boundaries of the eventuality; the PAST expresses anteriority. But given the possibility of combining with a variety of tenses, we must concede that the PAST we are positing is *not* deictic as in Greek but *relative* (Verkuyl 2011; Broekhuis and Verkuyl 2014): it does not express anteriority with respect to $t_u$ but with respect to a time $t$ which is a free variable TP. This triggers the *Now*-anchoring rule. The derivation of (66) follows in (67).

(66) Flavio avrà vinto.
 Flavio have.FUT.3sg won
 Flavio must have won.

(67)

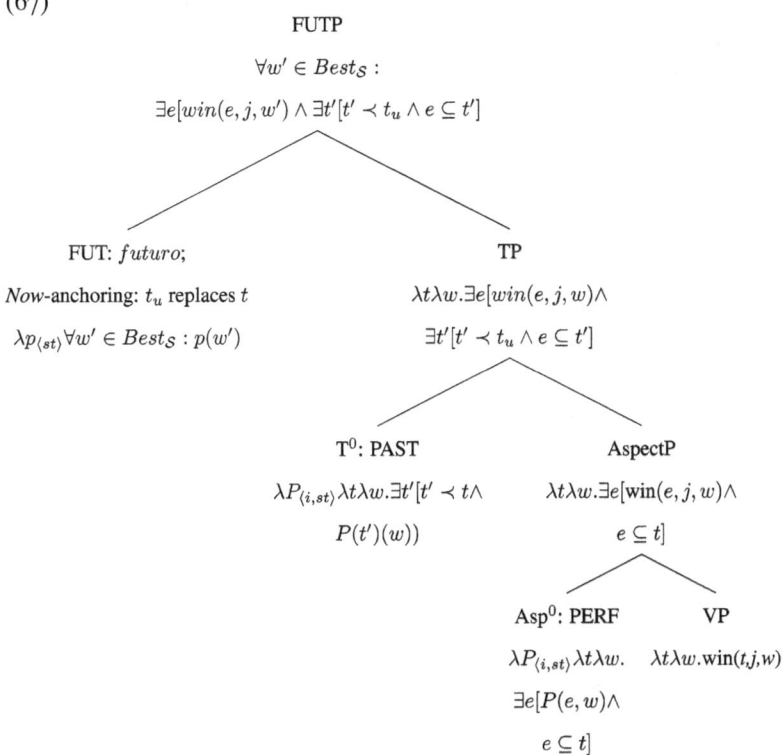

We can thus generalize that, regardless of whether the embedded PAST under FUT is a simple past or a perfect, the anteriority relation is expressed—only in the case of the simple past (Greek) it makes reference to $t_u$, but in the case of the perfect (Italian, English, Dutch, German) we have relative anteriority and reliance on the *Now*-anchoring rule. What is important is that the anteriority relation is in the scope of FUT. This analysis of Italian can be extended to cover Dutch, German, and English apparent perfects under FUT and MUST.

### 3.6.2 *Mood and T in Complement Clauses*

As we illustrated with Greek, the very same analysis can be extended to Italian embedded mood. In embedding, Mood does not provide anchoring to $t_u$ necessarily. In (69) we have a future of a past, where the future component is provided by the imperfective embedded under belief and the past relative to which the futurity is calculated is provided by the time on the main verb, to which mood is anaphoric (the counterfactuality is also provided by the imperfect; see Ippolito 2005).

(68) a. Crede    che Flavio vinca.
        believes that Flavio win.PRES.SUBJ.3sg
        He believes that Flavio will win.
     b. Crede    che Flavio abbia              vinto.
        believes that Flavio have.PRES.SUBJ.3sg won
        He believes that Flavio has won.

(69) Credeva         che vincesse.
     believe.3sg.IMPF that win.IMPF.SUBJ.3sg
     He believed that he would win.

# MOOD AND TENSE IN COMPLEMENT CLAUSES

(70)

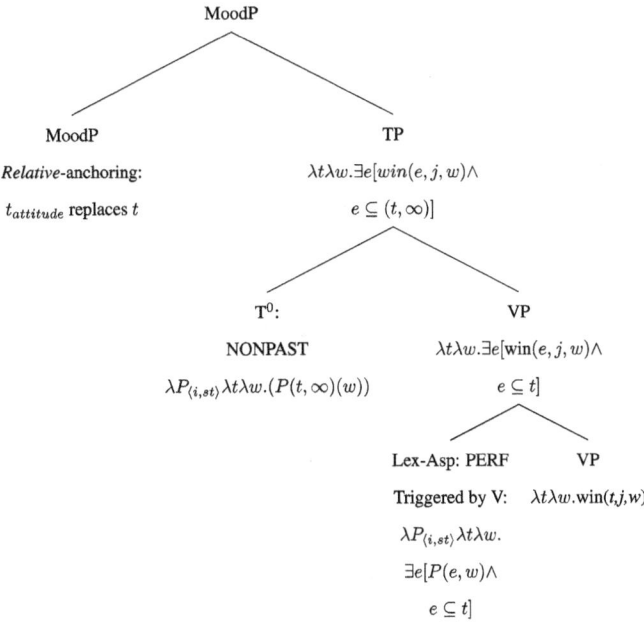

(71)

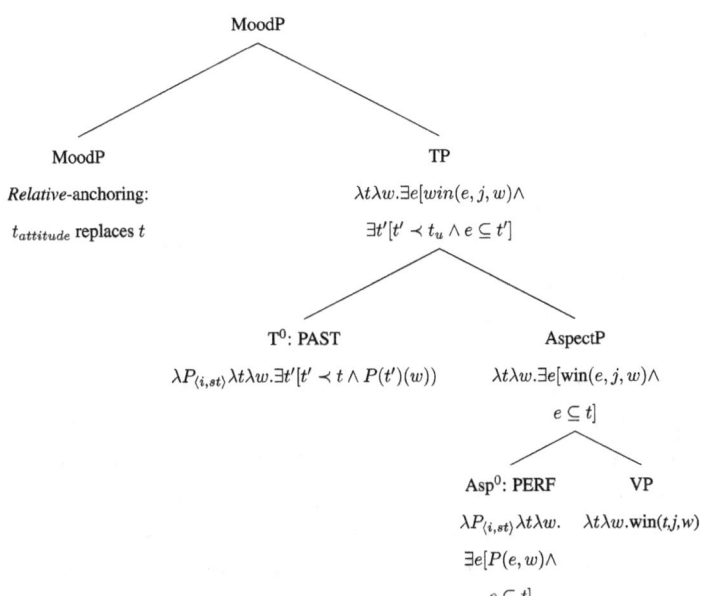

As we see, all modal particles introduce a perspectival time. Mood is no exception to this. When embedded, it functions as a mirror of the tense of the attitudes upon which it is dependent, i.e., it becomes anaphoric, and the left boundary $t$ will now be the time of the attitude, as mentioned in the discussion of Greek.

Having clarified the tense and mood interaction, let us revisit now some core patterns illustrating how attitude verbs restrict the temporal orientation of the complement.

### 3.7 Temporal Constraints Imposed by the Selecting Verb

*3.7.1 Indicative Selecting Verbs: No NONPAST*

Recall the relevant attitude classes, starting with the indicative in Greek:

(72)  Indicative verbs in Greek (*oti/pos, pu*):
  a. epistemic factives: *ksero, gnorizo* (know)
  b. emotive factives: *xerome* (be glad), *metaniono* (regret)
  c. doxastic (nonfactive): *pistevo* (believe), *nomizo* (think), *theoro* (consider), *vrisko* (find)
  d. certainty: *ime sigouros* (be certain), *ime pepismenos* (be convinced)
  e. conciousness: *exo epignosi* (be aware)
  f. pure assertives: *leo* (say), *dhiavazo* (read), *isxirizome* (claim), *dhilono* (declare, assert)
  g. verbs of denial: *arnoume* (deny), *ksexno* (forget)
  h. fiction verbs: *onirevome* (dream), *fandazome* (imagine)
  i. memory verbs: *thimame* (remember)
  j. perception verbs: *vlepo* (see), *akouo* (hear)

These attitudes, specifically doxastic, epistemic, certainty, memory, and dream/fiction verbs select indicative across a number of languages including French (as we saw earlier: Baunaz 2015; Puskás 2017), Spanish, Catalan (Quer 1998, 2001; Villalta 1998), Portuguese (Marques 2010, 2014), Serbian (Todorovich 2012), and Romanian (Farkas 1992), among others. They appear with present and past. Here are, again, some examples from Greek:

(73) O Nicholas kseri       oti/pos/*na    efije  i  Ariadne.
     the Nicholas knows.3sg that.IND/SUBJ left.3sg the Ariadne
     Nicholas knows that Ariadne left.

(74) O Nicholas ine sigouros oti/pos/*na    efije   i   Ariadne.
     the Nicholas s.3sg certain   that.IND/SUBJ left.3sg the Ariadne
     Nicholas is certain that Ariadne left.

(75) O Nicholas ine   pepismenos oti/pos/*na    efije   i
     the Nicholas is.3sg convinced   that.IND/SUBJ left.3sg the
     Ariadne.
     Ariadne
     Nicholas believes that Ariadne left.

(76) O Nicholas pistevi     oti/pos/*na    efije  i  Ariadne.
     the Nicholas believe.3sg that.IND/SUBJ left.3sg the Ariadne
     Nicholas believes that Ariadne left.

(77) O Nicholas exi epignosi      oti/*na      i  Ariadne ton
     the Nicholas has awareness.3sg that.IND/SUBJ the Ariadne him
     voithise.
     helped.3sg
     Nicholas is aware that Ariadne helped him.

(78) O Nicholas onireftike oti/pos/*na    efije   i   Ariadne.
     the Nicholas dreamt.3sg that.IND/SUBJ left.3sg the Ariadne
     Nicholas dreamt that Ariadne left.

(79) O Nicholas theori      oti/pos/*na    i  Ariadne ine
     the Nicholas consider.3sg that.IND/SUBJ the Ariadne is
     omorfi.
     beautiful
     Nicholas finds Ariadne to be beautiful.

(80) O Nicholas vriski    oti/pos/*na    i   Ariadne ine omorfi.
     the Nicholas find.3sg that.IND/SUBJ the Ariadne is  beautiful
     Nicholas finds Ariadne to be beautiful.

Since the indicative is an indicator of veridical commitment, its use after verbs of knowledge, belief, and certainty is expected—given the premises of our theory in the previous chapters.[10] Doxastic attitudes involve an individual anchor's (in this case, the main clause subject's cognitive mental state which relies on knowledge, belief, awareness, memory, perception, or imagination). In the doxastic attitude we include verbs like *vrisko* find) and *theoro* (consider), which in Greek take finite complements only.

Here is an example from French illustrating the stability of the pattern of indicative with knowledge, belief, certainty, and imagination:

(81)   Jean croit/est certain/imagine que Marie est partie.
       John believes/is certain/imagines that Mary is left.

These verbs, as we have mentioned already, do not combine with nonpast, but they do allow future reference with FUT in their complements:

(82)   O    Nicholas ine      sigouros oti/*na        tha
       the  Nicholas be.3sg   certain   that.IND/SUBJ FUT
       fiji              i    Ariadne.
       leave.nonpast3sg  the  Ariadne
       Nicholas is certain that Ariadne will leave.

(83)   O    Nicholas ine      pepismenos oti/*na       tha
       the  Nicholas is.3sg   convinces   that.IND/SUBJ FUT
       fiji              i    Ariadne.
       leave.NONPAST.3sg the  Ariadne
       Nicholas is convinced that Ariadne will leave.

In other words, future orientation is not excluded from the doxastic complement, but it is blocked by the use of indicative which is incompatible with the NONPAST and therefore necessitates the use of future.

Purely assertive verbs select the indicative in Greek and behave like epistemics and doxastics:

---

10. As we said earlier, *oti/pos* appear to be merely stylistic variants, we are therefore treating them as the same item. There may be stylistic or regional variation that does not appear to be relevant for the semantics.

(84) O Nicholas anakinose oti/pos/*na efije i Ariadne.
the Nicholas announced.3sg that.IND/SUBJ left.3sg the Ariadne
Nicholas announced that Ariadne left.

Verbs like *anakinose* (announce) are purely assertive and do not alternate with *na*.

Finally, verbs of negative assertion (mentioned in chaps. 1 and 2) also select the indicative:

(85) O Nicholas arnithike oti/*na i Ariadne ton
the Nicholas denied.3sg that.IND/SUBJ the Ariadne him
voithise.
helped.3sg
Nicholas denied that Ariadne helped him.

At first, the indicative appears striking given that DENY $p$ does not entail $p$. But—as we said in chapter 2—if we view these verbs as subjectively veridical, i.e., expressing full commitment to $\neg p$, it makes sense that they select indicative:

(86) 〚Nicholas denied that $p$〛 is true in the world of the utterance context $w$ iff:
$\forall w'[w' \in M(Nicholas) \rightarrow w' \in \{w'' \mid \neg p(w'')\}]$

In other words, if $i$ denies that p and $i$ is truthful, then $i$ knows $\neg p$ to be true. The condition might be weakened to $i$ believes $\neg p$ to be true. Regardless of which version we chose, the point here is that homogeneity explains why we get indicative with even negative assertives. The tense, again, is variable and there are no particular constraints.

Let us move on now to the subjunctive verbs.

### 3.7.2 Subjunctive Verbs: NONPAST

In Greek, the following verbs select subjunctive.

(87) Subjunctive verbs in Greek:
    a. volitionals: *thelo* (want), *skopevo* (plan)
    b. directives: *dhiatazo* (order), *simvulevo* (advise), *protino* (suggest)

c. modal verbs: *prepi* (must), *bori* (may)
d. effort verbs: *prospatho* (try)
e. permissives: *epitrepo* (allow); *apagorevo* (forbid)
f. implicatives: *katorthono* (manage), *anagazo* (force)

The very same classes select subjunctive in Italian too.

(88) Subjunctive verbs in Italian:
a. volitionals: *volere* (want)
b. directives: *ordinare* (order)
c. modal verbs: *è necessario* (it is necessary), *è possibile* (it is possible), *bisogna* (it is needed)
d. permissives: *impedire* (forbid)

Here are some examples with volitional verbs in Greek and Italian.

(89) a. Thelo    na/*oti         kerdisi           o  Janis.
       want.1sg that.SUBJ/IND win.NONPAST.3sg the John
    b. Voglio      che Gianni vinca/.
       want.1sg.SUBJ that John    win.3sg.SUBJ
       I want John to win.

Volitional verbs are future oriented and select the NONPAST, as mentioned earlier:

(90) Mas protinan       na/*oti           milisoume           me ton
     us  suggested.3pl that.SUBJ/IND talk.NONPAST-1PL with the
     Jani.
     John
     They suggested to us that we talk with John.

(91) Mas simvulepsan na/*oti          milisoume           me ton
     us  advised.3pl    that.SUBJ/IND talk.NONPAST-1PL with the
     Jani.
     John
     They advised us to talk with John.

(92) Skopevoun na/*oti           milisoun            me ton Jani.
     plan.3pl     that.SUBJ/*IND talk.NONPAST-3PL with the John
     They suggested to us that we talk with John.

We observe here again the correlation of *na* plus lower nonpast and future orientation. Notice the parallel with the *to*-infinitival or the subjunctive in English (which is, as we said, a bare infinitive). Epistemic modal verbs are independent in their lower tense:

(93) a. Bori/Prepi na/*oti    kerdise        o  Janis.
        can/must    that.SUBJ win.PAST.3sg the John
        It is possible that John has won.
     b. È       possibile che abbia          vinto.
        be.3sg possible  that  have.SUBJ.3sg won
        It is possible that John has won.

(94) a. Ine    pithano na/*oti kerdisi.
        is.3sg possible SUBJ    win.NONPAST.3sg
        He may win.
     b. È           possibile che vinca.
        be.3sg.IND possible  that win.3sg.SUBJ
        He may win.

As we saw in chapter 2 and in earlier discussions (Giannakidou and Mari 2016a, 2018), epistemic modals appear with all three tenses. The constraint for NONPAST concerns more narrowly the volitional class, which we discuss further in chapter 5.

It is also important to note that verbs of effort like TRY, and implicatives like MANAGE, pattern with volitional verbs and require NONPAST:

(95) O   Flavio prospathise na/*oti         milisi              me
     the Flavio tried.3sg   that.SUBJ/IND talk.NONPAST-3sg with
     ton Jani.
     the John
     Flavio tried to talk with John.

(96) O   Flavio katafere     na/*oti       milisi              me
     the Flavio managed.3sg that.SUBJ/IND talk.NONPAST.3sg with
     ton Jani.
     the John
     Flavio managed to talk with John.

(97) *O Flavio prospathise na          milise        me ton Jani.
    the Flavio tried.3sg    that.SUBJ/IND talk.PAST.3sg with the John

(98) *O Flavio katafere na          milise        me ton Jani.
    the Flavio tried.3sg that.SUBJ/IND talk.PAST.3sg with the John.

We will discuss the temporal constraints with this class in chap. 7. For now, we note the fact that verbs of effort and implicatives require NONPAST.

## 3.8 Conclusions

Our main findings in this chapter are the following. First, the choice of mood correlates not with finiteness but with a choice of embedded tense: the indicative complement, specifically, is incompatible with NONPAST, but the subjunctive of volitional and directive verbs requires it. NONPAST, and not the subjunctive or future, is responsible for anaphoric tense and future orientation. We articulated explicit syntax-semantics compositions to illustrate how the anaphoric (NONPAST), or independent (PAST, PRES(ENT)) tense of the embedded tense is derived in Greek and Italian.

Second, recall that the PAST and PRES are objectively veridical tenses but the NONPAST is an unspecified, indefinite, forward looking time. The observation that the subjunctive associates with an indefinite time is found already in Uriagereka (1988) and in earlier discussions of Greek and Romance subjunctive (for example, Tsoulas 1995), and is line of thought that persisted; for recent discussion see Uriagereka and Gallego (2020). In the syntactic literature, the interaction of the verb with tense centers around the question of types of head movement, and whether it is the moving Verb that projects upon movement or Tense. We have shied away for addressing more narrowly syntactic questions in our treatment of mood and tense; but the correlates we established are obvious and connect well with this literature. Translating roughly into Uriagereka and Gallego's recent work, what matters, in our analysis, is whether the embedded clause is V-centered (NONPAST) or T-centered hence tense independent with PAST or PRESENT.

Thirdly, we offered a syntax of subjunctive *na* where *na* is a possibility modal in nonassertive main clauses. This main subjunctive is licensed too, since it cannot appear in assertions, unless it is under a nonveridical operator, i.e., a modal verb, and it otherwise appears in questions and in hybrid imperatives. In subordinate clauses, on the other hand, *na* functions as a subordinator and has no meaning. It moves to the C position, where it cannot contribute modality. The Italian subjunctive remains in Mood in embedded clauses. The anaphoric property of the subjunctive, we showed, is due to the anchoring rules that are triggered in MoodP and the dependency to the higher tense of the attitude verb.

Finally, we found that within the subjunctive class there are further restrictions: some verbs strictly require NONPAST (volitionals), but others are flexible (modals). We will discuss the temporal properties of each class in the chapters that follow.

CHAPTER FOUR

# Solipsistic and Suppositional Belief

In this chapter, we focus on the indicative versus subjunctive choice with doxastic propositional attitude verbs, i.e., attitudes of belief, thought, certainty, memory, understanding, dream, imagination, and the like. Unlike verbs of knowledge, belief verbs are not objectively veridical— but they select the indicative mood. There are, in fact, two main patterns: (a) doxastic verbs *strictly* select the indicative, a pattern observed in Greek and most Romance languages, and (b) doxastic verbs are flexible and allow both moods, such as in Italian, Portuguese, and Yucatec Spanish (Bove 2020). Our main ideas are as follows.

Doxastic verbs that select the indicative are *subjectively* veridical: they have what Mari (2016a) calls "solipsistic" belief-style truth conditions, i.e., they express the attitude holder's $i$ doxastic commitment to the complement proposition, with no regard of what is actually the case (i.e., truth). Solipsistic is the classical analysis of belief since Hintikka (1962). Greek doxastic verbs express the Hintikka, solipsitic belief and select the indicative. Italian verbs can be construed solipsistically too, and in this case they follow the Greek pattern and select indicative.

The subjunctive is triggered when the doxastic verb is construed *suppositionally*. Suppositional belief means "believe but not know" (Mari 2016a). In this case, the doxastic predicate takes a nonveridical epistemic modal base M as an additional argument, just like the modal verbs, and obeys the Nonveridicality Axiom. When this happens, subjunctive will be selected, as is the case with modal verbs. There are, therefore, two ways of conceptualizing beliefs: (a) as veridical, solipsistic attitudes that do not address the actual world or knowledge, and lack any presuppositions, or (b) as nonveridical *suppositional* attitudes that engage with knowledge. Italian verbs are underspecified lexically and can be construed either way. This dualitty explains why doxastic attitude verbs are compatible with both indicative and subjunctive. By carefully distinguishing knowledge and *doxa* (belief), we will argue that, like Greek, Italian belief is strong doxa-wise but it is weak epistemic-wise. The flexibility in mood choice does not necessitate imposing ambiguity in the lexical entries of propositional attitude verbs. Our account offers a new way of understanding mood shift by acknowledging the similarity between propositional attitudes and modals.

Finally, the embedded mood has no semantic function itself (Giannakidou 2016b) but pragmatic: it updates the discourse with the information coming form the complement clause. The indicative anchors the complement proposition to the local attitude holder's doxastic space. We define an assertive indicative manifested in Greek by *oti* which adds $p$ to the doxastic space, and a presuppositional indicative manifested with *pu*, which requires that $p$ already be present in the doxastic space or the common ground. The subjunctive performs nonveridical update, which prevents the addition of $p$ to to the doxastic space or the common ground, it is therefore informationally (as well as epistemically) weaker.

With Italian-style subjunctive belief, the speaker believes that $p$ is true, but does not know that $p$ is true (to the best of her knowledge, she knows that she does not know whether $p$ is true). With Greek-style indicative belief (which, do not forget, is also an option in Italian), the speaker believes that $p$ is true and knowledge of whether $p$ is true or false is not relevant. The doxastic verb meaning is more flexible in Italian than it is in Greek. But as we will see next, Greek too has some doxastic verbs that allow the indicative subjunctive flexibility of Italian.

## 4.1 Veridical Belief and Doxastic Commitment

In the discussion that follows, we will use the label "doxastic" to refer to verbs that express attitudes of belief, thought, consciousness, consideration, dream, imagination, fiction, perception, and memory. These attitudes are also sometimes referred to as "cognitive."

Let us start by recalling that the epistemic and doxastic classes select indicative:

(1) Indicative verbs in Greek (*oti/pos, pu*):
  a. epistemic factives: *ksero, gnorizo* (know)
  b. emotive factives: *xerome* (be glad), *metaniono* (regret)
  c. doxastic (nonfactive): *pistevo* (believe), *nomizo* (think), *theoro* (consider), *vrisko* (find)
  d. certainty: *ime sigouros* (be certain), *ime pepismenos* (be convinced)
  e. conciousness: *exo epignosi* (be aware)
  f. pure assertives: *leo* (say), *dhiavazo* (read), *isxirizome* (claim), *dhilono* (declare, assert)
  g. verbs of denial: *arnoume* (deny), *ksexno* (forget)
  h. fiction verbs: *onirevome* (dream), *fandazome* (imagine)
  i. memory verbs: *thimame* (remember)
  j. perception verbs: *vlepo* (see), *akouo* (hear)

Let us focus first on "pure" doxastics, i.e., verbs that indicate belief, certainty, conviction, and dream/fiction. Here are some core examples from Greek repeated from earlier discussion:

(2) O Nicholas kseri oti/*na efije i Ariadne.
 the Nicholas knows.3sg that.IND/SUBJ left.3sg the Ariadne
 Nicholas knows that Ariadne left.

(3) O Nicholas ine sigouros oti/*na efije i Ariadne.
 the Nicholas is.3sg certain that.IND/SUBJ left.3sg the Ariadne
 Nicholas is certain that Ariadne left.

(4) O Nicholas ine pepismenos oti/*na efije i Ariadne.
 the Nicholas is.3sg convinced that.IND/SUBJ left.3sg the Ariadne
 Nicholas is convinced that Ariadne left.

(5) O Nicholas pistevi oti/*na efije i Ariadne.
 the Nicholas believe.3sg that.IND/SUBJ left.3sg the Ariadne
 Nicholas believes that Ariadne left.

(6) O Nicholas exi epignosi oti/*na i Ariadne ton
    the Nicholas has awareness.3sg that.IND/SUBJ the Ariadne him
    voithise.
    helped.3sg
    Nicholas is aware that Ariadne helped him.

(7) O Nicholas onireftike oti/*na efije i Ariadne.
    the Nicholas dreamt.3sg that.IND/SUBJ left.3sg the Ariadne
    Nicholas dreamt that Ariadne left.

(8) O Nicholas theori oti/*na i Ariadne ine omorfi.
    the Nicholas consider.3sg that.IND/SUBJ the Ariadne is beautiful
    Nicholas considers Ariadne to be beautiful.

(9) O Nicholas vriski oti/*na i Ariadne ine omorfi.
    the Nicholas find.3sg IND/SUB the Ariadne is beautiful
    Nicholas finds Ariadne to be beautiful.

Recall the initial puzzle: What do all these verbs have in common that renders them indicative selectors like knowledge verbs? Unlike knowledge which is grounded on objective veridicality, i.e., truth, these attitudes are purely *subjective*, and some may even completely lack a factual dimension. When I imagine or dream something, I do not care about what is the case in the actual world; in fact, I know that the content of my dream or imagination is *not* part of the world. Yet verbs of dreaming, imagination and fiction systematically select the indicative in Greek and the bulk of Romance languages, just like knowledge verbs. Why is that?

In our earlier discussion, we established that subjective veridicality is a precondition on assertion. We said that for the co-operative speaker to utter the sentence $p$, she must be veridically committed to $p$, which means that she knows or believes $p$ to be true. Recall the definition of subjective veridicality:

(10) Subjective veridicality:

(i.) A function $F$ that takes a proposition $p$ as its argument is subjectively veridical with respect to an individual anchor $i$ and an information state $M(i)$ iff $M(i)$ entails $p$.
(ii.) $M(i)$ entails $p$ iff $\forall w'[w' \in M(i) \rightarrow w' \in \{w'' \mid p(w'')\}]$.

Subjective veridicality implies $p$-homogeneity of the entire $M(i)$. When all worlds in $M(i)$ are $p$ worlds, $p$ is entailed in $M(i)$. This is a state of full commitment to p, and following Gricean Quality (*Be truthful*), as we said, it is a precondition on assertion. If p is negated, in a parallel manner, the sentence expresses the speaker's commitment to ¬p:

(11) *O Giacomo dhen ine giatros / Giacomo is not a doctor* is assertable by speaker *i* if and only if
$\forall w'[w' \in M(i) \to w' \in \{w'' \mid \neg doctor(Giacomo)(w'')\}]$

Again we have universal commitment, this time that all worlds in M(*i*) be ¬p worlds. We can therefore say that an unmodalized positive or negative sentence expresses veridical commitment of the speaker to p or ¬p. For this reason, the use of negation in a main clause never triggers the subjunctive.

When we look at doxastic verbs, we will argue that it is necessary to differentiate between two kinds of veridical commitment: *epistemic* commitment and *doxastic* commitment. Doxastic commitment is veridicality in an individual's doxastic space. Depending on the propositional attitude, we will identify several doxastic spaces in our discussion below, namely belief, imagination, thought, memory, and consciousness states. These states are anchored to the subject of the propositional attitude since it is her attitude that the sentence reports. The system we will develop in the next few chapters follows the earlier typology of propositional attitudes proposed in Giannakidou (1997, 1998, 1999, 2009), as well as some more recent work on Italian doxastics by Mari (2016a, 2017a, b). Here we develop a comprehensive, integrated system that will address the various classes of attitudes we identify as doxastic.

Recall the case of knowledge verbs such as *ksero, gnorizo, sapere, know*. The truth condition for knowledge, as can be recalled, is the following:

(12) 〚Nicholas kseri /knows *p*〛 will be defined iff the actual world *w* is a *p* world. If defined,
〚Nicholas kseri oti *p*〛 is true in *w* with respect to M(*Nicholas*) iff:
$\forall w'[w' \in M(Nicholas) \to w' \in \{w'' \mid p(w'')\}]$

KNOW *that*, or as we will call it, *indicative knowledge*, combines an objective veridicality presupposition with a subjectively veridical assertion: the information state of the subject, M(*Nicholas*), is homogeneous, i.e., all worlds are $p$ worlds.[1] Factivity is the objective veridicality condition that the actual world $w$ is a $p$ world:

(13) Factivity as objective veridicality:
A propositional function $F$ is factive iff $Fp$ presupposes objective veridicality, i.e., that $p$ is true in the actual world $w$.

Objective veridicality is, in other words, actuality. Crucially, indicative knowledge is objectively veridical, but knowing an answer to a question is not. This is the case of KNOW *whether*, which appears with a different complementizer— i.e., *whether*, Greek *an*, homophonous to the conditional connective mentioned earlier—indicating that the complement is a question. In this case, we might also have a *wh*-complement:

(14) a. O Nicholas kseri       an eftase       to treno stin ora tu.
        the Nicholas know.3sg if arrived.3sg the train on time its
        Nicholas knows whether the train arrived on time.
     b. O Nicholas kseri       pote eftase     to treno stin ora tu.
        the Nicholas know.3sg when arrived.3sg the train on time its
        Nicholas knows when the train arrived on time.

Here the complements of KNOW are not true propositions, but questions. This KNOW is not factive and must be distinguished from factive KNOW. An embedded polar question introduces both possibilities, $p$ and $\neg p$, it therefore does not entail $p$. Knowing the answer to a question is a different state than knowing *that*, which is the case of knowledge which is veridical, i.e., justified true belief.

Veridical functions need not be factive. Subjective veridicality simply requires that the individual anchor is in a state M that supports $p$, regardless of whether $p$ is actually (i.e., objectively) true. For instance, *Nicholas believes that Ariadne is a doctor* reflects that Nicholas is in a veridical belief state, but the sentence *Ariadne is a doctor* can be objectively false, i.e., Nicholas might have a false belief:

(15) ⟦Nicholas believes that $p$⟧ is true in the world of the utterance context $w$ iff:
$\forall w'[w' \in \text{Dox}(Nicholas) \rightarrow w' \in \{w'' \mid p(w'')\}]$

---

1. For these reasons, Giannakidou (1998, 1999) called knowledge verbs *strongly* veridical.

Here we are using Dox to refer specifically to a doxastic state and separate it from the epistemic space of knowledge.

(16) Belief state of an individual anchor $i$:
A belief state Dox($i$) is a set of worlds associated with an individual $i$ representing worlds compatible with what $i$ believes.

The truth condition of *believe* does not entail actual truth. However, following Hintikka's classical analysis, (16) renders *believe* subjectively veridical, because the whole M(*Nicholas*) entails $p$. We will generalize here that the class of verbs denoting private doxastic spaces are subjectively veridical because they denote variants of Dox that entail $p$ without entailing actual truth. This disregard for actual truth renders belief states under the classical analysis *solipsistic*.

Looking at languages following the Greek pattern, we must say that solipsistic belief verbs lack the objective layer of meaning and make no connection to the actual world. The truth condition is purely subjective and does not require the actual world to be a member of Dox. For the evaluation of an embedded $p$ "$i$ believes that $p$", the subject might even have just an opinion. An opinion seems more contestable than a belief: when one expresses an opinion, one does so knowing that there is a plurality of opinions or that their opinion can be controversial:

(17) O Nicholas theori/pistevi oti i ji ine epipedi.
the Nicholas consider/believe.3sg that.IND the earth is flat
Nicholas believes that the Earth is flat.
Nicholas considers Earth to be flat.

(18) O Nicholas vriski oti to omo psari ine nostimo.
the Nicholas finds.3sg that.IND the raw fish is tasty
Nicholas finds raw fish to be tasty.

People can have controversial opinions or personal tastes (which we take to be kinds of opinions) and may also believe false things; but this doesn't seem to affect the choice of indicative mood. For belief and opinion, the truth condition requires subjective veridicality only, namely that Dox(subject) entails $p$ while ignoring Dox(*speaker*), the actual world, and the common ground.

We proceed to zoom in on Greek, where belief is this kind of pure solipsistic doxa and lacks connection to knowledge, fact, or common ground. We then turn to Italian, where belief is a composite attitude with the veridical assertion of doxa and the nonveridical presupposition of not knowing.

## 4.2 Solipsistic Doxastic Commitment: The Indicative

In this section, we focus on the various doxastic classes and show how they can be construed solipsistically as denoting veridical commitment states. In section 3 we illustrate that Italian allows also a nonsolipsistic construal of belief.

### 4.2.1 Attitudes of Certainty, Opinion, Awareness, and Memory

Consider first attitudes of certainty, which tend to appear as combinations of BE with a certainty adjective:

(19) O Nicholas ine sigouros oti/*na efije i Ariadne.
the Nicholas us.3sg certain that.IND/SUBJ left.3sg the Ariadne
Nicholas is certain that Ariadne left.

(20) O Nicholas ine pepismenos oti/*na efije i
the Nicholas is.3sg convinced that.IND/SUBJ left.3sg the
Ariadne.
Ariadne
Nicholas is convinced that Ariadne left.

The cognitive states of certainty and conviction can be thought of as variants of belief. Dox therefore is the relevant model here. The attitude subject is doxastically committed to the complement, i.e., Dox entails $p$:

(21) 〚Nicholas ine sigouros (BE CERTAIN) oti $p$〛 is true in w iff
$\forall w'[w' \in \text{Dox}(\textit{Nicholas}) \rightarrow w' \in \{w'' \mid p(w'')\}]$

(22) 〚Nicholas ine pepismenos (BE CONVINCED) oti $p$〛 is true in w iff
$\forall w'[w' \in \text{Dox}(\textit{Nicholas}) \rightarrow w' \in \{w'' \mid p(w'')\}]$

Doxastic commitment is thus defined exclusively on Dox as follows:

(23) Doxastic commitment of $i$:
  (i.) An individual anchor $i$ is doxastically committed to a proposition $p$ iff Dox($i$) entails $p$.
  (ii.) An individual anchor $i$ is doxastically committed to a proposition $\neg p$ iff Dox($i$) entails $\neg p$.

(24) *Doxastic commitment* and entailment:
  (i.) For an individual anchor $i$, Dox($i$) entails $p$ iff all the words in Dox($i$) are $p$-worlds.
  (ii.) For an individual anchor $i$, Dox($i$) entails $\neg p$ iff all the words in Dox($i$) are $\neg p$ worlds.

Doxastic commitment characterizes, in other words, the veridical and antiveridical state of commitment that relies on belief. In embedded sentences, doxastic commitment is specifically tied to the subject of the main clause attitude verb. But in a main sentence, doxastic commitment is tied to the speaker. If the speaker reasons with pure belief, then it is doxastic commitment that satisfies veridicality for assertability and not knowledge. In most cases the speaker reasons with a mix of knowledge and belief, and they both form the foundation for veridical commitment. When we have embedding under attitudes, knowledge and doxa typically get separated and depend on the lexical meaning of the attitude verb.

From now on, we will differentiate between plain M and Dox to refer to a purely epistemic space (what one knows) and a doxastic space respectively. In the complements of the sentences (19)–(20), "Ariadne left" is anchored to the subject's Dox(*Nicholas*). The truth condition requires that Dox(*Nicholas*) be a commitment $p$-state. There are no $\neg p$ worlds in Dox(*Nicholas*). Both BE CERTAIN and BE CONVINCED denote doxastic states, but they differ from BELIEVE in that they might allow inference to previous states of non-belief. E.g., we may hypothesize that to be convinced of something means that you came to believe it from a previous state of not believing it. Likewise, if you are certain of $p$, this means that you have considered, and rejected, the possibility of not $p$. This adversarial component, however, is not part of the truth condition, and it is most likely an implicature:[2]

---

2. This kind of contrarianism appears also with adverbs such as *totally*, as has been argued by Beltrama (2016), who posits that they have a nonveridical presupposition.

(25) O Nicholas ine    pepismenos oti        i  Ariadne ton
     the Nicholas is.3sg convinced    that.IND the Ariadne him
     agapai, ke  pote  dhen skeftike oti  afto bori   na     min
     love.3sg, and never not    thought that this might that.subj not
     ine    alithia.
     be.3sg true
     Nicholas is convinced that Ariadne loves him, and he never thought
     that this might not be true.

(26) O  Nicholas ine    sigouros oti       i  Ariadne ton agapai,
     the Nicholas is.3sg certain  that.IND the Ariadne him love.3sg,
     ke  pote  dhen skeftike oti  afto bori  na      min ine    alithia.
     and never not    thought that this might that.subj not be.3sg true
     Nicholas is certain that Ariadne loves him, and he never thought
     that this might not be true.

With verbs of memory such as *thimame* (remember), we are looking at a set of worlds that we will call Mem(*subject*), that it to say, the set of propositions that are remembered by the attitude holder:

(27) Memory state of an individual anchor *i*:
     A state of memory Mem(*i*) is a set of worlds associated with an individual *i* representing worlds compatible with what *i* remembers.

The lexical entry for the generic predicate REMEMBER is as follows:

(28) $[\![i \text{ REMEMBER } p]\!]^{\text{Mem},i} = 1$ iff $\forall w'[w' \in \text{Mem}(i) \to w' \in \{w'' \mid p(w'')\}]$

What one remembers is a combination of knowledge and belief, so we can think of Mem(*i*) as a mixed space. One can have memories of actual events or episodes, and in this case a memory verb is construed factively as remembering a fact. The Greek verb will take the factive complementizer *pu*. Yet memories do not correspond always to true episodes in the world. People may have unclear memory, they may embellish or dramatize reality and construct memories, as is well known. People often have false or imagined memories; memory is therefore highly doxastic. We will revisit memory verbs later when we discuss flexible mood patterns.

Consciousness attitudes, finally, such as those meaning BE AWARE, are belief or knowledge based too. Without entering into unnecessary (for the purposes of mood) debates, we assume, with the linguistics literature on the matter, that the set of worlds representing consciousness is a subset of worlds of the belief space (e.g., Franke and Jäger 2011). It is generally assumed that one can hold beliefs without being conscious of them. We thus define a function Con that returns those worlds of Dox(*subject*) that are the worlds compatible with the attitude holder's conscious beliefs. Con(Dox(*subject*)), as a result, is a veridical doxastic commitment state. In addition, awareness attitudes are factive, as we see, since they can only be defined if $w \in p$ :

(29) Consciousness state of an individual anchor $i$:
A consciousness state Con(Dox($i$)) is a set of worlds associated with an individual $i$ representing worlds compatible with what $i$ is conscious about.

(30) $[\![i \text{ IS AWARE that } p]\!]^{w_0,M,Con,Dox,i}$ is defined iff $w_0 \in p$
If defined $[\![i \text{ is aware that } p]\!]^{w_0,M,Con,Dox,i} = 1$ iff:
$\forall w'[w' \in \text{Con}(\text{Dox}(i)) \rightarrow w' \in \{w'' \mid p(w'')\}]$,
and $\exists w'[w' \in \text{Dox}(i) \land w' \in \{w'' \mid \neg p(w')\}]$

Attitudes with this meaning *be aware* will select the indicative in Greek. But they allow both subjunctive and indicative in Italian.

(31) O Nicholas exei epignosi oti/*na i Ariadne tou
the Nicholas has awareness that.IND/*SUBJ the Ariadne him
leei psemata.
says lies
Nicholas is aware that Ariadne is lying to him.

(32) Sono cosciente che Anna è/sia a casa.
be.1sg.PRES.IND aware that Anna be.3sg.IND.SUBJ at home
I am aware that Ann is home.

We will discuss the reasons behind this variability later and again in chapter 7. As a preview, consider that while Con(Dox(*subject*)) is a doxastic commitment veridical state, Dox itself is nonveridical since, as indicated, Dox contains worlds where the subject is not aware of *p*.

To sum up, with attitudes of certainty and awareness the truth condition is anchored to variants of Dox(*subject*); in the case of awareness a subset or Dox(*subject*) that contains conscious beliefs. With memory predicates, veridical commitment is implemented in the state of memory. Certainty, awareness, and memory states are solipsistic in that they all have subjective veridicality in their truth condition and lack presuppositions or engagement with the common ground, both of which could result in weakening commitment.

*4.2.2 Attitudes of Thought and Opinion*

Consider now attitudes of thought and so-called "personal taste" (Lasersohn 2005):

(33)  O  Nicholas nomizi       oti/*na        efije     i   Ariadne.
      the Nicholas thinks.3sg that.IND/SUBJ left.3sg the Ariadne
      Nicholas thinks that Ariadne left.

(34)  O  Nicholas theori       oti/*na             i  Ariadne ine
      the Nicholas believe.3sg that.IND/SUBJ the Ariadne is
      omorfi.
      beautiful
      Nicholas considers Ariadne to be beautiful.

(35)  O  Nicholas vriskei       oti/*na             i  Ariadne ine
      the Nicholas believe.3sg that.IND/SUBJ the Ariadne is
      omorfi.
      beautiful
      Nicholas finds Ariadne to be beautiful.

*Nomizo* (think), *theoro* (consider) and *vrisko* (find) are doxastic verbs; and in Greek, they take *oti* complements. The English verbs have been discussed extensively in the context of predicates of personal taste and faultless disagreement (Lasersohn 2005). In Greek too, *theoro* (consider) and *vrisko* (find) cannot combine with "objective" predicates such as *wooden*:

(36)  O  Nicholas nomizi       oti/*na         to  trapezi ine xylino.
      the Nicholas thinks.3sg that.IND/SUBJ the table   is   wooden
      Nicholas thinks that the table is wooden.

(37) #O Nicholas theori      oti      to  trapezi ine xylino.
     the Nicholas considers.3sg that.IND the table  is  wooden
     Nicholas considers that the table is wooden.

(38) O Nicholas vriski    oti     i   Ariadne ine eksipni.
     the Nicholas find.3sg that.IND the Ariadne be smart
     Nicholas finds that Ariadne is smart.

We called verbs such as *theori, vriski, consider, find* verbs of opinion earlier. This explains why they require complements that contain disputable properties such as those meaning BEAUTIFUL and reject predicates like WOODEN which cannot be disputed. Having an opinion presupposes nonsingularity of perspective, i.e., that the matter is not objectively settled. There are differences of opinion on whether an entity is beautiful, but there are no differences of opinion in what counts as wooden. There is an objective criterion for being wooden, and it is a matter of fact, not of opinion whether an object is wooden or not.[3]

When it comes to mood choice, for the Greek counterparts of FIND and CONSIDER engagement with the possibility of *not p* doesn't seem to matter. The Greek opinion verbs behave solipsistically as pure beliefs when it comes to mood choice. For Greek, specifically, it becomes clear the *vrisko* FIND and *theoro* CONSIDER complements behave like belief complements in selecting indicative. Their truth condition is identical to that of *pistevo* "believe":

(39) [[Nicholas vriski/theori (finds, considers) oti $p$]] is true in $w$ with respect to Dox(*Nicholas*) iff: $\forall w'[w' \in \text{Dox}(\textit{Nicholas}) \rightarrow w' \in \{w'' \mid p(w'')\}]$

---

3. The expanding literature on predicates of personal state such as *tasty, modern, beautiful* is divided broadly into contextualists (Stephenson 2005, 2006, 2007; Glanzberg 2007; Stojanovic 2008; Saebo 2009; Kennedy and Willer 2016), and relativists (Lasersohn 2005, 2015; Egan 2007; MacFarlane 2007, 2014). Both sides posit a categorical distinction in adjectives between evaluative/subjective and nonevaluative/objective type: the former have, and the latter lack, a judge argument or parameter, it is argued. The English verb *find*, consequently, has been argued to combine only with judge-taking adjectives (Saebo 2009), and this is built as a presupposition, most prominently in Kennedy and Willer's "(radical) counterstance" presupposition. FIND and CONSIDER are argued to differ from BELIEVE in having the (radical) counterstance presupposition, which says that the property they embed must be disputable. We can think of counterstance as the adversarial inference we mentioned earlier.

Greek *theoro* (consider) and *vrisko* (find) are thus classical beliefs when it comes to mood choice, and although the verbs differ from *pistevo* in that the subject is indeed aware that there may be opposing views, the verbs remain nevertheless solipsistic. The subject holds on to her, albeit disputable, belief. The lexical entry contains no uncertainty. The intended counterstance may be just an implicature (*pace* Kennedy and Willer 2016) because it can be canceled:

(40)  Just like everybody else, I find Maria to be quite beautiful.

Examples like these show both commitment in the doxastic space and the cancellability of the contrarian component of FIND.[4]

The verb THINK is similarly construed as a belief verb:

(41)  ⟦Nicholas nomizi (thinks) oti $p$⟧ is true in $w$ with respect to Dox (*Nicholas*) iff
$\forall w'[w' \in \text{Dox}(Nicholas) \rightarrow w' \in \{w'' \mid p(w'')\}]$

Hence, it seems to be a robust generalization that, in Greek, attitudes of thought, opinion, and personal taste pattern solipsistically as beliefs and select indicative.

### 4.2.3  Dream and Fiction Attitudes

The last class we consider includes dream and fiction verbs such as *dream* and *imagine*. In this case, we do not have a doxastic model in the sense of beliefs about the world, but a fictional model, comprising the set of worlds compatible with the subject's dream or imagination, hallucination, etc. Giannakidou designated such models as $M_{dream}$ (see also Giorgi and Pianesi 1996), $M_{imagination}$, but we will use Fic to refer to the various such imaginative and dream states:

---

4. Let us also note here that recent studies of English taste predicates show systematic gradations in the intuitions about faultless disagreement: disagreements about *delicious, disgusting* are faultless by 99 percent of native English speakers, with *salty* and *sweet* being 70 percent faultless, *red, green* at 50 percent, *round, square* are judged faultless at 25 percent of participants (Cohen and Nichols 2010, Sklaviadis 2017). The overall empirical picture is thus more complicated than predicted by the categorical perspective of current analyses, e.g., by having or not a judge, having or not the presupposition of counterstance. For us, a judge, i.e., an individual anchor, is always present as a parameter of evaluation, for every sentence, as we made clear right at the beginning (see also Harris and Potts 2009).

(42) Dream state of an individual anchor *i* (Giannakidou, 1999):
A dream state Fic$_{dream}$ (*i*) is a set of worlds associated with an individual *i* representing worlds compatible with what *i* dreams.

(43) Imagination state of an individual anchor *i* (Giannakidou, 1999):
An imagination state Fic$_{imagination}$ (*i*) is a set of worlds associated with an individual *i* representing worlds compatible with what *i* imagines.

(44) a. O Nicholas onireftike oti/*na efije i Ariadne.
the Nicholas dreamt.3sg that.IND/*SUBJ left.3sg the Ariadne
b. Nicholas ha sognato che Ariadne è andata
Nicholas has dreamt that Ariadne be.3sg.PRES.IND gone
via.
away
Nicholas dreamt that Ariadne left.

(45) O Nicholas fandastike oti/*na efije i Ariadne.
the Nicholas imagined.3sg that.IND/*SUBJ left.3sg the Ariadne
Nicholas imagined that Ariadne left.

(46) [[Nicholas dreamt that *p*]]$^{Fic_{dream}, Nicholas}$ is 1 iff:
$\forall w'[w' \in Fic_{dream}(Nicholas) \rightarrow w' \in \{w'' \mid p(w'')\}]$

(47) [[Nicholas imagined that *p*]]$^{Fic_{imagination}, Nicholas}$ is 1 iff:
$\forall w'[w' \in Fic_{imagination}(Nicholas) \rightarrow w' \in \{w'' \mid p(w'')\}]$

When someone dreams or imagines something, the relevant private space is the set of dream or imagination worlds. The dream space is, according to Giorgi and Pianesi 1996, a prototypical private space. What one dreams entails nothing about the real world. This is something expressed also in Farkas (1985, 1992) who states that "fictional reality replaces the actual one". A dream or imagination state, as can be seen, fully supports *p* it is therefore committal and subjectively veridical. *Oti* anchors *p* to Fic$_{dream}$ (subject), we will say, and adds the embedded proposition to it.

Hallucinations are similar:

(48) O Nicholas ixe tin paraisthisi oti/*na efije
the Nicholas has the hallucination that.IND/that.SUBJ left.3sg
i Ariadne.
the Ariadne
Nicholas hallucinated that Ariadne left.

(49) Hallucination state of an individual anchor $i$ (Giannakidou 1999):
A hallucination state $\text{Fic}_{hallucination}(i)$ is a set of worlds associated with an individual $i$ representing worlds compatible with what $i$ hallucinates about.

(50) $[\![\text{Nicholas hallucinated that } p]\!]^{\text{Fic}_{hallucination}, Nicholas}$ is 1 iff:
$\forall w'[w' \in \text{Fic}_{hallucination}(Nicholas) \rightarrow w' \in \{w'' \mid p(w'')\}]$

The fiction, dream, and hallucination states are entirely dissociated from the actual world and are therefore private in the strictest sense. Fic is an alternative to Dox representing belief that is dissociated from reality: Fic, unlike Dox does not contain beliefs about the world but rather sets up an entirely fictional reality. The prerequisite for indicative is veridicality in Fic. All doxastic states we defined, Dox, Mem, and Fic, express belief-based commitments, though the belief can be mixed with knowledge (Mem), or can be belief about alternative realities (dream and fiction verbs).

The concept of objective *realis* is totally irrelevant, as it turns out, for the indicative mood. Veridical doxastic verbs are subjective and solipsistic, and select indicative complements. We can view this syntactically as a form of L(exical) selection:

(51) Generalization: Strict selection of indicative in Greek:
Solipsitic veridical verbs L(exically) select indicative *oti* complements.

(52) Greek doxastic verbs:
Solipsistic veridical doxastic V: [CAT: [V]; SEL: [INDICATIVE: *oti*]]
Lexicalizations: *pistevo, nomizo, onirevome*, and the rest of the verbs discussed here that strictly select indicative.

The Greek doxastics are therefore lexically specified as selecting complements marked indicative by *oti*. Mood selection is therefore like case selection, e.g., accusative or dative, for the direct object of the verb in a language that assigns case. And just as with case, mood alternations are not possible. Mood marking, thus, in strict selection, has no semantic effect as correctly pointed out in Giannakidou (2016) and Ambar (2016), unlike in optional cases, e.g., epistemic subjunctive in questions and relative clauses.

Generalizing, Solipsistic Veridical Doxastic V will select INDICATIVE also in most Romance languages (e.g., Spanish, French, ...):

(53) Veridical doxastic verbs:
Solipsistic Veridical Doxastic V: [CAT: [V]; SEL: [INDICATIVE] ]
Lexicalizations: *Penso, creer, penser, croire*, and the rest of the verbs in Romance (except Italian and Portuguese) that strictly select indicative.

Solipsistic veridical doxastic verbs are thus purely subjective, and this is reflected in the grammatical choice of indicative, which is the mood not only of knowledge but also of subjective veridical commitment— thus not *realis*, contrary to what the traditional descriptions have been.

Let us move on now to Italian which exhibits a more flexible mood pattern with doxastics, and therefore allows us to establish a nonsolipsistic belief construal with a nonveridical presupposition. Nonveridical belief contrasts with solipsistic belief in conveying an awareness by the main clause subject *i* that the complement is believed but not known.

## 4.3 Suppositional Belief and the Subjunctive

In contrast to Greek and the bulk of Romance languages, Italian allows belief and other doxastic verbs to select indicative as well as subjunctive:

(54) Credo/Penso che Maria sia/è incinta.
believe/Think.PRES.1sg that Mary is.SUBJ/IND.3sg pregnant
I believe that Mary is pregnant.

The Italian doxastics are therefore mood flexible. The indicative is also allowed with nonepistemic factives, but the subjunctive is the preferred form. Subjunctive might be taken to indicate some form of weakness, e.g., partitioning in the doxastic space (as is argued, e.g., by Homer 2008). The major argument against this idea is provided by verbs of certainty and conviction (Mari 2016a) which can select subjunctive. When one is certain or convinced, one is doxastically committed to *p*, i.e., there can be no ¬*p* worlds in Dox.

(55) Sono sicura         che Maria sia/è       incinta.
     am   certain.PRES.1sg that Mary be.SUBJ/IND.3sg pregnant
     I am certain that Mary is pregnant.

(56) Sono convinta         che Maria sia/è       incinta.
     am   convinced.PRES.1sg that Mary be.SUBJ/IND.3sg pregnant
     I am convinced that Mary is pregnant.

Moreover, as pointed out in Mari (2016a), dream verbs, which prototypically select indicative in Greek, can license subjunctive in Italian.

(57) Immagina          che Maria sia/è       incinta.
     imagine.PRES.3sg that Mary be.SUBJ/IND.3sg pregnant
     She imagines that Mary is pregnant.

It is very important to note the intuition that subjunctive with fictional predicates conveys a "do not know" component (see Mari 2016a, 2017b, c) . The sentence means that the attitude holder does not know whether Mary is pregnant—she just imagines that she is, to the best of her imagination.

Notably, the subjunctive is not an option for Italian *sapere* (know), which selects indicative. This is the case for all other languages that we are aware of. With factive KNOW the veridicality of the epistemic space is settled. With subjunctive BELIEVE and IMAGINE there is no epistemic certainty, but this does not mean that there is uncertainty in the doxastic space or in the imagination space (Mari, 2016a). Informally, the distinction between knowledge and belief in a language like Italian can be represented as in 59.

(58) Sa    che Maria è incinta.
     knows that Mary is pregnant
     She knows that Mary is pregnant.

(59) a. Knowledge: $p$ is presupposed; M is veridical
b. Belief: that $p$ is known is not presupposed; Dox is veridical

The above facts indicate clearly that (a) the difference between epistemic versus doxastic modal space matters in Italian, and (b) the Italian doxastic verbs are not lexically specified to select indicative, unlike Greek and other Romance doxastics.

### 4.3.1 Solipsistic and Suppositional Belief: Italian

As mentioned earlier, an obvious conjecture is that in Italian belief is "weak", and that it reveals uncertainty (Homer 2008). However, as we said, this cannot be correct because even the predicate meaning BE CERTAIN licenses the subjunctive. To make our way into the semantics of Italian doxastics, a better way to start is in the context of our analysis of modals, since these also select the subjunctive: in the subjunctive version, we can assume that belief verbs are construed with the nonveridical presupposition as "believe but not know". This "do not know" component is the nonveridical presupposition of modals. When added to the doxastic attitude, it imbues the doxastic verb with antiknowledge—just as with modal verbs. The nonveridical construal is always an option, we will argue, in the interpretation of doxastic statements in Italian, and plays the key role in triggering the subjunctive.[5]

Mari (2016a) proposes that the Italian doxastic verbs are underspecified lexically: they can be interpreted either as Hintikka beliefs (in the Greek style and selecting the indicative), or they can be interpreted *conjecturally*, as she calls it. The "do not know" presupposition adds, just as with modals, uncertainty to the lexical entry, and the doxastic verb acquires mixed veridicality. We will call such construals of doxastic attitudes *suppositional* doxastics. The two meanings of doxastics are, of course, closely related. The "believe but don't know" meaning can be understood under Gricean assumptions to be the more basic meaning of a

---

5. Why the antiknowledge option is not pursued in Greek or more extensively in other Romance languages is an interesting question of linguistic variation. Recall that the Italian flexibility in observed to some extent also in Portuguese, and in some dialects of Spanish as was recently revealed in Bove (2020). In Greek, the stability of indicative may have to do with the loss of infinitive, and in any case it is worth exploring historically too.

doxastic. If the speaker choses to report "*i* believes that *p*" rather than "*i* knows that *p*", then the speaker probably doesn't have sufficient evidence to say the latter. But "*i* believes that *p*" can always be strengthened to "*i* knows that *p*":

(60) a. Roberto believes that Carla had an offer from Harvard; in fact, he knows she did.
b. I know you think otherwise, but I believe he is lying. I truly do.

In these examples, belief is construed quite strongly as equivalent to knowledge or as contrasting with another's disbelief. Such uses of belief verbs are quite common, and rely of course on the context, as all strengthenings do. The Greek style solipsistic doxastic verbs can be understood as conventionalizations of strengthened belief, but Italian doxastics, apparently, can retain "believe but don't know". When construed this way, Italian doxastics obey the Nonveridicality Axiom of modals and combine a veridical assertion with a nonveridical epistemic presupposition. It is then no surprise that they select the subjunctive, just as modals do.

### 4.3.2 Nonveridical Epistemic Space with Suppositional Belief

Our specific proposal for suppositional doxastics in Italian will implement the system we employed for MUST, and we will present an analysis building on Mari (2016a) which is responsible also for revealing the empirical richness of the phenomenon. Suppositional belief statements and bare sentences differ in some important respects which are reminiscent of the difference between bare sentences and MUST discussed in chapter 2. Note that this is not peculiar to Italian. English also allows spelling out a series of differences between belief statements and bare assertions, which highlight the "lack of knowledge" component of belief. The most important test is parallel to the one that we used in chap. 2 to show that MUST lacks knowledge.

(61) Context: I look through the window and it is raining.
a. It is raining.
b. #I believe that it is raining.
c. #It must be raining.

In the context where knowledge of *p* is established, a mere belief statement is weak, just like a MUST statement is.

Belief statements and assertion have different effects on the common ground. The bare assertion is a proposal to update the common ground with *p*, while a belief statement cannot eliminate ¬*p* worlds. Denials are a good test to capture the difference.

(62) Context. I believe that God exists. I utter:
 a. God exists.
 b. I believe that God exists.

Only the bare assertion can be challenged. Neither the belief statement nor the prejacent embedded under it can be. Consider this more closely:

(63) A: I believe that God exists.
 B: No you are wrong. A: I only said that I believe it !

(64) A: God exists.
 B: No you are wrong. A: #I only said that I believe it !

We have put forth the same argument for future expressions (Giannakidou and Mari, 2018a), which we claimed are universal epistemic modals akin to MUST.

If we are correct, belief in some languages and under a suppositional interpretation becomes the attitude counterpart of MUST.[6] How can we reconcile these observations with the claim, which we have been defending based on the Greek data, that belief is strong and reveals doxastic commitment? Mari (2016a) proposes that we can distinguish between two beliefs: the classic Hintikka belief which is veridical and solipsistic, and the MUST-like belief which is suppositional. Mari used the label "credence" for the classical belief. Just like MUST, we argue, suppositional belief features two modal bases, a veridical doxastic one (just as with Hintikka belief) and a nonveridical epistemic modal base.

Greek verbs are lexically specified, as we showed, as solipsistic doxastics, hence the mood rigidity. Italian verbs, on the other hand, are underspecified in the lexicon. The indicative is a signal that the verb is used solipsistically; and the subjunctive is a signal to add the nonveridi-

---

6. See also Papafragou (2006) for a suggestion in this direction.

cal antiknowledge presupposition. The coexistence of a nonveridical M(*i*) (as with modals), and a veridical Dox(*i*) in a single lexical entry is sufficient to explain the licensing of the subjunctive in Italian and in other languages. Dox is the single modal base relevant for classical doxastics in Greek, French, and the languages that select indicative; but Dox is only one of the two parameters for suppositional belief. The two types of belief are given below (in a preliminary format), with our new terminology here:

(65) Solipsistic belief (also called "expressive" in Mari, 2016a):
$[\![i\text{ believe}_{sol} p]\!]^{\text{Dox},i} = 1$ iff $\forall w'[w' \in \text{Dox}(i) \to w' \in \{w'' \mid p(w'')\}]$

(66) Suppositional belief (called "conjectural" in Mari, 2016a):
$[\![i\text{ believe}_{sup} p]\!]^{\text{M,Dox},i}$ is defined iff M(*i*) is nonveridical (partitioned epistemic modal base). If defined, $\forall w'[w' \in \text{Dox}(i) \to w' \in \{w'' \mid p(w'')\}]$

Solipsistic belief is the subjectively veridical belief described in section 2. It only features a doxastic modal base, or variants thereof, and expresses doxastic commitment. Suppositional belief, on the other hand, while also expressing doxastic commitment, it also takes M as an argument and obeys the Nonveridicality Axiom: i.e., it has a presupposition, like MUST, that the epistemic space M is nonveridical. It is this that renders a suppositional belief verb akin to "believe but not know." In other words, Italian belief is *not* weaker *doxastically* than solipsistic belief.

One can view suppositional doxastics as mixed doxastics—mixed in the sense that they combine in their lexical entry belief and lack of knowledge. The two kinds of belief, crucially, can be expressed also by Greek and French modal adjectives which are attitudinal and have the structure in (66), which explains that they are subjunctive licensors.[7]

(67) Il est probable qu'il vienne.
it is probable that he come.SUBJ.3sg
It is probable that he comes.

(68) Ine pithano na erthi.
is probable that.SUBJ come.3sg
It is probable that he comes.

---

7. In French both subjunctive and indicative are possible with future orientation.

Here again, the matter is not settled in the epistemic modal base, but in those worlds that better comply with the stereotypicality conditions are worlds in which the prejacent is true. The subjunctive is thus predicted, as we elaborated in chap. 2.

It is important to acknowledge that this distinction between two types of belief is a more general phenomenon and does not concern just Italian. However, in Italian this distinction is made visible by the systematic flexibility of mood. In other languages, especially those lacking systematic mood distinctions in clausal complements, the distinction may surface in other ways, for example by using a modal verb as we noted already; recall *Ariadne believes that Jason might be sick*. We are not saying that mood is a prerequisite for the two kinds of belief to exist; we are saying that the subjunctive versus indicative distinction is a safe diagnostic to track the difference.

To provide a fuller picture, consider fictional predicates which are indicative selectors in Greek but flexible in Italian. As we have already noted, the interpretation with the indicative and the subjunctive mood are not identical: when the indicative is used, the fictional space of the attitude holder is described. When the subjunctive is used, the speaker reports a supposition and contrasts it with knowledge. Letting Fic be the set of propositions corresponding to the imagination of the attitude holder, the two resulting interpretations for *immaginare* in Italian are the following:

(69) Private or solipsistic imagination (Mari 2016a: "expressive fictional"):
$[\![i \,\text{immaginare}_{sol}\, p]\!]^{\text{Fic},i} = 1$ iff $\forall w'[w' \in \text{Fic}(i) \to w' \in \{w'' \mid p(w'')\}]$

(70) Suppositional imagination: (Mari 2016a: "conjectural fictional"):
$[\![i \,\text{immaginare}_{inq}\, p]\!]^{M,\text{Fic},i}$ is defined iff $M(i)$ is nonveridical (partitioned epistemic modal base). If defined, $\forall w'[w' \in \text{Fic}(i) \to w' \in \{w'' \mid p(w'')\}]$

As we have noted, predicates of certainty also license the subjunctive. Let us recall the examples:

(71) Sono sicura che Maria sia/è incinta.
am certain.PRES.1sg that Mary be.SUBJ/IND.3sg pregnant
I am certain that Mary is pregnant.

(72) Sono convinta che Maria sia/è incinta.
am convinced.PRES.1sg that Mary be.SUBJ/IND.3sg pregnant
'I am convinced that Mary is pregnant.'

We treat certainty just as we treat belief (in the same way as in a Hintikkean semantics, belief and certainty amount to the same; see Mari 2016a). We designate Cer as the domain of certainty.

(73) Solipsistic certainty:
$[\![i \text{ CERTAIN}_{sol} p]\!]^{\text{Cer},i} = 1$ iff $\forall w'[w' \in \text{Cer}(i) \to w' \in \{w'' \mid p(w'')\}]$

(74) Suppositional certainty:
$[\![i \text{ CERTAIN}_{sup} p]\!]^{M,\text{Cer},i}$ is defined iff = 1 iff $M(i)$ is nonveridical (partitioned epistemic modal base). If defined, $\forall w'[w' \in \text{Cer}(i) \to w' \in \{w'' \mid p(w'')\}]$

By using Cer instead of Dox we intend to signal that probably the modal base is construed based on different evidence. While doxa includes personal opinions, guesses and consideration of normalcy conditions, certainty involves inferential evidence (see discussion in Mari 2016a, 2017a, b). As with belief, certainty does not imply knowledge; unlike belief, to form a thought that can be qualified as certain, the speaker uses more reliable knowledge such as facts and evidential inferences.

Consider, finally, the role of negation. When doxastic verbs get negated, they can allow subjunctive (see Giannakidou 1995; Quer 1998, 2001). This was the use of the subjunctive that initiated the characterization "polarity subjunctive" in the literature:

(75) a. Dhen pistevo       oti/na         efije  i  Ariadne.
        not  believe.1sg that.IND/SUBJ left.3sg the Ariadne
        I don't believe that Ariadne left.
     b. Pistevo       oti/*na         efije  i  Ariadne.
        believe.1sg that.IND/SUBJ left.3sg the Ariadne
        I believe that Ariadne left.

If I don't believe that Ariadne left, then it is not the case that all worlds in Dox are worlds where Ariadne left. The subjunctive is therefore licensed because not believing lacks doxastic commitment:

(76)  $[\![i\ dhen\ pistevo(\text{not believe})\,p]\!]^{\text{Dox},i}$ is $= 1$ iff
$\neg\forall w'[w' \in \text{Dox}(i) \rightarrow w' \in \{w'' \mid p(w'')\}]$

The effect of negation on the attitude is thus simply understood as a consequence of the fact that Dox is no longer veridical, and the subjunctive is fully expected.

To sum up, in Italian, mood flexibility between indicative and subjunctive with doxastic verbs reveals that doxastic verbs can be construed as obeying the Nonveridicality Axiom of modals, i.e., as taking an epistemic nonveridical modal base as an additional argument. This component is absent from classical belief verbs, which we labeled solipsistic. These track only the doxastic dimension and have simple, unidimensional lexical entries lacking the nonveridical presupposition. With suppositional doxastics, what is known and what is believed coexist in the lexical entry, and it appears that Italian doxastic verbs are systematically construed this way.

Generalizing, we propose the following lexical entry for Suppositional Doxastic V, which will select SUBJUNCTIVE also in Romance languages:

(77)  Suppositional doxastic verbs:
Suppositional Doxastic V: [CAT: [V]; SEL: [SUBJUNCTIVE] ]
Lexicalizations: Italian doxastics, Greek memory verbs, SEEM (to be discussed next)

Italian doxastics can be construed suppositionally or veridically, and they will select the respective moods. In other words, Italian doxastics appear to be massively underspecified.

### 4.3.3 Summary: Typology of Doxastic Attitudes and Mood

Let us summarize our analysis of epistemic and doxastic verbs in Greek and Italian (see. Table 4.1).

(78)  Typology of doxastic verbs
   a. Indicative-selecting solipsistic doxastic verbs: They have a simple truth condition and assert doxastic commitment.

|  | Bare Sentence Assertion | Subjunctive Belief | Indicative Belief |
|---|---|---|---|
| doxastic commitment | X | X | X |
| epistemic com. (full) | X | | |
| epistemic com. (partial) | | X | |

   b. Subjunctive-selecting suppositional doxastic verbs: The doxastic commitment assertion is augmented with an epistemic nonveridical presupposition. Dox and M coexist in the lexical entry: full doxastic commitment in the truth condition and nonveridicality in the presupposition.
   c. Some doxastic verbs are lexically specified as solipsistic (Greek doxastics). Other verbs are underspecified and can accept the nonveridical presupposition. Underspecified verbs allow both moods.

Given this typology, we can see that there is a continuum between the assertion of the unmodalized veridical sentence and doxastic statements. By having postulated veridical commitment as precondition on assertion, we assume that, when asserting $p$, the co-operative truthful speaker is BOTH doxastically and epistemically committed to $p$. The speaker believes and knows (always relatively to the best of her knowledge) that $p$ is true.

With Italian-style subjunctive belief, the speaker believes that $p$ is true, but does not know that $p$ is true (to the best of her knowledge, she knows that she does not know whether $p$ is true). With Greek-style indicative belief (which, do not forget, is also an option in Italian), the speaker believes that $p$ is true and knowledge of whether $p$ is true or false is not relevant. The doxastic verb meaning is more flexible in Italian than it is in Greek. But as we will see next, Greek too has some doxastic verbs that allow the indicative subjunctive flexibility of Italian.

The view we developed negates two widespread assumptions. The first one is that that subjunctive belief is "weaker" than indicative belief. This view is incorrect, as we said: the doxastic component of suppositional belief is veridical, therefore as strong as that of solipsistic doxastics. Both solipsistic and suppositional doxastics express doxastic commitment and are therefore equally strong doxastically. It is the epistemic uncertainty of the nonveridical presupposition that creates weakness, just as with MUST. The second widespread assumption that our analysis challenges is that the choice of subjunctive depends on preference or desire (e.g. Villalta 2008). It became clear that the supposition doxastic has nothing to do with preference or desire; subjunctive depends entirely on the epistemic uncertainty introduced by the nonveridical M. We will offer more challenges to the relevance of preference for the subjunctive in the next chapter.

To complete the picture, it will be necessary to emphasize that the choice between indicative and subjunctive is not a choice about languages (Greek vs. Italian), but about how doxastic attitude classes lexicalize in the two types of languages. As a general observation, we have indeed posited that a systemic difference between the two languages is that, in Italian, doxastic verb meanings tend to be flexible (or, underespecified) — the verbs can therefore be construed also with epistemic nonveridicality. Greek lexical entries of doxastics, on the other hand, appear to be more rigidly solipsistic; the blocking of subjunctive is the reflex of that. Yet, Greek too has doxastics that seem to behave like Italian suppositional doxastics: memory, semblance, SEEM predicates, and perception verbs. We discuss these next.

## 4.4 More Flexible Doxastics: Memory, Semblance, Perception

### 4.4.1 Mood Flexibility with Memory Verbs

Recall that memory verbs can take subjunctive:

(79)  O   Nicholas thimate          na       kleini               tin
      the Nicholas remembered.3sg that.SUBJ close.NONPAST.3sg the
      porta, alla den ine sigouros.
      door, but not is sure
      Nicholas remembers closing the door, but he is not entirely sure.

The subjunctive is compatible with a context where Nicholas is not fully sure about his memory, and he has some doubt, i.e., he "does not know for sure". This is the by now familiar nonveridical supposition that denies knowledge. The solipsistic *oti* clause is incompatible with such reading:

(80) #O Nicholas thimate        oti      eklise     tin porta, alla
    the Nicholas remembered.3sg that.IND closed.3sg. the door, but
    den ine sigouros.
    not is sure
    #Nicholas remembers that he closed the door, but he is not entirely
    sure.

Note the exact parallel with the English -*ing* clause. The *that* vs. *ing* difference is reflected in Greek with the *oti* vs. *na* distinction.

Recall that with verbs such as *thimame* (remember), we are looking at Mem(*subject*), that is to say, the set of propositions that are remembered by the attitude holder:

(81) Memory state of an individual anchor $i$:
    A state Mem($i$) is a set of worlds associated with an individual $i$ representing worlds compatible with what $i$ remembers.

(82) $[\![i\ \text{REMEMBER-}oti/that\ p]\!]^{\text{Mem},i}$ is = 1 iff $\forall w'[w' \in \text{Mem}(i) \rightarrow w' \in \{w'' \mid p(w'')\}]$

Memory is construed solipsistically as a combination of knowledge and belief, as we said earlier, and takes indicative and *that*. What is remembered is indeed a combination of knowledge and belief. Memories are not photographic snapshots of the world but rather inner representations of events, construed, compensated for, vague or even made up by the person who remembers; hence Mem can contain also pure beliefs.

Memory can also be construed as remembering a fact, in which case we have *pu* and an epistemic M:

(83) O Nicholas thimate          pu      eklise      tin porta, (#alla
    the Nicholas remembered.3sg that.IND closed.3sg. the door, but
    den ine sigouros).
    not is sure
    Nicholas remembers the fact that he closed the door, (#but he is not entirely sure).

(84) $[\![i\ \text{REMEMBER-}pu/\text{the fact that}\ p]\!]^{\text{Mem},i}$ is = 1 iff $w \in p$; if defined, $\forall w'' \in \text{Mem}(i)(p(w''))$

Here we have the factive presupposition $p \in w$, plus commitment in Mem. The subjunctive variant, however, uses Mem, and the presupposition that $M_{epistemic}$ is nonveridical. In this case, what is remembered will be contrasted with what is known. What we remember does not always correspond to what is real.

(85) Suppositional memory:
$[\![i \text{ REMEMBER}_{sup} p]\!]^{M,Mem,i}$ is defined iff $M(i)$ is nonveridical (partitioned epistemic modal base). If defined,
$[\![i \text{ REMEMBER}_{sup} p]\!]^{M,Mem,i} = 1$ iff $\forall w'[w' \in \text{Mem}(i)) \rightarrow w' \in \{w'' \mid p(w'')\}]$

The interplay is crucially between veridical commitment in memory, but partition (nonveridicality) in the presupposition. The subjunctive is triggered, exactly parallel to Italian, in case the subject remembers but doesn't know for sure.

### 4.4.2 Semblance Verbs

Verbs meaning SEEM/APPEAR behave in a similar way to the memory verb and have considerable flexibility. We have not discussed these predicates thus far because in English they are raising construals, unlike the typical attitude verbs. The semblance anchor is the speaker. Implicative verbs and ability modals (to be discussed in chap. 6) have similar syntactic properties and are likewise also anchored to the speaker's doxastic state. It is useful to consider here semblance verbs both for their flexibility as well as because they raise important questions about perception and veridicality.

The key facts are below. We have used translations in English to capture accurately the meaning of the Greek sentences which differ minimally only in the use of complementizers. As we see, all three complementizers—*na, oti, pu*—are allowed:

(86) Ta paidia fenonde na ine kourasmena (ala bori ke
the children seem.3pl that.SUBJ be.3pl tired (but might and
na min ine).
subj not be.3pl)
The children seem to be tired (but they might not be).

(87) Ta paidia   fenonde  oti        ine    kourasmena (#ala bori  ke
     the children seem.3pl that.IND be.3pl tired        (but might and
     na  min  ine).
     subj not be.3pl)
     It is obvious that the children are tired (#but they might not be).

(88) Ta paidia   fenonde  pu         ine    kourasmena (#ala bori  ke
     the children seem.3pl that.IND be.3pl tired        (but might and
     na  min  ine).
     subj not be.3pl)
     The children are tired, and it is apparent.

It is in the nature of semblance predicates to show a flexible attitude sometimes as knowledge (using the appearance of P as evidence for P) and sometimes as suppositional belief, in which case they take the subjunctive. The subjunctive complement of SEEM, APPEAR allows the nonveridical inference: for any predicate P, and individual x, *x seems P to i* (the speaker) does not entail that *x is P* actually. In other words, appearances can be deceiving, and semblance verbs do not entail objective veridicality or knowledge. We call this variant "suppositional SEEM" to keep in line with our vocabulary so far:

(89) Suppositional SEEM (*fenome with subjunctive* in Greek):
     $[\![i\,\text{SEEM}_{sup}\,p]\!]^{M,\text{Dox},speaker}$ is defined iff $M(speaker)$ is nonveridical (partitioned epistemic modal base). If defined,
     $[\![i\,\text{SEEM}_{sup}\,p]\!]^{M,\text{Dox},speaker} = 1$ iff $\forall w'[w' \in \text{Dox}(speaker)) \to w' \in \{w'' \mid p(w'')\}]$

Suppositional SEEM, then, is much like suppositional belief and memory in Italian and Greek, only anchored to the speaker. The speaker expresses a belief that *i* has the property *P*, but at the same time she knows that she does not know that for sure.

The indicative complement correlates with solipsistic commitment, in which case *oti* is chosen, or with factivity in which case we have *pu*:

(90) Solipsistic SEEM (*fenete oti* Greek):
     $[\![i\,\text{SEEM}_{solipsistic}\,p]\!]^{\text{Dox},speaker}$ is $= 1$ iff $\forall w'[w' \in \text{Dox}(speaker)) \to w' \in \{w'' \mid p(w'')\}]$

(91) Factive SEEM (*fenete pu* Greek):
 $[\![i \text{ SEEM}_{factive} \, p]\!]^{\text{Dox},speaker}$ is = 1 iff $w \in p$; if defined $\forall w'[w' \in \text{Dox}(speaker)) \rightarrow w' \in \{w'' \mid p(w'')\}]$

We see that the lexical entry is flexible and can associate with both Dox and M. This flexibility affects veridicality which is itself reflected in the distinct mood choice. We want to repeat therefore that flexibility in mood choice does not necessitate imposing ambiguity in the lexical entries of propositional attitude verbs. It rather shows that the verb exhibits variability in being able to pick different modal bases, and in some cases it can take take an epistemic nonveridical one that denotes lack of knowledge. Here, Dox and M belong to the same realm of epistemic modality; we will see more interactions in the bouletic realm in chap. 5, including lexical entries able to combine with epistemic/doxastic base or bouletic ones (such as, for instance, the lexical entries of persuasion attitudes).

In Italian we observe indicative/subjunctive alternations, as one would expect. Just as in Greek, the attitude holder is always the speaker. When the speaker does not know, only the subjunctive is possible. In this case, there is epistemic uncertainty and the embedded clause expresses a likelihood judgment about *p*, very similarly to *credere*.

(92) Sembra che sia           arrivato.
     seems  that be.SUBJ.3sg arrived
     It seems that he has arrived.

When the speaker knows that *p* is false, both the indicative and the subjunctive are possible.

(93) Sembra    che ha/abbia           vent'anni.
     looks like tha have.IND/SUBJ.3sg twenty-years
     It looks like he is twenty years old.

When the subjunctive is used, the subjunctive enhances an effect that we find akin to "widening" of the common ground: in most similar worlds, which are not part of the common ground, he is twenty. The epistemic uncertainty of the SEEM relation seems to be generally producing this effect, therefore also in Greek. If you widen what can be known, it becomes more difficult to know for sure.

Note, finally, that the in Italian "suppositional belief" can also appear in the infinitival:

(94) Sembra essere contento.
  seems be happy
  He seems to be happy.

Let us move on now to perception verbs.

### 4.4.3 Perception Verbs

Perception mood patterns are very similar to semblance and memory: subjunctive and indicative are both possible:

(95) O Nicholas idhe     ton Flavio na
  the Nicholas saw.3sg the Flavio that.SUBJ
  kleini                              tin porta, ala i  porta dhen ine
  close.NONOPAST.IMPERF.3sg. the door, but the door not   is
  kleisti.
  closed
  Nicholas saw Flavio closing the door, but the door is not closed.

(96) O Nicholas idhe    oti      o Flavio eklise     tin porta, #ala
  the Nicholas saw.3sg that.IND the Flavio closed.3sg. the door, but
  i  porta den ine klisti.
  the door not is  closed
  #Nicholas saw that Flavio closed the door, #but the door is not closed.

Observe again the contrast in finiteness in English between an *-ing* or bare infinitival complement and a *that* complement. The subjunctive complement (equivalent to the *-ing* complement) conveys direct perception, seeing with Nicholas' own eyes. In addition, the closing of the door need not necessarily include the result state of the door being closed. The indicative complement, on the other hand, includes the result state. The difference, we will argue, illustrates that in the indicative complement we have a veridical doxastic state that includes the result, but in the subjunctive complement we have the presupposition of not knowing that the door is closed in all worlds.

For $p$ being indicative "Giacomo closes the door and the door is closed", we have the following. Anchoring again happens to the speaker's doxastic state:

(97) Seeing is believing (solipsistic SEE, indicative):
$[\![i \text{ SEE}_{belief}\, p]\!]^{\text{Dox},speaker}$ is $= 1$ iff $\forall w'[w' \in \text{Dox}(speaker)) \to w' \in \{w'' \mid p(w'')\}]$

Greek *vlepo oti* denotes solipsistic SEE. Here, seeing is understood as a solipsistic belief that the door is closed. It cannot be contradicted without producing Moore paradoxical effects. The subjunctive, on the other hand, reveals the following structure (Per is for "perception state"):

(98) Suppositional SEE (*vlepo na*):
$[\![i \text{ see}_{sup}\, p]\!]^{\text{M,Per},speaker}$ is defined iff M($i$) is nonveridical (partitioned epistemic modal base). If defined, $[\![i \text{ see}_{sup}\, p]\!]^{\text{M,Per},speaker} = 1$ iff $\forall w'[w' \in \text{Per}(speaker)) \to w' \in \{w'' \mid p(w'')\}]$

Here, the speaker perceives that Flavio closes the door, but doesn't know that the door is closed. The modal base is now strictly perception and the nonveridical epistemic presupposition is added. This explains both the direct perception effect and nonentailment to the result.

There is finally also a factive construal. This is parallel to the factive SEEM and REMEMBER: it contains the factive presupposition of objective veridicality, and then commitment in Per (or Dox; we don't think the difference is important here):

(99) O Nicholas idhe    pu       o  Flavio eklise       tin porta, #ala
     the Nicholas saw.3sg that.IND the Flavio closed.3sg. the door, but
     i    porta den ine klisti.
     the door not is closed
     #Nicholas saw that Flavio closed the door, #but the door is not closed.

(100) Factive SEE (*vlepo pu* Greek):
$[\![i \text{ SEE}_{factive}\, p]\!]^{\text{Per},speaker}$ is $= 1$ iff $w \in p$; if defined $\forall w'[w' \in \text{Per}(speaker)) \to w' \in \{w'' \mid p(w'')\}]$

We therefore find a systematic pattern of flexibility in Greek that allows us to see not just the mood flexibility but also an important distinction within the indicative between a solipsistic, subjective veridicality construal and a presuppositional factive one. This difference is hard to detect in Italian or any other Romance language, since these languages lack overt lexicalizations of the factive indicative. Importantly, the factive indicative shows that identifying the indicative with mere assertion is inadequate.

We think it is useful to consider that there are additional temporal constraints on the perception verb. Observe:

(101) Vlepo  ton Gianni na            pernai/*perasi/*perase
      see.1sg the John    that.SUBJ cross.PRES/NONPAST/PAST.3sg
      to   dromo.
      the street
      I see John cross the street.

Recall our discussion in chap. 3. The subjunctive complement accepts only the PRES form. Let us explain this by showing why the other options are bad. The NONPAST is bad because it forces future reference. PAST is bad because seeing requires simultaneity. The true perception reading forces simultaneity: you cannot be seeing *now* an event that happened in past; seeing and happening of the event must coincide. This is why a past complement of SEE (in the indicative) results in an "understand" reading. We take the attitude UNDERSTAND to be a doxastic attitude too, and the verbs UNDERSTAND (*katalaveno, comprendere*) select the indicative:

(102) Katalaveno       oti/*na       o   Giannis
      understand.1sg that.IND/SUBJ the John
      xtipise                tin porta.
      knock.NONPAST.3sg/PAST.3sg the door
      I understand that John knocked on the door.

Understanding is, in other words, another form of doxastic commitment.

Going back to perception verbs, with indicative seeing there is no problem with past or even future because the modal base is not Per. The reading is, in other words, not true perception. HEAR behaves similarly.

HEAR plus indicative is indirect perception, so temporally independent, but HEAR plus subjunctive is just like the seeing variant:

(103) Akouo    ton Gianni na
      hear.1sg the John  subj
      xtipai/*xtipisi/*xtipise                    tin porta.
      knock.PRES.3sg/NONPAST.3sg/PAST.3sg the street
      I hear John knock on the door.

(104) Akousa oti o   Giannis *xtipisi/xtipise            tin
      hear.1sg ind the John  *knock.NONPAST.3sg/PAST.3sg the
      porta.
      street
      I heard that John knocked on the door.

In both cases the direct perception reading forces the necessity of PRES.

### 4.4.4 Summary: Doxastic Verbs, Modals, and the Subjunctive

To sum up: what is crucial for licensing the subjunctive in all the cases of doxastic predicates in this chapter is the presence of a nonveridical epistemic modal base M in the presupposition of the lexical entry. This rendered suppositional doxastic verbs similar to modals: they both obey the Nonveridicality Axiom. We saw this to be the case with:

1. Modal verbs;
2. Belief, certainty, awareness, and opinion attitudes;
3. Imagination and fiction attitudes;
4. Memory attitudes;
5. Semblance attitudes;
6. Perception attitudes.

It becomes clear, then, that the subjunctive mood depends on whether the doxastic commitment expressed by the attitude is contrasted with lack of knowledge. When it does, the lexical entry contains the nonveridical presupposition of epistemic uncertainty in M. Some attitude verbs are solipsistic and cannot combine with a nonveridical M. These express "pure" subjective veridical commitment. Prototypical cases are Greek doxastic attitudes of belief, opinion, certainty, imagination, understanding, and the many similar verbs in Romance that follow the Greek pattern. But memory, semblance and perception are flexible.

The use of subjunctive is thus an indication of lack of knowledge. The subjunctive can be seen an antiknowledge marker, like modal verbs. It is the mood indicating that the attitude holder does not know $p$:

(105) Subjunctive as epistemic uncertainty:
For a proposition $p$ and an individual anchor $i$ (where $i$ is the speaker or a propositional attitude subject):
SUBJUNCTIVE ($p$) entails that $i$ does not know $p$ to be true.

The above is the broadest generalization for the subjunctive that explained the data we have discussed so far—and it can account for all uses of subjunctive to be discussed in this book, including cases of autonomous subjunctive in main clauses where, as we saw, the subjunctive itself seems to contribute a possibility modal. Epistemic uncertainty is expressed formally as obeying the Nonveridicality Axiom, which holds for modals as can be recalled:

(106) Nonveridicality Axiom of modals:
MODAL (M)($p$) can be defined if and only if the modal base M is nonveridical, i.e., M contains $p$ and $\neg p$ worlds.

Modals and attitudes are similar in that they can take a nonveridical epistemic M as their argument. We can therefore generalize as follows:

(107) Nonveridicality Axiom:
For any propositional attitude or modal verb $\alpha$, $\alpha$ obeys the Nonveridicality Axiom iff $\alpha$ ($p$) presupposes that the modal base M of the anchor $i$ of $\alpha$ is nonveridical, i.e., partitioned into $p$ and $\neg p$ worlds.

(108) Licensing condition for the subjunctive mood:
The subjunctive will be licensed in the complement of an attitude verb or modal $\alpha$ that obeys the Nonveridicality Axiom.

These simple generalizations capture a wide array of facts, as we saw, about the nature of subjunctive taking attitudes and modals.

At the same time, doxastic verbs at their truth conditional core—both when they select the subjunctive and when the select they indicative—denote veridical states, expressing doxastic commitment of the attitude holder to the complement proposition. In combining these two components, the subjunctive doxastics become similar to modals, which express commitment to Ideal worlds. The difference between attitudes and modals is that with modals there is no additional modal base, but with attitudes we have various kinds of doxastic models (Dox, Fic, Cer, Mem), combining with the epistemic M.

We want to emphasize two things: first, as we mentioned before, the use of subjunctive remains doxastic and does not add a preferential component to the lexical entry. This is important to remember because often attempts are made to render the subjunctive dependent to bouletic or preferential spaces. This is clearly a problematic assumption given the bulk of data we discussed here, and more discussion will follow in chap. 5.

Second, we found in Greek a systematic pattern of flexibility that allows us to see an important distinction within the indicative: we have a subjective veridicality construal reflected with *oti* and a presuppositional factive lexical entry reflected with *pu*. We found this pattern to be true of knowledge, memory, semblance, and perception verbs; it was therefore quite systematic. This difference is hard to detect in Italian or any other Romance language since these languages lack overt lexicalizations of the factive indicative (*pu*); but the two kinds of indicatives are significant in showing, as we will present next, that the indicative is not simply the mood of assertion—as some literature seems to assume (most notably Farkas's work). The indicative, as *pu* shows, is a mood sensitive also to presuppositional material, namely the objective veridicality (factivity) presupposition.

Let us now move on to develop this last piece of our theory by addressing the discourse functions of the mood particles.

## 4.5 The Update Functions of Mood Morphemes

In this section, we discuss the discourse function of mood morphemes in complementation. Semantically, as we mentioned already, the subjunctive and indicative contribute no independent modality in subordination; they rather reflect the veridical or nonveridical property of the scope of the higher verb. By contrast, in main clauses, the subjunctive may contribute a possibility modal, as can be recalled from our earlier discussions:

(109) Ti     na         theli?
      what that.SUBJ want-3sg
      What might he want?

(110) Na      tou       arese      to fagito?
      that.SUBJ he-GEN liked-3sg the food
      Might it be the case that he liked the food?

The subjunctive adds a possibility epistemic modal *might*. Importantly, these questions are reflective and open-ended, as we said. Giannakidou (2016) calls this subjunctive epistemic, and it has the following denotation:

(111) Epistemic subjunctive as a possibility modal:
      $[\![ \,?(\text{Subjunctive } p))]\!]^{M,i,S} = ?((\exists w' \in M(i) : p(w'))$; where '?' is the question operator

As we noted at the beginning of chap. 3, the subjunctive in main clauses does have the semantic contribution of a possibility modal. In complementation, however, the subjunctive is a subordinator, as can be seen clearly in Greek, and all the semantic action is in the (non)veridicality of the main attitude verb. We used the subjunctive as a diagnostic for whether the verb contains an epistemic uncertainty presupposition or not.

In subordination, mood morphemes can be subordinators themselves, as in Greek, or not, as in Italian; in both cases their function is to update the preceding discourse with the embedded proposition. We will call this "anchoring." The complement does not have access to the common ground since $p$ is embedded under $\alpha$, therefore $\alpha$ ($p$) cannot update the conversation with $p$. The proposition $p$ instead will be anchored to the local space Dox. Mood anchoring is comparable to the *Now*-Anchoring that we mentioned earlier. Syntactically, if *Now*-anchoring happens at the Mood node, mood anchoring happens at C.

Recall our mood generalizations:

(112) a. The subjunctive is sensitive to the nonveridicality in the presuppositional component of an attitude verb.

b. The indicative *oti* is sensitive to the veridicality of the truth condition.
c. The indicative *pu* is sensitive to the veridicality of the presupposition. It is selected by verbs that have a veridical presupposition (either a factive one, or a presupposition of subjective veridicality, as we explore further with emotives in chap. 7).

The subjunctive versus indicative difference appears to be not just a difference in veridicality (indicative) vs. nonveridicality (subjunctive), but also a difference at the level at which the sensitivity applies: the truth conditions (indicative) vs. the presupposition (subjunctive). But there is also *presuppositional* indicative, manifested in Greek *pu*. The indicative can therefore not be de facto identified with assertion, as we emphasized already.

The indicative *oti* performs that we will call *private assertion*:

(113) Indicative I: Private Assertion:
Add $p$ to the local Dox(*subject*).

Private assertion adds the indicative *oti* proposition to the local version of Dox(subject) we mentioned, established by the higher verbs $\alpha$ in the sentence. Embedded indicative in Italian functions in exactly the same way. Because it is an embedded clause, addition cannot happen to the common ground, as we said; only the propositional attitude sentence itself gets added to the common ground. The addition of $p$ to Dox and its variants narrows down the worlds in those spaces by intersection, as expected.

(114) $\text{Dox}(i) + p = \{w'$ in Dox where $p$ is true$\}$

Private assertion anchors $p$ to the main subject's private space, thus performing a kind of context shift. This addition is informative: it adds more information to Dox, and narrows down possibilities in it. The private spaces can be narrowed down informationally by adding propositions, just like unembedded assertions add to the context set $W(c)$. *Oti* is unnecessary in main clauses, where addition happens to the common ground, and this explains, without any additional assumptions, the absence of *oti* in main clauses. *Oti* performs only private assertion; it is not a lexicalization of the Assert operator.

Greek has another type of indicative, which performs exclusively *presuppositional anchoring*: *pu*. In this case, *p* is required to already be in the common ground:

(115) Indicative II (*pu*) indicative: Presuppositional anchoring
 *p* is already in the common ground.

*Oti* can also perform presuppositional anchoring when it introduces the complement of a knowledge verb, and *p* is already in the common ground. *Pu* can only perform presuppositional anchoring. Since *pu* is the specialized form for presuppositional anchoring, it will be the preferred form for this function, as is indeed the case: we find *pu* also with the emotive class we will discuss later. When a language does not lexicalize the difference, the indicative performs both private assertion and presuppositional anchoring. In a language with no mood distinction such as English, the complementizer *that* performs these two functions too.

In contrast to *oti*, *pu* cannot perform private assertion, and this is why it is excluded with doxastic verbs. The existence of a specified presuppositional indicative form suggests quite clearly that the indicative mood is not isomorphic to assertion, contrary to what was previously thought (e.g. Farkas 2003).

Presuppositional anchoring is not addition, but retrieval of a *p* that is common knowledge. We can think of it as a filter: the proposition added by the *pu* clause is already in the common ground, and does not add new information. This captures the distribution of *pu* with all the doxastic verbs we mentioned here, as well as the occurrence of *pu* with emotive factives (to be discussed further in chap. 7). Just as an illustration of the contrast with *oti*, recall that *pu* can't be used in a context where the speaker doesn't know *p*. Consider the answer to a question: How much did that book cost?

(116) Ksero *pu/oti kostise 25 dollaria.
 know.1sg that.*IND-pu.IND-oti cost-3sg 25 dollars
 I know that it costs 25 dollars.

In this context of seeking information, the person asking the question does not know how much the book costs. Hence that the book cost $25 is not part of the common ground, and *pu* cannot be used. Here we see that the complement of KNOW can convey new information and this enables *oti*: in the context above we have addition of new information. The embedded indicative then can add to the common ground, as suggested in the use of *oti* after KNOW.

On the other hand, when $\alpha$ obeys the Nonveridicality Axiom, the speaker does not know whether $p$ is objectively true, $p$ therefore cannot be added to Dox(*subject*), or the common ground, of course. The subjunctive, we propose, performs Nonveridical anchoring (see earlier discussions in Giorgi and Pianesi (1996), Giannakidou 1997, 1998, and Mari (2017a, b, c)):

(117) Subjunctive: Nonveridical anchoring
Do not add $p$ to Dox or the common ground.

The subjunctive mood is, in other words, a prohibition: do not add $p$. This follows, of course, from the nature of nonveridicality. Given that, main clause subjunctives are either nonassertions or possibility statements; and in chap. 3 we generalized that in all cases the subjunctive mood is an instruction *not* to add $p$ to the common ground.

A comparable update is the inquisitive anchoring with embedded questions (Greek *an*, "whether"). Inquisitive anchoring is a special case of nonveridical anchoring:

(118) Inquisitive anchoring
Update CG with ?$p$.

Inquisitive anchoring adds specifically a question to the common ground. The subjunctive does not add a question, but a question is indeed a nonveridical space, hence consistent with not updating with $p$. At this point, we want to offer some final thoughts on the effect of indicative versus nonindicative which, as is now clear, goes beyond mere mood choice in complement clauses.

Our approach acknowledges that indicative and subjunctive morphemes have sentential update functions (Portner 2009, 2018), just like, e.g., the mood imperative. The imperative too, like all other nonassertions, has a nonveridical foundation, i.e., the proposition that follows is not objectively true, or known to the speaker. In fact, as we will argue in chap. 5, the imperative has an antiveridical presupposition (that $p$ is objectively false, or is believed to be false by the speaker) at the time of utterance. Hence, one can generalize that nonindicative moods *all* require nonveridicality in the presupposition. Unlike the imperative, the subjunctive in complement clauses and adjuncts does not have illocutionary force because illocutionary force is a property of main contexts only. The imperative cannot embed for this reason.

The analysis we proposed here shares some similarities and differences with Farkas (2003). Farkas uses updates of private states, but unlike in our theory, for her the verb is responsible for the update of *p*. For us, it is the mood morpheme itself that is responsible for anchoring of the complement proposition *p* (see Mari, 2017a, b and the recent study in Mari and Portner 2019). Quer (2001), at the same time, proposes to consider mood in a dialogical perspective, where subjunctive implies disagreement and lack of endorsement (he calls it "model shift"). As we showed in the four preceding chapters, the subjunctive does not depend on disagreement but on the nonveridical presupposition of epistemic uncertainty. This characterizes all uses of the subjunctive.

## 4.6 Conclusions

In this chapter, we proposed a theory of mood choice that relied on the simple premise that what underlies mood choice is veridicality and nonveridicality. The indicative mood is selected by veridical predicates, i.e., epistemic verbs such as those meaning KNOW which are objectively veridical, i.e., they entail truth of the complement in the actual world, and solipsistic doxastics, which are subjectively veridical and entail truth of the complement in a doxastic space (Dox, Fic, Mem, Cer, Per and the like).

(119) Licensing condition for the indicative mood:
The indicative will be licensed in the complement of a propositional attitude that is veridical (objectively or subjectively).

The indicative is therefore the mood of truth but also of veridical—doxastic or epistemic—commitment.

The subjunctive, on the other hand, is the mood of nonveridicality. It is an indicator of epistemic uncertainty, i.e., nonentailment in the modal space, and it is licensed by verbs that obey the Nonveridicality Axiom:

(120) Nonveridicality Axiom:
For any propositional attitude or modal verb $\alpha$, $\alpha$ obeys the Nonveridicality Axiom iff $\alpha$ $(p)$ presupposes that the modal base M of the anchor $i$ of $\alpha$ is nonveridical, i.e., partitioned into $p$ and $\neg p$ worlds.

(121) Licensing condition for the subjunctive mood:
The subjunctive will be licensed in the complement of an attitude verb or modal $\alpha$ that obeys the Nonveridicality Axiom.

These simple generalizations capture a wide array of facts, as we saw, about the nature of subjunctive taking attitudes and modals.

Modal verbs and propositional attitude verbs are similar in that they presuppose nonveridical modal bases. Doxastic propositional attitudes take modal spaces as arguments due to their lexical meaning, and at their truth conditional core—both when they select the subjunctive and when the select the indicative—convey doxastic commitment of the attitude holder to the complement proposition. The use of subjunctive with doxastic propositional attitudes is in itself an argument against the association of the subjunctive with bouletic orderings, as we are about to discuss next in chap. 5. The concept of preference was shown to be unnecessary for the explanation of mood choice.

Doxastic verbs can be flexible in how they are construed: they can be construed veridically as pure doxastic commitments, but also suppositionally in which case they license subjunctive in the complement. Suppositional doxastics obey the Nonveridicality Axiom. Italian construes its doxastics suppositionally freely, and this option is explored to a lesser extent in Portuguese (see Marques 2004, 2010) and in some dialects of Spanish (e.g., Yucatec Spanish as recently showed in Bove 2020).

Next we show that the Nonveridicality Axiom–and not preference or gradability—is the determining factor also for subjunctive choice with bouletic attitudes.

CHAPTER FIVE

# Bouletic Attitudes: Volition, Hope, Promising, and Persuasion

In this chapter, we focus on some "classically' subjunctive and infinitival predicates such as verbs of volition and desire. We argue that the truth conditions of these predicates require the notion of *bouletic commitment*, the counterpart of doxastic commitment in the realm of doxastics. Like pure belief—which can be construed solipsistically, as we illustrated— some volitional verbs are also construed as solipsistic desires, defined on variants of the bouletic state Boul, on a par with variants of Dox that we defined in chap. 4. When construed solipsistically, volitional attitudes select indicative, as expected.

Bouletic attitudes can also be constructed suppositionally with the by now familiar nonveridical presupposition. In this case, the subjunctive is licensed, in agreement with what we have observed so far. WANT always selects the subjunctive or infinitive and is never compatible with indicative. We propose that this is because WANT features a nonveridical, partitioned Boul that does not entail $p$; it is therefore the bouletic counterpart to MUST, and only in Ideal worlds in Boul is $p$ entailed. In addition, WANT predicates have an antiveridical presupposition that $p$ is not true, or that $i$ believes it to not be true at the time of wanting. We label this *antifactivity*, and have mentioned it before as the property underlying all nonindicative moods, therefore also the optative and imperative.

The landscape of desiderative predicates that emerges is reminiscent of the landscape we just observed with doxastics—hence supporting our intended parallelism between the two realms. While our analysis necessitates the concept of *ordering*, in line with what much of the current literature proposes (Heim 1992; Giannakidou 1997, 1998, 2009; Portner 1997; Villalta 2008; Moulton 2014; Grano 2017, 2018 and references therein), bouletic preference does not play a role in our system. Within a unified analysis for doxastics and bouletics, nonveridicality as a partitioning of the relevant modal base becomes the core common to subjunctive licensing doxastics and bouletics. Preference ordering becomes unnecessary to explain mood choice, and this has repercussions for the *that* vs. *to* choice in English.

Finally, we find systematic correlations between the embedded tense and potential shift in the type of model an attitude can associate with. We find this to be the case with verbs of persuasion and assertive verbs, for example. When combining with a tense other than the NONPAST, PERSUADE shifts to the doxastic type of modal base. The lower tense is crucial in triggering the shift in the modal base, and our account offers a simple explanation for what otherwise could be thought of as lexical ambiguity. If models of evaluation are available for attitudes, and if doxastic/epistemic and bouletic are the two major types of models, shifts between the two are not unexpected but are in fact consistent with the properties of the lower tense. In addition, they illustrate one more similarity between attitudes and modals, many of which are also flexible in the type of modal base they associate with.

## 5.1 Introduction

Let us start with our main findings thus far about the layers in the attitude meaning that impact the licensing of the indicative and subjunctive. First, propositional attitudes that select the indicative are veridical in the following sense: they are construed solipsistically as epistemic or doxastic commitments of the attitude subject $i$ to the truth of the complement proposition $p$. Solipsistic doxastics have very simple truth conditions, supporting the complement proposition in the entire Dox (or its variants), and lack any presupposition whatsoever.

Second, doxastic verbs can also be construed suppositionally, in which case they trigger a subjunctive complement. Suppositional doxastics take an epistemic M as an additional parameter of evaluation, and presuppose, just like modal verbs, that M is nonveridical, i.e., that $i$ doesn't know $p$ to be true. The use of subjunctive mood reflects this epistemic uncertainty, while the indicative is a signal of veridical commitment:

(1) Licensing condition for the subjunctive mood:
The subjunctive will be licensed in the complement of a propositional attitude that obeys the Nonveridicality Axiom, i.e., the attitude presupposes that the attitude holder $i$ does not know that $p$ is true.

(2) Licensing condition for the indicative mood:
The indicative will be licensed in the complement of a propositional attitude that is veridical objectively (knowledge) or subjectively (solipsistic belief of all kinds).

When we say "nonveridical attitude", we intend to refer to a propositional attitude that obeys the Nonveridicality Axiom; and when we say a "veridical attitude", we intend to refer to a solipsistic attitude that conveys veridical commitment. The indicative is the mood of veridical commitment par excellence. The subjunctive, on the other hand, is the mood of nonveridicality, i.e., epistemic uncertainty.

Syntactically, as we said, mood selection is encoded in the subcategorization frame of the lexical entry of the verb. The flexible patterns suggest that lexical entries are underspecified and that subcategorization is not strict. By distinguishing the veridicality of the truth condition from nonveridicality in the presupposition (Nonveridicality Axiom), our system allows for mixed lexical entries that explain the flexible mood patterns without resorting to ambiguity, as most previous accounts have had to do. A mixed lexical entry with a nonveridical presupposition will always trigger the subjunctive, and the whole process of mood choice becomes a more flexible procedure as is indeed required by the empirical data.

Our goal in this chapter is to develop this theory further in the domain of bouletic, or volitional, verbs. These verbs involve in their truth condition a bouletic model, i.e., a set of worlds compatible with what $i$ wants, hopes, intends, is required to do, promises to do, and the like. These verbs typically come with future orientation, hence at present there is uncertainty as to whether the complement $p$ will come to be true. The literature also uses labels such as *desiderative, directive*, and we assume that these all refer to the same class of verbs. The tense of the complement of volitional verbs is the future-oriented NONPAST (discussed in chap. 3), the infinitival NONPAST, or actual future when we have indicative. The bouletic model comes in various forms, depending on the lexical meaning of the attitude, as is the case with doxastics.

We confirm that the presence of the nonveridical presupposition is key to understanding the selection of subjunctive with volitional verbs. We propose *bouletic* commitment as homogeneity of Boul, i.e., universal quantification over *p* worlds in Boul. Verbs that only have this component are "solipsistic bouletics", and will select indicative. This, we will argue, is an option with verbs meaning HOPE, PERSUADE, and PROMISE. We will also propose a novel semantics for pure volition without bouletic preference, quite different from much contemporary work (Heim 1992; Giannakidou 1997, 1998, 2009; Portner 1997; Villalta 2008; Moulton 2014; Grano 2017, 2018; Condoravdi and Lauer 2012).

The discussion proceeds as follows. In section 2, we offer our analysis of WANT, including discussion of previous accounts based on ordering. We argue that such accounts fail to unify the use of subjunctive with both bouletics and suppositional doxastics (which do not involve ordering in any sensible way). In ordering-based accounts, these two uses of subjunctive remain coincidental, but our theory succeeds in unifying these two core cases. In section 3, we discuss HOPE and PROMISE. In section 4, we discuss the dual patterns with Greek and Italian equivalents of verbs meaning PERSUADE. In section 5, we discuss dual patterns with verbs of assertion such as SAY and DENY. We close in section 6 with some general discussion about the typologies observed, which will help in our further exploration of implicative verbs, ability modals, and attitudes of emotion in the remaining chapters.

## 5.2 WANT: Bouletic Commitment, Antifactivity

Along with modals, verbs of desire such as those meaning WANT are strict subjunctive and infinitive selectors. They are never flexible and univocally reject the indicative. The pattern is remarkably stable across languages. Here are some basic examples from Greek and Italian:

(3) I   Ariadne theli     na/*oti          kerdisi               o   Janis.
    the Ariadne want.3sg that.SUBJ/IND win.NONPAST.3sg the John
    Ariadne wants (for) John to win.

(4) I     Ariadne epithimi    na/*oti           kerdisi              o   Janis.
    the  Ariadne desire.3sg that.SUBJ/IND win.NONPAST.3sg the John
    Ariadne desires (for) John to win.

(5) I     Ariadne efxete     na/*oti           kerdisi              o   Janis.
    the  Ariadne wish.3sg that.SUBJ/IND win.NONPAST.3sg the John
    Ariadne wishes (for) John to win.

(6) Gianni vuole/desidera che  Maria vada          a scuola.
    Gianni wants/desires    that Mary  go.SUBJ.3sg to school
    Gianni wants/desires that Mary goes to school.

Notice that the Greek verb *efxome* (wish) is not counterfactual but indeed a regular volitional verb. The subjunctive is typically followed by the familiar form glossed above as NONPAST which gives future orientation, as discussed in chap. 3. Generic PRES with stative verbs is also possible, but not with eventive verbs. PAST is excluded:

(7) I     Ariadne theli      panda na/*oti         ine    kalontymeni.
    the  Ariadne want.3sg always that.SUBJ/IND be.3sg well-dressed
    Ariadne wants to always be well-dressed.

(8) *I    Ariadne theli      na           grafei           to gramma tora.
    the  Ariadne want.3sg that.SUBJ write.PRES.3sg the letter    now
    *Ariadne wants to be writing the letter now.

(9) *I    Ariadne theli      na           egrapse          to gramma
    the  Ariadne want.3sg that.SUBJ write.PAST.3sg the letter
    xthes.
    yesterday
    * Ariadne wants to wrote the letter yesterday.

The pattern is almost parallel in Italian. PRES with statives is allowed although often with what we call a "generic" interpretation of the desire. We will return to this specific case at the end of our discussion and set it aside for now. PAST, as we mentioned, is otherwise banned 12.

(10)  Maria vuole che Susanna vada         vestita bene a scuola.
      Mary  wants that Susan    go.SUBJ.3sg dressed well at school
      (ok generic)
      Mary always wants that Susan dresses well at school.

(11)  Maria vuole che Susanna sia         contenta.
      Mary  wants that Susan    be.SUBJ.3sg happy
      (generic or coerced)
      Mary wants that Susan be happy.

(12)  *Maria vuole che Susanna sia         stata contenta.
       Mary  wants that Susan    be.SUBJ.3sg been  happy
      *Mary wants that Susan had been happy.

Recall that epistemic modals can combine a *na* complement with past.

(13)  I   Ariadne prepi/bori na      efije           xthes.
      the Ariadne must/may   that.SUBJ leave.PAST.3sg yesterday
      Ariadne must/may have left yesterday.

(14)  Maria crede   che Susan sia         stata contenta.
      Mary  believes that Susan be.SUBJ.3sg been  happy
      Mary believes that Susan has been happy.

Hence, there is no incompatibility with the subjunctive and PAST generally, and we will see in the next section that with HOPE the subjunctive can accept PAST; but the PAST is excluded in a volitional complement. Unless bearing on a generic situation (see below), event-directed volition is future oriented: you want at a now something that will happen in the future of that now. You cannot want something you already have; in that case you are happy to have it, i.e., you have an emotive attitude toward it and not a volitional one, it appears.

(15)  Gianni voleva che venisse                  anche Lucia.
      John   wanted that come.SUBJ.IMPERF.3sg also  Lucy
      John wanted Lucia to come as well.

As a convention for ease of exposition, we will say that the Greek and Italian attitude verbs presented here denote the volition meaning WANT. The Italian pattern can be replicated for French.

(16) a. Je veux que Marie vienne.
    I want that Mary come.SUBJ.3sg
    I want that Mary comes.
  b. *Je veux que Marie soit venue.
    I want that Mary be.SUBJ.3sg come
    *I want that Mary has come.
  c. Je veux que Marie soit heureuse.
    I want that Mary be.SUBJ.3sg happy
    I want Mary to be happy.

We will continue using uppercase to denote the abstract meaning that is realized by the specific Greek, French, and Italian words. WANT uniformly selects the subjunctive in the languages we know, but it contrasts with HOPE which, as we discuss further in the next section, can appear with either mood. The English verb *want* has been argued to have an ordering or preference component (*pace* Anand and Hacquard 2013; going back to Heim 1992; Giannakidou 1998, 1999; Portner 1997). Let us take a look at this idea first.

### 5.2.1 Against Bouletic Preference as Subjunctive Trigger with WANT

The general idea promoted in the literature is that volition attitudes, along with persuasion and intention attitudes, are "preference based attitudes", according to the initial characterization in Bolinger (1975) (for recent work, see Anand and Hacquard, 2013; Grano 2018). Most of the literature working on *to* vs. *that* distinction in English (Portner 1997; Moulton 2006; Anand and Hacquard 2013; Grano 2018) assumes a clear difference between *that*-selecting attitudes as being epistemic (Grano calls them "rational"), and *to*-selecting attitudes that are supposed to convey priority or dynamic modality (Portner 2009), also referred to as preference modality.[1]

In English, in other words, the semantic contrast correlates not with mood but with finiteness: finite complements express doxastic modality, but nonfinite complements are said to express preference modality:

(17) a. Mary wants/intends [for John to be happy].
  b. *Mary believes/claims [for John to be happy].

---

1. Here "preference" stands for "bouletic" preference, as, strictly speaking, any time an ordering source is used, there is a "preferential" component in the meaning of the verb.

(18)  a.  *Mary wants/intends [that John is happy].
      b.  Mary believes/claims [that John is happy].

The *for*-infinitive is sometimes distinguished as a special designator of preference; however, it is really unclear whether *for* actually conveys more than simply being the vehicle for obviation in English. *For* does not combine with *believe, claim*, surely, but this does not suggest preference: it could simply be that *for* is excluded because the obviating alternative with doxastic and assertive verbs such as *believe, claim* is *that*. The typical thesis, as we said, is that *(for) to* infinitives contribute preference modality, whereas *that* complements convey doxastic modality. Note that this distinction cannot hold in Italian or French were WANT also selects *that* clauses. But let's assume, for the sake of the argument, that *that*-subjunctive clauses are the correspondent of English infinitival.

In the initial and foundational characterization of bouletic attitudes (Heim, 1992; see later Villalta, 2008), these attitudes convey ordering of doxastic worlds according to a bouletic ordering source. According to Heim's (1992: 197) dynamic framework, the lexical entry for WANT is as follows:

(19)  Heim (1992), WANT:
      $c + a\ wants\ \phi =$
      $[\{w \in c : \text{for every } w' \in Dox_a(w)\}$
      $Sim_{w'} Dox_a(w) + \phi <_{a,w} Sim_{w'}(Dox_a(w)) + \neg \phi]$

According to this, WANT introduces the ordering source, ranking $\phi$ worlds higher than $\neg \phi$ worlds. And there is also an underlying nonveridical doxastic layer in desire. Giannakidou 1997,1998, 2009 builds on the partition of doxastic layer and calls WANT nonveridical. That alone suffices to explain the choice of subjunctive.

When we consider the Greek and Italian mood facts, the idea of bouletic preference becomes problematic, which is the reason why it didn't play much role in Giannakidou's early work. The subjunctive versus indicative choice is only parallel to the *to, that* contrast, not identical to it, yet the generalizations proposed for English have been routinely proposed as generalizations about verb classes across languages.

When one tries to generalize the observations about *to* vs. *that* complements in English and the idea that subjunctive is triggered by preference ordering, one is faced with a number of challenges. First, modal verbs of all modalities (priority, deontic, but also doxastic) select subjunctive and infinitive, as we saw; it is therefore impossible to say that the infinitive and the subjunctive correlate with one type of modality, namely bouletic (broadly construed). This is simply not the case.

Second, as Giannakidou (2009, 2016) points out, and we illustrated already in this book, temporal connectives such as those meaning BEFORE and WITHOUT select the subjunctive but do not convey volition or the like. Recall some of the data that we discussed earlier:

(20) Prin (na) vreksi, as pame spiti.
before SUBJ rain.3sg, that.OPT go.1pl home
Before it rains, let's go home.

(21) Andiamo a casa prima che piova.
go.IMP.1pl to home before that rain.SUBJ.3sg
Let's go home before it rains.

(22) Ekane tin metafrasi xoris na xrisimpopiisi leksiko.
did.3sg the translation without that.SUBJ use.3sg dictionary
He did the translation without using a dictionary.

The use of subjunctive in the examples above is clearly at odds with the idea that the subjunctive requires volition or preference. Rather, the subjunctive correlates with the nonveridical nature of BEFORE and WITHOUT.

Third, the suppositional doxastics we studied in chap. 4 do not convey preference either. Suppositional doxastics and modals do use ordering sources, in the way we showed in chap. 2 and 4, but the ordering is stereotypical or meta-evaluative and not preferential. Adding a subjunctive, crucially, does not alter the type of modality from doxastic to bouletic. Hence, the preference-as-bouletic ordering idea fails to capture this major aspect of the subjunctive choice, namely that the subjunctive correlates with epistemic uncertainty. And if one takes a look at the English infinitivals from the perspective of subjunctive doxastics, one has to admit that even in English it is not accurate to say that the infinitive reflects nondoxastic modality. Quite the contrary: ECM infinitives have been argued by Moulton (2009) to contribute doxastic modality, an analysis consistent with ours in chapter 4. Hence, the split *to-that* in terms of belief vs. preference/volition is not clear-cut in English either.

A final issue that we want to discuss is that most of the preference-based works in English that argue for a categorical difference in modality between *that* and *to* attribute the semantic difference not to the attitude predicate but to some head in the complement, specifically *for*. The idea that there is a modal in the complement clause appears in Bhatt (1999), Kratzer (2006, 2013), Moulton (2009), Anand and Hacquard (2013), Gosselin (2013), White (2014), Bogal-Allbritten (2016), Grano (2017), Gluckman (2018); for earlier references to this end, see Bresnan (1972), Stowell (1982), and Pesetsky (1992). Apart from lacking empirical evidence, this idea (namely that there is modality in the complement clause and that it is due to some modal head) leaves unexplained the selection problem: why is it that some verbs select the particular complement with the specific modality, while others require another modality, and some are compatible with both? The selection patterns become arbitrary in such approaches, and the dependence on the higher propositional attitude is at best only indirect.

Our approach, on the other hand, starts with the meaning of the higher verb as the key function. Understanding the (layers in the verb) meaning is then used as the basis for explaining the mood patterns. As we have argued, there is little to no evidence that the actual mood morphemes contain themselves any modality in embedding. Greek, in particular, which has main subjunctives, allows us to see that in the complement clause the subjunctive has no modal contribution. As we argued at the end of chap. 4, mood morphemes in complementation function strictly as anchors of the upcoming proposition. In the case of the indicative it is possible to have a modal particle below mood, specifically the future particle; but in this case, clearly, the modality is contributed by the future particle and not the mood morpheme. The key to understanding the choice of complement, then, is the meaning of the attitude verb.

With these in mind, let us proceed now with our new analysis of WANT.

### 5.2.2 A New Semantics for WANT

WANT is the prototypical volitional attitude, and one is tempted to treat it as parallel to BELIEVE. Just as BELIEVE expresses doxastic commitment, WANT could be seen as expressing bouletic commitment in the worlds consistent with one's desires, one might argue. However appealing this parallel may be, it turns out that wanting is weaker than believing; the predicate WANT is more akin to MUST.

A precondition for wanting $p$, we will argue, is for $p$ to *not* be true. Consider the following case:

(23) Context: I just received a letter from Bill:
#I want so much to receive a letter from Bill!

(24) Context: The door is open.
a. #I want to open the door.
b. #Open the door!

These examples suggest that a precondition for wanting something is to *not* have what you want at the time of wanting. Notice that the past *I wanted so much to receive a letter from Bill!* in the same context is fine because the wanting time is prior to the receiving time. If $p$ is already true, the appropriate attitude to have is *emotive*, i.e. one can be happy or sad about it (to be discussed in chap. 7). Crucially, when $i$ wants $p$, either $p$ is false at the time of desire, or the subject $i$ believes $p$ not to hold. For instance, $i$ might erroneously believe $p$ to not hold:

(25) Ariadne wants Flavio to buy her a nice gift for her birthday. He did just that, but it's a secret, she doesn't know!

In this sequence, Ariadne does not know that Flavio bought her a nice gift. The speaker knows that, but the speaker's knowledge is irrelevant for Ariadne's desires.

We will call this property of WANT *antifactivity*, and we define it below identifying wanting with the utterance time:

(26) Antifactivity presupposition of WANT attitudes:
$i$ WANT $p$ at $t_u$ can only be defined if $p$ is not true at $t_u$, or if $i$ believes that $p$ is not true at $t_u$.

Antifactivity is an antiveridicality presupposition, either an objective antiveridicality or a subjective one, as we see. Crucially, antifactivity characterizes not just WANT but other directive moods such as the optative and imperative. These too require, upon being issued, that the action has not been undertaken (Portner 1997; Kaufmann 2012). Issuing an imperative when the required effect already holds is redundant.² In this sense, WANT, imperatives and optatives are like the future, which is also antifactive at the time of utterance (Giannakidou and Mari 2018); the future orientation of WANT, imperatives, and optatives is therefore quite understandable.

Antifactivity manifests itself also with counterfactual desires and wishes:

(27) a. I wish John were here!
    b. Ariadne is fourteen years old, and does not have a driver's license, but she wants to drive this car.

Clearly, there is no contradiction in the above sentences. Ariadne wants something impossible given that she is only 14 and doesn't have a driver's license. The fact that she knows at $t_u$ that her desire cannot be true doesn't prevent her from having it. Likewise, counterfactual verbs express a subject's desire for something that is clearly not true at $t_u$.

Antifactivity is stronger than the nonveridicality presupposition, i.e., antifactivity entails nonveridicality. The presupposition of wanting is therefore stronger than mere not knowing or not believing required by the Nonveridicality Axiom.

Let us now define Boul as follows:

(28) Bouletic state of an individual anchor *i*:
    A bouletic state Boul(*i*) is a set of worlds associated with an individual *i* representing worlds compatible with *i*'s desires.

In a Portnerian perspective, Boul is useful for priority modality and indicates will of doing. According to Copley (2009), WANT also relates

---

2. Iatridou (2000: 243) has some examples that might seem like challenges to antifactivity: *I have what I want, I live in Bolivia because I want to live in Bolivia*. Crucially, these examples do not involve sentence complements: the WANT predicate is found in a *because* clause and in a free relative. Notice that our antifactivity presupposition is defined as a a precondition on uttering *i* WANTS *p*. At the same time, in *I have what I want*, *what I want* defines an object, not a proposition, i.e. the set of things or the unique thing that I want. The *because* clause, on the other hand, can be understood as a sort of coordination, or even a conditional, in which case the *because* clause would be equivalent to an *if*-clause, hence temporally prior to the main clause, consistent with antifactivity. Many thanks to Tom Grano for bringing these examples to our attention.

to plans and goals. Here we do not endorse any specific view but acknowledge that *want* can also be directed toward a state, as in *I want Flavio to be the winner*. In this case, I have my desire without necessarily having a plan or taking any action toward that end; our theory will easily accommodate these cases, by simply manipulating a temporal parameter (see below).

Given antifactivity and Boul, the lexical entry for WANT could look like this:

(29) Boul($i$): $\lambda w'(w'$ is compatible with what the subject $i$ wants in $w_0$ at $t_u$)

(30) Semantics of WANT. (First take, to be revised.)
$[\![i\,\text{WANT}\,p]\!]^{\text{Dox,Boul},t_u,i}$ is defined iff $\forall w' \in \text{Dox}(i) : \neg p(w')$ If defined,
$[\![i\,\text{WANT}\,p]\!]^{\text{Dox,Boul},t_u,i} = 1$ iff $\forall w'' \in \text{Boul}(i) : p(w'')$

The antiveridical antifactive presupposition of WANT already makes the subjunctive necessary, and indeed with WANT the subjunctive is unequivocal across languages and cannot be negotiated. Volition is always relative to reality or the belief about it; the temporal parameter can be fixed at any time provided by higher tense.

Now, when it comes to universal quantification in Boul, if WANT induces universal quantification over the entire bouletic space, as depicted above, an issue arises with how the account would handle the apparent nonmonotonicity of desire (Heim 1992).[3] Heim offers examples such as the following:

(31) I don't want to teach, but (since I have to) I want to teach Tuesdays and Thursdays.

There is also the possibility of conflicting desire reports such as:

(32) John wants it to rain so the picnic will be canceled, but he also wants it not to rain so he can go hiking.

These led Heim (1990) and Giannakidou (1997, 1998) to propose that Boul is partitioned. In our theory, this means that WANT becomes equivalent

---

3. We appreciate Tom Grano raising this key point.

to MUST: $p$ is true only in the Ideal set in Boul, and there are still worlds in Boul where $p$ is not true. In bouletic Ideal worlds, $p$ is true. In this case, *Ideal* is a function over the bouletic modal base. Here is, then, the semantics for WANT that we will adopt:

(33) $[\![i\,\text{WANT}\,p]\!]^{i,\text{Dox},\text{Boul},\textit{Ideal},S,t_u}$ is defined iff $\forall w' \in \text{Dox}(i) : \neg p(w')$ (antifactivity), and Boul is nonveridical:
$\exists w'' \in Boul : \neg p(w'') \land \exists w''' \in Boul : p(w''')$
If defined,
$[\![i\,\text{WANT}\,p]\!]^{i,\text{Dox},\text{Boul},\textit{Ideal},S,t_u} = 1$ iff $\forall w'''' \in \textit{Ideal}_S : p(w'''')$

Hence, WANT emerges as the bouletic counterpart of MUST, and it will select the subjunctive. In other words, WANT does not express bouletic commitment, unlike BELIEVE. At best, it expresses commitment in the Ideal worlds, just like MUST. HOPE, on the other hand, can indeed express bouletic commitment as we shall see.

Before turning to the semantics of HOPE, let us conclude with the generic WANT, illustrated in (16-c) and repeated here in (34). We see that there is no antifactivity proper.

(34) Je veux que Marie soit heureuse.
 I want that Mary be.SUBJ.3sg happy
 I want Mary to be happy.

We claim that here WANT describes a generic desire (see also the distinction WANT as desire and WANT as a principle for action in Condoravdi and Lauer 2012). We implement this by manipulating the temporal parameter of WANT. While when anchored to a context the temporal parameter leads to sensitivity to antifactivity relative to the time of the context, in the absence of the temporal parameter, antifactivity becomes irrelevant, and the desire is considered to hold no matter when and what.

## 5.3 Hoping

*Elpizo* (hope) and *spero* in Greek and Italian exhibit flexible mood and flexible tense:

(35) a. Elpizo      na           kerdisi/kerdise              o  Janis.
       hope.1sg that.SUBJ win.PERF.NONPAST/PAST.3sg the John
       I hope for John to win/to have won.
    b. Spero         che Gianni abbia       vinto/vinca.
       Hope.1sg.PRES that John   have.3sg.SUBJ won/win.3sg.SUBJ
       I hope that John has won.

(36) a. Elpizo    oti       kerdise o Janis.
       hope.1SG that.IND won.3sg the John
       I hope that John won.
    b. Elpizo    oti      tha kerdisi       o  Janis.
       hope.1sg that.IND FUT win.nonpast.3sg the John
       I hope that John will win.
    c. Spero         che il  Milan vincerà
       hope.1sg.PRES that the Milan win.3sg.FUT.IND
       I hope that Milan AC will win/has won.

Notice the correlation with tense: the past is now allowed with the subjunctive, something impossible, as we said, with WANT predicates. Recall:

(37) *I  Ariadne theli      na          egrapse        to gramma
      the Ariadne want.3sg that.SUBJ write.PAST.3sg the letter
      xthes.
      yesterday
      *Ariadne wants to wrote the letter yesterday.

In other words, the HOPE attitude is not restricted temporally: one can hope things about the past, the present, or the future. In sharp contrast with WANT, in Italian the indicative version is exclusively restricted to future orientation.

(38) a. Spero         che verrà.
       hope.IND.1sg that come.IND.FUT.3sg
       I hope that he will come.
    b.*Spero         che è           venuto.
       hope.IND.1sg that be.IND.3sg come
       I hope that he has come.

The indicative version, in Italian as in Greek, reveals that the speaker is expressing an attitude of expectation, rather than relying on reasonable evidence that can trigger a supposition about what will happen.

Equivalents of *hope* are also flexible in other languages, and the flexibility has created difficulty in handling this attitude. According to Anand and Hacquard (2013), English *hope* features a preferential and an epistemic layer. The epistemic layer comprises $p$ and $\neg p$ worlds—it is therefore nonveridical in our terminology—but, according to Anand and Hacquard, it is not nonhomogeneity that triggers the subjunctive but the preferential layer. The epistemic layer (even if partitioned) triggers the indicative. We saw why the preferential argument is not right, and Anand and Hacquard offer no new arguments. Overall, their account fails to appreciate the role of the partitioned modal space in licensing the subjunctive, and predicts indicative with the suppositional doxastics we discussed in chap. 4. In our approach, the nonveridical presupposition triggers the subjunctive in HOPE, in a way parallel to doxastics and modals.

Intuitively, hoping feels stronger than mere wanting. Often a flavor of planning or a path to realization is understood at the foundation of hope; one can therefore not have counterfactual hopes or contradictory hopes. Heim's sentences that we discussed earlier with WANT are pretty strange with HOPE:

(39) a. I don't hope to teach, but (since I have to) I hope to teach Tuesdays and Thursdays.
 b. #I hope not to teach, but (since I have to) I hope to teach Tuesdays and Thursdays.

It is rather odd to hope not to teach and then continue as above. Likewise, there are no conflicting hopes:

(40) #John hopes that it will rain so the picnic will be canceled, but he also hopes that it won't rain so he can go hiking.

We can assume that HOPE is stronger than WANT in that it contains a path to action—as opposed to mere wanting which doesn't, as we said. We will also maintain the idea that a nonveridical epistemic presupposition is a subjunctive trigger. The duality of patterning shows that HOPE can be construed solipsistically like pure bouletic commitment (thus stronger than WANT which shows commitment only in the Ideal bouletic alternatives) without the epistemic component:

(41) Solipsistic HOPE (indicative):
$[\![i\text{ HOPES that }p]\!]^{\text{Boul},i}$ is true in $w$ with respect to Boul($i$) iff:
$\forall w' \in \text{Boul}(i) : p(w')$

This construal of HOPE identifies hoping with pure bouletic commitment with no epistemic or doxastic uncertainty. HOPE is, in other words, the bouletic counterpart to belief and not WANT. The sense of a plan or action is a result of bouletic commitment, most plausibly an implicature: a rational agent can be bouletically committed to a proposition only if she has reasons to do so, and having some plan or other is a good enough justification. The Greek and Italian words *elpizo* and *spero* can be construed as solipsistic HOPE, and chose the indicative.

But the meaning HOPE can also be construed as having the extra non-veridical layer. Here Boul is a function over the modal base and stands for $Boul(M(i))$ returning those worlds in $M(i)$ that are compatible with $i$'s preferences.

(42) Suppositional hope (subjunctive):
$[\![i\text{ HOPE }p]\!]^{M_{epistemic},\text{Boul},i}$ is defined iff
$\exists w' \in M_{epistemic}(i) : \neg p(w') \land \exists w'' \in M_{epistemic}(i) : p(w'')$
If defined,
$[\![i\text{ HOPE }p]\!]^{M_{epistemic},\text{Boul},i} = 1$ iff $\forall w''' \in Boul : p(w''')$

The Greek and Italian words *elpizo* and *spero* can also be used to denote suppositional HOPE, in which case they select subjunctive. Hence, HOPE verbs are underspecified lexically as to which version of HOPE they convey. This dual strategy, as we see, is available at the bouletic realm as much as it was available at the doxastic realm, and the HOPE verb emerges as the obvious bouletic dual of the Italian BELIEVE verb.

It is also important to note another difference between HOPE and WANT predicates: the speaker believes $p$ to be *actually* possible in the case of HOPE (see discussion in Portner and Rubinstein 2013), but not with WANT. Example (43-a) is felicitous only if marrying Brad Pitt is inferred to be a possibility. This inference does not come about with (43-b):

(43) a. Spera          di sposare Brad Pitt.
       hope.PRES.3sg of marry   Brad Pitt
       I hope to marry Brad Pitt.
    b. Vuole          sposare Brad Pitt.
       want.PRES.3sg marry   Brad Pitt
       I want to marry Brad Pitt.

This also justifies using an epistemic modal base for HOPE but not for WANT, which allows unreasonable and unrealizable desires. Our account here succeeds in offering a relatively simple semantics for the flexibility of HOPE attitudes without resorting to preference or ambiguity.

## 5.4 Promising

The verbs meaning PROMISE also feature mood shifts, but their profile is yet different from HOPE and WANT. Like WANT, the PROMISE attitude is clearly future oriented; but promising is also said to involve commitment of *i* to act on bringing about *p*, and for this reason PROMISE is often characterized as performative in the Austinian sense. Neither WANT nor HOPE have this commitment to action on behalf of *i*.

Like HOPE, PROMISE is flexible in the mood it takes, as can be seen here with examples from Greek:

(44) a. I Ariadne iposxethike na fiji noris.
       the Ariadne promised.3sg that.SUBJ leave.NONPAST.3sg early
       Ariadne promised to leave early.
    b. I    Ariadne iposxethike oti       tha  fiji
       the Ariadne promised.3sg that.IND FUT leave.NONPAST.3sg
       noris.
       early
       Ariadne promised that she will leave early.

But if the PROMISE attitude comes with commitment to action, what does the use of the subjunctive show? The puzzle is observed already in Giannakidou 1997, where it is claimed that only the indicative version involves promise to act; the *na* version, Giannakidou argues, does not convey commitment to carry out the action indicated by the *na* clause. The dual pattern is puzzling from the performative perspective, clearly.

Past tense is excluded with the *oti* clause because of the nature of promise, which is future oriented and antifactive like WANT:

(45) #I     Ariadne iposxethike   oti          efije              noris.
     the Ariadne promised.3sg that.IND left.PAST.3sg early
     #Ariadne promised that she left early.

English does allow *promise* with past, but in this case the reading is emphatic, akin to swearing that the speaker or the promise subject is saying the truth. Italian is parallel to English in this respect. Greek promising lacks this flavor.

(46) Ti     prometto che me lo  ha detto.
     to you promise   that me that has said
     I promise you that he told me so.

We define a lexical entry for *performative* PROMISE which encodes future orientation as part of the lexical meaning of the attitude driven by the specific type of bouletic commitment which is *intention*, understood as intention (maybe a plan) to bring about $p$.

(47) Performative PROMISE (Greek: *iposxome oti*):
     $[\![\text{promise that } p]\!]^{i,\text{Boul}}$ is 1 iff:
     $\forall w' \in \text{Boul}(i) : \exists t' \succ t_u : p(w', t')$; where Boul is *intention to bring about*

This reveals intentional commitment of $i$ to $p$. In the case of PROMISE, it is commitment to bring about $p$ that may or may not involve a plan at the time of promising.

With the subjunctive version, PROMISE is gauged against uncertainty and has a suppositional layer: it is not certain that there will be a time in which $p$ will turn out to be true. This is *nonperformative* PROMISE, and triggers subjunctive.

(48) Nonperformative PROMISE (Greek: *iposxome na*):
$[\![\text{promise that } p]\!]^{M_{epistemic}, \text{Boul}, i}$ is defined iff
$\exists w' \in M_{epistemic}(i) : \neg p(w') \land \exists w'' \in M_{epistemic}(i) : p(w'')$
If defined,
$[\![\text{promise that } p]\!]^{M_{epistemic}, \text{Boul}, i}$ is 1 iff
$\forall w''' \in \text{Boul}(M(i)) : \exists t' \succ t_u : p(w''', t')$; where Boul is *intention to bring about*

Here we have the uncertainty about the outcome $p$; hence although there is intentional commitment in entailing $p$ in Boul, there is still non-veridicality in M. The Greek verb *iposxome* can be used in both ways. It is not clear to us that the difference is traceable in English since the description of English *promise* has always been that it is performative. In our theory, performativity is solipsistic promise, and nonperformative promise is promise with uncertainty.

Suppositional promise can be understood as pure intention. The verb meaning INTEND has this semantics too, we will argue. Notice that the Greek *protitheme* (intend) selects strictly the subjunctive:

(49) a. I    Ariadne protithete   na/*oti
     the Ariadne intends.3sg that.SUBJ/IND
     fiji                          noris.
     leave.NONPAST/PAST.3sg early
     Ariadne intends to leave early.

Intention is an attitude of plan to act, but unlike solipsistic promise, when $i$ intends to bring about $p$, $i$ is aware that this may not happen:

(50) INTEND (Greek: *protitheme*)
$[\![\text{intend that } p]\!]^{M_{epistemic}, \text{Boul}, i}$ is defined iff
$\exists w' \in M_{epistemic}(i) : \neg p(w') \land \exists w'' \in M_{epistemic}(i) : p(w'')$
If defined,
$[\![\text{intend that } p]\!]^{M_{epistemic}, \text{Boul}, i}$ is 1 iff
$\forall w''' \in \text{Boul}(M(i)) : \exists t' \succ t_u : p(w''', t')$; where Boul is *intention to bring about*

Verbs of intention across languages have this meaning, we will submit. Suppositional PROMISE is an intentional attitude rather than a performative one. We could designate the set for intention distinctively as Int, and we will use it again soon with PERSUADE.

In WANT, HOPE, INTEND, and PROMISE, the attitude remains the same but there is an observed difference in "strength", as was with doxastics. The strength change that mood brings about concerns whether the attitudes are construed as obeying or not obeying the Nonveridicality Axiom (solipsistically). Being strong refers to the latter case; weaker construals of the lexical meanings have the nonveridicality presupposition added. An additional aspect of strength, finally, had to do with what exactly Boul encompasses. In the case of wanting and hoping, it is pure desires, but in the case of promising and intending, it is intention to act that may (but doesn't have to) include a plan for action.

We move on now to examine cases where the choice of two moods is not simply about strength but also produces an apparent difference in the meaning of the attitude verb. Here, we will observe interactions between Boul and Dox.

## 5.5 Attitudes of Persuasion

Apparent meaning change is observed with attitudes of persuasion, assertive, and certain negative verbs. We will show that in these cases the difference in meaning indicates, in addition to the presence or not of a presuppositional nonveridical layer, also a shift in the type of state chosen (bouletic or doxastic). The lower tense is crucial in triggering the shift, as we shall see.

The attitude PERSUADE is manifested in English with the verbs *persuade, convince*, in Italian with *persuedere*, and in Greek with *pitho, ime pepeismenos*. Both moods are allowed:

(51) a. I Ariadne epise ton Nikolas na
 the Ariadne persuaded.3sg the Nicholas that.SUBJ
 fiji noris.
 leave.NONPAST.3sg early
 Ariadne convinced Nicholas to leave early.

b. I Ariadne epise         ton Nikolas oti      i   idea
   the Ariadne persuaded.3sg the Nicholas that.SUBJ the idea
   tou ine   kali.
   his is.3sg good
   Ariadne convinced Nicholas that his idea is good.

(52)  Gianni ha persuaso Maria che era      ora di partire.
      John   has persuaded Mary that be.IND.3sg time to leave
      John has persuaded Mary that it was time to leave.

(53)  Gianni ha persuaso Maria che fosse    ora di partire.
      John   has persuaded Mary that be.SUBJ.3sg time to leave
      John has persuaded Mary that it was time to leave.

Notice the change in meaning and the alteration in English between *convince to* (equivalent to *pitho na*), and *convince that* (equivalent to *pitho oti*). The English difference is discussed in a recent paper by Grano (2018). As in English, *pitho na* means convince someone to act, but *pitho oti* means to make someone believe that the complement proposition is true. This difference is brought about in Greek by the mood, in English by the *to* vs. *that* choice. Italian also allows the infinitive with the expected "convince to act" reading:

(54)  Gianni ha persuaso Maria a partire.
      John   has persuaded Mary to leave
      John has persuaded Mary to leave.

As in the case of the attitudes discussed so far, there is no evidence that we are dealing with preference. We will start our discussion of the English verb *persuade* with some comments from Grano (2018), who defends the following generalizations:

(55)  a. When *persuade* combines with a nonfinite control complement, the meaning is roughly "cause to intend";
      b. When *persuade* combines with a finite complement, the meaning is roughly "cause to believe".

For Grano, the semantic difference in the two patterns of *persuade* correlates with finiteness and control, in the spirit of the research mentioned earlier that posits a categorical divide between doxastic and preference attitudes. In Greek, this generalization is not transferable, since with both subjunctive and indicative we have finite clauses. Moreover, in Greek it is not even about control. Notice below the pattern of obviation:

(56) I Ariadne epise ton Nikolas na
 the Ariadne persuaded.3sg the Nicholas that.SUBJ
 fijoun ta paidhia noris.
 leave.NONPAST.3pl the children early
 Ariadne convinced Nicholas for the children to leave early.

In Greek, instead, the contrast is between subjunctive with NONPAST and future orientation versus indicative with PAST or PRES. The same holds in Italian: the imperfective indicative indicates PRES, whereas with the subjunctive version (*fosse*, 53) the question whether it was time to leave is open, and forward shifting of the time of evaluation is conveyed. This specific subjunctive pattern is by now familiar for all bouletics.

Are the Greek, Italian, and English verbs of persuasion ambiguous? Not really. Our method of explanation should be obvious by now: the verbs can be construed with or without a nonveridical presupposition, and accordingly they select indicative or subjunctive. In addition, with PERSUADE, a state (or, model, or modal base) shift happens from bouletic to doxastic. Modal verbs are flexible in the types of modal bases they combine with, and can combine with epistemic or deontic or circumstantial modal bases. Some propositional attitude predicates, then, such as PERSUADE have similar flexibility, and are therefore crucial in revealing that the relation between epistemic and bouletic attitudes is more fluid and less categorical.

Grano, however, assumes a more strict divide, and distinguishes between what he calls "rational" and "preference" attitudes. Belief is a rational attitude, and desire a preference attitude — intention having features of both. Given our own analysis of volitionals without ordering, the distinction is not motivated. But in his framework, the divide entails the following analysis for *persuade*:

(57) PERSUADE (Grano 2018: 49):
 a. persuade = cause to have a rational attitude
 b. *p* finite = information that *p* is true
 c. *p* for / to= preference for *p* to be true
 d. RATIONAL + PREFERENCE = INTENTION

(58) a. #I persuaded John to quit smoking, although he still doesn't intend to.
b. I persuaded John to quit smoking, although he still doesn't want to.

*Persuade*, according to Grano, targets rational attitudes, which include belief and intention but not desire. Intention and desire constitute a semantically natural class (preference-based attitudes) to the exclusion of belief. In addition, he proposes that there is another class of attitudes that crosscuts this distinction, including belief and intention but not desire, and this is the class that includes persuasion verbs. Grano's account has insights that are not incompatible with what we are proposing. For instance, he suggests that rational attitudes are those that have a Hintikkean semantics—the ones that we call solipsistic. Non-rational attitudes, such as desire reports, have a semantics that is either non-Hintikkean thus nonveridical (as in Heim 1992; Giannakidou 1997, 1999, and as we suggested here, i.e., equivalent to MUST), or Hintikkean but "context-sensitive in a way that may nullify some of the effects of a Hintikkean semantics as in von Fintel 1999." (Grano 2018: 14).

In our approach, the choice is fundamentally between a solipsistic versus a suppositional construal of PERSUADE on a par with the other cases we have discussed thus far. And intention, as we said, is suppositional and contains epistemic uncertainty. In the case of PERSUADE, we will postulate that there is a shift also in the modal base chosen. Consider first the subjunctive variant which is persuade to act. The resulting lexical entry is as follows:

(59) PERSUADE someone to act (with NONPAST):
$[\![i \text{ PERSUADE NONPAST} j, p]\!]^{M_{epistemic}, \text{Boul}, i, j}$ is defined iff
At $t_u$: $\exists w' \in M_{epistemic}(i) : \neg p(w') \land \exists w'' \in M_{epistemic}(i) : p(w'')$
If defined,
$[\![i \text{ PERSUADE NONPAST} p]\!]^{M_{epistemic}, \text{Boul}, i, j} = 1$ iff
$\forall w''' \in \text{Boul}(i) : \exists t' \in [t, \infty) : (w''', t')$; where Boul is a function that triggers worlds of $M_{epistemic}(i)$ where *i intends j to bring about p*.

Boul now is the set of worlds $w'$ compatible with *i* having the intention to bring about *p*. It is, in other words, an intentional space. The choice of subjunctive and the ensuing NONPAST follows from the nature of Boul since they are future oriented, and the intention to act excludes doxastic alternatives. The effect is similar to PROMISE and INTEND. An interesting difference between PERSUADE and PROMISE lies in who is in charge of bringing about, i.e., who intends to bring about $p$. With PROMISE it is the subject, with PERSUADE it is the object.

Persuade plus PAST or present, on the other hand, produces the meaning "cause to believe," and there is no reference to action. This is a veridical solipsistic construal; we shift to a doxastic model:

(60) Doxastic PERSUADE (indicative):
 $[\![i \text{ is convinced that } p]\!]$ is true in $w$ with respect to Dox($i$) iff:
 $\forall w' \in \text{Dox}(i) : p(w')$

In this construal, to be convinced means to believe. As expected, doxastic persuasion is fully compatible with PAST and PRESENT tenses, just like other doxastic verbs. Interestingly, the HOPE meaning in the solipsistic construal can sometimes also give the flavor of a doxastic reading. Consider:

(61) Elpizo oti kerdise o Janis.
 hope.1SG that.IND won.3SG the John
 I hope that John won. Sounds like "I believe that John won and this is desirable."

In other words, a bouletic verb, when combining with a tense other than the NONPAST—which is its natural choice because of the nature of desire to be future oriented—may shift to the doxastic type of modal base. Doxastic spaces are more naturally compatible with past and present, since only facts about the past or the present can be known or believed. The lower tense is therefore crucial in triggering the shift in the modal base because it brings about constraints that have to do with the nature of the predicates in question.

Our account offers a simple explanation for what otherwise could be thought of as lexical ambiguity. If models of evaluation are available for attitudes, and if doxastic/epistemic and bouletic are the two major types of models, shifts between the two are not unexpected but are in fact consistent with the properties of the lower tense. And these shifts are exactly the shifts we observe with modal verbs when they associate with different types of modal bases. Grano's postulated difference between rational and preference attitudes therefore can be rethought as shifting between doxastic and bouletic spaces, and this is again another similarity between propositional attitudes and modals.

## 5.6 Verbs of Assertion

Verbs of assertion display a similar change of model (or modal base) and correlation with tense reminiscent of persuasion verbs. We illustrate below with the Greek verbs *leo* and *arnoume* (examples from Giannakidou 2016; and Giannakidou and Staraki 2013). The contrast is now a lexical contrast in English:

(62) a. O  Janis lei   oti      efijan noris.
        the John says that.IND left.3pl early
        John *says* that they left early.
     b. O  Janis lei   na       figoun                 noris.
        the John says that.SUBJ leave.NONPAST.3pl early
        John *wants* for them to leave early.

(63) a. O  Janis arnithike oti      efijan noris.
        the John denied    that.IND left.3pl early
        John *denied* that they left early.
     b. O  Janis arnithike na       fiji                   noris.
        the John says      that.SUBJ leave.NONPAST.3sg early
        John *refused* to leave early.

The choice of *na* and NONPAST correlates with action or thought of the future. The difference in mood lexicalizes in distinct verbs in English (*refuse, deny* and *say, want*). With both *lei* and *arnithike*, the subjunctive complement acquires a volitional, intentional meaning; the *oti* complements, on the other hand, with veridical past or present tense remain assertive.

For assertive verbs, the model of reported conversation is relevant (following Giannakidou 1997, 1999):

(64) Reported conversation state of an individual anchor *i*:
     A reported conversation information state $M_{rc}(i)$ is a set of worlds

associated with an individual *i* representing worlds compatible with what *i* knows or believes to be true of the reported conversation.

The model of reported conversation is a doxastic or epistemic space (or, more likely, mixed); the *oti* complement adds the proposition to the reported conversation, with a possible intent to also add it to the common ground. This is, however, only possible intent:

(65)  O  Janis lei  oti        efijan    noris, alla dhen ton  pistevo.
      the John says that.IND left.3pl early, but not   him  believe.1sg
      John says that they left early, but I don't believe him.

(66) $[\![\text{Nicholas said that } p]\!]^{i,M_{rc}} = 1$ in $w$ with respect to $M_{rc}(Nicholas)$ iff:
$\forall w' \in M_{rc}(Nicholas) : p(w')$

Hence, the speaker can believe or disbelieve the reported sentence, but the subject of SAY has to accept it as part of the conversation. This renders *leo* veridical and allows the indicative.

*Leo na*, on the other hand, contains a bouletic component (again, Boul is a function over $M(i)$).

(67) Bouletic assertive verb:
$[\![i \text{ SAY } p]\!]^{i,M_{epistemic},Boul}$ is defined iff
$\exists w' \in M_{epistemic}(i) : \neg p(w') \land \exists w'' \in M_{epistemic}(i) : p(w'')$
If defined,
$[\![i \text{ SAY } p]\!]^{i,M_{epistemic},Boul} = 1$ iff $\forall w''' \in Boul: p(w''')$

In other words, verbs that denote SAY can use a bouletic argument, and in this case they produce a bouletic meaning. The verb ASK is similar: *Ariadne asked what time it is* versus *Ariadne asked me to read her a story*. These systematic switches in verbal meaning need not be thought of as ambiguities but rather as flexibility in what kind of modal space verbal meanings can take as arguments for their truth condition. We find, then, that there are interactions between Dox and Boul, and attitude verbs can combine with both. As we mentioned before, this argues against the strict separation of attitudes often assumed in the literature between epistemic (or rational) versus priority (or preference). A single attitude can take a priority or an epistemic base and shift in meaning accordingly.

In Italian, there is meaning shift, but the resulting interpretations are similar to the alternations we observed with doxastics. With the indicative there is full commitment of the speaker (and possibly request of adding $p$ to the common ground); with subjunctive, there is no full commitment, and the speaker is in a state of uncertainty of whether $p$ is true (see Mari 2015a, 2016a). As we see, in Italian there is no shift to bouletic worlds. Instead, it is worth noting that reportative SAY triggers subjunctive in Italian. The relevant lexicalization is not truthfulness in the reportative space but epistemic uncertainty that the reported status of $p$ enhances.

(68) La gente dice che è incinta.
the people say that be.IND.3sg pregnant
People say that she is pregnant.

(69) La gente dice che sia incinta.
the people say that be.SUBJ.3sg pregnant
People say that she is pregnant.

(70) Subjunctive SAY, Italian:
$[\![i \text{ say } p]\!]^{i, M_{epistemic}, M_{rc}}$ is defined iff
$\exists w' \in M_{epistemic}(i) : \neg p(w') \wedge \exists w'' \in M_{epistemic}(i) : p(w'')$
If defined,
$[\![i \text{ say } p]\!]^{i, M_{epistemic}, M_{rc}} = 1$ iff
$\forall w''' \in M_{rc}(M_{epistemic}(i)) : p(w''')$

With Italian *dire*, thus, the model does not change; we find, once again, that lexical meanings of the verbs can differ for the same class crosslinguistically (SAY). Notice, significantly, that the tense in Italian remains the same, unlike in Greek, where the shift to the bouletic modal base correlates with the use of nonpast—which itself necessitates subjunctive. In Italian, there is no shift in tense, therefore also no shift in the modal base. This lends support to our idea that tense and modal base shift correlate, just as they do with modal verbs.

Regarding DENY, recall our earlier discussion in chapter 2:

(71) O Nicholas arinthike oti/*na i Ariadne ton
the Nicholas denied.3sg that.IND/SUBJ the Ariadne him
voithise.
helped.3sg
Nicholas denied that Ariadne helped him.

(72) O Nicholas arinthike *oti/na voithisi tin
 the Nicholas denied.3sg that.IND/SUBJ help.NONPAST.3sg the
 Ariadne.
 Ariadne
 Nicholas refused to help Ariadne.

We see the familiar correlation: subjunctive with NONPAST, indicative with PAST (or present). The indicative version is a negative assertion (briefly mentioned in chap. 1). DENY is a variant of SAY, but this time the commitment of the subject $i$ is to $\neg p$, i.e., negative commitment. Negative commitment, as we said in chap. 2, is homogeneous, subjective (at least doxastic) commitment to $\neg p$, and it therefore selects indicative.

If $i$ denies that $p$, and $i$ is truthful, then $i$ knows or believes $\neg p$ to be true. The point here is that subjective commitment of the solipsistic construal predicts indicative with even negative assertive verbs. Ultimately, subjective commitment is a positive, in other words, veridical stance to the prejacent proposition, i.e., either to $p$ or its negation— as opposed to the nonveridical stance which does not allow $i$ to fully commit to $p$.

The subjunctive version comes with NONPAST and shifts the modal base to a bouletic one: all bouletic worlds are $\neg p$ worlds. In Italian we do not have NONPAST, therefore no forward shifting with the subjunctive, hence no triggering of a bouletic M either. Rather, the indicative versus subjunctive shift reflects whether $p$ is settled in the common ground, and, as we have made explicit earlier, mood morphemes can indicate whether $p$ should be appended to the mental space of the attitude holder or to the common ground. In Italian, DENY is a typical example of the shift to the common ground.

(73) Maria nega cha ha ucciso Marco.
 Mary denies that have.IND.3sg killed Marco
 Mary denies that she has killed Marco.

(74) Maria nega cha abbia ucciso Marco.
 Mary denies that have.SUBJ.3sg killed Marco
 Mary denies that she has killed Marco.

In the subjunctive case, it is common knowledge that Mary has killed Marco. In the indicative case, all participants but Mary are committed to *p*. In this case, nonveridicality is part of the common ground, rather than the epistemic space (see Mari 2017a, b).

(75) Subjunctive DENY, Italian:
$[\![i \text{ deny } p]\!]^{i,\text{CG},M_{rc}}$ is defined iff
$\exists w' \in \text{CG}: \neg p(w') \wedge \exists w'' \in \text{CG}: p(w'')$
If defined,
$[\![i \text{ say } p]\!]^{i,\text{CG},M_{rc}} = 1$ iff
$\forall w''' \in M_{rc}(\text{CG}) : \neg p(w''')$

Note that the same analysis can be extended to subjunctive SAY in Italian, where there is free variation between nonveridicality in the modal base and nonveridicality in the CG. There is an obvious connection between the two (Mari 2015, 2017a, 2019): if the speaker is uncertain about *p* and shares the C(ommon) G(round) set with the interlocutors, then the CG also does not settle *p* and nonveridicality can be a property of either the belief model or the CG.

## 5.7 The (Non)veridicality Theory of Mood Selection

Now that we finished the analysis of the major bouletic attitudes, we want to take stock in this final section to put together the landscape of mood selection as it emerges from the study of doxastic, bouletic, and modal attitudes. The result is a semantic typology of propositional attitudes based on their (non)veridicality and a small number of premises that allow predictions for other attitudes and larger sets of data.

Here are the basic premises that hold crosslinguistically in Greek, and Italian, French:

(76) Two kinds of propositional attitude verbs (includes modal verbs):
 (i.) Solipsistic attitude verbs in ii: no presupposition.
 (ii.) Presuppositional attitude verbs: mixed lexical entry with presupposition(s) and a truth condition.

(77) Veridical attitudes:
 (i.) Epistemic attitudes are veridical.
 (ii.) Solipsistic attitudes are veridical: they entail that *p* is true in the anchor's *i* modal space.

(iii.) The modal space is a variant of: epistemic (*M*), doxastic (Dox(i)), or bouletic (Boul(i)).

BELIEVE is the prototypical doxastic solipsistic attitude, and HOPE the prototypical solipsistic bouletic.

Nonveridical attitudes, on the other hand, obey the Nonveridicality Axiom, as can be recalled:

(78) Nonveridical propositional attitudes and modals:
A propositional attitude verb and a modal (ATTITUDE) is nonveridical if ATTITUDE obeys the Nonveridicality Axiom.

(79) Nonveridicality Axiom:
(i.) For ATTITUDE, ATTITUDE obeys the Nonveridicality Axiom iff ATTITUDE $p$ presupposes that the modal base M of the anchor $i$ of ATTITUDE is nonveridical, i.e., partitioned into $p$ and $\neg p$ worlds.
(ii.) An ATTITUDE that obeys the Noniveridicality Axiom is called nonveridical.

The nonveridical modal base is in most cases epistemic, which means that the nonveridical space induces epistemic uncertainty.

The mood morphemes indicative and subjunctive are sensitive to the assertion (indicative) and the presupposition (subjunctive, indicative *pu* in Greek). Here are the licensing conditions for subjunctive and indicative:

(80) Licensing condition for the *subjunctive* mood:
The subjunctive is licensed in the complement of a nonveridical ATTITUDE.

(81) Licensing condition for the *indicative* mood:
The indicative is licensed in the complement of a veridical ATTITUDE.

The mood morphemes mark the scope of ATTITUDE as veridical or nonveridical; at the same time, as illustrated in chap. 4, they provide anchoring instructions about informational update of the upcoming proposition in the scope of the ATTITUDE.

Factivity characterizes epistemic verbs of knowledge but also emotive factive verbs, as we will discuss in chapt.7. We also established antifactivity as antiveridicality presupposition— that $p$ is not true, or that $i$ believes $p$ to not be true— of desire verbs such as WANT and nonassertive moods such as the imperative.

(82) Antifactivity presupposition of ATTITUDE:
ATTITUDE is antifactive if $i$ ATTITUDE $p$ at $t_u$ presupposes that $p$ is not true at $t_u$, or that $i$ believes that $p$ is not true at $t_u$.

The ATTITUDE here is a propositional attitude verb. We have not found any modal verbs that are anti-factive. Modal verbs, even in the weakest form of possibility always allow $p$ as an option in the modal base. They are, in other words, nonveridical but never antifactive.

Regarding porpositional attitude verbs specifically, the picture we are building looks as in fig. 5.1:

(83) DOXASTIC:
  a. Solipsistic doxastics: *oti*-belief in Greek, indicative belief in Italian.
  b. Suppositional doxastics: subjunctive belief in Italian.

(84) BOULETIC (HOPE type) / PERSUADE:
  a. Solipsistic bouletic: *oti*-HOPE in Greek, indicative HOPE in Italian.
  b. Suppositional bouletic: subjunctive-HOPE in Italian.

(85) BOULETIC (WANT type):
Suppositional only; subjunctive across languages.

(86) SAY:
  a. Solipsistic SAY. *oti*-SAY in Greek; indicative-SAY in Italian: total commitment to $p$ the attitude holder aligns with the common ground.
  b. Suppositional SAY. Subjunctive-SAY in Italian: partial commitment the attitude holder does not align with the common ground.

| Notion | Value | Attitude Type | Greek | Italian |
|---|---|---|---|---|
| Doxastic | Solipsistic | Belief | *pistevo, nomizo* (believe, think) | *credere, pensare,* ' (believe, think), *essere sicuro* (be certain), *essere convinto* (be convinced) |
| | | Dream Imagine | *onirevome* (dream) *fandazome* (imagine) | *sognare* (dream) *immaginare* (imagine) |
| | Suppositional | Belief | | *credere* (believe), *pensare* (think), *essere sicuro* (be certain), *essere convinto* (be convinced) |
| | | Memory | *thimame* (remember) | *ricordarsi* (remember |
| | | Perception | *vlepo, akouo* (see, hear) *fenome* (seem) | *sembrare* (seem) |
| | | Epistemic modal verbs | epistemic modal verbs | *è necessario, possible, probabile*; (it is necessary, possible, probable) |
| Bouletic | Solipsistic | Want | *thelo* (want) | *volere* (want) |
| | | Deontic Modals | deontic modals | *è necessario* (it is necessary) |
| | Suppositional | Hope | *elpizo* (hope) | *sperare* (hope) |
| | | Promise | *iposxome* (promise) | *promettere* (promise) |
| | | Persuade | *pitho* (persuade) | *persuadere* (persuade) |
| | | Say Deny | *leo* (say) *arnoume* (deny) | *dire* (say) *negare* (deny) |

FIGURE 5.1 Notions, values and attitude types: solipsistic and suppositional variants

As figure 5.1 shows, Greek lexicalizes attitudes as solipsistic (when not antifactive). Italian has a preference for the suppositional lexicalization. French is in between: it lexicalizes nonfactive epistemics as solipsistic but has a preference for suppositional bouletic. We can conceive the lexical realizations in each language as different instantiations of lexical concepts for attitude verbs (which we refer to as "notions"). While we can foresee blocking rules for Greek and Italian (in Greek the suppositional version is blocked, whereas Italian blocks the solipsistic version), as we have extensively argued in our discussion in chap. 3, any theory of mood will have to allow for flexibility intra- and cross-linguistically. Recall, indeed, that there is flexibility even in Greek with both bouletic and doxastic attitudes (of memory, semblance, and perception).

No theory of blocking will be able to account for such complexity of pattern in mood shift, which can be the result of diachronic variation and contact across verb classes. What we hope to have shown is that propositional attitude verbs have different lexicalizations, which we think of as manifestations of an abstract meaning or notions (see early discussions in Giannakidou 1997, 1998 and Mari 2003). Attitude classes can be understood as attitude concepts, and the two variants can be seen as the linguistic realization of the values of these conceptual categories (in our specific case, solipsistic and suppositional). Which variant is realized in which language and for which type of verb can be predicted to some extent by the nature of the verb—recall that memory, perception, and semblance are by nature more flexible, and can be vague or gappy. No theory can fully predict the multifactorial variation observed, but the one we developed so far makes a good job of establishing the possible constraints as they follow from the attitude's layers of meaning.

CHAPTER SIX

# Ability Modals, Temporality, and Implicatives

In this chapter we want to accomplish three tasks. First, we want to explain why the subjunctive/infinitive is chosen with ability modals and implicative verbs, instead of a finite tensed clause when a language makes it available. The selection of the subjunctive is expected with ability modals since, as modals, they obey the Nonveridicality Axiom. We propose a new analysis of ability modality (building on earlier work by Giannakidou 2001; Mari 2010, 2013, 2015a, 2017c; Giannakidou and Staraki 2012; and Thomason 2005) by treating the modal ABLE as the dispositional counterpart of epistemic MUST, entailing action to $p$ only in the Ideal worlds.

Implicatives, on the other hand, appear to pose a challenge for the subjunctive since it looks like—at least in Karttunen's initial approach—they entail that $p$ is true. We offer an analysis of MANAGE as an aspectual operator presupposing that a volitional agent $i$ tried to bring about $p$, without, in fact, entailing actualization of $p$. This presupposition alone suffices to license the subjunctive, which, as we argued, is triggered by a nonveridical presupposition. Our challenging of Karttunen's idea that MANAGE $p$ entails $p$ echoes recent voices in the literature (Baglini and Francez 2015; Nadathur 2016), but our own account relies on the affinity between managing and trying, and the nonveridicality of trying.

Under certain circumstances, ability modals do allow entailment to $p$, i.e., the entailment that the ability was actualized and led to $p$ ("actuality' entailment"). The actuality entailment renders the prejacent true at a past time, and depends crucially, we newly argue, on ABLE being embedded under PAST. We offer a thorough analysis of this phenomenon based on Mari (2016b), consistent with the fact that the choice of subjunctive mood is not affected. We show that the actuality entailment depends on PAST, not perfective aspect as previously thought. In our analysis, implicative operators and ability modals in the veridical reading are not equivalent, contrary to Bhatt (1999). Extending our theory of mood thus far, we argue that when the actuality entailment arises, the modal remains nonveridical in the presupposition.

## 6.1 Core Patterns of Ability Modals and Implicatives

Ability in English is expressed through modal verbs and expressions such as *can, be able to, be capable of*, and similar expressions:

(1)  a. Ariadne can solve this problem.
     b. Ariadne is able to solve this problem.
     c. Ariadne is capable of solving this problem.

In Greek, Italian, and French, lexicalizations of ability relate to the possibility modal *bori, pouvoir, potere* (see Staraki (2013, 2017) for an extensive presentation for Greek; Mari (2015a) for Italian and French). The ability modal appears to be homophonous to the possibility modal but, unlike the latter, the ability modal has personal syntax:

(2)  Ta pedia    borun   na/*oti           pane           sto     spiti
     The children can.3pl that.SUBJ/IND go.IMPF.3pl to-the home
     mona tus.
     alone them
     Ability: The children are able to go home on their own.
     Permission: The children are allowed to go home by themselves.

Here we see the verb *boro* in the third person plural, agreeing with the plural *children*. As we showed earlier, the epistemic *bori* is invariant in the third person singular, almost particle-like. With the personal *boro*, the epistemic reading is excluded:

(3)  Ta pedia    bori    na/*oti           ine            sto     spiti
     The children can.3sg that.SUBJ/IND go.IMPF.3pl to the home
     mona tus.
     alone them
     Epistemic only: The children may be home alone (as far as I know).

(4) Ta pedia borun na/*oti ine sto spiti
the children can.3pl that.SUBJ/IND go.IMPF.3pl to-the home
mona tus.
alone them
Permission only: The children are allowed to be home alone.

Notice here that the stative predicate *be home alone* cannot combine with the ability *borun*; the only possible reading with the stative is that of permission.

In Italian and French, we have similar effects (see Kronning 1996). Ability and epistemic modals have the same morphosyntactic profile,[1] but ability is incompatible with stative meaning:

(5) a. Gianni può aprire la porta con il naso.
      John can open the door with the nose
      John can open the door with his nose.
   b. Gianni può essere malato. (epistemic only)
      John can be ill
      John might be ill.

(6) a. Jean peut ouvrir la porte avec son nez.
      John can open the door with his nose
      John can open the door with his nose.
   b. Jean peut être malade. (epistemic only)
      John can be ill
      John might be ill.

We immediately note that abilitative modals require a nonstative predicate, as ability is ability to act. The abilitative/epistemic distinction correlates with embedding of eventive and statives respectively, as can be recalled from our discussion in chapter 3. The Italian ability modal selects an infinitive and not a subjunctive. This is because obviation is not tolerated, and it is obviation that allows the subjunctive generally in Romance. In Greek, the infinitive is not an option because all sentential complements must be finite, as we know. We will continue to take the infinitive and the subjunctive to be equivalent, and specifically in the case of ability modals—and similar control verbs—we will argue that they contain

---

1. Note, nonetheless, that only nonepistemic CAN in French can pronominalize.

*zero* tense, although it is a morphological nonpast. Zero tense is thus another possible denotation for a morphological nonpast, to be distinguished from NONPAST which has future orientation and which we have discussed extensively thus far. We also assume, following Giannakidou and Staraki (2013) and Staraki (2013), that the Greek ability verb *boro* is a separate lexical item from the possibility modal *bori* which is invariant. Finally, we acknowledge that abilitative but not epistemic modals can be pronominalized.

As modal verbs, *boro, pouvoir, potere* ability modals are expected to obey the Nonveridicality Axiom which requires that the modal base be nonveridical. They are also objectively nonveridical: ABLE (the children go home) does not entail that the children went, will, or are going home. Ability itself is a disposition, i.e., a state, which can be a precondition for action. However, the mere disposition does not entail that action is taken. The ability of Ariadne to solve this problem does not entail that she does or did solve the problem. Pure ability is thus nonveridical (Giannakidou 2001; Mari 2010b, 2015, 2016b; Mari and Schweitzer 2011; Mari, Beyssade and Del Prete 2013) and does not trigger actual truth of the prejacent clause.

*6.1.1 Ability and Action*

Portner (2009: 135) characterizes the modality expressed by ability expressions *dynamic* and considers it a subcase of volitional modality, thereby distinguishing ability from epistemic or modality deontic (which are characterized by Portner as *priority* modals). Unlike epistemic modals, where the key anchor is the speaker, with ability verbs the subject is important, i.e., she has the ability to do something. From this perspective, the ability modal looks more like an attitude verb—where we saw the key individual anchor is the subject. The term "root" modal is used sometimes to reflect this similarity. The subject of the ability modal is typically agentive (see also Hackl 1998; Staraki 2013), in contrast with the subjects of epistemic or deontic modalities, and "controls" the action or state expressed by the complement clause (something not observed typically with propositional attitudes).

The proper treatment of ability has not been an easy task. One dimension of complication has to do with the quantificational force of the ability modal. Kenny (1975, 1976) argued that ability cannot simply be analyzed as a possibility operator within modal logic; likewise Giannakidou (2001) and Thomason (2005) propose analyses of CAN as a universal quantifier (hence like MUST). Thomason rejects the existential analysis as weak: "To put it roughly, Cross's theory of the *can* of ability is based on equivalence between *I can* and *If I tried I might*. This doesn't seem right; *If I tried I would* is a more intuitive conditional explication. This raises a fairly complex and delicate issue, one that is crucial for the logical analysis of ability." (Thomason 2005: 7). The data discussed in Giannakidou 2001, and Giannakidou and Staraki (2013), support this stronger analysis of ability which we will adopt in this chapter.

Another fact about ability is that can be understood in terms of enabling factors as well as temporal constraints. As Thomason, again, puts it: "In general, ability can depend on favorable circumstances, on the presence of appropriate knowledge, and on non-epistemic properties of the agent. I can truly say I can't write a check either because my bank balance is negative, or because I don't know where my checkbook is, or because my hand is injured. I believe that the same sense of *can* is involved in each case." (Thomason 2005: 3). Additionally, ability can be understood as a general disposition of the subject (holding generically) or as being anchored to a specific situation and time. An example like *I can lift a fifty pound rock* would be most plausibly understood as generic; it attributes a property to an agent that holds under a wide variety of times and circumstances, perhaps to all that are Ideal, as we will argue here (see also Thomason 2005: 3). J.-H. Lee (2006) further shows that, in Korean, generic and time-bound CAN are realized by lexically distinct verbs, showing that the difference between generic ability and time-bound ability can be lexicalized in a language. So, abilities may be generic or time-bound dispositions for action; but neither generic, nor time bound abilities imply acting on the ability. Ability is therefore nonveridical and the choice of subjunctive in Greek is expected.

Ability expressions, however, can also be used to refer to real actions. Aristotle expresses this difference in the following way (On Interpretation 23a, 7-13): "'Possible' itself is ambiguous. It is used, on the one hand, of facts and things that are actualized; *it is possible for someone to walk, inasmuch as he actually walks*, and in general we call a thing *possible2*, since it is now realized. On the other hand, *possible1* is used of a thing that might be realized; it is possible1 for someone to walk, since in certain conditions he would." Notably, Aristotle aims to distinguish two readings of possible, and *possible2* expresses an "actualized possibility" (*puissance en acte*, as Mari and Martin 2009 put it). "In fact, if *possible2* expresses an actualized possibility, on this reading, ABLE *p* entails *p*, since actualizing an ability involves performing an action" (Mari and Martin 2009: 9).

This actualized ability, as one may think of it, has been studied recently in a number of works under the label "actuality entailment" coined by Bhatt (1999) who discussed Hindi and Greek examples. Bhatt attributes the entailment to the perfective aspect on the modal verb. We give below two examples from Greek (from Giannakidou and Staraki 2013). Recall that Greek, unlike English, has a perfective/imperfective distinction in the past (as well as in the nonpast; see chap. 3 for details):

(7) John was able to escape.

(8) O Janis borese na apodrasi (#ala
 the John can.perf.past.3sg that.SUBJ escape.perf.nonpast.3sg (but
 dhen apedrase).
 not escaped)
 John was able to, and he did escape (#but he did not).

(9) O Janis boruse na apodrasi (ala
 the John can.impf.past.3sg that.SUBJ escape.perf.nonpast.3sg (but
 dhen apedrase).
 not escaped)
 John could/was able to escape (but he did not).

The sentence with perfective aspect *borese* entails that John escaped, an entailment lacking with imperfective aspect, as we see. The imperfective sentence is a statement of pure ability and is nonveridical, since it does not imply *p*. The perfective ability statement is also in the past, and it is factual: it implies that John engaged in a series of actions the result of which was the fact that he escaped.

French and Italian are similar to Greek and have also been thoroughly discussed in the literature (see, e.g., for French, Hacquard 2006, 2009, 2014; Mari and Martin 2007, 2009, Homer 2010; for Italian, Hacquard, 2006; Mari, 2010b, 2015a, 2016b).[2]

---

2. Several authors do not subscribe to an aspectual analysis, and it has been argued that causality plays a key role (Giannakidou and Staraki 2013).

(10) Jean a pu        prendre le train, #mais il ne l'a
     John has can.PAST.PART to take the train, but he not that-has
     pas pris.
     not taken
     John managed to take the train, #but he did not do it.

(11) Gianni ha potuto      prendere il treno, #ma non lo ha
     Gianni has can.PAST.PART to take the train, but not that has
     preso.
     taken
     Gianni managed to take the train, #but he did not take it.

The *imparfait* cancels the actuality entailment in French (*a contrario*, see Mari and Martin 2007 Mari 2010b, 2015 Giannakidou and Staraki 2013; Davis et al. 2009).

(12) John pouvait   prendre le train, mais il ne l'a     pas pris.
     John can.IMPF to take the train, but he not that-has    taken
     John could have taken the train, but he did not take it.

(13) Gianni poteva     prendere il treno, #ma non lo ha preso.
     John can.IMPF to take the train, #but not that has taken.
     John managed to take the train, #but he did not take it.

Bhatt and others (Hacquard 2006, Piñón 2003) argue that the actuality entailment with ability is an aspectual phenomenon. Bhatt suggests actualized ability has the logical structure PERF(ABLE $p$), whereas pure ability is GEN(ABLE $p$), and most of the literature assumes some variant of this idea. Mari and Martin 2007, 2009; and Giannakidou and Staraki 2013 challenge the given wisdom, and offer alternative accounts. In this chapter, we will discuss thoroughly the relevant facts in Greek, French, and Italian, and offer an analysis of the actuality entailment that is consistent with the ability modal obeying the Nonveridicality Axiom (following some ideas in Mari 2016b). The effect will be derived from the ability being in the scope of PAST, the role of which has been underappreciated in previous accounts.

### 6.1.2 *Implicatives*

Bhatt points out a similarity between the action reading of ability and implicative verbs such as MANAGE:

(14)  I   Ariadne katafere/borese         na/*oti
      The Ariadne managed.could.PERF.3sg that.SUBJ/IND
      ftiaksi         to aftokinito.
      fix.NONPAST.3sg the car
      Ariadne managed to/was able to fix the car.

(15)  a. Mario è riuscito   a riparare la  macchina.
         Mario is managed to repair    the car
      b. Mario ha  potuto riparare la   macchina.
         Mario has could   to repair the car
         Mario managed to repair the car.

Notice that PRES (which is the present progressive in English) is either odd or doesn't produce the actuality entailment:

(16)  #John is managing/is being able to fix the car.

(17)  John is forcing Ariadne to sign the papers.
      *Does not entail* that Ariadne signed or is signing the papers.

(18)  John is getting Ariadne to sign the papers.
      *Does not entail* that Ariadne signed or is signing the papers.

The implicative structure is therefore not inherently veridical, i.e., it does not entail *p*. Whether or not the veridical inference will be possible depends largely on tense. It is important to make this observation right at the beginning because the role of tense tends to be overlooked in almost all the accounts we know. None of the existing accounts explains why the intended veridicality entailment doesn't arise with PRES. On the contrary, under Bhatt's account, and because PRES is not generic, the veridicality inference should be allowed, contrary to fact.

Crucially, the future also doesn't license the veridical inference:

(19)  I   Ariadne tha  kataferi/boresi          na
      The Ariadne will manage.PERF.3sg/can.PERF.3sg that.SUBJ
      ftiaksi       to aftokinito.
      fix.PERF.3sg the car
      Ariadne will manage/will be able to fix the car.

Despite the presence of perfective aspect, embedding under FUT doesn't give actuality. This casts doubt on the idea that implicatives inherently entail *p*, and it also shows that actualization, contrary to what is claimed in most of the literature, cannot be simply due to perfective aspect. It seems rather to be an effect of PAST. Our own analysis is inspired by this observation: ability, unlike epistemic modals, can be in the scope of a semantic PAST. Epistemic modality in all accounts we know is higher than tense and this explains in our theory why there is no actuality entailment with epistemic modality.[3]

The semantics of MANAGE has been an issue of considerable debate. Karttunen (1971) and Karttunen and Peters (1979) present the earliest discussions. Karttunnen posits that MANAGE *p* entails *p*—which would render MANAGE veridical. The use of a nonveridical tense, however—i.e., the morphological nonpast—is inconsistent with a veridical analysis. The literature typically focuses on English, and the problem of tense and mood choice is not adequately appreciated, but it sheds new light on implicatives as we will show.

Unlike the ability modal, MANAGE does presuppose trying; and it implicates that it took (some or considerable) effort to bring about *p*:

(20) John didn't manage to fix the car *entails* that *John made an effort to fix the car.*

(21) John managed to fix the car *entails* that *John made an effort to fix the car.*

TRY itself is nonveridical (Giannakidou 2013) and selects the subjunctive. In addition, the TRY component often (but not always) gives rise to a difficulty reading. Difficulty, on the other hand, seems to not be a necessary component of actualized ability:

(22) O    Janis borese na           pji   deka bires—ke   itan efkolo!
     the John could  that.SUBJ drink ten  beers—and was easy
     John was able to drink ten beers—and it was easy!

---

3. Observe *musted*. Even when morphological past appears, e.g., epistemic *could* is not necessarily about the past: *Flavio could be home now.*

(23) O Janis katafere na          pji    deka bires—#ke itan efkolo!
     the John managed that.SUBJ drink ten   beers—and was easy
     John managed to drink ten beers—and it was easy!

In the ability sentence, John is a heavy drinker, and ten beers were easy to drink; but notice the contrast with MANAGE, which is odd with the statement of ease. Difficulty is thus not an intrinsic component of ability, at least not in the way it appears to be of MANAGE.[4] Bhatt (1999) argues that the ability modal in the perfective is an implicative verb, whereas the pure ability has the structure GEN(able). But in light of the contrast with *manage* above, simply reducing the ability modal to an implicative is not desirable. We will argue that implicatives and ability modals differ importantly in that only the actualized ability entails *p*. We will treat MANAGE as a nonactualization (therefore nonveridical) aspectual operator, explaining the use of subjunctive—a long-standing puzzle that none of the existing analyses addresses.

Our discussion proceeds as follows. In section 2, we offer an analysis of the ability modals in Greek, Italian, and French as MUST in the realm of ability. In section 3, we consider and reject previous accounts of the actualized reading of ability. In section 4, we offer our own analysis. In section 5 we discuss implicatives. We will argue that the choice of the subjunctive is justified because the implicative presupposes TRY, and trying is nonveridical. We will also follow recent analyses of the assertion of MANAGE that argue that MANAGE only entails the means to bring about the prejacent (Nadathur 2016). This analysis derives nonveridicality for MANAGE *p*, and the subjunctive is justified by nonveridicality both by the assertion and the presupposition.

## 6.2 Ability Modality

Giannakidou (2001) offers an analysis of the ability modal—which we will designate as ABLE—as a universal quantifier. We will start by

---

4. Some degree of effort can be implicated with ability, as in the example from Giannakidou and Staraki (2013) *O Janis borese na sikothi*. (John was able to stand up. It was a difficult thing!). Standing up is normally easy, but with *borese* we need a context in which it takes effort to stand up, i.e., John was sick or John is a nonwalking infant. In any case, there appears to be a contrast between ability modals and MANAGE when it comes to difficulty, something that the literature typically overlooks.

presenting that analysis; then we will adjust it to the framework developed in chapter 2 so that a full parallel to epistemic MUST will be established.[5]

### 6.2.1 Some Background Notions

As we mentioned at the beginning, it has been common to admit that the semantics of mere possibility is too weak for ability verbs. Giannakidou (2001), Thomason (2005), and Portner (2009) are recent discussions (see also references therein); Chierchia and McConnell-Ginet (1992: 238) also admit that the analysis of *can* as a possibility modal is "certainly not right".[6]

The problem with mere possibility is that it conceptualizes ability as occasional, i.e., it makes $ABLE\ i\ p$ true in case there is some (and possibly random) outcome associated with a manifestation of $i$'s ability (see Thomason 2005; Kenny 1975, 1976; and Mari and Martin 2009; Mari 2012, 2015a, 2017c on this point). The basis of our discussion, then, is that in all ideal worlds consistent with $i$'s abilities, $i$ carries out $p$ — but the mere circumstantial modal analysis of possibility cannot capture this. The individual anchor $i$, crucially, is the sentence subject, i.e., the subject argument of ABLE. In Greek, Italian, and French, the relevance of the agent is suggested clearly by the fact that the ability modal is a personal verb, as we mentioned, contrary to the epistemic modal of possibility *bori* which has impersonal syntax.[7] The same holds, as we showed in (1), for the deontic modal.

Giannakidou (2001), to our knowledge, is the first explicit analysis of the ability modal as a universal modal. The reasoning is justified as follows. In an example like *John can swim*, for each world we consider, John will have the ability to swim in that world. Though this definition seems to work in worlds where John knows indeed how to swim (and he knows that he knows that) due to training or natural talent, in worlds where John didn't learn how to swim, or hasn't discovered his natural talent yet, $p$ is clearly not true, Giannakidou argues. Therefore, we need to restrict the

---

5. See also Maier (2016) for the role of ordering sources with dispositional modality.
6. See Hackl (1998) for an existential analysis.
7. It therefore follows that the ability modal is lexically distinct from the possibility one, hence one should not expect the possibility analysis to carry over to ability in the first place. As for the question of why the possibility paradigm is explored and not *prepi*, the answer can simply be because in Greek the latter lacks personal syntax entirely.

set of worlds in the modal base to those worlds in which people have abilities to do things (because of proper training, natural talents, or whatever other reason), and where people are aware of these abilities. Giannakidou calls these worlds the *ability modal base*; following the standard Kratzerian framework, the ability base is a function from $w$ to worlds $w'$, at least as normal as $w$, compatible with what an agent $i$ is capable of doing at $w$.

(24)   $K_{ability}(i)(w) = \{w' : \forall p[i \text{ is capable of } p(w) \rightarrow p(w')]\}$ (Giannakidou 2001: 702).

This is a good start; but a problem is raised by this definition, namely that whenever the agent has an ability in a world, she actualizes that ability in that world ($p$ is true). We will develop here an account that does not encode this notion of obligatory actualization. Within this modal base, we need to partition between worlds where $i$ undertakes action to bring about $p$, and worlds in which $i$ has not taken such action.

The truth condition for *boro* given by Giannakidou is as follows:

(25)   For all worlds w' in $K_{ability}$, there is a world $w''$ in $K_{ability}$ such that $w'' <_w w'$, and for every other world $w''' <_w w''$ in $K_{ability}$, $p$ is true in $w'''$. (ABILITY CAN; Giannakidou 2001: (132))

Given the fact that abilitative modals can give rise to actuality entailments, the role of the ingredients involved in turning ability into action is crucial. The notion of ability needs some rethinking in order to better understand the role of tense as well as the nature of the relation between ability and action. We proceed now to offer an analysis within our current system.

### 6.2.2 *ABLE and MUST: The Structure of the Ability Modal Base*

The analysis we offer here is exactly parallel to epistemic MUST. We start by reminding the key features of MUST. Recall the epistemic modal base:

(26)   $M(i)(t_u)(w_0) = \lambda w'(w'$ is compatible with what is known by the speaker $i$ in $w_0$ at $t_u$)

Recall that our notation $M(i)$ corresponds to the Kratzerian notation using set intersection $\cap f(w_0, i, t_u)$, where this returns the set of worlds compatible with what is known in $w_0$ by $i$. Modality, in our framework, is always subjective, allowing also for cases where the epistemic agent $i$ is a collective individual or group of people (and this may be used to capture what others would call objective modality). The epistemic modality is, as we said, dependent to knowledge at $t_u$, as is often acknowledged in the literature (see Portner 2009; Hacquard 2006, 2010; Giannakidou and Mari 2016a, b 2018a, b).

Now, when it comes to ABLE, we will continue using K to designate the modal base, and $i$ will be the subject of ABLE. Ability is parametric to time; people have different abilities at different times. Ability as a general predisposition is thought to be atemporal (recall that Bhatt uses GEN), and certain abilities may indeed be atemporal, e.g., such as the ability to talk, to walk, to breath etc. However, abilities are also skills, and they become parametric to time and training, age, and so forth. The ability to drive, to speak French, to cook well are such abilities — and one can actually argue that all abilities are of this type.[8]

(27)  $K(i)(t_u)(c) = \lambda w'(w'$ is compatible with what the subject $i$ is capable of doing in $w_0$ at $t_u$)

K encompasses what $i$ can do at $t_u$. Knowledge is always anchored to $t_u$, but this is not so for ability. Time sensitive variants of ABLE, as in Korean, or embedding ABLE under PAST (the specific configuration producing actuality entailment) have the temporal argument of K affected: it is, by default, $t_u$ if ABLE is in the present tense, but the temporal parameter can be in the past or future depending on whether ABLE is embedded under PAST or FUT. Unlike epistemic modality which doesn't scope under tense, the ability modal is often characterized as root modal and has regular syntax that allows it to appear under tense. The actuality entailment is a case where ABLE has narrow scope below PAST, and, anticipating our analysis of the phenomenon, the K parameter in this case is set to a time prior to $t_u$.[9]

---

8. See also discussion in Menendez-Benito (2013) on the possible ingredients of an abilitative modal base.
9. The same, we will argue, holds for deontic modals: the deontic MUST can scope below PAST. In this case, an actuality inference is also triggered, although it is only an implicature; more discussion follows in section 4.

The modal base of epistemic MUST, as we noted, is nonveridical about the proposition $p$ denoted by its prejacent, and contains both $p$ and $\neg p$ worlds. To derive the truth conditions of MUST we assumed with the literature (see, e.g., Portner, 2009) that MUST uses a set of propositions $S$ which describe shared stereotypical/normalcy conditions. Given the epistemic modal base $M(i)(t_u)(w_0)$, in chapter 2, we have defined Ideal$_S$ as a function over $M(i)(t_u)(w_0)$. The output Ideal$_S$ is a subset of $M(i)(t_u)(w_0)$:

(28)  Ideal$_S$ $(M(i)(t_u)(w_0)) = \{w' \in M(i)(t_u)(w_0) : \forall q \in S(w' \in q)\}$

So defined, Ideal$_S$ delivers the worlds in the epistemic modal base, a subset of $M(i)$, in which all the propositions in $S$ are true. $S$ is a set of propositions that corresponds to common ground norms. Since only those worlds are considered in which *all* the propositions in $S$ are true, the function Ideal$_S$ determines a cut-off point. (The set Ideal$_S$ is also parametric to time. Unless otherwise stated, we consider that Ideal$_S$ is determined at the actual world and at the utterance time).

The basic truth condition of MUST requires that $p$ is true in the Ideal set of $M(i)$. Tense comes from below MUST and can be either a semantic present (PRES) or past. (FUT is a case of MUST scoping above a NON-PAST, a case that we will not consider here.) Given a set Ideal$_S$ and the utterance time $t_u$,

(29)  $[\![\text{prepi/devere/must (PAST }(p))]\!]^{M,i,S}$ is defined only if $M(i)$ is nonveridical and is partitioned into Ideal$_S$ and $\neg$Ideal$_S$ worlds. If defined,
$[\![\text{prepi/devere/must (PAST }(p))]\!]^{M,i,S} = 1$ iff $\forall w' \in \text{Ideal}_S : \exists t' \prec t_u : p(w', t')$

(30)  $[\![\text{prepi/devere/must (PRES }(p))]\!]^{M,i,S}$ is defined only if $M(i)$ is nonveridical and is partitioned into Ideal$_S$ and $\neg$Ideal$_S$ worlds. If defined,
$[\![\text{prepi/devere/must (PRES }(p))]\!]^{M,i,S} = 1$ iff $\forall w' \in \text{Ideal}_S : p(w', t_u)$

(To keep things simple here, we ignore the role of the metaevaluation, although we do seem to get the Positive Polarity Item effect: *John is not able to sing* only has the expected MUST above negation reading). Echoing Giannakidou and Mari (2016a, b), we said that we can think of Ideal$_S$ as the "inner" domain of MUST, and $M(i)$ as the "outer" domain. The outer domain is a nonveridical epistemic space that does not as a whole support $p$; but the Ideal$_S$ space is veridical: all worlds are $p$ worlds. In other words, MUST is nonveridical with respect to M, but veridical with respect to Ideal$_S$. This accounts for why we say that MUST expresses partial commitment: it expresses commitment to $p$ in the Ideal$_S$ subset of $M(i)$. This makes it stronger than MIGHT, and grants MUST *mixed* veridicality status. Because of the nonveridical $M(i)$, MUST satisfies the licensing condition for the subjunctive we posited, and this explains why the complement of MUST appears in the subjunctive.

ABLE works in a parallel way but now we have $K(i)(t_u)(w_0)$. We define Ideal$_\mathcal{R}$ as a function over $K(i)(t_u)(w_0)$. The output Ideal$_\mathcal{R}$ is a subset of $K(i)(t_u)(w_0)$:

(31)  Ideal$_\mathcal{R}$ $(K(i)(t_u)(w_0)) = \{w' \in K(i)(t_u)(w_0) : \forall q \in \mathcal{R}(w' \in q)\}$

Now Ideal$_\mathcal{R}$ delivers the worlds in K, a subset of $K(i)$ where all abilities are carried out. The function Ideal$_S$ determines a cut-off point, as with epistemic MUST.

*What are the Ideal worlds with ability?* In our account, circumstances establish a divide between worlds in which the ability is actualized and those in which it is not. To actualize abilities at least two preconditions must be met. First, the circumstantial preconditions must be satisfied, and again, normality plays a role: the world has to function in the normal way with the usual causal laws. Second, the agent must want to bring about $p$. Volition has been recognized as a precondition of ability several times in the literature (see discussion in Mari and Martin 2007; Giannakidou and Staraki 2013, which develop an account based on volitional causation). The volitional agent $i$ might not be the entity denoted by the subject, but there is a notion of *plan* and possibly of *goal* underlying abilitative modality (Thomason 2005; Mari 2016b; Mari 2015a among others). In this respect, parametrizing the ABLE modal to the volitional agent $i$ is going to be critical if we want to understand the entailment of actuality. Notice, crucially, that nonvolitional agents are impossible:

(32) #The wind was able to break the window.

Now let us consider the lower tense.

### 6.2.3 Zero Tense, Obligatory Control

With epistemic MUST, as can be recalled, the lower tense can be quite free: a present, past, or nonpast (in which case the MUST is predictive). However, the complement of ABLE lacks this flexibility and only accepts morphological nonpast forms, perfective or imperfective:

(33)   a. I     Ariadne bori    na         odigisi                    (tora).
          the Ariadne can  that.SUBJ drive.perf.nonpast.3sg  now
          Ariadne is capable of driving right now.
       b. I     Ariadne bori    na         odigi.
          the Ariadne can  that.SUBJ drive.impf.nonpast.3sg
          Ariadne can drive (generally).

Recall that in French and Italian we only have infinitives, the tense of which is also nonpast. In Greek, as can be seen, two nonpast forms are possible: the perfective (which we have seen so far to be a semantic NON-PAST and which forward shifts), and the imperfective nonpast, which is a semantic PRES or the generic tense, and does not forward shift. The imperfective version above is a statement that Ariadne has generally the ability to drive, but the perfective statement is that Ariadne has at present the ability to undertake driving. In other words, the perfective vs. imperfective contrast with the nonpast marks a divide between general ability versus the time-space-bound ability (a difference that can be lexicalized in some languages, e.g., in Korean, Lee 2008). Perfective aspect still does not entail that Ariadne is driving now, but it anchors the ability to now.

Importantly, there is no forward shifting despite the use of nonpast with perfective; this is because the ability holds at the time of utterance, though acting on the ability may happen afterwards.

The ability, crucially, cannot be followed by a lower past. As we can see here, if we try to embed a past tense under ABLE, only the epistemic reading arises, and the difference between perfective and imperfective goes away (for reasons that are not relevant right now):

(34) I   Ariadne bori na         odigise             (xthes).
      the Ariadne can  that.SUBJ drive.perf.nonpast.3sg now.
      Epistemic reading only: Ariadne could have driven yesterday
      #Ariadne is capable of having driven yesterday.

(35) I   Ariadne bori na         odigouse            (xthes).
      the Ariadne can  that.SUBJ drive.impf.nonpast.3sg.
      Epistemic reading only: Ariadne could have driven yesterday
      #Ariadne is capable of having driven yesterday.

This also holds in Italian, as we showed in section 1. We repeat the examples:

(36) a. Gianni può aprire la porta con il naso.
        John   can open  the door with the nose
        John can open the door with his nose.
     b. Gianni può essere malato.
        John   can be    ill
        John might be ill.

Notice the oddity of the English examples too. And in Greek, even with higher past, only the morphological non-past forms in the complement of ABLE are available:

(37) I Ariadne borouse na odigisi/*odigise.
     the Ariadne could.3sg that.SUBJ drive.perf.past.3sg/drive.
     imperf.past.3sg

(38) *Ta paidia borousan na odigisan/odigousan (xthes).
     the children could.3spl subj drive.perf.past.3pl/drive.imperf.
     past.3pl now.

We must conclude, therefore, that the ability modal is incompatible with lower past, which means that the embedded clause cannot refer to a time prior to the ability time (unlike with epistemic modals). The reason for this follows from the relation between ability and action: ability is a precondition for action, action therefore cannot precede ability temporally. The ability to do the action coincides with and is sustained through the action in the worlds where the action is carried out (for Italian and French, see Mari, 2010b, 2012, 2015, 2016b). This also follows from the nature of ability as a necessary means (Giannakidou and Staraki 2013) to carry out the action.

The only morphological tense that can be used is the nonpast, as we said; but at the same time, the nonpast cannot forward shift the ability. In other words, it does not behave like the semantic NONPAST that we are by now familiar with. What is it then, semantically?

We will assume that ABLE embeds semantically a zero tense. Zero tense characterizes a number of Greek verbs that seem to have raising-like behavior (Grano 2015, based on earlier discussion by Spyropoulos 2008). The ability modal is certainly one of these, and it does exhibit distinctive syntactic behavior in that it does not obviate, i.e., it appears to be obligatory control, a property that characterizes also English ABLE :

(39) *I   Ariadne bori  na    tragoudisi    i  Maria.
     the Ariadne able that.SUBJ sing.nonpast.3sg the Mary
     *Ariadne can for Mary to sing.

Notice the contrast with *thelo* (want):

(40) I   Ariadne theli  na    tragoudisi    i  Maria.
     the Ariadne want.3sg that.SUBJ sing.NONPAST.3sg the Mary
     Ariadne wants for Mary to sing.

Grano proposed zero tense for the nonpast with similar verbs such as *tolmo* (dare), and aspectual ones like those meaning START and FINISH:

(41) a. *I   Ariadne tolmise   na       antimilisi         i
        the Ariadne dared.3sg that.SUBJ talk-back.nonpast.3sg the
        Maria.
        Mary
        *Ariadne dared for Mary to talk back.
     b. *I   Ariadne arxise    na       antimilisi         i
        the Ariadne started.3sg that.SUBJ talk-back.nonpast.3sg the
        Maria.
        Mary
        *Ariadne started for Mary to talk back.

When you dare do something, the daring and the doing coincide: you cannot first dare and then do. The same with START. With this class of verbs, then, the embedded nonpast must logically coincide with the actions, since it is a means for the action. The property of obligatory control thus correlates with this form of coincidence tense, which we understand zero tense to be. A zero tense is truly anaphoric, i.e., it identifies with the value of the tense of ABLE, DARE, or START.

We are ready now to give the truth condition. Given a set Ideal$_\mathcal{R}$, the utterance time $t_u$, $T$ the set of times, and $i$ the main clause subject:

(42) $[\![\text{ABLE (zero-T}p))]\!]^{K,i,\mathcal{R}}$ is defined only if K($i$) is nonveridical and is partitioned into Ideal$_\mathcal{R}$ and ¬Ideal$_\mathcal{R}$ worlds. If defined,
$[\![\text{ABLE (zero-T } p))]\!]^{K,i,\mathcal{R}} = 1$ iff $\forall w' \in \text{Ideal}_\mathcal{R}: \exists t \in T : p(w',t)$

(43) $[\![\text{GEN (ABLE } (p))]\!]^{K,i,\mathcal{R}}$ is defined only if K($i$) is nonveridical and is partitioned into Ideal$_\mathcal{R}$ and ¬Ideal$_\mathcal{R}$ worlds. If defined,
$[\![\text{GEN (ABLE } (p))]\!]^{K,i,\mathcal{R}} = 1$ iff $\forall w' \in \text{Ideal}_\mathcal{R} : p(w'))$

As we see, the generic version, in accordance with our observations and the literature on genericity, has no temporal information whatsoever. A zero tense takes the value of the higher tense, but unlike NONPAST, zero tense doesn't move the time forward.

We therefore have a difference between temporal and atemporal (generic) ABLE. Aspect brings about the two versions, but semantically it plays no role other than distinguishing a generic from an episodic version of ability. With the above analysis as the base, we move on now to deal with the cases where the acting on $p$ is entailed. The property of obligatory control, as we noted, is used as a diagnostics for zero tense.

## 6.3 The Actuality Entailment: Previous Accounts

In this section, we consider previous explanations of the actuality entailment that rely mostly on aspect. Giannakidou and Staraki (2013) offer an account in terms of causality—and aspects of that account become relevant in our own analysis later.

Bhatt (1999) is the first to discuss actuality entailments, and he observes that they arise when the modal is in the perfective. We have given examples in Greek, French, and Italian here is an original one in Hindi from Bhatt:

(44) a. Yusuf havaii-jahaaz uraa sak-taa hai/thaa (lekin
    Yusuf air-ship fly can.IMPF be.PRES/be.PAST (but
    vo havaii-jahaaz nahii uraa-taa hai/thaaa).
    he air-ship neg fly-IMPF be.PRES/be.PAST)
    Yusuf was able to fly airplanes (but he doesn't/didn't fly airplanes).
  b. Yusuf havaii-jahaaz uraa sak-aa (#lakin us-ne havaii-jahaaz
    Yusuf air-ship fly can-PFV (but he-erg air-ship
    nahii uraa-yaa).
    neg fly-PFV)
    Yusuf could fly the airplane (#but he didn't fly the airplane).

Bhatt's observation has been that the perfective aspect triggers actualization and is replicated across a variety of languages that show the perfective versus imperfective contrast (recall for French, Hacquard 2006; Mari and Martin 2007; Homer 2010; Mari and Schweitzer 2011; for Italian, Hacquard 2006; Mari 2015a; for Greek, Giannakidou and Staraki 2013, among others).[10] In addition, remember that the perfective under future does not license actuality, as we showed earlier:

(45) I Ariadne tha kataferi/boresi na
    The Ariadne will manage.PERF.3sg/can.PERF.3sg that.SUBJ
    ftiaksi to aftokinito.
    fix.perf.3sg the car
    Ariadne will manage/will be able to fix the car.

Despite the presence of PERF, embedding under FUT doesn't give actuality, as we noted — and this fact alone challenges the assumption that actuality is due to perfectivity.

But let us accept, for the sake of the present discussion, the role of perfectivity in Bhatt's account and subsequent accounts in the same spirit. In the actualization reading, ability modals are argued to be identical to implicatives:

---

10. The literature on actuality entailments has been rapidly expanding, and it would be impossible to render justice here to the variety of works across languages; see also for Spanish, Borgonovo and Cummins (2007); for Blackfoot, see Davis et al. (2010) and Louie (2014). We do not discuss purely syntactic approaches such as Demirdache and Uribe-Etxebarria (2008). For an overview, see Hacquard (2014).

(46) a. Jean a pu          prendre le train, #mais il ne
       John has can.PAST/PART take    the train, #but he not
       l'a      pas pris.
       that-has not taken
       John was able to/managed to take the train, #but he did not do it.
   b. Gianni ha potuto prendere il treno, #ma non lo ha preso.
      John has can take the train, but not that has taken
      John was able to/managed to take the train, #but he did not take it.

The *imparfait* cancels the actuality entailment in French (*a contrario*, see Giannakidou and Staraki 2013; Davis et al. 2009).

(47) a. Jean pouvait    prendre le train, mais il ne l'a      pas
       John can.IMPF to take    the train, but  he not that-has not
       pris.
       taken
       John could have taken the train, but he did not take it.
   b. Gianni poteva    prendere il   treno, #ma non lo   ha preso.
      John  can.IMPF take       the train, but not that has taken
      John was able to/managed to take the train, #but he did not take it.

Bhatt (1999) proposes that the modal is ambiguous and that in addition to a non-implicative $can_1$, there is an implicative $can_2$ that behaves just like the implicative *manage to*. Bhatt also argues that the imperfective conveys generic information, which prevents the actuality entailment from arising.

Mari and Martin (2007) observe that imperfectivity *cannot* cancel the implication with implicative verbs, and can be seen in the examples below which are replicated for Greek too; Mari and Martin argue that there is no such thing as an implicative modal.

(48) a. Jean arrivait        à prendre le train, #mais il ne l'a
       John manage.IMPF to take    the train, but  he not that-has
       pas pris.
       not taken
       John managed to take the train, #but he did not take it.

b. Gianni riusciva      a prendere il   treno, #ma non lo  ha
   John   manage.IMPF to take    the train, but  not that has
   preso.
   taken
   John managed to take the train, #but he did not take it.
c. O   Janis kataferne          na   perni to   treno, #ala dhen
   the John managed.IMPF.3sg SUBJ take  the train, but  he
   to  eperne.
   not take.IMPF.3sg
   John managed to take the train, #but he did not take it.

(49) O   Janis boruse           na perni to   treno, ala dhen to
     the John managed.IMPF.3sg to take  the train, but not   it
     eperne.
     took.IMPF.3sg
     John could take the train, but he did not take it.

For now, we will describe the previous accounts in order to illustrate the current extent of available analyses. Since Bhatt (1999), theoreticians have built on the assumption that the modal is nonimplicative, non-veridical, and the actualization is the effect of aspect or causality. The debate has been very active since Bhatt (1999) and, most prominently, Hacquard (2006, 2009, 2010). Given the mismatch between implicative verbs—which remain implicative with the imperfective—and modals—which are only implicative in the perfective—two different accounts seem to be needed, and this is what we provide in section 5.

### 6.3.1 Identification of Events across Worlds

Hacquard (2006, 2009) observed that the actuality entailment does not arise when the modal has an epistemic interpretation.

(50) Jean a   pu              prendre le   train, comme il  a
     John has can.PAST.PART to take  the train, as       he has
     pu              ne pas le prendre.
     can.PAST.PART not    it take
     John might have taken the train, and he might not have taken it.

To the best of our knowledge, Hacquard (2006, 2009) remains the only work that aims at providing an explanation for the implicative-epistemic ambiguity of the modal in the perfective in French. She proposes that modal bases are parametric to events, and the interpretations of modals depend on them being anchored to different event types. Hacquard proposes a structural account for the ambiguity, such that the epistemic modal scopes above tense and aspect (consistent with what is known in the literature), and the goal-oriented modal is interpreted below temporal and aspectual operators—a position that we also endorse and which is consistent with the empirical evidence. Because we are not trying to explain the ambiguity of the modal but only actuality entailments, we focus on the theory that Hacquard offers to derive this entailment.

Hacquard seeks to maintain a nonimplicative reading of the modal. Let us consider (46-a), repeated here in (51):

(51) Jean a pu prendre le train, #mais il ne l'a pas pris.
John has can.PAST.PART to take the train but he not that-has not taken
John managed to take the train, #but he did not take it.

The modals that trigger the actuality entailment are said to be modifiers of event descriptions. The modalized event description denotes a set of events such that there is *at least one world compatible with the circumstances* in the actual world such that John takes the train in this world.

(52) $[\![_{Mod}$ can $[_{GV}$ john take the train$]]\!]^{w,B,\leqslant,c}$ = $[\![can]\!]^{w,B,\leqslant,c}$ $(\lambda w' [\![$John take the train$]\!]^{w',B,\leqslant,c})$ = $\lambda e. \exists w'$ compatible with the circumstances in $w$ such that take-the-train$(e, J, w')$

The ability modal, as we see, is simply an existential, which is a major difference with our approach (and the motivating literature we referenced in our earlier discussion). However, we will not focus on that here. Under the scope of aspect, the modal receives a "root" (the term is used by Hacquard) interpretation from being anchored to a wordly event that is introduced by aspect. The world that is introduced by aspect is the actual world. The time of predication of the temporal property is then restricted as past, and the following interpretation is obtained: "There is an event in the actual world that is located in a past interval, and there is a world that is compatible with the circumstances in the actual world in which the event is an event of John taking the train." To obtain the actuality entailment, the event located in the actual world at a past time must bear the same description as the "possible" event. To this end, Hacquard proposes the following principle.

(53) Preservation of Event Descriptions Across Worlds: for all worlds $w1$, $w2$, if e occurs in $w1$ and $w2$ and $e$ is a $P$-event in $w1$, then ceteris paribus, $e$ is a $P$-event in $w2$.

It has gone unnoticed in the literature that Hacquard's account functions properly only in the case in which the modal base contains only $P$-event worlds. This is certainly an unsuitable solution because an existential modal claim is compatible with all worlds being $P$-event worlds, but also with some of the worlds being $\neg P$-event worlds. The latter possibility, however, is blocked under Hacquard's view. We explain why.

Given the compatibility of existential modals with there being $\neg P$-event worlds in the modal space, it would have to be possible to extend the truth conditions in the following way.

(54) $[\![$Jean a pu prendre le train$]\!]^{w,b,c,\leqslant} = 1$ iff $\exists e[e$ in $w \wedge \tau(e) \subseteq t \wedge t \prec t_u \wedge \exists w'$ compatible with the circumstances in $w$ such that takes-the-train$(e, J, w') \wedge \exists w''$ compatible with the circumstances in $w$ such that $\neg$takes-the-train$(e, J, w'')]$

As we said, the modalized event description denotes a set of events such that there is at least one world compatible with the circumstances in the actual world, such that John takes the train in this world. There might be other worlds in the modal base in which John does not take the train. According to the principle 53, given (54), the actual world can turn out to be one in which the event is a $\neg P$-event. For this reason, it is not possible, under Hacquard's account, to extend the truth conditions as in (54).

Hacquard can still advance the counterargument that the problematic portion above is not part of the truth conditional content, but rather an implicature that can be canceled, just as it happens with the *some-all* pair: "Some of the students got an A, in fact, all of them did". Nonetheless, it is an implicature that *must* be canceled under Hacquard's view to obtain the entailment. If there are accessible $\neg P$-event worlds, the entailment cannot go through. Again, given the preservation of event descriptions across worlds, if some of the accessible worlds are $\neg P$-event worlds, the actual world can be identified with either a *P*-event world or a ¬*P*-event world.

Interpreting the above with a sympathetic eye, we can still concede that the principle of event identification goes through before the calculation of the implicature: the actual world is identified as being a *P*-event world in virtue of 53 and *then* the implicature (that there are ¬*P*-event worlds in the modal base) is calculated. This would be the only way to save the account, but there are several questionable assumptions that be must endorsed for it to work. Moreover, even admitting that there is such a principle of preservation of events, we would have to define a precise algorithm allowing the computation of this (pragmatic?) principle and of the implicature of existential modal quantification that the modal base contains ¬*P*-event worlds. It is unclear to us whether such a difficult enterprise would provide insights worth the effort.

### 6.3.2 Action Dependent Abilities

Mari and Martin (2007) build on the clash between the stativity of the modal and the perfective aspect. They propose that the perfective introduces a "boundedness condition," and they newly distinguish two cases: the "bare case," where no adverbs are used 51, and the cases in which temporal adverbs are used, as in (55).

(55) #Le robot a pu repasser les chemises à un stade
 the robot has can.PAST.PART iron the skirts at one stage
 bien précis de son développement, mais cette fonction n'a
 well precise of his development, but this function not-has
 jamais été utilisée.
 never been used
 the robot could iron skirts at a precise stage of its development, but this function has never been used.

They propose that the boundedness condition of the perfective aspect can be satisfied in two different ways. When the adverbs are used, they provide the temporal boundaries within which the possibility holds. In this case, there is no actuality entailment. When there are no adverbs, however, the boundaries of the action itself satisfy the boundedness condition of the perfective. In this case, the action ontologically precedes the attribution of the ability, and thus the actuality entailment arises. Let us explain while walking through the definition of action-dependent abilities (ADA) that Mari and Martin (2007) introduced to explain the entailment.

(56) Action Dependent Abilities (ADA):
(i) ADAs require an action to exist: an ADA *ontologically depends* on the corresponding action.
(ii) A unique and nonrepeatable performance suffices to *imply* the corresponding ADA.
(iii) ADAs have the same temporal boundaries as the action on which they depend and are thus bounded.

Clause (i) has the purpose of explaining the actuality entailment: the action has to *ontologically exist* in order to attribute the action-dependent ability to the agent. However, the actuality arises even when the existence of the action is not established, as in questions, in which the speaker is not asking whether John had the possibility of taking the train but whether he actually took it. As "No" is a possible answer to this question, we see that the action need not 'exist' to obtain the entailment.

(57) Il devait    partir.    Est-ce qu' il  a   pu
     he must.IMPF to leave.              he has can.PAST.PART
     prendre le   train?
     take    the train
     He had to leave. Did he manage to take the train?

Claim (ii) states that performing an action *implies* that the performer of the action had the ability to perform it. So far so good. However, why do we choose to utter an abilitative statement in some cases but not in others? Consider the following scenario. I see a dog running. Then, I utter (58):

(58) Ce chien a    pu              courir.
     this dog has can.PAST.PART   run
     This dog managed to run.

Since the ability to run is implied by the running itself, I can feel entitled to utter an abilitative statement. In the absence of any further information, the hearer would mostly likely respond:

(59) Wait a minute: there were some impediments?

In other words, the performance of an action does not always seem to justify the attribution of an ability to act, post facto. In a context in which the speaker knows $p$ but chooses to utter the weaker $\lozenge p$, the Gricean maxim is violated. The question then arises what renders such a weaker statement felicitous. The constraints on the context of use of implicative modals must therefore be spelled out.

Mari and Martin (2007) importantly propose (iii), namely that ADA has the same temporal boundaries as the action. They explain this temporal coincidence by the fact that the ability ontologically depends on the action. However, as we have seen, the action need not exist in order to derive the entailment. Other proposals explaining this coincidence have been advanced. We focus on the cases where the entailment arises, and return later to the cases in which temporal adverbs are used (55).

### 6.3.3 Actualistic Present Perfect

Homer (2010) shows that the perfective on a stative leads to actuality entailment beyond modal verbs. Example (60) entails that the house has been sold.

(60) La maison a coûté 200000 euros.
the house has cost.PAST.PART 200000 euros
The house has costed 200000 euros.

Homer's explanation resorts to an actualistic operator ACT. The schematic LF proposed by Homer for modal sentences giving rise to the Actuality Entailment is in (62).

(61) Jean a pu prendre le train.
John has can.PAST.PART take the train
John managed to take the train.

(62) [PRES [PERF [PFV [Q ACT [pouvoir [Jean prendre le train]]]]]]

The analysis for (61) is in (63).

(63) [[Jean a pu prendre le train]]$^{c,s}(c_w)$ = 1 iff there is a past interval t s.t., there is an eventuality $e$ of $s(Q)$ in t in $c_w$ s.t. no proper part of $e$ is an eventuality of $s(Q)$ and $e$ is simultaneous with a state in $c_w$ of John taking the train being possible.

Homer encodes in the semantics of ACT the simultaneity between the state of John taking the train being possible and of the event $e$, which is an event, presumably, in this case, of John taking the train.

Piñón (2011) observes that (63) does not entail the existence of an eventuality $e$ in which John takes the train. Homer (2010: 11) explains that a pragmatically determined event is entailed. As a consequence, one can legitimately wonder with Piñón (2011) how an actuality entailment is ensured given that in any realistic context there are a number of available values for $Q$.

In spite of the several insights that previous accounts have provided, the role of PAST is systematically underappreciated, and there seems to be an overemphasis on event semantics. As can be recalled, under future, perfective aspect and events cannot license the actualization reading of ability. The causality-based theory of Giannakidou and Staraki (2013) also relies on event semantics, though it emphasizes the role of ability as a causal factor in bringing about the veridicality entailment. The causality account and its underlying assumptions seem to be better suited for implicatives, and we will have to say more on this in section 5. In our next discussion, we offer our own analysis, which capitalizes on the PAST.

## 6.4 New Account: Actualizing ABLE Is Scoping below PAST

### 6.4.1 ABLE under PAST

The analysis that we adopt here follows Mari (2016b), for whom the key to understanding the actuality entailment lies in the following: (a) the relative scope of PAST, i.e., it is a necessary condition that PAST scopes higher that ABLE; (b) the presence of zero tense; and (c) the modal structure of the inner domain (the quantificational domain) of the ability modal, where Ideal$_\mathcal{R}$ is parametrized to a volitional agent $i$. Recall the truth condition:

Given a set Ideal$_\mathcal{R}$, the utterance time $t_u$, and $i$ the main clause subject:

(64)  $[\![$ABLE (zero-T$p$))$]\!]^{K,i,\mathcal{R},t}$ is defined only if K($i$) is nonveridical and is partitioned into Ideal$_\mathcal{R}$ and ¬Ideal$_\mathcal{R}$ worlds. If defined,
$[\![$ABLE (zero-T $p$))$]\!]^{K,i,\mathcal{R},t}$ = 1 iff $\forall w' \in$ Ideal$_\mathcal{R}$: there exists a time $t$ such that $p(w',t)$

Recall that the zero tense does not function prospectively but identifies with $t$, the time of evaluation for ABLE. The ability to do the action coincides with the action in the worlds where the action is carried out. This follows from the nature of ability, as we noted, which is a prerequisite to carry out the action and is sustained as the action is carried about, not prior to it.

Crucially, the logical form of actualized ability has PAST above ABLE. This means that the $t$ variable will be set to a time prior to now. There is no need for a special operator PERF, as the morphological form perfective nonpast is now a zero tense. As we said, a zero tense is a kind of anaphor, taking the value of the higher tense, in this case past, but unlike NONPAST, zero tense doesn't move the time forward. Unlike previous approaches, in our theory PERF plays no role and is therefore unnecessary. Notice that English also shows the actuality effect despite the fact that it doesn't employ aspect. The following analysis, which we adopt and extend here, is from Mari (2016b).

(65) a. ABLE = $\lambda p^{s \to \langle i \to t \rangle} \lambda w^s \lambda t^i \forall w'[w' \in \text{Ideal}_\mathcal{R}(w)(t) \land p(w')(t)]$
  b. PAST = $\lambda p^{s \to \langle i \to t \rangle} \lambda w^s \lambda t^i \exists t'[t' \prec t \land p(w)(t')]$
  c. VP = $\lambda w^s \lambda t^i p(w)(t)$

(66) Mari (2016b).

  a. ABLE (VP) = $\lambda w \lambda t. \forall w'[w' \in \text{Ideal}_\mathcal{R}(w)(t) \land [\lambda w \lambda t. p(w)(t)](w')(t)]$
   = $\lambda w \lambda t. \forall w'[w' \in \text{Ideal}_\mathcal{R}(w)(t) \land p(w')(t)]$
  b. PAST(MOD(VP)) =
   $\lambda w \lambda t. \exists t'[t' \prec t \land [\lambda w \lambda t. \forall w'[w' \in \text{Ideal}_\mathcal{R}(w)(t) \land p(w')(t)]](w)(t')]]$
   = $\lambda w \lambda t. \exists t'[t' \prec t \land \forall w'[w' \in \text{Ideal}_\mathcal{R}(w)(t') \land p(w')(t')]]$
  c. $t$ is fixed as $t_u$ and $w$ is the world of evaluation.
   Truth conditions: $\exists t'[t' \prec t_u \land \forall w'[w' \in \text{Ideal}_\mathcal{R}(w)(t') \land p(w')(t')]]$
   *Paraphrase*: There is a past time at which there is a world accessible from the world of evaluation, at which $p$ is true (e.g., John takes the train).

(67)

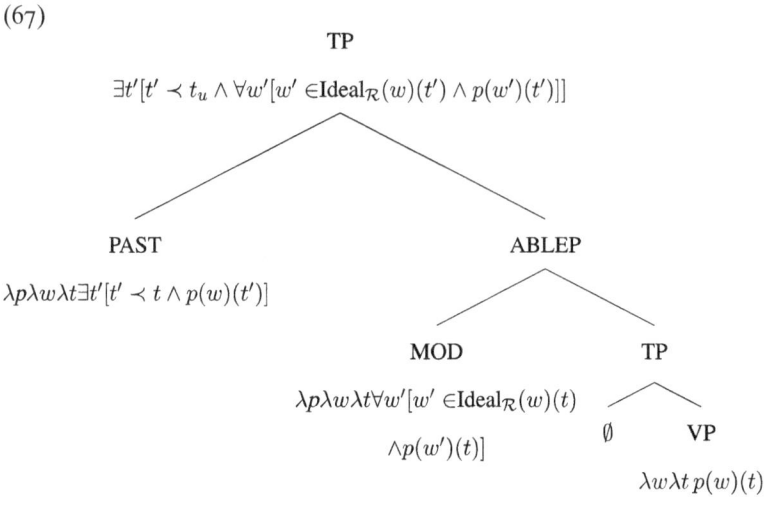

Recall that we have theorized the inner domain of abilitative modal as anchored to a volitional agent *i*. According to Mari (2016b), the agent *i* has a *goal*. We now add with Elgesem (1997), reinterpreting Belnap (1992), that the volitional agent projects a choice into the modal base (see Fig. 6.1): in this space, for each point in time the options are closed past and present-wise, whereas they are open future-wise. In Belnap, choices are conceptualized as sets of points in a branching structure where, at each point, the future is open (is a set of choice points) and the present and past are closed (choices have been made). The branching-time model recognized in Mari (2016b) representing a space where the agent achieves a goal becomes the choice space of *i*.

How does the entailment arise? Given the modal-temporal setting underlying the choice space of the agents, the answer that Mari provides is straightforward: in the veridical past, the choice space is closed. Moreover, given zero tense, there is no forward shifting of the prejacent with respect to the time at which the modal base is projected. In other terms, given the point of evaluation at which the modal base (the choice space) is projected—which is past, and at which *p* becomes true–, and given that it is the same time at which the choice space is projected, the actuality entailment arises because, at that time, the choice space is closed.

Had a prospective aspect intervened between the modal and the VP, the entailment would have not arisen, as with the French or Italian "imperfetto" (imperfect).

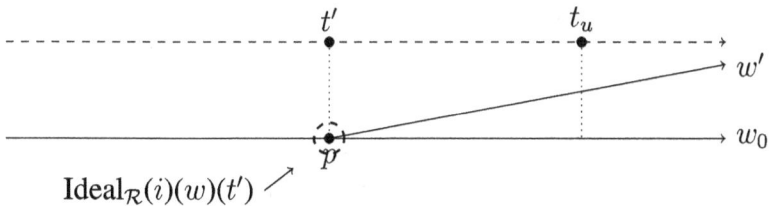

FIGURE 6.1 Choice space à la Belnap.

### 6.4.2 No Entailments When the Modal Is Not Agentive and Abilitative

Note that Mari (2016b) and our account here rely on the specific type of modal base that abilitative modal triggers — given the anchoring to the volitional agent $i$, the scoping of ABLE below PAST, and the presence of zero tense: the modal base is a choice space which has the specificity of being closed-past and present-wise. It follows that if a modal cannot embed under PAST, it won't be able to get the actualization entailment.

That this prediction is on the right track is evidenced by the fact that epistemic modals cannot occur in the past. Below, the invariant (hence epistemic) form *boruse* (existential modal in the third singular) with past is simply ungrammatical:

(68) Ta pedia *boruse/bori na odhijisoun.
 the children could.3sg/can.3sg that.SUBJ drive.3pl
 The children can drive.

Recall that the invariant *bori* is the epistemic CAN. We see that it cannot occur itself in the past. Past can scope below it, of course, as we have observed:

(69) Ta pedia bori na odhigousan.
 the children can.3sg that.SUBJ drove.3pl
 The children could have driven.

Given that the epistemic modal *bori* doesn't inflect for tense, aspect and person, we can actually think of it as a particle, since it is invariant just like particles *na, tha,,* etc.

Importantly, the ability personal *boro* can have a use as a permissive modal. We can call it deontic use. Deontic *boro* indeed combines with past, and actualization is possible. Recall our initial example:

(70) Ta pedia     borun        na          pane         sto      spiti  mona
    the children can.3pl that.SUBJ go.impf.3pl to-the home alone
    tus.
    them
    Ability: The children are able to go home on their own.
    Deontic: The children are allowed to go home by themselves.

(71) Ta pedia     borusan      na          pane         sto      spiti  mona
    the children could.3pl that.SUBJ go.IMPF.3pl to-the home alone
    tus.
    them
    Ability: The children were able to go home on their own, and they did.
    Deontic: The children could (were allowed to) go home by themselves.

As we can see, deontic and ability *boro* behave similarly. However, with the permissive reading, actualization is possible but not entailed; the above sentences are nonveridical:

(72) Ta pedia     borusan      na          pane         sto      spiti  mona
    the children could.3pl that.SUBJ go.IMPF.3pl to-the home alone
    tus,    ala dhen pigan.
    them, but not    went.3pl
    Deontic: The children could (were allowed to) go home by themselves, but they didn't.

If we consider deontic MUST, actualization is still cancelable, as expected:

(73) Ta pedia     eprepe          na          pane         sto      spiti
    the children MUST.PAST.3pl that.SUBJ go.IMPF.3pl to-the home
    mona tus,    ala dhen pigan.
    alone them, but not    went.3pl
    Deontic: The children had to go home by themselves, but they didn't.

Hence, the fact that the ability modal base depends on a volitional agent who has a choice (choice space) is key to explaining the effect of the PAST with ability in a branching-time framework, and why it is either impossible or, at best, weak, with other modals.

Consider now this example, whereby the set of alternatives is projected not from $i$ who triggers the choice space, but by the information provided by the adverb (between 3 and 5 pm; see Mari and Martin (2007) for the first observation of this phenomenon). Here the space does not have the same structure as the choice space, and this is crucial to the derivation of the entailment.

(74) Jean a pu entrer entre 3 heures et 5 heures,
John has can.PAST.PART to enter between 3 hours and 5 hours,
mais il n'est pas entré (adapted from Mari and Martin, 2007)
but he did not enter
John had the opportunity to enter between 3 and 5, but he did not enter.

This is also observed for deontic modals, when they are combined with an overt temporal adverb.

(75) Il a dû lire ce livre pendant tout le
He has must.PAST.PART read this book during whole the
mois de septembre et il ne l'a même pas touché.
month of September and he not that-has even touched
He had to read this book during the whole month of September and he did not even touch it.

Actuality entailments are specific to abilitative modals with intentionality (and thus choices).

Likewise, the entailment does not arise with past-oriented deontic modality. Here again, there is no agentivity, no choices, and nothing in the structure of the possibilities makes it possible for the entailment to arise (see Mari 2016b; Castroviejo and Oltra-Massuet 2016). Note that these are generic readings.

(76) Pour entrer tu dois avoir acheté les billets.
to get-in you must.2sg have bought the tickets
You must have bought the tickets to get in.

(77)  Tu dois    être un garçon pour pouvoir utiliser ces toilettes.
      you must.2sg be  a  male  to  can  use  this restroom.
      You must be a male to use this restroom.

Given this derivation of the entailment, our proposal faces the question of the triviality of the modal or by Gricean reasoning, of why the speaker is choosing to use the modal in comparison with the bare assertion. Our proposal is that the modal bears its nonveridicality presupposition, as in any other of its uses, excluding the aleithic.

### 6.4.3 The Nonveridicality of the Modal with the Entailment

How is the nonveridical presupposition of ABLE consistent with actualization?

Recall our distinction between the inner and the outer domain of the modal. In our theory Ideal$_\mathcal{R}$ is parametrized to $i$ and it is represented as a choice space, with its own specific structure. However, the outer domain does not have this structure. The abilitative modal base is partitioned between worlds in which $p$ is carried out and those in which it is not. To put it otherwise, an abilitative modal base is such that certain preconditions must be met in order for the action to be carried out (which include the agent volition and the normalcy of the circumstances, at the very least) and by partitioning the modal base we encode the idea that the action can fail. Note that, when this presupposition that the action can fail is not satisfied, the modal is not felicitous (see Mari, 2016b for extended discussion).

Consider the following scenario from Mari (2016b). As is well known, Usain Bolt is the fastest runner in the world, and can run 100 meters in 9.58 seconds.

(78)  Usain Bolt a  pu           battre le record du    monde
      Usain Bolt has can.PAST.PART break the record of-the world
      des  100 mètres grâce  à  son entrainement.
      of-the 100 meters thanks to his training
      Usain Bolt was able to break the 100-meter world record thanks to his training.

Breaking the world record is never taken for granted, and the possibility that even Usain Bolt does not break it is open at a time prior to the race.

The sentence is felicitous. Sentence 80, instead, is infelicitous in Context 1 and felicitous in Context 2 described in (79).

(79) a. Context 1: Usain Bolt is in his best shape and at the climax of his career.
b. Context 2: Usain Bolt is recovering from a long cold and is far from his highest standards.

(80) (#)Usain Bolt a pu courir 100 mètres en 15 secondes aujourd'hui.
Usain Bolt has can.PAST.PART run 100 meters in 15 seconds today
Usain Bolt was able to run 100 meters in 15 seconds today.

Consider context 1, (79-a), in which sentence (80) is infelicitous. Since Usain Bolt can run 100 meters in 9.58 seconds, it is taken for granted that, in his best shape, he can run 100 meters in 15 seconds, and the possibility that he does not run 100 meters in 15 seconds was not open. Sentence (80) is instead felicitous in context 2 (79-b), where Usain Bolt is recovering from a very bad cold. In this context, running 100 meters in 15 seconds is not granted; the possibility of $\neg p$ was open before $p$ becomes true.

The unmodalized sentence (81), on the other hand, is felicitous in both contexts (79-a) and (79-b). It is veridical, and does not require that $\neg p$ be an open possibility (see Mari 2016b for further discussion).

(81) Usain Bolt a couru 100 metres en 15 secondes.
Usain Bolt has run.PAST.PART 100 meters in 15 seconds
Usain Bolt has run 100 meters in 15 seconds.

Given the partitioning of the nonveridical modal base between worlds in which the action succeeds and worlds in which it does not, we can derive the inferences of difficulty which, as we mentioned, is a cancelable one. In other words, it is the nonveridicality of the modal base that lies at the foundation of the difficulty premise of ABLE (Mari 2016b).

To sum up, we have argued that the ability modal has a nonveridical modal base and will therefore select the subjunctive if the language allows it. The actualization entailment is derived by simply acknowledging (a) that ABLE scopes under PAST and (b) the ramifications of choice. There was no need to appeal to perfective aspect. The phenomenon, therefore, is not aspectual but rather modal/temporal and articulates at-issue and non-at-issue content by locating nonveridicality in the presupposition.[11]

Let us move on now to examine the class of implicative verbs.

### 6.5 Implicative Verbs and the Choice of Infinitive, Subjunctive

Karttunen (1971) identifies implicative verbs, illustrated by *manage*, as verbs giving rise to an implication as follows (examples from Baglini and Francez 2016):

(82) Solomon managed to build the temple implies that Solomon built the temple.

(83) Solomon didn't manage to build the temple implies that Solomon didn't build the temple.

It is often assumed that the verb *manage* contributes no truth-conditional content beyond that of the prejacent. Karttunen (1971: 350) writes: 'All that takes place when John manages to do something is that he does it. While intending to do is one thing and doing another, managing to do is inseparable in space and time from doing; it is the same event." In other words, this original analysis renders MANAGE $p$ equivalent to $p$, therefore, from our perspective, veridical.

*6.5.1 The Puzzle from the Perspective of Greek and Italian*

If the meaning MANAGE is veridical as per Karttunen's analysis, why do implicative verbs select the subjunctive and the infinitive?

(84) I Ariadne katafere na/*oti
the Ariadne managed.3sg that.SUBJ/IND
ftiaksi to aftokinito.
fix.PERF.NONPAST.3sg the car
Ariadne managed to fix the car.

---

11. For further developments in this direction, see Laca 2018, 2019.

(85) Mario è riuscito a riparare la macchina.
Mario is managed to repair the car
Mario managed to repair the car.

The occurrence of the subjunctive and infinitive is quite unexpected if semantically MANAGE *p* is identical to *p*, as hypothesized by Kartunnen. From the perspective of Greek and Italian (and almost all of Romance, actually) the subjunctive choice appears at odds with our idea that subjunctive depends on nonveridicality. Most of the literature focuses on English where this problem is literally invisible. But for us, this discrepancy becomes the springboard to argue that MANAGE *p*, in fact, is not veridical, and does not entail *p*.

Karttunen (1971) and Karttunen and Peters (1979) further observe that *manage* has presuppositional content. The sentences above presuppose (or "conventionally implicate") that Ariadne and Mario tried to fix the car, and that it took some sustained effort to do it. This has been referred to sometimes in the literature as the "effort" presupposition. Now, it has also been noted that the effort component can be rather weak sometimes. For instance, Coleman (1975) gives examples such as the following:

(86) a. Harry managed to insult Ursula without even trying.
b. My neighbors managed to schedule their one wild party of the year on the night before my German exam.

Here we see that the effort can even be explicitly denied without contradiction. Coleman therefore concludes that the MANAGE presupposition varies between one of effort, difficulty, and/or sheer coincidence, depending on the context of utterance. We will argue, however, that even in the case of mere coincidence, the use of a MANAGE word seems to presuppose that some effort was produced. This can be seen below:

(87) a. Harry didn't manage to insult Ursula (#without even trying).
b. #My neighbors didn't manage to schedule their one wild party of the year on the night before my German exam.

At least some effort seems to be undeniably present with MANAGE, though arguably not difficulty. In the (87-a) example, for instance, the coincidence reading is lost, and the effort presupposition is sustained. Likewise in the (87-b) example which is odd exactly because the effort inference survives but it is implausible. We think it reasonable, therefore, to posit a TRY presupposition for MANAGE. Let us formulate this initially as a generalization:

(88) TRY presupposition of MANAGE:
*i* MANAGE *p* presupposes that *i* tried *p*; where *i* is the subject of MANAGE.

The TRY component is key, we will argue, to understanding why the subjunctive mood is chosen, and why the verb meaning MANAGE *p* is not equivalent to the veridical assertion of *p*. Notice that the verbs meaning TRY also select subjunctive and infinitive:

(89) I    Ariadne prospathise/dhokimase na/*oti
     the Ariadne tried.3sg/attempted.3sg that.SUBJ/IND
     ftiaksi        to aftokinito.
     fix.nonpast.3sg the car
     Ariadne tried/attempted to fix the car.

The choice of subjunctive and zero tense (following our analysis of morphological perfective nonpast with ability modals) with verbs meaning TRY and MANAGE sheds new light on the puzzle of implicatives. It allows us to address the meaning of MANAGE knowing that the equivalence between PAST *p* and MANAGE *p* is simply not straightforward, *pace* Kartunnen. Recall again that whether we get implication to *p* (*p* to be true) depends on whether we have a higher PAST or not. PRES and FUT block the inference, as we mentioned at the beginning:

(90) #John is managing/is being able to fix the car.

(91) I    Ariadne tha kataferi    na      ftiaksi to aftokinito.
     the Ariadne will manage.3sg that.SUBJ fix.3sg the car
     Ariadne will manage to fix the car.

None of the existing accounts explains the effect of tense, specifically why the intended implication to *p* doesn't arise with PRES or FUT. At the same time, even with the past, the inference to *p* seems to be variable when it comes to other members of the implicative class (e.g., DARE, ALLOW below):

(92) I   Ariadne tolmise        na       antimilisi.
     the Ariadne dared.3sg SUBJ talk.back.nonpast.3sg
     Ariadne dared to talk back.

(93) I   daskala epetrepse   tin Ariadne na   fiji        noritera, ala
     the teacher allowed.3sg the Ariadne SUBJ leave.3sg earlier,   but
     telika  dhen xriastike.
     finally not  needed.3sg
     The teacher allowed Ariadne to leave early but in the end it was
     not necessary.

As we see, not all implicatives give rise to a veridical inference: the *allow* sentence does not imply *p*. Implicatives as a class, therefore, cannot simply be identical to bare *p* in implying *p*. The fact that they do not embed past further argues against the equivalence:

(94) *I  Ariadne katafere       na        eftiakse       to aftokinito.
     the Ariadne managed.3sg that.SUBJ fix.PAST.3sg the car
     *Ariadne managed to have fixed the car.

(95) *Flavio è riuscito   ad aver riparato la   macchina.
     Flavio is managed to have repaired the car
     *Flavio managed to have fixed the car.

The exclusion of past is at odds with the idea that the MANAGE sentence is simply equivalent to the unembedded past sentence. Crucially, implicatives do not convey a propositional attitude; they are not propositional attitude verbs. So, wherever inferencing is done, it is done indeed by the speaker who chooses to use MANAGE instead of the unembedded sentence, and in so doing she chooses to do something substantially more than merely asserting *p*.

It appears that there are two main issues about MANAGE. The one issue is whether the MANAGE sentence asserts *p* or not. If it does, it is veridical and the choice of subjunctive seems puzzling. The second issue is the presupposition of TRY. TRY is nonveridical, as we shall see, and if MANAGE has a presupposition of TRY, as we are arguing, then it is of mixed veridicality, *even if it entails p*. Nonveridicality in the presupposition is the prerequisite for the choice of subjunctive in our theory, and will override veridicality (objective or subjective), since the subjunctive is sensitive to what the sentence presupposes, not what it asserts.

### 6.5.2 Veridicality of Aspectual Operators: Actualization of an Event

We will backtrack now to Giannakidou's (2013a) discussion of the absence of NPIs in progressives because that paper offers a first handle of TRY within the analysis of aspectual operators and actualization. Giannakidou argues that the progressive operator PROG is veridical in entailing some actualization of *p*, and it therefore does not allow NPIs:

(96) *O    Janis  egrafe           olo to  proi        kanena  grama.
     the J.       wrote.IMPF.3sg   all the morning     any     letter
     *John was writing any letter all morning.

(97) O    Janis  prospathise na          grapsi       kanena grama pu
     the J.     tried.3sg   that.SUBJ    write.3sg    any    letter that
     na    itan leptomeres.
     SUBJ was detailed
     John tried this morning to write some letter or other that was detailed enough.

NPI and the subjunctive are not licensed because PROG *p* is a veridical clause, lacking a proper NPI and subjunctive licenser. Veridical PROG contrasts with nonveridical TRY which doesn't entail realization of *p*, and therefore allows NPIs, as we can see, as well as subjunctive relative clauses (which are kinds of NPIs). If MANAGE presupposes TRY *p*, then the analysis of TRY carries over to the presupposition of MANAGE.

How is PROG veridical? Giannakidou (2013) relies on Sharvit's (2003) analysis. As we can see, that analysis poses an actuality component ((98-a)) and a modal component (that itself relies on earlier work by Landman 1992 and others):

(98) For any event *e*, property of events P, and world *w*, *e* belongs to PROG(w)(P) iff:

   a. *e* is an event in *w*; and

b. for any realistic continuation branch C for *e* relative to *w*, there is an event *e'* and a world *w'* such that $< e', w' >$ is in C and *e'* belongs to P(*w'*). (Sharvit 2003: 414)

According to this analysis, in order to evaluate a sentence such as *Mary was crossing the street (when a bus hit her)*, we build a continuation branch based on the evaluation world and the ongoing event given by the VP. We stay in the evaluation world until Mary gets hit by a bus, at which point we shift to a maximally similar world in which a bus does not hit her and which is a reasonable option, and continue to trace the progression of the event. Under normal circumstances, the continuation branch will contain an event in which Mary successfully crosses the street, and so the sentence is judged true. In a sentence like *Mary was landing on the moon (when the phone rang)*, on the other hand, we have a non-realistic evaluation branch and therefore the sentence is judged to be false, or true only in a fictional/dream context.

The important thing is clause *a*, that an event is physically realized in the world. This physical realization, Giannakidou argues, suffices to give us veridicality: a rational speaker chooses to use PROG [cross the street] when she knows that there is an actual, though arguably not completed but ongoing, event *e* of crossing the street. All worlds compatible with the speaker's beliefs, knowledge, and perceptions are worlds where the street is physically being crossed, though the event may not be completed. Likewise, in degree-based approaches of the progressive (Piñón 2008), progressive events are realized, in the actual world, to a degree higher than zero. Partial unfolding of the event makes the progressive actual, therefore veridical.

It appears, then, that when we consider events, the veridicality of the sentence correlates with actualization, and actualization is physical realization in the actual world of some portion of the event. The progressive is characterized by Giannakidou as an actualization function ACTUAL:

(99) ACTUAL is veridical (Giannakidou 2013a):
(i) When an eventuality P is actualized, P is at least partially physically realized in the actual world.
(ii) Actualization happens with actualization functions (ACTUAL).
(iii) Application of ACTUAL to P entails veridicality: the speaker knows that P is at least partly realized.

ACTUAL refers abstractly to functions like the progressive (PROG), the perfective, and the PAST tense. In choosing any of these functions, the speaker knows or believes that there is (at least some) physical realization of the event P. This knowledge renders PROG veridical and explains why the progressive and the perfective past are a bad context for NPIs, subjunctives, and other polarity items. Lacking a result, Giannakidou concludes, doesn't have any implications: an actualized event can be a complete one (perfective) or an incomplete, ongoing one (progressive).

### 6.5.3 No Actualization with TRY

As we noted, Giannakidou observes that Greek *prospatho* TRY contrasts with PROG in that it allows NPIs and subjunctive in relative clauses. The contrast suggests that TRY, unlike the progressive, must be nonveridical — a fact supported by the choice of subjunctive, and challenging analyses unifying TRY with progressive (Sharvit 2003). The contrast places TRY in the context of "intentional activity" that can involve both mental and physical action (Kamp 1999, 2007; Grano 2011).

The existence of the incremental theme has been central to the discussion of TRY. Sharvit (2003), cited in Grano (2011), argues that *try* is different from *want*, in that it entails existence of the theme:

(100)  a. John wanted to cut a tomato, but there were no tomatoes to cut.
       b. John tried to cut a tomato, #but there were no tomatoes to cut.

(101)  a. Mary wanted to push a cart, but there were no carts to push.
       b. Mary tried to push a cart, #but there were no carts to push.
       (Sharvit 2003: 405)

She then goes on to say: "Intuitively, it seems that *try* differs from its cousins *want, expect, believe*, etc. in that it doesn't simply express an attitude of some individual toward some proposition, but it also expresses some activity . . . This required "action" is extensional, in the sense that it has to go on in the actual world for the sentence to be judged true." (Sharvit 2003: 407). Action, however, as Giannakidou points out, renders TRY an actualization operator, akin to the progressive. But then the nonlicensing of NPIs and subjunctive with TRY becomes a problem.

Is TRY really an actualization operator? Grano (2011) suggests that *try* does not necessarily involve physical action and does not always imply the physical existence of the incremental theme. He offers the following cases; notice especially the contrast with PROG:

(102) John tried to find a book, but there was no book.

(103) a. John was eating an apple. Entails: Part of the apple was consumed.
b. John tried to eat an apple. He looked everywhere but there was no apple, so no apple was consumed.

(104) Context: John is severely injured and cannot move his arm:
a. #John was raising his arm.
b. John tried to raise his arm. (But he didn't.)

These examples are problematic for the assumption that TRY involves action like the progressive, and lead Giannakidou and Grano to the conclusion that although we tend to think of TRY as involving physical action, in fact it does not. According to Kamp (1999, 2007: 1), TRY (as well as FAIL, SUCCED) is a device for *intentional* activity indicating *conceptual continuity* which often exists between things we intend to find or do or make, and the events in the real world that result when we try to realize those plans and intentions. In *i* TRY P, where P is a predicate of events, an agent *i* has the intention or a plan to set a path for action that will count as P, but what Kamp seems to be saying is that there is a conceptual continuum between the plan/intention and the action, a continuum that includes pure intention. Grano (2011), likewise, proposes that TRY, unlike the progressive, contains a preparatory phase of the event that need not involve physical action P but just mental action (e.g., planning, etc.). TRY is, therefore, nonveridical:

(105) Nonveridicality of TRY:
$TRY(i, p)$ does not entail $ACTUAL(p)$; where $p$ is an eventuality description.

This renders TRY nonveridical. The verb *try* itself and its cognates in Greek and Italian are TRY operators.

We could now argue that TRY $p$ is a presupposition of implicatives. However, a possible worry arises: the agentivity of TRY is too strong when it comes to implicatives proper (see Mari, 2010b, 2015a):

(106)  He managed to be dumped by his girlfriend without even trying to be dumped.

We propose to introduce a weaker notion of trying, which we define as follows:

(107)  Unintentional TRY: *un*-TRY:
*un*-TRY $(i, p)$ is true iff $i$ brings about some action(s) $A$ that can result in $p$ being true.

In prototypical cases, the implicative MANAGE seems to require an intentional TRY. However, since the more underspecified definition in (107) covers a larger number of cases, we will use *un*-TRY.

This definition of *un*-TRY allows a series of actions, unrelated to the literal content $p$ that can lead to $p$ be true, but TRY itself doesn't directly address $p$; i.e., if you are trying to eat an apple, you maybe at the store right now doing grocery shopping, but you haven't taken action that can be characterized as "eating an apple". This is in line, as we now discuss, with recent proposals on implicatives.

### 6.5.4 MANAGE, un-TRY, and the Subjunctive

Putting it all together now, we will propose that MANAGE has the following presupposition:

(108)  MANAGE presupposes un-TRYING:
MANAGE $(i, p)$ is defined only if $i$ *un*-TRY $p$ is true.

This presupposition alone is sufficient to explain the use of the subjunctive: *un*-TRY $(i, p)$ does not entail that any part of $p$ is actualized. As we have been arguing, the subjunctive is sensitive to the presence of a nonveridical presupposition. The presupposition that the subject agent $i$ tried $p$ does not entail that in all trying worlds $i$ succeeded in bringing about $p$.

In fact, *i* might actually not be engaged in the activity described by *p* at all, as we just mentioned. Here is another example below:

(109)  John managed to fix the car. He called the mechanic and the mechanic did it.

In this case, the managing of fixing the car does not involve John engaging in the fixing of the car at all. John simply initiated a series of events by calling the mechanic, and this event, followed by other events (such the mechanic coming to see the car, taking it to his workshop, etc.) led eventually to the fixing of the car. John's trying and managing to fix the car did not involve the proposition or eventuality *John fixed the car*. There is no trying world where John actually fixed, or was engaged in physical activity that can be successfully described as "fix the car".

But calling the mechanic was indeed a crucial enabling factor, a *necessary means* or a *catalyst* (Baglini 2010; Giannakidou and Staraki 2013; Baglini and Francez 2016) for the event of fixing the car to come to be. It was the act that initiated a number of events that are related causally to bringing about the result state of the car being fixed. We can encode this as follows:

(110)  MANAGE $(i, p)$ asserts that there is a *causal* path, i.e., a sequence of eventualities $S$ such that $S$ is a necessary means for $p$.

If this is the assertion of MANAGE, then all it entails is that there is a causal path, initiated and sustained through the necessary means $S$, and that the last stage of the path is $p$. From this perspective, MANAGE $p$ is nonveridical in its assertion, as well as its presupposition, and this explains why it invariably selects the subjunctive. At no time does the speaker know that John fixed the car himself:

(111)  Epistemic uncertainty of MANAGE:
*i* MANAGE *p* does not entail that the speaker knows that *i* undertook action *p*.

Hence the use of the subjunctive is not a surprise, but rather follows the patterns we have observed with the modal verbs and attitudes. And

MANAGE appears to be both nonveridical in the presupposition (having a TRY component and epistemic uncertainty) and in the assertion.[12] Crucially, ability can trigger and sustain a causal path as argued in Giannakidou and Staraki (2013), and it is for this reason that ABLE and MANAGE seem similar—although, as we have shown, they are not identical: ABLE does not have a presupposition of trying.

Our analysis, which owes some inspiration to Giannakidou and Staraki's (2012) causal analysis of of ability and Baglini's (2010) analysis of *get*, is very close in spirit to a recent proposal by Nadathur (2016). Below is Nadathur's proposal (Nadathur 2016: (24)):

(112) A statement of the form I(X), with implicative I and complement X:

    a. presupposes the existence of a causal factor (ancestor or set thereof) A for X, where A is causally necessary for X in the context of utterance;

    b. asserts that A was met in the world of evaluation. Consequently, ¬I(X) asserts that A was not met;

    c. If I is a two-way implicative, I(X) also presupposes that A is the only open prerequisite for X in the utterance context (all A-independent causal ancestors are presumed to be resolved in the X-conducive way).

The presupposition of A's existence, significantly, does not presuppose that A holds, Nadathur asserts. This lexical entry misses the presupposition of TRY, but if we just focus on the assertion, we read that all the so-called implicative verb asserts is the existence of means A which are causally necessary to bring about X. Our view of the assertion and Nadathur's are therefore quite close. And in both versions, we do not get the veridical entailment to *p*.

## 6.6 Conclusions

In this chapter we have shown that ability modals, even when giving rise to the actuality entailment, are no exception to our generalization about

---

12. It is possible to also postulate a decompositional analysis of MANAGE as *un-TRY p and p*. That would be compatible with the facts discussed here, and it would render MANAGE of mixed veridicality, again predicting the subjunctive. In that analysis, *p* is entailed but the nonveridicality of the presupposition would be sufficient for subjunctive.

modality: like epistemic modals, ability modals are also subject to the Nonveridicality Axiom. The nonveridicality presupposition accounts for why ability modals select the subjunctive. The veridical actuality entailment, on the other hand, is due to the ability modal scoping under PAST. In addition, we proposed an account of implicatives that radically differs from Kartunnen in deriving nonveridicality for MANAGE in both presupposition and assertion. Mood and tense choice were key elements in advancing our new arguments for the nonveridical semantics of MANAGE.

As a side effect of our analysis, the phenomenon of obligatory control with implicatives and ability modals was correlated with the lexical semantics of ability and implicativity: ability and causal path for an action have to hold concurrently with the action. Therefore the morphological nonpast cannot forward shift but contributes the coincidental. Zero tense requires a local relation to the ABLE time. This fact, we think, creates a useful frame within which to understand, and not simply stipulate, obligatory control.

CHAPTER SEVEN

# Propositional Attitudes of Emotion: Gradability and Nonveridicality

In this chapter, we complete our theory by considering the mood patterns observed in the complements of propositional attitudes of *emotion*. A precise treatment of emotion is lacking in the formal semantics literature, and the notion is often reduced to concepts such as preference (as with bouletics), gradability, or expressivity. In dealing with emotion attitudes, we will articulate a precise semantics for emotion as a gradable nonveridical space, on a par with modals and the other partitioned attitudes that we have discussed.

Descriptively, emotion attitudes include (at least) three types of attitudes. First, there are attitudes known as *emotive* such as, e.g., the English *be happy, regret, be surprised, be angry*, which often appear with gradable psychological adjectives; these designate various kinds of emotion toward a fact or something that the subject perceives as a fact. Emotive predicates can be positive or negative. Second, there are attitudes that we will label 'epistemic emotives', such as *be aware, remember*. Such attitudes combine an emotive component with an epistemic component in their meaning. Finally, we have attitudes of fear, known also as *verba timendi*, such as, e.g., the English *fear, be afraid*. Fear, in contrast to the emotive predication, never relates to a fact, as we shall see. As we just alluded to, emotive predicates are often treated as factive. Verbs of fear, on the other hand, have not been claimed to be factive. All classes express psychological states of emotion and show variable, i.e., flexible, mood patterns.

## 7.1 Introduction: The Puzzles of Emotion Attitudes

Let us start with emotive predicates, which are the most frequently discussed. Across European languages, these predicates select both the indicative and the subjunctive. French and Italian, for example, select subjunctive, but Greek chooses the indicative complementizer *pu*.

(1) a. Jean regrette que Marie ait lu ce livre.
John regrets that Mary have.SUBJ.3sg read this book
b. Gianni rimpiange che Maria abbia letto questo libro.
John regrets that Mary have.SUBJ.3sg read this book
c. John regrets that Mary has read this book.

(2) O Pavlos lipate pu/*na/*oti efije i Roxani.
the Paul regrets that.IND-pu/SUBJ/IND-oti left.3sg the Roxani
Paul regrets/is sad that Roxanne left.

Crucially, the assertive indicative—*oti*—is not possible, as we see. In chap. 4 we proposed that *pu* is the *presuppositional* indicative because it appears with the emotive class of verbs that have been claimed to have a factive presupposition. As we noted there, *pu* appears also with the epistemic factive *know*, and with memory or perception verbs adding the presupposition that the *pu* clause is a fact. We will revisit these cases later in the chapter. The key observation at this initial stage is that the emotive class is marked with the presuppositional indicative in Greek, which itself suggests that the verbs belonging to it must have a veridical presupposition (albeit not necessarily a factive one). From the point of view that *pu* is sensitive to the presupposition, *pu* is indeed like the subjunctive—which is sensitive to the presupposition of an attitude. But unlike the subjunctive, which needs a nonveridical presupposition, the presuppositional indicative needs a veridical presupposition.[1]

---

1. Giannakidou (2016) claims that *pu* has expressive content in the sense of Potts (2007), i.e., containing expressive indices. But *pu* can be used also with, epistemic *know* and perception verbs, and in these cases there is no emotion. Hence, it seems more plausible to argue that it is the presuppositional aspect of these predicates that *pu* responds to, not the emotion. Yet, given that *pu* is a complementizer and that expressive meaning is typically expressed high in the structure, it is also reasonable to assume, with Giannakidou

Because emotive verbs are thought to be factive (Kiparsky and Kiparsky 1968, Karttunen 1971) the use of subjunctive is unexpected (Giannakidou 1998, 2006, 2016). Their nonemotive cousins meaning *know* strictly select the indicative:

(3) a. Jean sait que Marie a lu ce livre.
    John knows that Mary has read this book
   b. Gianni sa che Maria ha letto questo libro.
    John knows that Mary has read this book
   c. John knows that Mary has read this book.

If emotive attitudes are factive, why do they take the subjunctive in Romance languages? If both *know* and emotives have a factive presupposition that their complement is objectively true, how can we explain the contrast vis-à-vis the subjunctive?

Giannakidou (2016) observes three types of languages:

(4) Flexibility in mood choice with emotive verbs:
   a. Languages that require subjunctive (Spanish, Italian, French);
   b. Languages allowing subjunctive and indicative (Portuguese, Catalan, Turkish);
   c. Languages where emotives select indicative (Greek, Hungarian, Romanian, Bulgarian).

Giannakidou's previous version of the theory (Giannakidou 1994, 1998, 2009, 2016) predicts indicative after emotives and derives the languages in (c); see also Marques (2004), Baunaz (2015). Emotives have also been argued to denote preference (Villalta 2008). Unfortunately, none of the approaches offers a satisfactory way to address the variation observed because the treatment is monolithic, i.e. the selecting predicate is either veridical or nonveridical, or preferential or non-preferential. In the approach we have developed in this book, the variation in the patterns of mood indicates layers in the attitude meaning, specifically between what a selecting verb *asserts* and what it *presupposes*. This allows us to

---

(2016), that if there is expressive content, this complementizer is in a perfect place to encode it.

combine in a single lexical entry a veridical with a nonveridical component, i.e., what we called *mixed* (non)veridicality. Mixed (non)veridicality, we showed, turns out to be massive, and it is the underlying cause of subjunctive choice in most cases, and certainly of mood flexibility.

In our study of various attitudes so far, we found that the subjunctive is sensitive to the presuppositional content of the predicate and will be triggered by a nonveridical presupposition in the lexical entry of the predicate. Recall:

(5) Licensing condition for the subjunctive mood:
The subjunctive will be licensed in the complement of an attitude or modal verb (ATTITUDE) iff ATTITUDE obeys the Nonveridicality Axiom.

(6) Licensing condition for the indicative mood:
The indicative will be licensed in the complement of ATTITUDE iff ATTITUDE is veridical (objectively or subjectively).

When we say "nonveridical attitude", we refer to a propositional attitude or a modal that obeys the Nonveridicality Axiom, i.e., the attitude presupposes that the attitude holder $i$ is in a nonveridical state with regards to $p$. This nonveridical state is most typically a state of epistemic uncertainty: $i$ does not know that $p$ is true. But the nonveridicality condition on the presupposition applies generally as a condition that the relevant space be partitioned. From our study of emotive predicates, it will become clear that the nonveridicality requirement generalizes to this class of predicates too. Emotives too obey the Nonveridicality Axiom. On the other hand, when we say a "veridical' attitude", we intend to refer to a solipsistic attitude that lacks the nonveridical presuppositional layer. Epistemic attitudes are both presuppositional and veridical.

Recall also that, pragmatically, the subjunctive mood is a prohibition: do not add $p$ to a subjective space, or the common body of knowledge (the common ground). Not adding $p$ is consistent only with a nonveridical state. The discourse function, therefore, of the subjunctive and its sensitivity to a nonveridical presupposition are interlinked. As said earlier, this generalizes to other non-indicatives such as the optative and the imperative moods which have also been argued to have a nonveridical— or as we argued in chap. 5, *antifactive*—presupposition.

Our licensing conditions explained why suppositional doxastics in Italian, bouletic verbs in general, modals and implicatives select the subjunctive: they all have a nonveridical presupposition. Verbs of awareness and perception can also be construed with this presupposition, as we saw earlier and will revisit here; they are therefore also compatible with the subjunctive. The meaning of these attitudes is multilayered, and mood flexibility is a diagnostic for that.[2]

Emotives, we will argue here, have mixed veridicality. They convey a presupposition of a nonveridical emotive space which has a positive and a negative extent. But unlike modals, suppositional doxastics and volitions, the emotive class also has a veridical presupposition of factivity or, as we will show, subjective veridicality. The indicative is possible because of this veridical presupposition.

Crucially, a similar mood variability is observed with awareness predicates— indicative in Greek, but subjunctive in Italian:

(7) O Nicholas exei epignosi oti/*na      i   Ariadne tou leei
    the Nicholas has  awareness that.IND/SUBJ the Ariadne him says
    psemata.
    lies
    Nicholas is aware that Ariadne is lying to him.

(8) È molto/poco cosciente che tu   sia         stanco.
    is very/little aware    that you be.SUBJ.3sg tired
    He is very/little aware that you are tired.

(9) Maria è più   cosciente di Gianni dell'accaduto.
    Mary is more aware       of John   of happened
    Mary is more aware than John of what has happened.

We will discuss this alternation as part of the analysis we will develop for emotive predicates.

---

2. Giannakidou (2016), in a similar vein, acknowledges the subjunctive after emotives as a subspecies of what she calls *evaluative* subjunctive. The emotive subjunctive, it is claimed, is a case where the subjunctive functions modally, though not as a modal in the assertion but at the level of presupposition. The emotive subjunctive introduces the presupposition that the individual anchor considered ¬p possible at a time prior to the assertion (see also for Italian Giorgi and Pianesi 1996). Thus in this case too, the subjunctive is an indicator of a nonveridical epistemic state prior to the assertion. We will revisit this idea in section 2 below.

Finally, we will contrast emotives with verbs of fear, which seem to lack the veridical factivity presupposition. Predicates of fear do allow both subjunctive and indicative, but this correlates with prospective or past/present orientation in the lower clause:

(10)  O Pavlos *fovate* *pu/*oti/na          vgi
      the Paul fears that.IND-pu/ND-oti/SUBJ go.NONPAST.3sg
      ekso.
      outside
      Paul is afraid to go outside.

(11)  O Pavlos *fovate*    *oti/na          i    aitisi  tou
      the Paul fears.3sg that.IND-oti/SUBJ the request his
      aporifthike.
      was-denied.3sg.
      Paul is afraid that his request was denied.

The subjunctive version is a fear to perform an action. The action is not realized yet (hence NONPAST above), and the fear does not imply that the action is not desirable. For instance, Paul might fear to go outside because it is raining and he doesn't want to get wet, while at the same time he wants to go outside because he has a date he has been looking forward to for the entire week. The indicative statement, on the other hand, reads like a statement of belief, qualified with a negative emotive adverb: *Paul believes that, unfortunately for him, his request was denied*. In both cases, there is no factive presupposition.

Notice the parallel in Italian:

(12)  Paul ha paura di andare fuori.
      Paul has fear to go    outside
      Paul is afraid to go outside.

(13)  Paul ha paura di aver svegliato il  bambino.
      Paul has fear of have woken    the baby
      Paul is afraid of having woken up the baby.

In both cases, Italian licenses the infinitive, which we take to be equivalent to the subjunctive, and the past vs. nonpast distinction is made. We will argue that verbs of fear, like emotives, convey an emotional stance which is partitioned. This explains why they select the subjunctive and infinitives. Verbs of fear lack the veridical presupposition of emotives, therefore never select *pu*. The indicative indicates that the verb of fear is used as a verb of belief. Fear attitudes, thus, have a dual life as predicates of fear to act, and as believing something unfortunate.

Verbs of fear have yet a third dimension in their meaning, revealed in an additional selection pattern, with a special complementizer manifested in English with *lest* and in Greek with the complementizer *mipos*:

(14) O Pavlos fovate mipos dhi         tin Maria.
     the Paul fears  lest  see.NONPAST.3sg the Mary
     Paul is afraid lest he see Mary.

Here, seeing Mary is truly undesirable for Paul. *Mipos* emerges from a historical path that fused the subjunctive negation *mi* (Veloudis 1980; Giannakidou 1997, 1998; Chatzopoulou 2012, 2019)—which might appear here as "expletive"—with the indicative complementizer *pos*.[3] Synchronically, it also has uses as an epistemic possibility adverb, exclusively allowed in questions:

(15) Mipos irthe   i   Maria?
     maybe came.3st the Maria
     Did Mary come, perhaps?

(16) #Mipos irthe   i   Maria.
     maybe came.3sg the Maria
     *Perhaps Mary came.

As a possibility modal, *mipos* and questions convey the same kind of nonveridicality: nonveridical equilibrium, not bias, as we noted in chap. 2. Note that *mipos*, is used also as an interrogative complementizer, roughly equivalent to "whether":

(17) Me rotise    an/mipos efaga.
     me askee.3sg if/whether ate.1sg
     'She asked me if/whether I ate.'

---

3. Expletive negation with verbs of fear has been analyzed by Yoon (2012) as a subjunctive marker, and this is consistent with our approach here. Yoon adds that there is an additional presupposition (or conventional implicature) of expressive meaning in the sense of Potts 2007; we consider this possibility in section 5. Expletive negation is instead analyzed as a modifier of the ordering source by Mari and Tahar (2020).

The *mipos* version of the indirect question has a presupposition, absent in the *an/if* version, that the possibility of eating was under discussion. The reading of *mipos*, likewise, with verbs of fear, we will argue, has a presupposition that the possibility raised by the complement was under discussion. The fear space has the additional presupposition of being non-veridical, as with all emotive spaces. The sentence in this case asserts that in all fear worlds the possibility of *p* is resolved positively.

French and Italian express this same meaning with the subjunctive, and French interestingly uses the expletive negation *ne*.

(18) a. Carlo teme che arrivi un temporale.
Charles fears that come.SUBJ.3sg a storm
Charles fears that a storm is arriving.
b. Charles crains qu'une tempête ne soit
Charles fears that-a storm NE be.SUBJ.3sg
en train d'arriver.
arriving
Charles fears that a storm is arriving.

(19) a. Carlo teme sia arrivato un temporale.
Charles fears that come.SUBJ.3sg arrived a storm
Charles fears that a storm has arrived.
b. Charles crains qu'une tempête ne soit arrivée.
Charles fears that-a storm NE be.SUBJ.3sg arrived
Charles fears that a storm has arrived.

To summarize, there are three types of fear:

(20) Varieties of fear:
a. Fear to do something (subjunctive).
b. Fear as a doxastic attitude toward something unfortunate that happened (indicative); and
c. Fear that an unfortunate possibility will be realized/has been realized. (special complementizer / subjunctive (+ expletive negation))

We proceed with the discussion as follows. We consider first the factivity presupposition of emotives in section 2 and conclude that emotives have a subjectively veridical presupposition and not a factive one. The emotive attitude can be directed also to a perceived or believed fact. In section 3, we offer our analysis of emotion space as a partitioned nonveridical space. We rely on the gradable, scalar nature of emotive verbs, and define a morphism between the emotive scale and possible worlds, such that we get a divide into worlds where the emotions hold (positive extent), and those where it doesn't (negative extent). The existence of a scale thus creates a nonveridical presupposition, in effect unifying the scalar with the truth-based aspects of mood choice. In section 4 we extend our analysis to awareness predicates. In section 5 we discuss the consequences for the complementizer system of Greek and revisit verbs of memory and perception that are also compatible with *pu*. We discuss fear predicates in section 6.

## 7.2 The Veridical Presupposition of Emotive Attitudes

In this section, we discuss the factive presupposition of emotive predicates. We also consider the possibility of a negative presupposition.

Emotive predicates are known to have a "factive" presupposition:

(21) O Pavlos lipate pu efije i Roxani.
 the Paul regrets that.IND left the Roxani
 Paul is sad that Roxanne left.

(22) O Pavlos *dhen* lipate pu efije i Roxani.
 the Paul not regrets that.IND left the Roxani
 Paul is not sad that Roxanne left.

(23) Roxanne left.

The positive and negative sentence both entail that Roxane left. This has been the standard observation since Kiparski and Kiparski (1970), who argued that the complement is a fact, i.e., a presupposed true statement. This is also the reason why these verbs are characterized as presuppositional: the emotive verb presupposes some fact and asserts the subject's emotion toward that fact. The status of the emotive complement as a factive is also consistent with certain syntactic properties that it has, e.g., syntactically the complement is a weak island (Roussou 1994; Varlokosta 1994; Giannakidou 1998; Baunaz 2015, among others), it blocks quantifier movement, anaphor and NPI licensing, and the like.

Huddleston and Pullum (2002) call into question the factivity of the complement. They call emotives *not entailing*, and give examples like these below:

(24) Falsely believing that he had inflicted a fatal wound, Oedipus regretted killing the stranger on the road to Thebes. (Klein 1980, quoted in Gazdar 1979: 122).

It is not true objectively that Oedipus inflicted a fatal wound. Egré (2008) offers similar examples:

(25) John wrongly believes that Mary got married, and he regrets that she is no longer unmarried. (Egré 2008: (30)).

These examples show that one can have an emotive attitude toward something that one *believes* to be a fact, but may not actually be a fact. In the normal case, we are happy or sad about something that we know happened; but one may only believe that something happened (a believed fact) and feel happy or sad about it. Hence, the alleged factivity presupposition need not be satisfied as objective veridicality; mere subjective veridicality, i.e., the emotive subject's belief of $p$ is enough.

(26) Subjective veridicality presupposition of emotives:
$[\![i \text{ V-emotive } p]\!]^{\text{Dox},i}$ is defined iff $\forall w' \in \text{Dox}(i) : p(w')$.

The presupposition of *know*, on the other hand, is objective veridicality, namely $w_0 \in p$:

(27) $[\![i \text{ knows } p]\!]^{w_0,M,i}$ is defined iff $w_0 \in p$.
If defined $[\![i \text{ knows } p]\!]^{w_0,M,i} = 1$ iff: $\forall w' \in M(i) : p(w')$

The factivitity of *know* and its equivalents is unquestionable; *know* is veridical in both the presupposition and the assertion, subjectively and objectively. Emotive verbs, on the other hand, in the counterexamples above, do not rely on objective veridicality—but on doxastic commitment of $i$ to the truth of the complement.

Baker (1970) suggested further that emotives express a negativity, a "contrariness" between a perceived fact and some mental or emotional state. According to Baker, we say that we are *surprised* when a certain fact does not conform to our expectations; *relieved* when it does not conform to our fears; *disappointed* when a (perceived) fact is not in line with our hopes. Likewise, Baker claims that we say that a certain fact is odd or strange if it seems counter to our view of what is logical. Emotives, as a class, appear to convey this perceived contrariness—and this allows them to license NPIs:

(28) a. *Ariadne believes/dreams that she talked to anybody.
   b. *Ariadne knows that she talked to anybody.
   c. Ariadne regrets that she talked to anybody.
   d. Ariadne is amazed that we got any tickets at all!

Very much in agreement with Baker (and later Linebarger 1980), Giannakidou (1997, 2006, 2016) argues that the appearance of NPIs with emotive verbs is due to the fact that emotive verbs trigger an implicit negative inference. Giannakidou (2006) suggested that the component of emotives responsible for implicit negation is a counterfactual conditional. The implicit negation is a non-cancelable counterfactual conditional with a negative protasis:

(29) a. John regrets that I bought a car. Entails John would prefer it if I had not bought a car.
   b. John regrets that I bought a car; #in fact he wouldn't want me to buy a car.

Negating *John would want me to buy a car* creates oddity, suggesting that this inference is "not merely a conversational implicature, as argued in Linebarger, but rather something stronger, perhaps a presupposition or a conventional implicature in the sense of Potts (2005). In fact, since emotive factives convey an expressive attitude toward the propositional content of their complement, it makes sense to argue that they all encode conventionally this negative attitude." (Giannakidou 2006: 595). Giannakidou (2016) later suggests that the negative component is a presupposition: $i$ has a *belief or expectation that not p was true prior to the assertion*. It is because of this presupposition that we get the perceived contrariness, and the NPI sanctioning, it is claimed. We give below Giannakidou's (2016) version of the presupposition:

(30) Negative (nonveridical) presupposition of emotive factives:
*i* is surprised that *p* is defined if only if: *i* believed that ¬*p* at a time t' ≺ $t_u$ (where $t_u$ is the utterance time).

A similar idea is also found in Giorgi and Pianesi (1996), where a counterfactual presupposition is advocated. On the other hand, Giannakidou and Mari (2016a, b) present challenging examples that show the negative inference to be softer than a presupposition. Observe the following example, where the continuation "and she always knew that" is felicitous:

(31) Arianna è contenta/felice/triste/irritata/ ... che Nicolas
Arianna is happy/glad/sad/irritated/ ... that Nicholas
abbia partecipato alla maratona, e ha sempre
has.SUBJ.3sg participated to the marathon, and has always
saputo che lo avrebbe fatto.
known that that have.COND.3sg done
Arianna is happy/glad/sad/irritated that Nicholas participated in the marathon, and she always knew that he would do it.

Example (31) clearly does not convey that the speaker had an expectation or belief that ¬*p* prior to $t_u$. Notice the contrast with *surprise* where the negative inference cannot be canceled:

(32) Ariadne is surprised that Nicholas participated in the marathon, #and she always knew that he would do it.

If we take it that the negative component is presuppositional, we then have to explain why it can get systematically canceled with non-*surprise* types of emotives (positive *be glad, happy*, and even negative *irritated, sad*). The strength of the negative inference seems to be limited to attitudes of surprise which are inherently akin to a change in expectation; but on the basis of that, it will be unjustifiable to conclude that negativity is a presupposition of *all* emotives. In many cases it has to be understood as an implicature.

Let us proceed now to the meaning of the emotive component. The nature of emotion will make obvious a nonveridical presupposition.

## 7.3 Gradability, Emotiveness, and Nonveridicality

Emotion predicates express emotions. Emotions are "attitudes" in a broad sense; but in a more narrow and accurate sense, they are psychological states toward facts, perceived facts, or potential facts (as is the case with fear). Emotive states are gradable: one can be *very* sad, *a little bit* sad, *terribly* sad—or, on the other hand, not sad at all, or only a little bit sad. It is therefore no accident that emotional attitudes often employ adjectives that are gradable and scalar. The gradable nature of emotion, we argue (following our earlier work, Giannakidou and Mari 2016a, b), is responsible for their nonveridical content.

### 7.3.1 The Presupposition of Nonveridicality of the Emotive Space

No attention has been paid in the mood literature to the fact that emotives are gradable predicates, with the exception of Villalta (2008) who, however, does not capitalize on what gradability tells us about veridicality. For us, gradability and nonveridicality will be the starting point. Gradability is diagnosed by a number of tests in many works (see indicatively Kennedy 2007; and Giannakidou and Mari 2016a, b). Gradable predicates are, first, compatible with degree modifiers, e.g., *very*; so are emotives:

(33) a. John is *very* tall.
 b. Gianni è *molto* alto.
 c. O Janis ine *poli* psilos.

(34) a. John is *very* irritated/happy that Mary came.
 b. Gianni è *molto* irritato/contento che venga anche Maria.
 c. O Janis ine *poli* thimomenos pu irthe i Maria.

Second, gradable predicates and emotives can be used in comparative sentences:

(35) a. John is *taller* than Mary.
 b. Gianni è *più alto* di Maria.
 c. O Janis ine *psiloteros* apo ti Maria.

(36) a. I am more/less irritated than you.
　　 b. Sono più/meno irritato di te.
　　 c. Ime pio/ligotero thimomeni apo sena.

Emotion predicates, therefore, can be understood on a par with gradable predicates which denote *scales*. The scales of emotion, in contrast to scales such as tallness, length, or time, do not rely on objective measure (e.g., meter or inches, minutes or seconds) but are purely subjective: what is frightening or irritating or surprising differs from person to person, and there is no objective way of measuring or building fine-grained differences of emotion. In this respect, the scales of emotive predicates are akin to the scales of predicates of personal taste (see Muñoz 2019 for a recent discussion that embeds emotion predicates in the discussion of personal taste). Emotion scales are construed by individual anchors based on their own emotions and perceptions.

In all analyses of gradability, gradable predicates introduce degree scales and map individuals onto points on the scales. Fine-grade distinctions, as we just said, are impossible with emotion, which lacks precise measurement. What is distinctive, however, is a designated degree available in all scales, and which functions as a *threshold* between the positive extent of the scale and the negative extent. For instance, if I say *John is tall*, I am saying that John exceeds the degree $d$ that is the threshold or standard of what counts as tall in the context. If John's height maps onto a degree $d'$ below $d$, then John cannot be said to be tall, he is not-tall. Let $\mathcal{D}$ be a set of ordered degrees, and $\mathcal{I}$ a set of individuals. We assume, quite standardly, that a scalar predicate has the analysis in 37:

(37) $\lambda P.\lambda x.\lambda d.P(x) \geqslant d$

Variables $x$ and $d$ take their value in the sets $\mathcal{I}$ and $\mathcal{D}$. Given the threshold $d$, two equivalence classes are determined: one above $d$ in which $i$ has the property, and one below $d$ in which $i$ does not have it. Since we are now considering emotion scales, the space above $d$ is the space in which $i$ has the emotion, and the space below $d$ is the portion of the scale where $i$ does not have the emotion. This is key to understanding the mapping to veridicality we proposd.

We are now going to map scales into modal spaces. We propose that there is a morphism $\mathcal{H}$ from degrees $\mathcal{D}$ and individuals $\mathcal{I}$ to worlds.

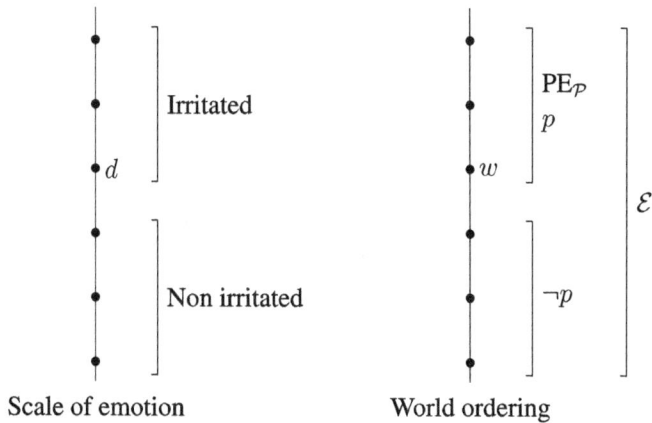

FIGURE 7.1 Emotion as a nonveridical space

(38)  $\mathcal{H}(\mathcal{D})(\mathcal{I}) = W$

The modal base $\mathcal{E}$ for "emotion" that we obtain via this mapping is nonhomogeneous.[4],[5] The worlds in the modal base are partitioned into those in which $i$ has the emotion and those in which she does not. This partition is driven by the threshold $d$. Note (Fig. 7.1), that in the worlds in which $i$ has the sentiment, $p$ is true. In other worlds, $W$ is a set of worlds ordered by $\leq_{S_i}$. The set of worlds is partitioned into two equivalence classes of worlds. One is the set of worlds in which the attitude holder has the emotion and $p$ is true. The other one is the set of worlds in which the attitude holder does not have the emotion and $p$ is false.

This partitioning allows us to define *Positive-Extent-worlds* (PE) for $p$:

(39)  $\text{PE}_\mathcal{P} = \{w' \in \mathcal{E}_\mathcal{P} : w'$ where the propositions in $\mathcal{P}$ are true $\}$

Here, the set $\mathcal{P}$ is the singleton set $\{p\}$. So $\text{PE}_\mathcal{P}$ contains all the worlds in which $p$ is true. In $\text{PE}_\mathcal{P}$ $i$ has sentiment $\mathcal{S}$. But not all worlds in $\mathcal{E}$ are PE worlds for $p$. $\mathcal{E}$ only partially supports $p$. $\text{PE}_\mathcal{P}$ is a subset of $\mathcal{E}$ (the emotive

---

[4]. Klecha (2014) proposes an account of gradable adjectives like *important* that incorporates degrees into the denotation of the adjectives, combining a degree-based semantics and ordering sources à la Kratzer. Here we propose an analysis of scalar emotive predicates in modal terms.

[5]. On emotivity and nonveridicality, see also Beltrama (2015).

space). The complement of PE$_\mathcal{P}$ contains $\neg p$ worlds. The semantics we propose here may remind the reader of the Best ordering used for modals (Portner 2009), but our ordering source merely contains $p$.

Hence, the gradability of the emotive predicate triggers an emotion space $\mathcal{E}$ and partitions it into $p$ and $\neg p$ worlds. The emotion space is thus a nonveridical space. Now that we have the semantics for the emotive component, let us put it together with the presupposition of subjective veridicality in the doxastic space.

(40) Presuppositions of emotive verbs:
$[\![i \text{ V-emotive } p ]\!]^{Dox(i),\mathcal{E}}$ is defined iff
Dox($i$) contains only $p$ worlds (subjective veridicality), and
The emotion space $\mathcal{E}$ is nonveridical and contains $p$ and $\neg p$ worlds (emotive nonveridicality)

The emotion and the doxastic space are independent of one another, as emotion is not a kind of belief. The emotive verb obeys the Nonveridicality Axiom and presupposes that the emotion space is partitioned, just as with other subjunctive licensers, i.e., modals, suppositional doxastics, and bouletics. The partitioned space is not epistemic, as was the case with those—it can therefore not be said that the emotion expresses epistemic uncertainty. Given the partition, subjunctive is absolutely expected and consistent with the predictions we have made so far.

As an illustration, consider an emotive sentence, say *I am happy that Bridget came today*. There are $p$ worlds in my emotion space, but also $\neg p$ worlds, worlds where I do not have the emotion. The sentence asserts that $p$ worlds are worlds in which I am happy, and $\neg p$ worlds are those in which I am sad. The emotive space describes my emotional state in terms of the propositions that make the emotion true. The attitude, just like any other attitude, introduces in the assertion a quantification over those worlds in which the emotion that they denote is true.

### 7.3.2 *The Assertion of Emotives*

On the analysis that attitudes and MUST modals introduce universal quantification, emotives are no exception: they introduce universal quantification over the positive extent of the emotion modal base, asserting that, in all worlds compatible with the sentiment, $p$ is true.

The mechanics is thus similar to the mechanics we proposed for doxastics, bouletics, and modals. An ordering source carves out the positive extent of the modal base, that part of the modal base in which the prejacent is true.

(41)  $PE_{\mathcal{E}} = \{w \mid \forall q \in PE\, q(w)\}$

The positive extent is thus defined as the set of worlds in which all the relevant propositions (compatible with the emotion at hand) are true. In these worlds $p$ is true. The truth condition is then universal quantification over these worlds. Thus the final analysis for emotive is as follows:

(42)  Emotives: final analysis:
$[\![i\,\text{V-emotive}\,p]\!]^{w,Dox(i),\mathcal{E}}$ is defined iff
Dox($i$) contains only $p$ worlds (subjective veridicality).
$\mathcal{E}$ is nonveridical and contains $p$ and $\neg p$ worlds (emotive nonveridicality).
If defined:
$[\![i\,\text{V-emotive}\,p]\!]^{w,Dox(i),\mathcal{E}}$ is true iff $\forall w' \in PE_{\mathcal{E}} : p(w')$

This analysis entails that, had $p$ not been realized, the attitude holder would have not had the emotion. The counterfactual flavor is thus not hard-wired in the semantics, but it is calculated given the presupposition of subjective veridicality (and potentially factivity) and the nonveridical structure of the modal base. This is, we believe, a welcome result, consistent with the intuitions about emotives.

With this analysis at hand, we will move on to capture awareness predicates, which also behave like emotives.

## 7.4 Attitudes of Awareness

Awareness is arguably a layer of epistemic nature, supplementary to the knowledge layer (see also Jäger and Franke 2011). Languages differ as to how they construct this epistemic space, which is independent of knowledge itself within a single agent, i.e., the idea being that one can know something without being aware that she does (see also discussion in Stanley 2008 about knowledge and certainty).

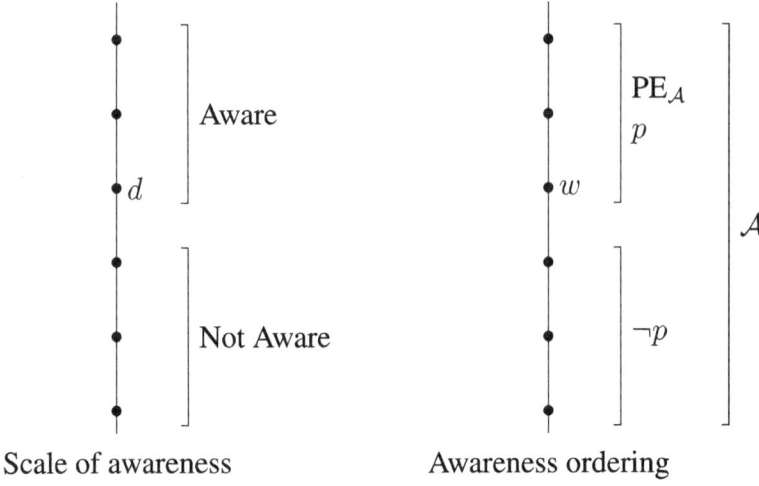

FIGURE 7.2 The nonveridical space of awareness.

The knowledge space is binary in the sense that one can only know or not know a particular fact. One cannot know a fact B more than one can know a fact B; if $i$ knows A and $i$ knows B then both A and B are known to $i$. The awareness space, on the other hand, can indeed be conceived of as gradable, on a par with the emotive space, to the point that one is aware of some of the facts she knows and not of others. The awareness space, in this respect, can be partitioned in two: those worlds in which the propositions of which I am aware are true and those worlds in which the propositions of which I am not aware are not true.

Note that $p$ is objectively true in all worlds. In the Figure 7.2, we only picture the awareness space $\mathcal{A}$, which is partitioned between $p$ and $\neg p$ worlds, in a way parallel to the emotive space. Here $p$ worlds are worlds in which the attitude holder is in a state of awareness of $p$, and $\neg p$ worlds are worlds in which the attitude holder is not aware of $p$.

Italian illustrates that the epistemic *be aware* space can also be understood as gradable, producing nonveridicality on a par with emotives, as in the schema above. This explains why the awareness predicate selects the subjunctive in Italian:

(43) È molto/poco cosciente che tu sia stanco.
 is very/little aware that you be.SUBJ.3sg tired
 He is very/little aware that you are tired.

(44) Maria è più cosciente di Gianni dell'accaduto.
    Mary is more aware of John of happened
    mary is more aware than John of what has happened.

The space for *essere cosciente* now is gradeable $\mathcal{A}$, partitioned into positive extent (PE) and negative extent, just as with emotives.

(45) Awareness in Italian:
    $[\![i \text{ sono cociente } p ]\!]^{M(i),\mathcal{A}}$ is defined iff $M(i)$ contains only $p$ worlds (subjective veridicality)
    $\mathcal{A}$ is nonveridical and contains $p$ and $\neg p$ worlds (awareness nonveridicality).
    If defined: $\forall w' \in \text{PE}_\mathcal{A} : p(w')$

(46) Sono cosciente che Anna è/sia     a casa.
    am aware that Anna be.SUBJ.3sg at home
    I am aware that Ann is home.

For Italian, the assertion of BE AWARE will be like that of the emotive, dividing the awareness space between $p$ and $\neg p$ worlds, thereby producing nonveridicality as reflected in the choice of the subjunctive. We see that the space of "awareness" is conceptualized as a partitioned one, including worlds of awareness and worlds of nonawareness. Awareness worlds (the Positive Extent $\text{PE}_\mathcal{A}$) are $p$ worlds. We see that awareness is lexicalized along the pattern of emotivity.

In Greek, by contrast, awareness verbs select indicative, thus aligning with knowledge verbs. We propose that $\mathcal{A}$ in Greek is simply a veridical, nonpartitioned epistemic or solipsistic space. And since it has a veridical presupposition, the awareness verb is exactly construed like KNOW:

(47) Awareness in Greek:
    $[\![i \text{ exi-epignosi that } p ]\!]^{w,i,\mathcal{A}}$ is defined iff $w \in p$.
    If defined $[\![i \text{ exi-epignosi that } p ]\!]^{w,i,\mathcal{A}} = 1$ iff $\forall w' \in \mathcal{A}(i) : p(w')$

(48) O Nicholas exei epignosi oti/*na     i Ariadne tou
    the Nicholas has awareness that.IND/SUBJ the Ariadne him says
    leei psemata.
    lies
    Nicholas is aware that Ariadne is lying to him.

Greek lexicalizes "be aware" as a knowledge verb and Italian lexicalizes it as a gradable emotive. In Greek, notice that the construction *exo epignosi* literally means "have knowledge". Hence awareness predicates are a genuine case of semantic variation in the two languages.

Let us now ask the more general question: Why do we have this systematic difference between Greek and Italian in epistemic and doxastic verbs? We will answer that this difference illustrates a prototypicality effect. In Italian belief verbs can be subjunctive selectors and are not prototypically solipsistic, like the indicative selecting belief verb that we find in Greek. Now, if epistemic and belief verbs set the standard for subjunctive and indicative, as it is reasonable to assume, then languages seem to choose among possible lexicalizations of epistemic and doxastic attitudes those that better align with the general pattern set by the prototypical case of belief.

Finally, we want to reiterate that since the consciousness predicate can be a subjunctive selector, preference cannot be the key in determining mood, *pace* Villalta (2008). This is a point that we made earlier in view of the fact that doxastics remain doxastic when they shift to subjunctive in Italian. Gradability, offers the necessary structure for nonveridicality by providing a threshold for $p$ and $\neg p$ worlds that mirrors the positive and negative extent of the scale. The connection between evaluating (via a gradable space) and nonveridicality has broader applications, as seen also in recent work by Beltrama (2015).

With this result, let us now address the implications of the semantics we have proposed for mood morphemes. We will then move to predicates of fear.

## 7.5 Presuppositional Indicative Complementizer *pu*

At this point, it will be very useful, we think, to go back to the pragmatic contribution of mood morphemes that we established in chapter 4 and ask the question of how the mood sensitivities are consistent or even dictate their pragmatic behavior. We will revisit the flexible patterns with knowledge, memory, and perception verbs, addressing not just indicative vs. subjunctive distinction, but also the dimension of assertive versus presuppositional indicative that emerges in the *pu* versus *oti* distinction in Greek.

## 7.5.1 Updates of Mood Morphemes and Their Sensitivity to (Non)veridicality Connected

Thus far, we have been arguing for the following generalizations:

(49)  a. The subjunctive is sensitive to nonveridicality in the presuppositional component of an attitude verb or modal. Nonveridicality is partitioning of an epistemic space (epistemic uncertainty), or partitioning of a modal space more broadly, as we saw this to be the case with bouletic and emotive spaces.
  b. The indicative is sensitive to veridicality in both presupposition and assertion.
  c. Indicative *oti* is sensitive to the veridicality of assertion. It is selected by veridical epistemic and solipsistic verbs.
  d. The indicative *pu* is sensitive to the veridicality of the presupposition. It is selected by verbs that have a veridical presupposition (either a factive one or a presupposition of subjective veridicality).

The subjunctive versus indicative difference appears to be not just a difference in veridicality (indicative) versus nonveridicality (subjunctive), but also a difference at the level at which the sensitivity applies: the presupposition (subjunctive), and the assertion as well as presupposition (indicative). The presuppositional indicative manifested in Greek *pu* is, from this perspective, quite significant. *Pu* performs presuppositional anchoring, we argued in chap. 4. Given that the emotive complement, as we showed, has a presupposition of belief of *p*, we will refine presuppositional anchoring here as:

(50) Presuppositional indicative *pu*: Presuppositional anchoring
  Presuppositional indicative (Greek *pu*) can be used iff *p* itself or *i*'s belief of *p* is already in the common ground.

This allows for the cases where the presupposition is not factive, but subjective veridicality. The existence of an indicative marker like *pu* is important because it illustrates that the indicative can also be sensitive to presupposition, specifically a veridical presupposition. Hence, the indicative vs. subjunctive opposition does not simply map onto assertion vs. presupposition — although indeed the subjunctive remains sensitive to presuppositional content only. Our prediction is that *pu* will be possible with other lexical entries as long as they contain a veridical presupposition. This is indeed what we find with attitudes meaning KNOW, REMEMBER, and verbs of perception, which we will discuss next.

But before we proceed, consider that most languages that have subjunctive vs. indicative are unable to make the distinction drawn in Greek between *oti* and *pu*, or assertive versus presuppositional indicative. Italian, French, and the other European languages *lack* presuppositional indicative. Lacking this category, the only choice in these languages for emotives, consistent with the mood requirements that have emerged in this book, is the use of subjunctive. With emotive verbs, the assertive indicative can simply not be an option, because assertive indicative requires veridicality in the assertion:

(51) Assertive Indicative: Private Anchoring
Assertive Indicative (Greek *oti*, and indicative in Romance) adds the complement propostion $p$ to Dox(*subject*), or some variant thereof.

This explains why languages that lack the distinction between assertive and presuppositional indicative won't be able to use the indicative when a predicate has veridicality in the presupposition, like the emotives. Another important thing to consider is also the stereotypicality effects we pointed out earlier with the awareness predicate. The nonveridicality presupposition, by itself, is enough to license the subjunctive in the stereotypical doxastic predicate and, by extension, to all predicates that have it.

The subjunctive, as we said, performs nonassertive anchoring.

(52) Subjunctive Nonassertive Anchoring:
Do not add $p$ to M, Dox, or the common ground.

The discourse behavior of the mood morphemes follows their semantic sensitivity to veridicality and nonveridicality. Greek and Romance subjunctive can be used only if the relevant states (M, variants of Dox, and the emotive space) are presupposed by $i$ to be *nonveridical* spaces. If $i$ is in a state of uncertainty, then $i$ cannot utter $p$ with the intent to add it to the common ground or her epistemic of doxastic space; hence the presuppositional sensitivity of the subjunctive follows from the semantics and is not merely stipulated (as, e.g., in Farkas 2003).

## 7.5.2 Knowledge, Memory and Perception

Recall some data that we have presented earlier in the book. The verb *ksero* (know) may also combine with *pu, na*:

(53) O Janis kseri na kolibai.
 The John knows.3sg that.SUBJ swim.IMPERF.3sg
 John knows how to swim.

(54) O Pavlos kseri$_F$ pu efije i Roxani.
 the Paul knows.3sg that.IND left.3sg the Roxani
 Paul knows that Roxanne left.

KNOW *na* does not presuppose or add *na* to the common ground. It is merely a statement of *how-to* ability: John knows how to swim. The *pu* variant seems to be equivalent to the *oti* variant. The choice of *pu* has a mere rhetorical effect and makes the complement topical. Typically, as indicated, the word KNOW *kseri$_F$* is in focus, which highlights that Paul knows (and is not ignorant of, thus the focus is contrastive) the already given proposition that Roxanne left. The *oti* variant of this statement is a mere statement of knowledge with no contrast or any particular discourse weight on either KNOW or the complement.

(55) O Pavlos kseri oti efije i Roxani.
 the Paul knows.3sg that.IND left-3sg the Roxani
 Paul knows that Roxanne left.

Consider now the memory verb *thimame* (remember). The default, as we said, is the indicative *oti*, but *na* can also be used:

(56) O Nicholas thimate na kleini tin
 the Nicholas remember.3sg that.SUBJ close.NONPAST.3sg. the
 porta, alla den ine sigouros.
 door, but not is sure
 Nicholas remembered closing the door, but he is not entirely sure.

The *na*-version is compatible with a context where Nicholas is not fully sure about his memory, and allows some doubt. He is, thus, in a nonveridical state. The *oti* clauses are incompatible with such context:

(57) #O  Nicholas thimate         oti      eklise     tin porta, alla
      the Nicholas remembered.3sg that.IND closed.3sg the door,  but
      den ine sigouros.
      not is sure
      #Nicholas remembered that he closed the door, but he is not
      entirely sure.

Note the exact parallel with the English -*ing* clause. The *that* vs.*ing* difference is reflected in Greek with the *oti* vs. *na* distinction. We have discussed these cases before in chapter 4.

In Italian, *ricordarsi* (remember) is also able to license both indicative and subjunctive:

(58) Si     ricorda    che era          andato al    mare.
     REFL remembers that be.IMPF.3sg gone    at the sea
     He remember that he was gone at the seaside.

(59) Si     ricorda    che fosse        andato al    mare.
     REFL remembers that be.IMPF.SUBJ.3sg gone    at the sea
     He remember that he was gone at the seaside.

With the indicative, that he went to the seaside is part of the common ground, or it is at least in the memory space of the speaker. This is equivalent to the *pu*-memory in Greek. With the subjunctive version, two interpretations are possible: (a) the attitude holder has a fuzzy memory, or (b) the memory is not shared in the common ground. In both cases, there is nonveridicality either at the level of the memory space of the individual anchor or in the collective space (we come back later to the nonassertive update in the common ground). We consider here only the case of fuzzy memory, which is equivalent to the *na*-memory of Greek.

Memory verbs, finally, can also take a *pu* complement. In this case, just as we saw with *ksero* know, they can't be used in the following context where the speaker doesn't know *p*. Consider the question: How much did that book cost?

(60) Thimame       *pu/oti           kostise  25 dollaria.
     remember.1sg that.IND-pu/IND-oti cost.3sg 25 dollars
     I remember that it cost 25 dollars.

(61) Ksero     *pu/oti   kostise 25 dollaria.
      know.1sg that.IND cost.3sg 25 dollars
      I know that it cost 25 dollars.

In this context, the person asking the question does not know how much the book costs, in other words, the price of the book is not known in the common ground. In this case, *pu* cannot be used, in accordance with what we predict. The *oti* variant is a perfect answer.

Now, consider a case when *pu* and *oti* are both felicitous:

(62) Thimame      pu/oti   to vilvio kostise 25 dollaria.
      remember.1sg that.IND the book cost.3sg 25 dollars
      I remember that the book cost 25 dollars.

In this case, the *pu*-memory corresponds to common knowledge.

We can capture these alterations as follows. Recall that with verbs such as *thimame* (remember), we are looking at Mem (subject), that is to say, the set of propositions that are remembered by the attitude holder:

(63) Memory state of an individual anchor $i$:
     A state Mem($i$) is a set of worlds associated with an individual $i$ representing worlds compatible with what $i$ remembers.

(64) $[\![i \text{ remember-}oti/that\, p]\!]^{Mem,i}$ is $= 1$ iff $\forall w' \in \text{Mem}(i) : p(w')$.

Memory is construed solipsistically as a combination of knowledge and belief, as we said earlier, and takes indicative and *that*. What is remembered is indeed a combination of knowledge and belief. Memories are not photographic snapshots of the world but rather inner representations of events, construed, compensated for, with certain degree of vagueness by the person who remembers; Mem can contain also pure beliefs.

Memory can also be construed as remembering a fact, in which case we have *pu* and an epistemic M:

(65) O Nicholas thimate          pu       eklise     tin porta,
      the Nicholas remembered.3sg that.IND closed.3sg. the door,
      (#alla den ine sigouros).
      but   not is sure
      Nicholas remembers the fact that he closed the door, (#but he is not entirely sure).

(66) $[\![i \text{ REMEMBER-}pu/\text{the fact that } p]\!]^{w_0,\text{Mem},i}$ is $= 1$ iff $w_0 \in p$; if defined,
$\forall w' \in \text{Mem}(i) : p(w')$

Here we have the factive presupposition $w_0 \in p$, plus commitment in Mem.

The subjunctive variant, however, uses Mem, and the presupposition that $M_{epistemic}$ is nonveridical. In this case, what is remembered will be contrasted with what is known. In the *na* version the memory seems unclear or vague; the *oti* memory is more precise and commital. The difference illustrates that in the *oti* complement we have a veridical doxastic state, but in the *na* complement we have a vague memory, with uncertainty about the door being closed in all worlds.

(67) Suppositional memory:
$[\![i \text{ REMEMBER}_{sup} \, p]\!]^{M,\text{Mem},i}$ is defined iff $M(i)$ is epistemic and nonveridical (partitioned epistemic modal base). If defined,
$[\![i \text{ REMEMBER}_{sup} \, p]\!]^{M,\text{Mem},i} = 1$ iff $\forall w' \in \text{Mem}(i) : p(w')$

The interplay is crucially between veridicality in memory but partition (nonveridicality) in the presupposition. The subjunctive is triggered, exactly parallel to Italian doxastics.

Consider finally, verbs of perception like *see*:

(68) O Nicholas idhe ton Flavio na kleini
the Nicholas saw.3sg the Flavio that.SUBJ close.impf.nonpast.3sg
tin porta, alla i porta dhen ine kleisti.
the door, but the door not is closed
Nicholas saw Flavio closing the door, but the door is not closed.

(69) O Nicholas idhe oti o Flavio eklise ton porta,
the Nicholas saw3sg that.IND the Flavio closed.3sg. the door,
#alla i porta den ine klisti.
but the door not is closed
#Nicholas saw that Flavio closed the door, but the door is not closed.

Observe again the contrast between an *-ing* complement and a *that* complement in English. The complement conveys direct perception, seeing with Nicholas' own eyes. In the *na* version seeing seems more vague, like with the memory verb, and the memory of closing of the door need not necessarily include the result state of the door being closed. The *oti* memory version includes that state. The difference again illustrates that in the *oti* complement we have a veridical doxastic state that includes the result, but the *na* complement conveys uncertainty about the door being closed.

For *p* being "Flavio closes the door and the door is closed":

(70) Solipsistic SEE (*vlepo oti*)
$[\![i \text{ vlepo/SEE}_{belief} \, p]\!]^{\text{Dox},i}$ is = 1 iff
$\forall w' \in \text{Dox}(i) : p(w')$

(71) Suppositional SEE (*vlepo na*):
$[\![i \text{ SEE}_{sup} \, p]\!]^{M,\text{Dox},i}$ is defined iff $M(i)$ is epistemic and nonveridical (partitioned epistemic modal base).
If defined, $[\![i \text{ SEE}_{sup} \, p]\!]^{M,\text{Dox},i} = 1$ iff $\forall w' \in \text{Dox}(i) : p(w')$

The *pu* variant, again, is like *thimame* and KNOW: the complement is now a fact marked with *pu*:

(72) O Nicholas idhe$_F$ pu o Flavio eklise ton porta.
the Nicholas saw.3sg that.IND the Flavio closed.3sg. the door
Flavio closed the door. Nicholas saw it.

To sum up: the mood alternations we see here are systematic and completely predicted by our main ideas, repeated here:

(73) a. The subjunctive is sensitive to nonveridicality in the presuppositional component of an attitude verb.
b. The indicative *oti* is sensitive to the veridicality of assertion. It is selected by factive and veridical solipsistic verbs.
c. The indicative *pu* is sensitive to the veridicality of the presupposition. It is selected by verbs that have a veridical presupposition.

Let us move on now to see how this theory explains the behavior of fear attitudes.

## 7.6 Attitudes of Fear

The mood patterns with fear predicates are a choice between indicative and subjunctive, correlating expectedly with prospective nonpast (subjunctive) and past or present tense (indicative), in agreement with the general pattern observed in this book. We also observe a special complementizer in Greek (*mipos*) and English (*lest*).

### 7.6.1 Three Empirical Patterns

Here are the generalizations specific to fear attitudes:

(74) Varieties of fear attitude:
  a. Fear to do something (subjunctive).
  b. Fear as a doxastic attitude toward something unfortunate that happened (indicative).
  c. Fear that an unfortunate possibility will be/has been realized (special complementizer *mipos/lest*; subjunctive with expletive negation in French).

Let us consider these in turn.

(a) Fear to do something: Subjunctive or infinitive with nonpast.

(75) O   Pavlos fovate *pu/*oti/na vgi           ekso.
     the Paul   fears  that.SUBJ go.NONPAST.3sg outside
     Paul is afraid to go outside.

(76) Paul a peur   de sortir.
     Paul is afraid of going out
     Paul is afraid to go out.

(77) Paolo ha  paura di uscire.
     Paul  has fear  of go out
     Paul is afraid to go out.

*Pu*, as we see, is impossible with predicates of fear, which leads us to postulate that there is no factivity or subjective veridicality presupposition. The subjunctive/indicative version is a fear to perform an action. The fear does not imply that the action is not desirable. As we said earlier, Paul might fear to go outside because it is raining and he doesn't want to get wet, while at the same time he really wants to go outside because he has a date he has been looking forward to for the entire week. Likewise, I may fear for some reason to do something I want very much to do, such as give a talk in front of a big audience.

(b) Fear as a doxastic attitude toward something unfortunate that happened, is happening or will happen: assertive indicative.

(78) a. O    Pavlos fovate oti/*pu/na                           i    aitisi   tou
       the Paul    fears    that.IND-oti/IND-pu/SUBJ the request his
       aporifthike.
       was-denied.3sg
       Paul is afraid that his request was denied.
    b. O    Pavlos fovate oti/*pu/na                           i    aitisi   tou
       the Paul    fears    that.IND-oti/IND-pu/SUBJ the request his
       tha    aporifthi.
       FUT be-denied.NONPAST.3sg
       Paul is afraid that his request will be denied.
    c. O    Pavlos fovate oti/*pu/na                           vrexi.
       the Paul    fears    that.IND-oti/IND-pu/SUBJ rain.PRES.3sg
       Paul is afraid it is raining (unfortunately).

The indicative statement reads like a statement of belief, qualified negatively: *Paul believes that, unfortunately for him, his request was denied.* The use of *oti* is expected, and likewise note how the English words *fear, be afraid* acquire the same doxastic flavor. The unfortunate reading is due to the nature of fear: we tend to fear something unpleasant, threatening, or uncomfortable. In a Gricean manner, the choice of FEAR instead of a regular doxastic verb violates manner and brings about the unfortunate reading.

There is a parallel in Italian, but the indicative version is only allowed with the first-person subject and has the flavor of politeness (see Tahar, 2018 and references therein). In French, the indicative cannot be used, and the subjunctive is mandatory across all these interpretations. In addition, expletive negation is also mandatory with fear predicates in this use:

(79) a. Paolo ha paura che la sua richiesta sia stata negata.
Paul has fear that the his request be.SUBJ.3sg been denied
Paul is afraid that his request was denied.
b. Paolo ha che la sua richiesta sia negata.
Paul has fear that the his request be.SUBJ.3sg denied
Paul is afraid that his request will be denied.
c. Ho paura che piove.
am afraid that rain.IND.3sg.
I am afraid that it is raining.

(80) J'ai peur qu'il #pleut/ne pleuve.
I have fear that-it rain.IND.3sg/expletive-negation rain.SUBJ.3sg.
I am afraid that it is raining.

The use of so-called expletive negation with fear predicates is quite common, and is found even in languages typologically unrelated to French such as Korean and Japanese (Yoon 2012). Yoon in fact argues, based exactly on the parallel between the subjunctive mood and expletive negation, that expletive negation is the realization of subjunctive mood in languages that lack mood morphology (Korean, Japanese). In line with Yoon's work, the expletive negation can be understood as contributing the negative component — a desirability scale in Yoon's approach.

We extend our theory of emotion scale and (non)veridicality to verbs of fear. Like emotives, verbs of fear convey an emotional stance which is partitioned between a positive and a negative extent. This explains why they select the subjunctive and infinitives. But verbs of fear lack the veridical presupposition of emotives, therefore they never select the *pu*. The indicative is triggered because the verb of fear is used as a verb of belief. In Italian, the indicative is possible only when there is hedging. Fear attitudes, thus, have a life as true predicates of fear to act and as belief in something unfortunate.

Verbs of fear have yet a third dimension in their meaning, revealed in an additional selection pattern, with a special complementizer manifested in English with *lest* and in Greek with *mipos*.

(c) Fear of a possibility: *mipos, lest*.

(81) O Pavlos fovate mipos di           tin Maria.
    the Paul fears lest see.NONPAST.3sg the Mary
    Paul is afraid lest he see Mary.

English employs the special complementizer *lest* which is construed with a subjunctive. The *lest* complement is admittedly of higher register in English, therefore not as common and somewhat marked. Greek *mipos*, on the other hand, is a quite common word with other related uses, and the pattern of *mipos* with the fear predicate is likewise quite common and unmarked.

*Mipos* emerges from a historical path that fused the subjunctive negation *mi* with the indicative complementizer *pos*. Synchronically, it also has uses as a possibility epistemic adverb, but only in questions (Giannakidou 2009):

(82) Mipos irthe    i   Maria?
    maybe came.3st the Maria
    Did Mary come, perhaps?

(83) #Mipos irthe   i   Maria.
    maybe came.3sg the Mary
    *Perhaps Mary came.

The above shows a link between *mipos* and interrogatives. Recall that, as a possibility modal, *mipos* and questions convey the same kind of nonveridicality: nonveridical equilibrium, not bias, as we noted in chap. 2. Crucially, *mipos* is used also as an interrogative complementizer, equivalent to "whether":

(84) Me rotise    an/mipos efaga.
    me asked.3sg if/whether ate.1sg
    She asked me if/whether I ate.

The *mipos* version of the indirect question has a presupposition, absent in the *an/if* version, that the possibility of eating was under discussion. The reading of *mipos*, likewise, with verbs of fear has a presupposition that the possibility raised by the complement was under discussion. The fear space has the additional presupposition of being nonveridical, like all emotive spaces. The sentence in this case asserts that in all fear worlds the possibility of *p* is resolved positively. We will extend this analysis to *lest*.

### 7.6.2 The Semantics and Pragmatics of Fear

Consider first the case of subjunctive fear to do something:

(85)  O   Pavlos fovate *pu/*oti/na                  vgi
      the Paul  fears  that/IND-pu/IND-oti/SUBJ  go.NONPAST.3sg
      ekso.
      outside
      Paul is afraid to go outside.

(86)  Paul a peur  de sortir.
      Paul is afraid of going out
      Paul is afraid to go out.

(87)  Paolo ha  paura di uscire.
      Paul  has fear  of go out
      Paul is afraid to go out.

This, one could say, is the most prototypical case of fear. The attitude bearer Paul fears to do some future action that will bring some kind of discomfort, in this case to go out. Notice the infinitive and nonpast in English, along with the subjunctive in Greek and Italian. Notice also the absence of expletive negation in French. Recall that we argued that the fear does not imply lack of desirability, because Paul might actually want to go out to meet his friend, but it's raining and it is uncomfortable; or maybe there are riots raging on the streets and he fears getting hurt. Since fear is an emotion, it is reasonable to postulate a scale of emotion specific to fear. The scale is subjective, relatively coarse, and lacks a precise objective measure (see Fig. 7.3). Key is the threshold $d$ that partitions the scale for any individual $i$:

This partitioning allows us to define *Positive-Extent-worlds* (PE) for *p*:

(88)   $PE_\mathcal{P} = \{w' \in \mathcal{E}_\mathcal{P} : w'$ where the propositions in $\mathcal{P}$ are true $\}$

Here, the set $\mathcal{P}$ is the singleton set $\{p\}$. So $PE_\mathcal{P}$ contains all the worlds in which *p* is true. These are the feared worlds. But not all worlds in $\mathcal{E}$ are

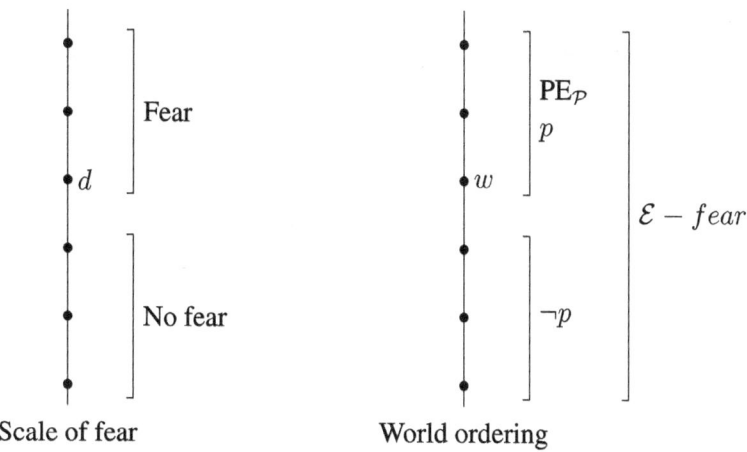

FIGURE 7.3 The nonveridical space of emotivity specific to fear.

PE worlds for $p$, $\mathcal{E}$ only partially supports $p$: $PE_\mathcal{P}$ is a subset of $\mathcal{E}$ (the fear space). The complement of $PE_\mathcal{P}$ contains $\neg p$ worlds. These are the worlds where $i$ does not fear to do $p$. The structure is exactly parallel to the one we posited for the general emotive case. Recall that the semantics we propose may remind the reader of the Best ordering used for modals (Portner 2009), but our ordering source merely contains $p$.

Fear, unlike the emotive class, lacks the factive presupposition. Here is the lexical entry:

(89) Fear predicate (FEAR to):
$[\![i\, FEAR\, p]\!]^\mathcal{E}$ is defined iff $\mathcal{E}$ is nonveridical and contains $p$ and $\neg p$ worlds (emotive nonveridicality).
If defined: $[\![i\, FEAR\, p]\!]^\mathcal{E} = 1$ iff $\forall w' \in PE\text{-}fear_\mathcal{E} : p(w')$

Words such as *fovame, be afraid, aver paura* and the like denote FEAR to and select the subjunctive, as expected, since the presupposition is nonveridical. *Pu* is not licensed because there is no veridicality presupposition.

The indicative version *FEAR that*, on the other hand, is a case where fear is grammaticalized as a kind of solipsistic belief just as in the case of awareness, memory, or perception with indicative (see Tahar, 2018).

(90) a. Paolo ha paura che la sua richiesta sia stata
Paul has fear that the his request be.SUBJ.3sg been
negata.
denied
Paul is afraid that his request was denied.
b. Paolo ha paura che la sua richiesta sia negata.
Paul has fear that the his request be.SUBJ.3sg denied
Paul is afraid that his request will be denied.
c. Ho paura che piove.
am afraid that rain.IND.3sg
I am afraid that it is raining.

(91) J'ai peur qu'il #pleut/ne pleuve.
I have fear that-it rain.IND.3sg/expletive-negation rain.SUBJ.3sg
I am afraid that it is raining.

(92) *Doxastic* fear, I:
$[\![i\,\text{FEAR}_{belief}\,p]\!]^{\text{Dox},i}$ is = 1 iff $\forall w'' \in \text{Dox}(i) : p(w'')$ (fear that)
Implicature triggered by expletive negation: $p$ is undesirable by $i$.

It is, in other words, the choice of model (emotive or *Dox*) that produces the apparent difference in meaning, just as with modal verbs, bouletics, and the other attitudes we have observed in the course of this investigation. Solipsistic doxastic fear conveys that $i$ has the belief that $p$ is, will be, or was true (we have abstracted away from time here) and that $p$ is undesirable by $i$. Recall that expletive negation can be used (though not in Greek), and we argue that it is a reflex of the undesirability, essentially following Yoon (2012). We add the undesirability clause as an implicature above and it follows from Gricean manner, as we said earlier, because FEAR is chosen rather than an expected doxastic verb such as BELIEVE. It is also conceivable that undesirability is a presupposition of doxastic fear, though clearly it is not a factive presupposition:[6]

(93) *Doxastic* fear, II:
$[\![i\,\text{FEAR}_{belief}\,p]\!]^{\text{Dox},i}$ can be defined iff $p$ is undesirable by $i$;
if defined, $[\![i\,\text{FEAR}_{belief}\,p]\!]^{w,\text{Dox},i} = 1$ iff $\forall w' \in \text{Dox}(i) : p(w')$

---

[6]. For an extensive discussion about the presuppositions and implicatures of *craindre* (fear) in French, see Mari and Tahar 2020.

Whichever version one chooses, the bottom line is that FEAR TO and FEAR THAT differ in the choice of model and the premise of desirability. FEAR TO can be fear to do an otherwise highly desirable thing—you might want to fly but you can still have fear to do it, you might want very much to talk to someone but fear to do it. In other words, the emotion of fear is independent of desirability or lack thereof. Fear THAT is not, in essence, fear at all.

Fear *lest/mipos*, finally, can be thought of as a variant of FEAR TO. It is important to note that many languages lack this specific variant (e.g., Italian) and employ the subjunctive FEAR TO for this version. Just like doxastic fear, fear *lest* considers both $p$ and $\neg p$, and expresses that $p$ is undesirable. In addition, we will argue, there is a contextual requirement that whether $p$ or $\neg p$ is under discussion:

(94) Presupposition 1: Whether Maria is coming or not is under discussion. This is consistent with the fact that *mipos* is interrogative complementizer.
Presupposition 2: The fear space is nonveridical, as is the case with FEAR TO.
Assertion: In all fear worlds the question is resolved positively, i.e., $p$ is the case.
Implicature or presupposition: $p$ is undesirable.

The use of *mipos* has remained mysterious in the Greek literature for quite a while, and the analysis we offer here is new. Recall that in French and Italian the subjunctive is used (which is explained by (ii) below) and French adds the use of *ne* (Tahar, 2018).

(95) Fear predicate (FEAR to):
$[\![i\,\text{FEAR}\,p]\!]^{\mathcal{E}}$ is defined iff:
(i) whether $p$ is/was/will be true or not is under discussion ($p$ or $\neg p$); and
(ii) $\mathcal{E}$ is nonveridical and contains $p$ and $\neg p$ worlds (emotive nonveridicality).
If defined: $[\![i\,\text{FEAR}\,p]\!]^{\mathcal{E}} = 1$ iff $\forall w' \in \text{PE-fear}_{\mathcal{E}} : p(w')$

*Mipos* and *lest*, in this analysis, need a question presupposition to be licensed. In this sense they are like the subjunctive. We can think of them as special subjunctives, since they presuppose a nonveridical space, differing from the "regular" subjunctive in that they presuppose a question.

According to Mari and Tahar (2019) expletive negation reverses the ordering source by creating a negative ordering of undesirability. In this case, the scale is determined by the propositions in the extension of the fear predicate in a given context and the extension of fear is conceived as the complement of the positive extension. Since this move is not necessary, expletive negation is disposable. The reasons for its use have historical roots in Latin that Mari and Tahar (2019) explain by tracing expletive negation to prohibitive negation, used to create negative preferences with imperatives and bouletics more generally.

## 7.7 Conclusions

In this chapter, we considered the mood patterns observed with propositional attitudes of emotion. In our discussion, we relied on the gradable, scalar nature of emotion, and we articulated a precise semantics for emotion which capitalized on its scalar nature. We proposed a morphism between emotion scales and worlds which renders the emotive space nonveridical, thus sanctioning the subjunctive. Emotive predicates also have a presupposition of subjective veridicality or factivity, which is responsible for licensing the Greek presuppositional complementizer *pu*. Languages that lack this complementizer typically resort to the subjunctive (though the indicative may still be an option; Quer 2001). Emotion predicates will come with lexical entries that are akin to the mixed veridicality patterns of modals, bouletic attitudes, and suppositional doxastics that we are, by now, familiar with. Verbs of awareness can also be construed as containing emotive scales—and in this case they select subjunctive, as expected. This is the case of Italian. Again as expected, Greek grammaticalizes awareness as a knowledge predicate.

Overall, we found again that the apparent changes of meaning reflect not ambiguity but flexibility with respect to the kind of modal bases emotion predicates can take as arguments. They can take an emotive modal base, an epistemic, or a doxastic one, as was the case with doxastic fear. The meaning shifts observed reminded us of the meaning shifts that we encountered in the study of modal verbs and bouletic attitudes. Acknowledging this possibility of flexible modal base association, therefore, accomplishes two highly desirable goals: it highlights the similarities between attitudes and modals, and offers a simple and systematic account of meaning shifts with propositional attitudes that avoids ambiguity.

CHAPTER EIGHT

# Epilogue: Truth and Veridicality in Grammar and Thought

We set out at the beginning to investigate the question—central for language, central for thought—of how truth and the constructs of truth we identified as subjective veridicality are conceptualized in the grammar of human language. We established a number of phenomena that are particularly revealing for such an exploration: modality, propositional attitudes, temporal dependencies, and mood selection. In this final chapter, we want to highlight what the central findings of our investigation have been, and what the implications might be for other related phenomena.

## 8.1 What We Found

One important thing that we found was that knowledge is the only realm of truth—the realm traditionally called factive or *realis*, and which we identified with objective veridicality. Knowledge verbs are the only verbs that engage with the world directly and whose complement sentences can refer to actual facts. In any other embedding, the world and reality are accessed only *privately* and indirectly, via subjective representations that individuals construct—which we called "models", "information states", and "modal bases"—based on their beliefs, memories, imagination, desires, expectation, and of course also knowledge. When a choice is made to use a modal expression or a propositional attitude verb, the speaker (as is the case with modals) or the propositional attitude bearer (as is the case with attitude verbs) is expressing a stance toward truth by admitting essentially that she lacks knowledge. These stances form veridicality commitments that can be stronger or weaker, depending on the modal or the chosen attitude.

The semantics of modal verbs and propositional attitudes is a privileged locus within which to observe how individuals rely on their own conceptualization of reality, through language, in the attempt to structure possibilities according to their knowledge, beliefs, priorities, and expectations. Propositional attitude and modal meanings, in our theory, emerge as stances toward propositions that can be *veridical* or *nonveridical*. Our approach has been that, contrary to what previous literature has proposed, propositional attitude verbs and modal expressions are in fact quite similar—differing essentially only in what kind of individual anchor they have: the speaker for modals, the attitude subject for propositional attitudes. The logic of and constraints in reasoning are essentially the same, as we showed. Both modals and attitudes can be flexible with respect to modal bases they associate with—and this has allowed us explain much of of the meaning and mood shifts observed within and across languages without resorting to ambiguity. Importantly, the shifts in the modal base correlate with temporal shifts in the embedded clause, and explain the orientation of some attitudes to the future or past as well as potential changes in meaning that may look initially like ambiguity.

## 8.2 Veridical and Nonveridical Stance

We have distinguished two stances individual anchors take toward propositional content: the veridical and the nonveridical stance. Veridicality relates to knowledge and solipsitic commitment, as we showed. Modalization, on the other hand, is the prototypical nonveridical stance, i.e., acknowledging lack of knowledge, belief, or certainty. Recall: the speaker has a choice to use an unmodalized sentence in the simple past or present tense, or to use a modal verb:

(1) a. It is raining.
    b. It must be raining.
    c. It may be raining.

The modal sentences do not entail that it is raining, or that the speaker knows or believes that it is raining. By uttering the sentence "It is raining," on the other hand, the speaker puts forth her knowledge or belief that it is raining. Putting forth her knowledge means that the speaker intends $p$ to be added to the common ground and become public knowledge. Upon adding *p* to the common ground, a listener might object to it if they know otherwise, e.g., if they just came back from outside and noticed that it is no longer raining. But insofar as the speaker is concerned, and *given what she thinks at the time of utterance*, it is true that it is raining.

When the speaker has knowledge, we say that the speaker is in a veridical state regarding the proposition *It is raining*. And being in a veridical state means that the speaker is fully committed to the proposition *It is raining*. We can think of the veridical stance as the mental state (or attitude) of commitment to truth. This is not commitment in the sense of commitment to act; veridical commitment is independent of action since it relies purely on knowledge and belief. The veridical stance is commitment to truth motivated by information that the speaker possesses, and which we can think of as the body of evidence.

Veridical stance is a precondition for assertion, we argued:

(2) Veridical information state as a prerequisite for assertion:
A sentence *S* is assertable if and only if the speaker is in a veridical state about *p* denoted by *S*.

That veridicality is a precondition on assertion follows from Gricean Quality, of course, which is the foundation of cooperative communication. There are, of course, noncooperative conversations such as advertising, propaganda, so-called bullshit (Frankfurt 2005), or types of political speech where truthfulness is not required. These cases deserve full consideration, and it is our hope that the framework we proposed in this book offers a number of tools that will be helpful for the analysis of noncooperativity and deceptive language.

In languages that have mood distinctions, indicative is the mood by default associated with a veridical state. The veridical stance relies on a homogeneous epistemic or doxastic state that does not allow both *p* and $\neg p$, and creates commitments of the individual anchors. Commitments are kinds of certainties that the anchors have about the truth of propositions. We say "kinds" of certainties because, as we saw, veridical commitments can be doxastic (belief based), or they can be based on memory— which we argued can be construed as a kind of belief—or on perception, desire, and expectations, i.e., what we just called the body of evidence, which is rational and follows stereotypical rules. Expectation can be understood as comprising elements of both desire and belief, as we saw in chap. 5, and some verbs (e.g., verbs of persuasion, assertive verbs) vacillate between the two options and may be anchored to either state. Veridical commitment can even be purely fictional, as is the case with dreams and fictional attitudes, in which case the subjective veridical stance replaces reality completely.

The nonveridical stance, on the other hand, is the case when the individual anchor reasons with uncertainty, and cannot be fully committed to the truth. Reasoning with uncertainty is one of the features of the human thought that most puzzles theoreticians across disciplines in a large variety of domains. In the nonveridical stance, the mental state allows both options $p$ and $\neg p$, and this produces all sorts of weakening in the meaning of a propositional attitude verb or a modal. This nonveridical weakening typically takes the form of a presupposition. Hence, in the subjective realm, while the veridical stance typically dominates the assertion, the nonveridical stance manifests itself as a presupposition. In the objective realm, that is with knowledge, veridicality characterizes both.

We have argued for a unified theory of attitudes and modals, touching upon a deeper mechanism in human linguistic and cognitive behavior, one that acknowledges uncertainty while expressing partial commitment. It is refreshing, we think, to recognize this—and, to our eyes, surprising how seriously this possibility has been overlooked in previous literature. Scholars talk about "weak" and "strong" modals or attitudes, presuming monolithic characterizations of the meanings. But we have shown that uncertainty and commitment can coexist in a lexical entry (what we called "mixed" veridicality). We have shown this to be a quite general case, and for this reason we avoided using the terms "weak" and "strong", since they are, from this perspective, too vague. The only meaningful application of "weak" and "strong" is to distinguish between what we called *solipsistic* and *suppositional* attitudes.

## 8.3 Mood Choice

Our overall conclusion about the grammatical phenomenon of indicative versus subjunctive choice in embedded clauses—complements, adjuncts, relative clauses— is that indicative is the mood of objective truth and of the veridical stance; and the subjunctive is the mood chosen when the individual anchor has a nonveridical stance toward the proposition $p$. Having a nonveridical stance toward $p$ means that the subjunctive is chosen when the anchor cannot be committed to the proposition. When the anchor cannot be committed to the proposition, there is uncertainty: the modal base is partitioned into $p$ and $\neg p$ worlds, and does not entail $p$.

As a quick summary, we distinguished between two types of attitudes:

(3) Veridical propositional attitudes:
 (i.) Epistemic attitudes are veridical (objectively and subjectively)
 (ii.) Solipsistic attitudes are veridical only subjectively: they entail that $p$ is true in the anchor's $i$ modal space.

(4) Nonveridical propositional attitudes:
 A propositional attitude is nonveridical if it obeys the Nonveridicality Axiom.

The Axiom states the following:

(5) Nonveridicality Axiom:
 (i.) For ATTITUDE, ATTITUDE obeys the Nonveridicality Axiom iff ATTITUDE $p$ presupposes that the modal base M of the anchor $i$ of ATTITUDE is nonveridical, i.e., partitioned into $p$ and $\neg p$ worlds.
 (ii.) An ATTITUDE that obeys the Noniveridicality Axiom is called nonveridical.

(6) Nonveridicality of modals:
 All (non-alethic) modals obey the Nonveridicality Axiom.

The principles that guide mood choice in our theory are the following:

(7) Licensing condition for the *subjunctive* mood
 The subjunctive is licensed in the complement of a nonveridical ATTITUDE.

(8) Licensing condition for the *indicative* mood
 The indicative is licensed in the complement of a veridical ATTITUDE.

We have also seen cases where the subjunctive itself is a modal category, akin to a possibility epistemic modal (in questions, relative clauses).

Doxastic attitudes such as those of belief have often been considered the prototypically solipsistic attitudes, and bouletic attitudes such as those of desire have been treated as the prototypically nonveridical attitudes. We have nonetheless shown that the matter is more nuanced than this. Doxastic lexical entries can be weakened with the infusion of the nonveridicality presupposition of epistemic uncertainty, as was shown to be systematically the case with Italian, but also happens to be the case with memory and perception attitudes in both Greek and Italian. Bouletics, conversely, can become solipsistic as in the case of HOPE and PROMISE.

These fine-grained distinctions have led us to argue that we can spell out general tendencies about mood selection, whereby Greek is a language that predominantly goes solipsistic, whereas Italian is a language that predominantly goes suppositional; and these tendencies generate more indicative and subjunctive respectively.

## 8.4 What Mood Flexibility Tells Us

We observed that mood flexibility with propositional attitudes is much more rampant than previously thought, and we took that flexibility to indicate flexibility in the attitude meaning $\alpha$, specifically that it is possible for $\alpha$ to be construed as obeying or not obeying the Nonverdicality Axiom. Mood shift does not necessitate ambiguity of $\alpha$ — but indicates that some attitude verbs can be underspecified with regards to whether they are construed with nonveridicality or not, as well as with respect to the types of modal spaces they take as arguments.

We observed potential shifts between bouletic and doxastic states with a single lexical entry. We found this to be the case in chap. 4 with Italian doxastics (Mari 2016a) and in chap. 5 with verbs meaning HOPE as well as with verbs of persuasion and assertion. The lexical shift in English between *deny* and *refuse* happens in Greek with different modal bases. When combining with a tense other than the NONPAST, the verb meanings were shown to shift to the doxastic state. Our account thus offered a simple explanation for what otherwise could be thought of as lexical ambiguity, and because the shift also correlates with the embedded tense, it renders tense a key factor. The shifts from doxastic to deontic modals are very similar and depend on tense in a very tight way. Indeed, we have a chain of semantic dependency that starts with the propositional attitude or modal verb and affects complementizer choice, mood choice, and embedded tense. These multidependencies are, in addition, one more reason to acknowledge that propositional attitudes and modal verbs are closer in their composition and logic than previously believed.

And here are some questions that arise. Why is it that some attitude types have flexibility and others do not? Why are the Greek doxastics construed only solipsistically, but in the same language attitudes of memory, perception, and persuasion are construed flexibly, as in Italian? Why is it that bouletics such as WANT are rigid in mood in both Greek and Italian, but HOPE and PROMISE words can be flexible? Why do some attitudes pose temporal restrictions on the arguments, and others do not? While it is impossible to give conclusive answers to all of these questions, we offered some concrete ideas that can help pave the way toward a more comprehensive understanding of the cognitive and conceptual aspects of the meanings of attitudes and modals.

Regarding volitional predicates, crucially, nothing in our analysis necessitates the concept of *preference* for the subjunctive selecting predicates, in stark contrast with what much of the current literature proposes (Heim 1992; Giannakidou 1997, 1998, 2009; Portner 1997; Villalta 2008; Moulton 2014; Grano 2016, 2018 and references therein). The concept of preference for the subjunctive became problematic in the realm of doxastics and epistemic modals, as we showed, since these remain doxastic with the subjunctive; and it is unnecessary for volitional attitudes too. The ingredients of veridicality (bouletic commitment) and the layers of meaning (specifically the presence or not of a nonveridical presupposition indicating lack of knowledge, as well as antifactivity) are sufficient to derive the mood patterns in Greek, Italian, and French—and have the welcome result of avoiding the empirically problematic overgeneralizations that preference accounts would have to make.

Our analysis has repercussions for the *that* vs. *to* choice in English, as we discussed further in chap. 5, thus challenging the idea that preference plays any role in that choice either. We also suggested that in English too the regulating factor behind the *that* vs. *to* choice is not finiteness but temporal restrictions, as they are derived from the attitude meaning. In contrast to many accounts again, in the theory we proposed the action in mood choice lies in the meaning of the attitude predicate, and *not* in the syntax of the complement clause. It is the verb meaning that enables syntactic choice, not the other way round. If complementizer choice could affect the meaning of the verb, there would in effect be no selectional restrictions; the higher verb would be able to combine with any complementizer or infinitive and the meaning would change accordingly. But this is clearly not the case. Flexibility is rampant but also systematically constrained, based on the clear parameters we identified in our work. The semantics of the predicate, we illustrated, offers an empirically more reliable foundation for explaining the properties of complement choice. It is the lexical meaning of the attitude $\alpha$ that determines the distribution of complementizers and morphological moods.

## 8.5 Anchoring, (Non)veridicality, and Informativity

Recall that in Greek mood morphemes appear as subordinators. As subordindators, they do not have inherent meaning, but contribute to the update of the embedded proposition $p$. Because we have embedding (and this characterizes both attitude verbs and modals which we jointly call attitudes $\alpha$), the prejacent $p$ cannot be directly added to the common ground under $\alpha$. The update will thus be mediated by $\alpha$. Semantic subjectivity, in other words, is mirrored in the way the information updates work.

An unembedded, unmodalized indicative assertion— which contains past or present tense, but not future because future, we argued, is a modal (Giannakidou and Mari 2018)— adds $p$ to the common ground. With an attitude of knowledge, $p$ is already in the common ground. With a solipsistic attitude, the private space replaces the common ground and what we called *private assertion* adds $p$ to Dox(*subject*):

(9) Indicative update: Private Assertion
 Add $p$ to the local Dox(*subject*).

Because $p$ is embedded under attitude $\alpha$, $\alpha$ acts syntactically as the barrier, i.e., the local context of update; the assertion of $p$ under $\alpha$ cannot access the common ground. That much should be clear from our discussion. The indicative (in Greek: *oti*) proposition is a signal to add $p$ to the local Dox(*subject*). The addition of $p$ to Dox, narrows down the worlds in those spaces by intersection, as expected:

(10) Dox($i$) + $p$ = {$w'$ in Dox where $p$ is true}

This private assertion anchors $p$ to the main subject's private space, thus performing a kind of context shift from the common ground. The private spaces can expand by adding propositions, just like unembedded assertions add to the context set $W(c)$. Embedded indicative in Italian functions in exactly the same way. *Oti* is unnecessary in main clauses, where addition happens in the common ground, and this explains, without any additional assumptions, the absence of *oti* in main clauses.

The indicative can also perform presuppositional anchoring, we said, as revealed with the complementizer *pu* in Greek. In this case, $p$ is required to already be in the common ground:

(11)   *PU*-anchoring: Presuppositional anchoring
       $p$ is already in the common ground.

Hence again the indicative does not add to the common ground. The fact that Greek lexicalizes an assertive and a nonassertive distinction in the indicative suggests quite clearly that the indicative mood is not fully isomorphic to assertion, contrary to what was previously thought.

On the other hand, when $\alpha$ obeys the Nonveridicality Axiom, the speaker does not know whether $p$ is objectively true, $p$ therefore cannot be added to Dox(*subject*), or the common ground, of course. The subjunctive, we proposed, performs Nonveridical anchoring:

(12)   Subjunctive: Nonveridical anchoring
       Do not add $p$ to Dox or the common ground.

The subjunctive mood is, in other words, a prohibition: do not add $p$. Given that, main clause subjunctives are either nonassertions or possibility statements; and in chap. 3 we generalized that in all cases the subjunctive mood is an instruction *not* to add $p$ to the common ground. A comparable update is the inquisitive anchoring with embedded questions (Greek *an*, "whether"). Inquisitive anchoring is a special case of nonveridical anchoring, we said:

(13)   Inquisitive anchoring
       Update common ground with ?$p$.

Inquisitive anchoring adds specifically a question to the common ground. The subjunctive does not add a question, but a question is indeed a nonveridical space, hence consistent with not updating with $p$. At this point, we want to offer some final thoughts on the effect of indicative versus nonindicative which, as is now clear, goes beyond mere mood choice in complement clauses.

The nonveridical state emerges as the underlying state for *all* nonindicative moods, including those which appear to affect the illocutionary force such as imperatives, optatives, and, of course, questions. Giannakidou (2013b) characterizes nonveridical assertions as *inquisitive*, thus similar to questions in that they have "nontrivial inquisitive content; and they are informationally weaker than past or present positive and negative assertions." (Giannakidou 2013b: 45). Hence, she concludes, from the point of view of nonveridicality, assertions do not behave as a uniform class, therefore a categorical distinction between assertion (trivial inquisitive content) and nonassertion (trivial informative content) is not desirable.[1] More desirable, and indeed reliable, is the semantic difference in veridicality.

Ciardelli et al. (2014) offer the following fact:

(14) Fact (Inquisitiveness in terms of possibilities):
   a. $\phi$ is inquisitive iff there are at least two possibilities for $\phi$.
   b. $\phi$ is an assertion iff there is exactly one possibility for $\phi$.

By Fact (14), and given that the two possibilities for $\phi$ are $\phi$ and $\neg\phi$, inquisitiveness becomes synonymous with nonveridicality:

(15) Veridical and nonveridical modal spaces, homogeneity (Giannakidou and Mari, 2018b):
   a. A modal space M is *veridical* with respect to a proposition $p$ iff it is positively homogeneous: $\forall w' \in M : p(w')$.
   b. A modal space M is *nonveridical* with respect to a proposition $p$ iff it is nonhomogeneous: $\exists w' \in M : p(w') \land \exists w'' \in M : \neg p(w'')$.
   c. A modal space M is *antiveridical* with respect to a proposition $p$ iff it is negatively homogeneous: $\forall w' \in M : \neg p(w')$.

---

1. Biased questions, at the same time, convey substantial information; hence, though inquisitive, their informative content is nontrivial. This suggests that the divide between inquisitiveness and informativity does not map straightforwardly onto assertion vs. question. Giannakidou and Mari (2019) take this up further to argue that the question itself is a modal structure—an idea that we hope to pursue in future work.

Inquisitive and nonveridical sentences convey nonveridical states, i.e., states with polar partitioning into $p$ and $\neg p$ worlds. So, inquisitive and nonveridical sentences boil down to the same thing. This is, we think, an important link to establish. A question, we argued, is like a possibility modal and conveys non-veridical equilibrium; a biased question is like a MUST modal and conveys bias. Veridicality and nonveridicality thus transcend the illocutionary force divide (assertion vs. question). Likewise, imperatives can be thought of as denoting nonveridical spaces, and they certainly have a antiveridical (or, antifactive) presupposition. But, contrary to how most researchers think about it, nonassertion is not the cause of nonveridicality; it is its effect. A nonhomogeneous state is what all nonassertions have in common.

In information nonbiased questions, there is nonveridical equilibrium, true uncertainty as to where the actual world is, i.e., in the positive or the negative space. The equilibrium is disrupted when the question is manipulated by material that creates bias. Universal modals are also manipulators of the nonveridical equilibrium, as we showed, and create bias toward $\phi$. What is common in all nonveridical/inquisitive states is that the epistemic agent has a choice about where to place the actual world: in the positive or in the negative space.[2] The notion of bias is useful for both questions and modality, as we showed—and this is a novel insight that emerged from our work. Bias, as we defined it, is much more precise than the impressionistic characterizations *weak, strong* used in the literature. The attitudes and modals that the literature calls strong are in fact biased, and still do not entail or add $p$.

The final lesson from our work concerns the division of labor between informativity and (non)veridicality. Roughly, the proposed distinction in Ciardelli et al. is the following:

(16) Inquisitiveness and Informativity:
   a. A question $?\phi$ has trivial informative content.
   b. An assertion $Assert\phi$ has trivial inquisitive content.

Our discussion has shown that nonveridical assertions also have nontrivial inquisitive content, hence they are informationally weaker than veridical

---

2. Disjunctions, Giannakidou 2013b notes, come with partitioned spaces too. The partition can be the expected polar one, e.g., *it rained or it didn't rain*, but it doesn't have to be; it can also be between two positive choices, $p$ and $q$.

(past or present) and negative assertions. Informativity thus correlates directly with (non)veridicality and not with illocutionary force. Other moods can also be understood in this way, e.g., the conditional mood, which we didn't discuss here because Greek and Italian do not have it. The misnomers used in the literature, likewise, such as the so-called indicative versus subjunctive conditionals, can now be understood in the light of the theory we have developed here. The notion of veridical commitment has been applied to the conditional protasis in recent work by Liu (2018), where veridicality is characterized as *elastic* precisely to capture the flexibility and gradience of commitment that (non)veridicality establishes and which we discussed extensively in this book.

In the end, what seems to matter for the veridicality judgment is whether a sentence presents the epistemic agent, i.e., the individual anchor, with one or more possibilities about the world, i.e. whether it reflects a homogeneous or nonhomogeneous stance. Superficially, this appears to correspond to the contrast between assertion versus nonassertion. However, nonveridical assertions show us that the contrast is just that: superficial. The more fundamental distinction is between a partitioned or homogeneous modal space, and this matters not only for propositional attitudes, modality, and mood choice—which is already quite a lot. It matters also for negative polarity and free choice items, evaluative adverbs (Liu 2012), as well as adverbs such as *totally* (Beltrama 2018), to mention just some of the recently discussed linguistic phenomena that demonstrably show this sensitivity.

It seems, therefore, unavoidable to conclude that nonveridical partitioning vs. homogeneity (veridicality, antiveridicality, commitment) is telling us something very essential about the logic of human language.

# References

Abraham, W. (2020). *Modality in Syntax, Semantics, and Pragmatics*. Cambridge: Cambridge University Press.

Abusch, D. (2004). On the Temporal Composition of Infinitives. In J. Gueron, J. Lecarme (eds.), *The Syntax of Time*, 27–53. Cambridge. MA: MIT Press.

Agouraki, Y. (1991). A Modern Greek Complementizer and Its Significance for Universal Grammar. *UCL Working Papers in Linguistics* 3:1–24.

Ambar, M. (2016). On Finiteness and the Left Periphery: Focusing on Subjunctive. In Blaszczak, J., A. Giannakidou, D. Klimek-Jankowska and M. Krzysztof (eds.), *Mood, Aspect, Modality Revisited: New Answers to Old Questions*, 129–180. Chicago: University of Chicago Press.

Anand, P. and A. Brasoveanu (2010). Modal Concord as Modal Modification. In *Proceedings of Sinn und Bedeutung* 14: 19–36.

Anand, P. and V. Hacquard (2013). Epistemics and Attitudes. *Semantics and Pragmatics*, 6:1–59.

Arregi, K. and P. Klecha (2015). The Morphosemantics of Past Tense. In T. Bui and D. Ozyıldız (eds.), *Proceedings of NELS 45*, Amherst, MA: GLSA.

Asher, N. and M. Morreau (1995). What Some Generic Sentences Mean. In G. Carlson and F.J. Pelletier (eds.). *The Generic Book*, 300–338. Chicago: University of Chicago Press.

Baker, Carl L. 1970. Double Negatives. *Linguistic Inquiry* 1:169–86.

Baunaz, L. (2015). On the Various Sizes of Complementizers. *Probus, 27(2)*: 193–236.

Banauz, L., and G. Puskás (2015). On Subjunctives and Islandhood. Unpublished manuscript, University of Geneva.

Baglini, R., and I. Francez (2016). The Implications of Managing. *Journal of Semantics 33(3)*: 541–560.

Bhatt, R. (1999). *Covert Modality in Non-finite Contexts*. PhD Dissertation, University of Pennsylvania.

Beaver, D. and J. Frazee (2016). Semantics. In *The Handbook of Computational Linguistics*. Oxford: Oxford University Press. DOI: 10.1093/oxfordhb/9780199573691.013.29.

Beltrama, A. (2018). Totally Between Subjectivity and Discourse. Exploring the Pragmatic Side of Intensification. *Journal of Semantics 35(2)*: 219–261.

Beltrama, A. (2016). *Bridging the Gap: Intensifiers Between Semantic and Social Meaning*. PhD dissertation, University of Chicago.

Beltrama, A. (2015). Great Pizzas, Ghost Negations: The Emergence and Persistence of Mixed Expressives. *Sinn und Bedeutung 19*.

Bertinetto, P.M. (1979). Alcune ipotesi sul nostro futuro (con alcune osservazioni su potere e dovere), *Rivista di grammatica generativa 4*, 77–138.

Bonami, O. and G. Godard (2008). Lexical Semantics and Pragmatics of Evaluative Adverbs. In L. McNally and C. Kennedy (eds.). *Adverbs and adjectives: Syntax, semantics and discourse*, 274–304. Oxford: Oxford University Press.

Borgonovo, C. and S. Cummins (2007). Tensed Modals. In L. Eguren and O. Fernandez Soriano (eds.). *Coreference, modality, and focus*. John Benjamins Publishing Company, Amsterdam/Philadelphia. 1–18.

Boogaart, R., and R. Trnavac, (2011). Imperfective Aspect and Epistemic Modality. In A. Patard and F. Brisard (eds.), *Cognitive Approaches to Tense, Aspect, and Epistemic Modality*, 217–248. Amsterdam: John Benjamins.

Bogal-Allbritten, E. A. (2016). *Building meaning in Navajo*. PhD Dissertation, University of Massachusetts - Amherst.

Bolinger, D. (1975). On the Passive in English. In *The First LACUS Forum* 1:57–80.

Bove, K.P. (2020). Mood Selection in Yucatec Spanish: Veridicality as the Trigger. *Lingua* 241 (2020) 102858.

Bresnan, J. W. (1972). Stress and syntax: A Reply. *Language*, 48:326–42.

Broekhuis, H., and H. J. Verkuyl, (2014). Binary Tense and Modality. *Natural Language and Linguistic Theory* 32(3): 973–1009.

Bulatović, A. G. (2008). *Modality, Futurity, and Temporal Dependency: The Semantics of the Serbian Perfective Nonpast and Future*. PhD diss., University of Chicago.

Castroviejo, E. and I. Oltra-Massuet. (2016). On Capacities and Their Epistemic Extensions. In C. Tortora, M. den Dikken, I. L. Montoya and T. O'Neil (eds.), *Romance Linguistics 2013: Selected Papers from the 43rrd LSRL*. Amsterdam: John Benjamins.

Chatzopoulou, A. (2019). *Negation and Nonveridicality in the History of Greek*. Oxford: Oxford University Press.

Chatzopoulou, A. (2012). *Negation and Nonveridicality in the History of Greek*. PhD diss., University of Chicago.

Chierchia, G. and S. McConnell-Ginet. (1990). *Meaning and Grammar: An Introduction to Semantics*. Cambridge, MA: MIT Press.

Ciardelli, I., J. Groenendijk, and F. Roelofsen. (2013). Inquisitive Semantics: A New Notion of Meaning. *Language and Linguistics Compass* 7(9): 459–476.
Cipria, A. and C. Roberts. (2000). Spanish Imperfecto and Pretaerito: Truth Conditions and Aktionsart Effects in a Situation Semantics. *Natural Language Semantics* 8(4): 297–347.
Cohen, J., and S. Nichols (2010). Colors, Color Relationalism, and the Deliverances of Introspection. *Analysis* 70(2): 218–228.
Coleman, L. (1975). The Case of the Vanishing Presupposition. In *Proceedings of the First Annual Meeting of the Berkeley Linguistics Society*, 78–89.
Comrie, B. (1976). *Aspect: An Introduction to the Study of Verbal Aspect and Related Problems*. Cambridge: Cambridge University Press.
Condoravdi, C. (2002). Temporal Interpretation of Modals: Modals for the Present and for the Past. In D. Beaver, Luis D. Cassillas Maritinez, Brady Z. Clark, S. Kaufmann (eds.), *The Construction of Meaning*, 59–88. Stanford, CA: CSLI Publications.
Condoravdi, C., and S. Lauer. (2012). Imperatives: Meaning and Illocutionary Force. *Empirical Issues in Syntax and Semantics* 9: 37–58.
Copley, B. (2002). *The Semantics of the Future*. PhD Diss., MIT.
Copley, B. (2009). *The Semantics of the Future*. New York: Routledge.
Cui, Y. (2015). *Modals in the Scope of Attitudes: A Corpus Study of Attitude-modal Combinations in Mandarin Chinese*. PhD diss., Georgetown University.
Davis, H., M. Louie, L. Matthewson, I. Paul, A. Reis Silva, and T. Peterson. (2010). Perfective Aspect and Actuality Entailments: A Cross-Linguistic Approach. *The Proceedings of SULA 5: The Semantics of Under-Represented Languages in the Americas*, 17–32. Amherst, MA: GLSA.
Davis, H., L. Matthewson, and H. Rullmann, (2009). Out of Control Marking as Circumstantial Modality in St'át'imcets. In L. Hogeweg, H. de Hoop and A. Malchukov (eds.), *Cross-linguistic semantics of tense, aspect and modality*, 205–244. Oxford: John Benjamins.
De Marneffe, M., C. Manning, and C. Potts. (2012). Did it Happen? The Pragmatic Complexity of the Veridicality Judgement. *Computational Linguistics* 38: 300–333.
Demirdache, H. and M. Uribe-Etxebarria. (2008). On the temporal syntax of non-root modals. In *Time and modality*, 79–113. Dordrecht: Springer.
Dendale, P. (2001). Le future conjectural versus devoir épistmique: différences de valeur et restrictions d'emploi. *Français Moderne*, 69(1): 1–20.
De Swart, H. (2007). A Cross-linguistic Discourse Analysis of the Perfect. *Journal of Pragmatics* 39(12): 2273–2307.
De Swart, H., G. Legendre, M. Putnam, and E. Zaroukian. (2015). Introduction. In G. Legendre, M. Putnam and E. Zaroukian (eds.), *Advance in OT Syntax and Semantics: From Unidirectional to Bidirectional OT*. Oxford: Oxford University Press.

Dowty, D. (1979). *Word Meaning and Montague Grammar*. Dordrech: Kluwer.
Egan, A. (2007). Epistemic Modals, Relativism, and Assertion. *Philosophical Studies* 133:1–22.
Egré, P. (2008). *Question-embedding and Factivity*. Paris: HAL Archives.
Farkas, D. (1982). *Intentionality and Romance Subjunctive Relatives*, PhD diss., Indiana University Linguistics Club, Bloomington, Indiana.
Farkas, D. (1985). *Intensional Descriptions and the Romance Subjunctive*. New York: Garland.
Farkas, D. (1992). On the Semantics of Subjunctive Complements. In P. Hirschbueler and K. Koerner (eds.), *Romance Languages and Modern Linguistic Theory*, 69–104. Amsterdam: Benjamins.
Farkas, D. (2003). Assertion, Belief and Mood Choice. In ESSLLI, *Conditional and Unconditional Modality Workshop*, 18–29. Vienna.
Frana, I. and Menendez-Benito, P. (2019). Evidence and Bias: The Case of the Evidential Future in Italian. *Proceedings of SALT* 29, 727–747.
Frankfurt, H. G. (2005). *On Bullshit*. Princeton, NJ: Princeton University Press.
Franke, M. and T. de Jäger. (2011). Now That You Mention It: Awareness Dynamics in Discourse and Decisions. In A. Benz, C. Ebert, G. Jäger, and R. van Rooij (eds.), *Language, Games, and Evolution*, 60–91. Berlin: Springer-Verlag.
Gazdar, G. (1979). *Pragmatics: Implicature, Presupposition, and Logical Form*. New York: *Academic*.
Geurts, B. and J. Huitink. (2006). Modal Concord. In P. Dekker and H. Zeijlstra (eds.), *Concord and the Syntax-Semantics Interface*, 15–20. ESSLLI, Malaga.
Glanzberg, M. (2007). Context, Content, and Relativism. *Philosophical Studies* 136(1): 1–29.
Giannakidou, A. (1994). The Semantic Licensing of NPIs and the Modern Greek Subjunctive. In Ale de Boer, Helen de Hoop, and Rita Landeweerd (eds.), Language and Cognition 4, *Yearbook of the Research Group for Theoretical and Experimental Linguistics*. 4:55–68. Groningen: University of Groningen.
—— (1995). Subjunctive, Habituality and Negative Polarity. In M. Simons and T. Galloway (eds.), *Semantics and Linguistic Theory (SALT) V*, CLC Publications, 94–112. Ithaca, NY: Cornell University.
—— (1997). *The Landscape of Polarity Items*. PhD dissertation, University of Groningen.
—— (1998). *Polarity Sensitivity as (Non)veridical Dependency*. Amsterdam: John Benjamins.
—— (1999). Affective Dependencies. *Linguistics and Philosophy* 22:367–421.
—— (2001). The Meaning of Free Choice. *Linguistics and Philosophy* 24:659–735.
—— (2002). Licensing and Sensitivity in Polarity Items: From Downward Entailment to Nonveridicality. In M. Andronis, A. Pycha and K. Yoshimura (eds.), *CLS 38: Papers from the 38th Annual Meeting of the Chicago Linguistic Society*, Parasession on Polarity and Negation, 1–21.

—— (2009). The Dependency of the Subjunctive Revisited: Temporal Semantics and Polarity. *Lingua* 120:1883–1908.

—— (2011). Non-veridicality and Time: The Dependency of the Subjunctive Revisited. In Musan, R. and M. Rathert (eds.), *Tense across Languages*. Berlin: Mouton de Gruyter, 59–90.

—— (2012). The Greek Future as an Epistemic Modal. In the *Proceedings of ICGL 10*, 48–61.

—— (2013a). (Non)veridicality, Evaluation, and Event Actualization: Evidence from the Subjunctive in Relative Clauses. In Trnavac and Taboada (eds.), *Nonveridicality and Evaluation: theoretical, computational, and corpus approaches*. Emerald, Studies in Pragmatics, 17–47.

—— (2013b). Inquisitive Assertions and Nonveridicality. In Maria Aloni, Michael Franke, F. Roelofsen (eds.), *The dynamic, inquisitive, and visionary life of φ: A Festschrift for Jeroen Groenendijk, Martin Stokhof and Frank Veltman*, University of Amsterdam, 115–26.

—— (2014). The Prospective as Nonveridical: Polarity Items, Speaker Commitment, and Projected Truth. In D. Gilberts and J. Hoeksema (eds.), *The Black Book. Feestschrift for Frans Zwarts*, 101–124.

—— (2016). The Subjunctive as Evaluation and Nonveridicality. In J. Blaszczak, A Giannakidou, D. Klimek-Jankosfa and K. Migdalski, *Revisiting Mood, Aspect and Modality: What is a Linguistic Category*, 177–217. University of Chicago Press.

Giannakidou, A., & L. L. S. Cheng. (2006). (In) Definiteness, Polarity, and the Role of Wh-morphology in Free Choice. *Journal of Semantics* 23(2):135–83.

Giannakidou, A. and A. Mari. (2012a). Italian and Greek Futures as Epistemic Operators. *Proceedings of CLS 48*, 247–62.

—— (2012b). The Future of Greek and Italian: An Epistemic Analysis. *Proceedings of Sinn und Bedeutung* 17:255–270.

—— (2013). A Two Dimensional Analysis of the Future: Modal Adverbs and Speaker's Bias. *Proceedings of the Amsterdam Colloquium 2013* (19): 115–22.

—— (2016a). Emotive Predicates and the Subjunctive: A Flexible Mood OT Account Based on (Non)veridicality. In *Proceedings of Sinn und Bedeutung* 20: 288–305.

—— (2016b). Emotive-factive and the Puzzle of the Subjunctive. *Proceeding of CLS 2015* 51: 181–95.

—— (2016c). Epistemic Future and Epistemic MUST: Nonveridicality, Evidence, and Partial Knowledge. In Blaszack, J., A. Giannakidou, D. Klimek-Jankowska, K. Mygdalski (eds.), *Mood, Aspect and Modality: What is a linguistic Category?*, University of Chicago Press.

—— (2017). La dimension Epistemique du futur: le rule des adverbes. In L. Baranzini and L. de Saussures (eds.), *Le Futur dans les langues Romanes*. Peter Lang AG. pp. 233–261.

—— (2018a). A Unified Analysis of the Future as Epistemic Modality: The View from Greek and Italian. *Natural Language and Linguistic Theory* 36(1): 85–129.
—— (2018b). The Semantic Roots of Positive Polarity: Epistemic Modal Verbs and Adverbs. *Linguistics and Philosophy* 30(4): 461–87.
—— (2019). Questions and Modality. Unpublished manuscript, University of Chicago and Institut Jean Nicod Paris.
Giannakidou, A., and E. Staraki. (2013). Rethinking Ability: Ability as Modality and Ability as Action. In A. Mari, C. Beyssade, and F. Del Prete (eds.), *Genericity*, 250–75.
Giannakidou, A. and F. Zwarts. (1999). Aspectual Properties of Temporal Connectives. *Greek Linguistics* 3. Amsterdam: University of Amsterdam.
Giorgi, A. and F. Pianesi. (1996). Tense and Aspect. From Semantics to Morphosyntax. Oxford: Oxford University Press.
Glanzberg, M. (2007). Context, Content, and Relativism. *Philosophical Studies* 136(1): 1–29.
Gluckman, J. D. (2018). *Perspectives on Syntactic Dependencies*. PhD dissertation, UCLA.
Goodhue, D. (2018). Must p is Felicitous Only if p is Not Known. *Semantics & Pragmatics* (forthcoming).
Gosselin, L. (2015). L'expression de l'opinion personnelle Je crois / pense / trouve / considère / estime que p. *L'information grammaticale* 144: 34–40.
Grano, T. (2011). Mental Action and Event Structure in the Semantics of "try." In *Semantics and Linguistic Theory* 21: 426–43.
—— (2015). *Control and restructuring*. Oxford: Oxford University Press.
—— (2017). The Logic of Intention Reports. *Journal of Semantics* 34(4), 587–632.
—— (2018). *Belief, Intention, and the Grammar of Persuasion*. Paper presented at Chicago Linguistic Society 54, April 2018.
Grosz, P. (2010). Grading Modality: A New Approach to Modal Concord and its Relatives. In *Proceedings of Sinn und Bedeutung* 14: 185–201.
Hackl, M. (1998). *On the Semantics of Ability Attributions*. Unpublished Manuscript. MIT.
Hacquard, V. (2006). *Aspects of Modality*. PhD Diss., Cambridge, MA: MIT.
—— (2009). On the Interaction of Aspect and Modal Auxiliaries. *Linguistics and Philosophy* 32(3): 279–315.
—— (2010). On the Event Relativity of Modal Auxiliaries. *Natural Language Semantics* 18(1): 79–114.
—— (2014). Actuality Entailments. In L. Matthewson, C. Meier, H. Rullmann, TE Zimmermann (eds.), *Companion to Semantics* London: Wiley.
Hacquard, V. and A. Wellwood. (2012). Embedding Epistemic Modals in English: A Corpus-based Study. *Semantics and Pragmatics* 5(4): 1–29.
Harris, J. A. and C. Potts. (2010). Perspective-shifting with Appositives and Expressives. *Linguistics and Philosophy* 32(6): 523–552.

Haspelmath, M. (1997). Indefinite Pronouns. *Oxford Studies in Typology and Linguistic Theory*. Oxford: Oxford University Press.

Heim, I. (1992). Presupposition Projection and the Semantics of Attitude Verbs. *Journal of Semantics* 9(3): 183–221.

Holton, D., P. Mackridge, and I. Phillipaki-Warburton. (1997). *Greek: A Comprehensive Grammar of the Modern Language*. London: Routlege.

Homer, V. (2008). Disruption of NPI Licensing: The Case of Presuppositions. In *Semantics and Linguistic Theory* 18: 429–46.

—— (2015). Neg-raising and positive polarity: The View from Modals. *Semantics & Pragmatics* 8: 1–88.

Hintikka, J. (1962). *Knowledge and Belief*. Ithaca, NY: Cornell University Press.

Huddleston, R. and G. K. Pullum. (2002). *The Cambridge grammar of English Language*, 1–23. Cambridge: Cambridge University Press.

Huitink, J. (2012). Modal Concord. A Case Study in Dutch. *Journal of Semantics* 29(3), 403–37.

—— (2014). Modal Concord. Submitted to The Blackwell Companion to Semantics, edited by Lisa Matthewson, Cécile Meier, Hotze Rullman and Thomas Ede Zimmermann (forthcoming).

Iatridou, S. (2000). The Grammatical Ingredients of Counterfactuality. Linguistic Inquiry 31: 231–270.

Iatridou, S. and H. Zeijlstra. (2013). Negation, Polarity and Deontic Modals. *Linguistic Inquiry* 44: 529–568.

Kamp, H. (1995). Discourse Representation Theory. In Jef Verschueren and Jan-Ola Östman and Jan Blommaert (eds.), Handbook of Pragmatics: Manual, 253–257. Amsterdam and Philadelphia, John Benjamins.

Kamp, H. (1999–2007). Intentions, Plans, and Their Execution: Turning Objects of Thought into Entities in the External World. Unpublished manuscript, University of Stuttgart.

Kamp, H. and U. Reyle. (1993). *From Discourse to Logic: Introduction to Model theoretic Semantics of Natural Language, Formal Logic and Discourse Representation Theory*. Dordrecht: Kluwer Academic Publishers.

Kang A. and S. Yoon. (2018). Two Types of Speaker's Ignorance Over the Epistemic Space in Korean. *Proceedings of the Linguistic Society of America*1, 21:1–15

Karttunen, L. (1971). Implicative Verbs. *Language* 47: 340–358.

—— (1972). Possible and Must. *Syntax and Semantics*, 1–20. New York, Academic Press.

Karttunen, L. and P. Stanley Peters. (1979). Conventional Implicature. In C. Oh and D. A. Dinneen (eds.), *Syntax and Semantics 11*, Presupposition, 1–56. New York: Academic Press.

Karttunen, L., & A. Zaenen (2005). Veridicity, In G. Katz, J. Pustejovsky and F. Schilder (eds.), *Annotating, Extracting and Reasoning about Time and Events*.

Dagstuhl Seminar Proceedings, Schloss Dagstuhl, Germany. Internationales Begegnungs- und Forschungszentrum (IBFI).

Kaufmann, M. (2012). *Interpreting Imperatives, Studies in Linguistics and Philosophy* 88, Netherlands: Springer.

Kennedy, C. (2007). The Grammar of Vagueness. *Linguistics and Philosophy* 30: 1–45.

Kennedy, C. and M. Willer. (2016). Subjective Attitudes and Counterstance Contingency. In *Semantics and Linguistic Theory* 26: 913–33.

Kenny, A. (1976). Human Ability and Dynamic Modalities. In J. Manninen, and R. Tuomela (eds.), *Essays on explanation and understanding*, 209–32. Dordrecht: D. Reidel.

—— (1975). *Will, freedom and power*. Oxford: Blackwell.

Klecha, P. (2014). *Bridging the Divide: Scalarity and modality*. PhD Diss., University of Chicago.

Klein, E. (1980). A Semantics for Positive and Comparative Adjectives. *Linguistics and Philosophy* 4:1–45.

Kiparsky, P. and C. Kiparsky (1968). Fact. *Linguistics Club*, Indiana University.

Knobe, J. and G.S. Szabo. (2013). Modals with a Taste of the Deontic. *Semantics and Pragmatics* 6: 1–42.

Kratzer, A. (1977). What 'Must' and 'Can' Must and Can Mean. *Linguistics and Philosophy* 1(3): 337–55.

—— (1981). Partition and Revision: The Semantics of Counterfactuals. *Journal of Philosophical Logic* 10(2): 201–16.

—— (1990). *How specific is a fact*. Amherst: University of Massachusetts.

—— (2006). *Decomposing Attitude Verbs*. Honoring Anita Mittwoch on her Eightieth birthday at The Hebrew University of Jerusalem.

—— (2013). *Modality and the Semantics of Embedding*. Presentation at the Amsterdam Colloquium.

Krifka, M. (2015). Bias in Commitment Space Semantics: Declarative Questions, Negated Questions, and Question Tags. *Proceedings of SALT* 25: 328–45.

Krönning, H. (1996), *Modalité, cognition et polysémie: sémantique du verbe modal 'devoir'*. Uppsala/Stockholm: Almqvist & Wiksell International.

Kush, D. (2011). Height-relative Determination of (Non-Root) Modal Flavor: Evidence from Hindi. In N. Ashton, A. Chereches and D. Lutz, (eds.), *Semantics and Linguistic Theory* 21: 413–25.

Laca, B. (2008). *On Modal Tenses and Tensed Modals*. Unpublished Manuscript, Université Paris 8 / CNRS.

—— (2018). Modals and Perfect Morphology. *Catalan Journal of Linguistics* 17: 43–76.

—— (2019). On the Interaction Between Modal and Aspectual Periphrases. Borealis: An International Journal of Hispanic Linguistics, 8(2): 83–109.

Landman, F. (1992). The Progressive. *Natural Language Semantics* 1(1): 1–32.

Lasersohn, P. (2005). Context Dependence, Disagreement, and Predicates of Personal Taste. *Linguistics and Philosophy* 28: 643–86.

Lassiter, D. (2016). Must, Knowledge, and (In)Directness. *Natural Language Semantics* 24(2): 117–63.

Lauer, S. (2013). *Towards a Dynamic Pragmatics*. PhD diss., Stanford University.

Lee, C. (2006). Contrastive Topic/Focus and Polarity in Discourse. *Where Semantics Meets Pragmatics* 16: 381–420.

Lee, E. (2008). Argument Structure and Event Structure: The Case of Korean Imperfective Constructions. *Journal of East Asian Linguistics* 17(2): 117–39.

Lekakou, M., & J. Quer. (2016). Subjunctive Mood in Griko: A Microcomparative Approach. *Lingua* 174: 65–85.

Linebarger, M. C. (1980). *The Grammar of Negative Polarity*. PhD diss., MIT.

Liu, M. (2019). The Elastic Nonveridicality Property of Indicative Conditionals. *Linguistic Vanguard*5(3).

—— (2012). *Multidimensional Semantics of Evaluative Adverbs*. Leiden: Brill.

Liu, M. (2019). The Elastic Nonveridicality Property of Conditionals. *Linguistics Vanguard* 5(s3).

Louie, M. (2014). Actuality Entailments in Blackfoot (Sleepers and Imposters). *WSCLA 2014*, Unpublished manuscripts. Memorial University.

Lyons, J. (1977). *Semantics*. Cambridge University Press.

MacFarlane, J. (2014). *Assessment Sensitivity: Relative Truth and its Applications*. Oxford: Oxford University Press.

MacFarlane, J. (2007). Relativism and disagreement. *Philosophical Studies* 132: 17–32.

Marques, R. (2004). On the System of Mood in European and Brazilian Portuguese. *Journal of Portuguese Linguistics* 3: 89–109.

Maier, J. (2016). Modal Predicates. *Linguistics and Philosophy* 39: 443–57.

Mari, A. (2003). *Principles d'identification et de catégorisation du sens: le cas de 'avec' ou l'association par les canaux*. Paris: L'Harmattan.

—— (2005). Intensional and Epistemic Wholes. In E. Machery, M. Werning, and G. Schurz (eds.), *The compositionality of Meaning and Content*. Vol. I, Foundational issues. Frankfurt: Ontos Verlag.

—— (2009). Future, Judges and Normalcy Conditions. Austin, TX: Chronos.

—— (2010a). On the Evidential Nature of the Italian Future. Unpublished manuscript. Institut Jean Nicod. https://jeannicod.ccsd.cnrs.fr/ijn_00678549/document.

—— (2010b). Temporal Reasoning and Modality. *Temporality: Typology and acquisition*, Paris VIII, March 2010.

—— (2012). *Pouvoir* au passé composé: L'effet épistémique et lecture habilitative. In L. de Saussure and A. Rhis (eds.), *Etudes de sémantique et de pragmatique Françaises*, 67–99. Geneva, Peter Lang.

―― (2014). *Each Other*, Asymmetry and Reasonable Futures. *Journal of Semantics* 31(2): 209–61.

―― (2015a). *Modalités et Temps. Des Modèles aux Données.*. Bern: Peter Lang AG.

―― (2015b). French Future: Exploring the Future Ratification Hypothesis. *Journal of French Language Studies* 26, 353–378.

―― (2015c). Overt and Covert Modality in Generic Sentences. *Cahiers Chronos* 27, 265–288.

―― (2016a). Assertability Conditions of Epistemic (and Fictional) Attitudes and Mood Variation. *Proceedings of SALT* 26: 61–81.

―― (2016b). Actuality Entailments: When the Modality is in the Presupposition. In *Lecture Notes in Computer Science*, 191–210. Dordrecht: Springer Verlag.

―― (2017a). *Believing and Asserting. Evidence from Mood Shift*. Workshop: Inquisitiveness Below and Beyond the Sentence Boundary. Amsterdam, December 18–19.

―― (2017b). *Belief and Assertion. Evidence from Mood Shift*. Workshop: Questioning Speech Acts. Kostanz, September 14–16.

―― (2018a). The French Future: Evidentiality and Information Increase. In A. Foolen et al. (eds.). *Evidence for Evidentiality*, 199–226. Amsterdam: John Benjamins.

Mari, A. (forthcoming). Private and Public Commitments: Bridging the Semantics and Pragmatics of Subjunctive Belief. *Cahiers Chronos*.

Mari, A., C. Beyssade, and F. Del Prete. (2013). Introduction. In A. Mari, C. Beyssade and F. Del Prete (eds.), *Genericity*, 1–92. Oxford: Oxford University Press.

Mari, A. and F. Martin. (2007). Tense, Abilities and Actuality Entailment. In *Proceedings of the Amsterdam Colloquium*, 151–56.

Mari, A. and F. Martin. (2009). On the Interaction between Aspect and Verbal Polysemy: (Im)-perfectivity and (Non)-implicativity. Unpublished Manuscript, Institut Jean Nicod and University of Stuttgart.

Mari, A. and P. Portner (2019). Mood Variation with Belief Predicates: Modal Comparison in Semantics and the Common Ground. Unpublished manuscript. Institut Jean Nicod Paris and Georgetown University.

Mari, A. and S. Schweitzer (2011). Calculating the Epistemic Interpretation of Past Modals via K. *Proceedings of the 29th West Coast Conference on Formal Linguistics*.

Mari, A. and C. Tahar. (2020). Negative Priorities: Evidence from Prohibitive and Expletive Negation. *Proceedings of Sinn und Bedeutung* 24.

Marques, R. (2010). Modality, Context Change Potential and Mood Selection in European Portuguese. In Becker, M., and E. Remberger (eds.), *Modality and Mood in Romance: Modal Interpretation, Mood Selection, and Mood*

*Alternation*, La Linguistische Arbeiten 533:133–161. Berlin: Walter de Gruter GmbH.

Marques, R. (2004). On the System of Mood in European and Brazilian Portuguese. *Journal of Portuguese Linguistics* 3: 89–109.

Matthewson, L. (2010). Cross-linguistic Variation in Modality Systems: The Role of Mood. *Semantics and Pragmatics* 3.9: 1–74.

Matthewson, L. (2012). On the (Non)-future Orientation of Modals. In *Proceedings of Sinn und Bedeutung* 16: 431–46.

Mayol, L. and E. Castroviejo (2013). (Non)integrated Evaluative Adverbs in Questions: A Cross-Romance study. *Language* 89(2): 195–230.

McCawley, J. D. (1981). The Syntax and Semantics of English Relative Clauses. *Lingua* 53(2–3): 99–149.

—— (1988). *The Syntactic Phenomena of English*. University of Chicago Press.

Menendez-Benito, P. On Dispositional Sentences. In A. Mari, C. Beyssade, and F. Del Prete (eds.), *Genericity*, 276–292. Oxford: Oxford University Press.

Montague, R. (1969). On the Nature of Certain Philosophical Entities. *Monist* 53(2): 159–194.

Morency, P., S. Oswald, and L. de Saussure. (2008). Explicitness, Implicitness and Commitment Attribution: A Cognitive Pragmatic Approach. *Belgian Journal of Linguistics* 22(1): 197–219.

Moss, S. (2015). On the Semantics and Pragmatics of Epistemic Vocabulary. *Semantics and Pragmatics* 8: 1–81.

Moulton, K. (2009). Natural Selection and the Syntax of Clausal Complementation. PhD Diss., University of Massachusetts Amherst.

—— (2006). Small Antecedents: Syntax or Pragmatics. *North East Linguistics Society (NELS)* 37, University of Illinois, Urbana-Champaign.

Muñoz, Patrick. 2019. On Tongues: The Grammar of Experiential Evaluation. PhD diss., University of Chicago.

Murray, S.E. (2016). *The Semantics of Evidentials*. Oxford: Oxford University Press.

Nadathur, P. (2016). Causal Necessity and Sufficiency in Implicativity. In *Semantics and Linguistic Theory* 26: 1002–1021.

Papafragou, A. (2006). Epistemic Modality and Truth Conditions. *Lingua, 116(10)*, 1688–1702.

Papafragou, A. (2000). Modality: Issues in the Semantics-Pragmatics Interface. Brill.

Pavlou, N. (2018). *Morphosyntactic Dependencies and Verb Movement in Cypriot Greek*. PhD Dissertation, University of Chicago.

Pesetsky, D. (1992). *Zero syntax*, vol. 2. Unpublished Manuscript. Cambridge, MA:MIT.

Philippaki-Warburton, I. (1994). The Subjunctive Mood and the Syntactic Status of the Particle na in Modern Greek. *Folia Linguistica* 28(3–4): 297–328.

Philippaki-Warburton, I. (1998). Functional categories and Modern Greek Syntax. *The Linguistic Review* 15:(2–3): 159–86.

Philippaki-Warburton, I., and I. Veloudis (1984). The Subjunctive in Complement Clauses. *Studies in Greek Linguistics* 5: 87–104.

Pietrandrea, P. (2005). *Epistemic Modality. Functional Properties and the Italian System.* Benjamin.

Piñón, C. (2003). Being Able To. *In Proceedings of WCCFL* 22: 384–97.

Piñón, C. (2008). Verbs of Creation. *Event structures in Linguistic Form and Interpretation*, 493–521. Berlin/New York: Mouton de Gruyter.

Portner, P. (2018). *Mood.* Oxford University Press.

—— (2009). *Modality.* Oxford University Press.

—— (2007). Imperatives and Modals. *Natural Language Semantics* 15(4): 351–383.

—— (1997). The Semantics of Mood, Complementation, and Conversational Force. *Natural Language Semantics* 5(2): 167–212.

Portner, P. and A. Rubinstein. (2012). Mood and Contextual Commitment. In A. Chereces (ed.), *Proceedings of SALT* 22, 461–487. Ithaca, NY: CLC Publications.

Potsdam, E. (1997). NegP and Subjunctive Complements in English. *Linguistic Inquiry* 28(3): 533–41.

Potts, C. (2007). The Expressive Dimension. *Theoretical linguistics* 33(2): 165–98.

Quer, J. (1998). *Moods at the Interface.* OTS Utrecht, PhD diss.

—— (2001). Interpreting mood. *Probus* 13: 81–111.

Quer, J. (2009). Twists of Mood: the Distribution and Interpretation of the Indicative and the Subjunctive. *Lingua* 119: 1779–87.

Rivero, M. L. (1994). Clause Structure and V-movement in the Languages of the Balkans. *Natural Language & Linguistic Theory* 12(1): 63–120.

Rivero, M. L., and A. Terzi. (1994). *Imperatives, Illocutionary Force, and V-movement.* Unpublished manuscript, University of Ottawa.

Rizzi, L. (1997). The Fine Structure of the Left Periphery. In *Elements of Grammar*, 281–337. Dordrecht: Springer.

Roberts, I. and A. Roussou, 2003. *Syntactic change: A Minimalist Approach to Grammaticalization* Cambridge: Cambridge University Press.

Rouchota, V. (1994). *The Semantics and Pragmatics of the Subjunctive in Modern Greek: A Relevance-Theoretic Approach.* PhD diss., University of London.

Roussou, A. (1994). *The Syntax of Complementisers.* PhD diss., University of London.

—— (2000). On the Left Periphery: Modal Particles and Complementisers. *Journal of Greek Linguistics* 1(1): 65–94.

—— (2009). In the Mood for Control. *Lingua* 119: 1811–36.

Rubinstein, A. (2014). On Necessity and Comparison. *Pacif Philosophical Quaterly* 95: 512–54.

Sæbø, K. J. (2009). Judgment Ascriptions. *Linguistics and Philosophy* 32(4): 327–52.

Saussure, L. de and P. Morency. (2011). A Cognitive-Pragmatic View of the French Epistemic Future. *Journal of French Language Studies* 22: 207–23.

Sharvit, Y. (2003). Trying to be Progressive: the Extensionality of Try, *Journal of Semantics* 20: 403–445.

Sitaridou, I. (2014). Modality, Antiveridicality and Complementation: The Romeyka Infinitive as a Negative Polarity Item. *Lingua* 148: 118–146.

Sklavadis, S. (2017). Predicates of Personal Taste: An Experimental Approach. Unpublished manuscript, University of Chicago.

Smirnova. A. (2012). The Semantics of Mood in Bulgarian. Proceedings of the 48th Annual Meeting of the Chicago Linguistic Society.

—— (2013). Evidentiality in Bulgarian: Temporality, Epistemic Modality, and Information Source. *Journal of Semantics* 30(4): 479–532.

Smith, C. S. (1991). *The Parameter of Aspect*. Dordrecht: Kluwer Academic Publishers.

Spyropoulos, V. (2008). Finiteness and Control in Greek. In *New Horizons in the Analysis of Control and Raising*, 159–183. Doordrecht: Springer.

Stanley, J. (2008). Knowledge and certainty. *Philosophical Issues* 18(1): 35–57.

Staraki, E. (2013). *Greek modality*. PhD diss., The University of Chicago.

—— (2017). *Modality in Modern Greek*. Newcastle: Cambridge Scholars Publishing.

Stephenson, T. (2005). Assessor Sensitivity: Epistemic Modals and Predicates of Personal Taste. In J. Gajewski, V. Hacquard, B. Nickel, and S. Yalcin (eds.), *New Work on Modality*, MIT Working Papers in Linguistics 51, 179–206. Cambridge, Massachusetts: MITWPL.

Stephenson, T. (2006). A Parallel Account of Epistemic Modals and Predicates of Personal Taste. In *Sinn und Bedeutung* 11: 1–24.

Stephenson, T. (2007). Judge Dependence, Epistemic Modals, and Predicates of Personal Taste. *Linguistics and Philosophy* 30(4): 487–525.

Stojanovic, I. (2008). The Scope and the Subtleties of the Contextualism, Litteralism, Relativism Debate. *Language and Linguistics Compass* 2(6): 1171–88.

Stowell, T. (1982). The Tense of Infinitives. *Linguistic Inquiry* 13(3): 561–70.

Tahar, C. (2018). *On the Pragmatic Content of the So-called Expletive Negation*. Paper presented at SLE 2018 51st Annual Meeting of the Societas Linguistica Europaea Workshop: The Semantics and Pragmatics of Apprehensive Markers in a Cross-linguistic Perspective, Institut Jean Nicod.

Tasmowski, L. and P. Dendale. (1998). Must/will and doit/futur Simple as Epistemic Modal Markers. Semantic Value and Restrictions of Use. In J. E. van der Auwera (ed.), *English as a Human Language. To honour Louis Goossens*, 325–36. Munich: Lincom Europa.

Terzi, A. (1997). PRO and Null Case in Finite Clauses. *The Linguistic Review* 14(4): 335–60.
Thomason, R. (2005). *Ability, Action and Context*. Unpublished manuscript. University of Michigan.
Todorovic, N. (2012). *The Indicative and Subjunctive Da-Complements in Serbian: A Syntactic-Semantic Approach*. PhD diss., University of Chicago.
Trnavac, R., and M. Taboada (2012). The Contribution of Nonveridical Rhetorical Relations to Evaluation in Discourse. *Language Sciences* 34(3): 301–18.
Tsangalidis, A. (1998). Will and Tha: *A Comparadive Study of the Category Future*. Thessaloniki: University Studio Press.
Tsimpli, I. M. (1990). The Clause Structure and Word Order of Modern Greek. *UCL Working Papers in Linguistics* 2: 226–255.
Tsoulas, G. (1995). *Subjunctives as Indefinites*. In G. Borgato (ed.), Teoria de Linguaggio e Analisi Linguistica, Unipress, Padova.
Tsoulas, G. (1993). Remarks on the Structure and Interpretation of Na-clauses. *Studies in Greek Linguistics* 14: 191–206.
Tzevelekou, M. A. Tsaggalidi, A. Psaltou-Joycey. (2012). *To Xroniko Sistima tis Neas Ellinikis: Meletes apo ti Skopia tis Ellinikis os Ksenis Glossas* [The tense system in Modern Greek: Studies from the perspective of Greek as a Foreign Language], Athens: Patakis Publications.
Uriagereka, J. and A. Gallego, (to appear). *Interclausal Dependencies*. To appear in Cambridge University Press.
Uriagereka, J., (1988). *On Government*. PhD diss., University of Connecticut.
Werner, A. (2018). Mood Alternations in the Diachrony of German: The Architecture of Epistemic Weakening. Unpublished manuscript, University of Vienna.
Willer, M. (2013). Dynamics of Epistemic Modality. *Philosophical Review* 122: 45–92.
Wiltschko, M. (2016). The Essence of a Category. Lessons from the Subjunctives. In J. Blaszak, A. Giannakidou, D. Klimek and K. Migdalski (eds.), *Mood, Aspect, Modality revisited. New answers to Old Questions*, 218–254. Chicago: University of Chicago Press.
Valencia, V. S., T. Van der Wouden, and F. Zwarts. (1993). Polarity, Veridicality, and Temporal Connectives. In P. Dekker and M. Stokhof (eds.), *Proceedings of the 9th Amsterdam Colloquium*, 587–606. Amsterdam: ILLC, University of Amsterdam.
Van der Wouden, T. (1994). *Negative Contexts*. PhD diss. University of Groningen.
Varlokosta, S. (1994). *Issues on Modern Greek sentential complementation*. PhD diss., University of Maryland.
Veloudis, Y. (1980). *Negation in Modern Greek*. PhD diss., University of Reading.
Verkuyl, H. (2011). Tense, Aspect, and Temporal Representation. In J. Van Benthem and A. ter Meulen (eds.), *Handbook of Logic and Language*, 971–988. Amsterdam: Elsevier.

Villalta, E. (2008). Mood and Gradability: An Investigation of the Subjunctive Mood in Spanish. *Linguistics and Philosophy* 31(4): 467–522.

Von Fintel, K. (1999). NPI Licensing, Strawson Entailment, and Context Dependency. *Journal of Semantics* 16(2): 97–148.

von Fintel, K. and A. Gillies (2010). Must... stay... strong! *Nat. Language Semantics* 18: 351–383.

von Fintel, K. and S. Iatridou (2008). How to Say Ought in Foreign: The Composition of Weak Necessity Modals. In J. Guéron and J. Lacarme (eds.), *Time and Modality*, 115–141. Dordrecht: Springer.

White, A. S. (2014). Factive-implicatives and Modalized Complements. In Iyer J. and L. Kusmer (eds.), *Proceedings of the 44th annual meeting of the North East Linguistic Society*, University of Connecticut, 267–78.

Xherija, O. (2016). Revisiting the Secrets of BEFORE: Lessons from Modern Greek. In M. Köllner and R. Ziai (eds.), *Proceedings of the Student Session of the 28th European Summer School in Language, Logic and Information*, 219–227.

Yalcin, S. (2007). Epistemic Modals. *Mind* 116: 983–1026.

Yoon, S. (2011). Rhetorical Comparatives: Polarity Items, Expletive Negation, and Subjunctive Mood. *Journal of Pragmatics* 43(7): 2012–33.

——— (2012). *NOT in the Mood: The Syntax, Semantics and Pragmatics of Evaluative Negation*. PhD diss., University of Chicago.

Zeijlstra, H. (2004). *Sentential Negation and Negative Concord*. PhD diss. University of Amsterdam. Utrecht: LOT Publications.

Zeijlstra, E. (2017). Universal quantifiers PPIs. *A Journal of General Linguistics* 2(1):1–25.

Zanuttini, R. (1992). *Negation and Clausal Structure: A Comparative Study of Romance Languages*. PhD diss., Penn State University.

Zimmermann, M. (2011). Discourse Particles. In K. von Heusinger, C. Maienborn, and P. Portner (eds.), *Semantics (HSK 33.2)*, 2011–38. Berlin: Mouton de Gruyter.

Zwarts, F. (1995). Nonveridical Contexts. *Linguistic Analysis* 25(3–4): 286–312.

# Index

Page numbers in italics refer to figures.

ability
    and action, 228–31, 241–43, 249–51, 255
    actualized, 229–30, 233
    Aristotle on, 229–30
ability modals, 225–60. *See also* modals
actuality entailment, 230–31, 236, *237*, 243–52, 254, 257–58, 270–71
actualization, 229–30, 258–60
    as complete/incomplete veridical, 264–66
    as effect of PAST, 233
    not possible with TRY, 266–68
adverbs
    manipulation by, 101–4
    with modal verbs, 89–104: *definitely*, 83, 92, 93, 94, 98, 102–3; *maybe*, 67, 83, 84, 91, 94, 97–103, 109, 279, 303; *perhaps*, 67, 84, 100, 102; *probably*, 67, 74, 83, 89, 90, 92–93, 96–98, 102–4, 109
    possibility epistemic, 279–80, 303
    temporal, 249, 257
agents, volitional, 239, 252, 254–56
Aktionsart, 114, 132
analysis, existential, of CAN, 228–29
anchors, individual (*i*), 182, 310
    defined, 7, 43, 58
    and ability/deontic, 235
    and bouletic state, 202
    and consciousness state, 157
    and doxastic attitudes, 140, 152–53, 155, 216–17
    and dream/fiction states, 161–62; information space of, 40–43, 45, 51;
    and memory state, 156, 174, 297; and veridicality/nonveridicality, 59–61, 64, 150
anchoring, 58, 179, 184
    assertive vs. nonassertive, 294
    inquisitive, 317
    inquisitive/nonveridical, 187
    *Now*-, 107, 120–23, 125, 128, 133–36
    presuppositional, 186, 293–94, 316–17
antifactivity
    ATTITUDE and, 222
    presupposition and, 48, 276, 318
    and WANT, 191, 201–4, 222
antiknowledge markers
    doxastic verbs and, 155, 165
    modal expressions as, 22–24, 51
    subjunctive as, 182
antiveridicality, 65, 187, 318
    antifactivity and, 191, 201, 203, 319
    and negation, 8
    subjective, 61
    *See also* nonveridicality; veridicality
Aristotle
    on ability, 229–30
    on possibility, 66, 229–30
    on truth, 1, 3–4
assertion, 150–51
    bare, 23, 52, 77, 167, *171*
    of emotives, 288–89
    negative, 63, 219
    private, 185–86, 316
    verbs of, 16, 28, 34, 138, 140–41, 149, 216–20

and veridicality, 41–42, 43, 60–61, 63, 105, 109, 299, 311
attitudes, propositional
  blocking and, 223
  bouletic, 191–224; of assertion, 216–20; doxastic mixed with, 215–16; of hoping, 204–8; INTENT, 210–11; of persuasion, 211–16; and plan for action, 203, 206–7, 209–11; of promising, 208–11; solipsistic vs. suppositional, 214, 223, 313; WANT, 194–204
  doxastic, 140, 147–88; of awareness, 157-158, 289–92; of certainty, 154, 158, 160, 164, 169–70; fictional, 150, 160–62, 164, 169; of memory, 156, 158, 173–75; of opinion, 158–60; of perception, 179–81, 298–99; of personal taste, 153, 159–60; private, 160–62, 169, 185–86; of semblance, 175–78; of solipsistic/conjectural imagination, 169, 222–23
  emotion, 274–81
  and modals, 2–3, 10–11, 16–22, 312
  nonveridical vs. veridical, 193, 220–23, 224
  rational, 207, 213–14
  solipsistic vs. suppositional, 222, 223
  strength of, 211

bases, modal
  ability, 236–39
  and ambiguity, 67
  circumstantial, 93
  combined, 213
  as nonveridical, 45, 65–66, 69–70, 79, 104, 182; epistemic, 69, 79–80, 85, 221; existential, 100; and necessity, 85–87, 96, 98, 102; possibility, 105
  as restricting, 66
  shift in, 20, 192, 213–16, 217–19, 255–57
  *See also* modals; verbs
BEFORE and WITHOUT, 199
belief
  Hintikkean, 147, 153, 165, 167
  HOPE and, 207
  lacks factivity, 42–43
  pure vs. weakened, 30
  state of, and subjective veridicality, 62–63, 147–48, 152–53
  suppositional: and solipsistic, 17–18, 30, 147–89, 192, 222; and subjunctive, 147–48, 163–73, 192–93
  *See also under* attitudes; commitment; mood; verbs
bias
  absence of, 54
  positive, 55, 71–88, 100; of MUST, 87–88, 102–5
  in questions, 318n, 319
Boul
  defined, 202–3
  doxastic spaces with, 215
  homogeneity of, 194
  and HOPE, 207–8
  interactions with Dox, 216–17
  *See also* WANT; *see also under* attitudes; commitment
bouletic state. *See* Boul
Bulgarian, 76

certainty, attitudes of, 154–56, 158, 160, 164–65, 169–70
choices
  defined, 254
  with French doxastics, 256–57
choice space and modal base, 254, 255–57
clauses
  embedded: complement, 3, 10–23, 28–30, 107–45; mood and, 10–16, 21, 24–29, 30–39, 107–45 *passim*; relative, 24–27
  main: future in, 131–36; subjunctive in, 13–14, 107–10, 131, 144–45, 184
combinations, nonharmonic, 101–4
commitment
  bouletic, 191–224
  doxastic: solipsistic, 154–63; and veridical belief, 148–54
  epistemic, 53–55, 60–61; vs. doxastic, 151–154
  full, 41–42, 51, 87, 150–51
  and informativity, 65, 88
  levels of, ranked, 87–88
  partial, 55, 85–87
  scale of, 53–55
  trivial, 53, 55, 65, 71, 86
  types of, 54–55, *172*

# INDEX

veridical, 51–55, 60–61, 148–63, 311–12;
  as prerequisite for assertion, 41–42,
    60–61, 105, 311
  weakened, 31, 53, 55
complementizer (C)
  in Greek, 12–14, 35–39, 110–11, 148, 175,
    183, 185–86, 298–99; *an* as, 152, 317;
    *mipos* as, 279–80, 302–4; *pu* as, 156,
    175–77, 274, 292–99, 308, 317
  subordinating particle as, 12–14, 110–11
  *whether* as, 152
  *See also* particles, subordinating, in
    Greek
conjecture, 93, 168–69
consciousness, state of, 157–58
continuity, conceptual, with TRY, FAIL,
  SUCCEED, 267
control, obligatory, with zero tense, 240–43
conversation, reported, 216–17

*de dicto*, narrow-scope reading, 26
*de re*, wide-scope/specific interpretation, 26
difficulty
  with ABLE, 259–60
  with TRY, 233, 261–62

emotion
  defined, 285
  with factives, 281–84
  gradability of, 285–89
  and modality, 274–81
  scale of, 286–87
  threshold in, 286, 287, 292, 304–5
English
  bouletic preference in, 197–200
  conjecture in, 93–94
  "fear lest" in, 302–4, 307–8
  HOPE equivalents in, 206
  imperfective nonpast in, 112–13
  *-ing* vs. *that* in, 178–79
  MUST examples in, 23–24, 73–74, 95, 98,
    102–3
  ordering/preference in, 197–200
  present implicative in, 232
  PROMISE in, 209
  "subjunctive" in, 10, 31–32
  supposition in, 166–67
  veridical past/present in, 8
epistemic weakening, 45, 51, 65, 72, 87

equilibrium, nonveridical, 54–55, 70–71, 85,
    86–88, 319
  and possibility, 99–101, 105, 279, 303
  *See also* questions
eventive verbs. *See* verbs: stative: vs.
  eventive
events, identification of, 246–49
evidentiality, in contexts with MUST, 76–78

facts/factivity
  doxastic verbs lack, 17–18, 63
  emotive, 28, 138, 281–82
  epistemic, 138–40
  knowledge and, 42–43, 62, 164–65
  modal sentences vs., 4–5
  and objective veridicality, 62, 152
  presupposition and, 281–84
  truth as, 7
  and veridicality, 5, 22, 62, 138–40, 179–80
  *See also under* verbs
force, illocutionary, 14, 44, 108–9, 319
free choice items (FCIs)
  and nonveridicality, 7–9, 15, 54
  *See also* negative polarity items (NPIs)
FUT, 57, 205
  and epistemic necessity, 67, 71–77
  as nonveridical, 57
  *See also* future
future, 4, 33, 57, 67, 75, 114, 208, 232–33
  epistemic, 114–15
  equivalent to MUST (FUT), 129; in
    Dutch and German, 129
  modal, in Italian, 131–37
  with modal spread, 92
  orientation toward, with NONPAST,
    18–21, 107, 118–24, 132, 140, 193–95,
    202, 216
  *See also* FUT; NONPAST; tense

German, use of modal in, 27–28
gerunds, 114
Gitksan, FUT analogue in, 123
gradability
  of emotive predicates, 286, 287, 288, 292
  and nonveridicality, 285–88
Gricean Quality, of truth, 5, 41, 52, 150–51,
    311. *See also* truth

Hindi
  actuality entailment in, 243–44

modal particle *gaa* in, 123–24
homogeneity, 41, 42–43, 85–86, 98–99, 105, 318
   and antiveridicality, 141
   and entailment, 59–62, 63
   and informativity, 65
HOPE
   modal flexibility of, 32, 204–8
   with plans/goals, 206–7

imperative, 10, 14, 44, 107–9, 187–88, 319
implicatives, 228, 231–34, 260–71. *See also* modals
indicative
   in French, 11–12
   in Greek, 6, 17–18, 32–34, 39–43, 176; with bouletic, 215; with certainty/awareness, 154–58; with KNOW, 12–13; with memory/perception, 36–38; with opinion, 153; with SAY, 217; two types of, 185–86; verbs that take, 16, 149–50
   as independent, 14
   in Italian, 12, 29–30, 31, 32, 34, 36, 37; with assertion, 185, 317; with awareness, 157; with KNOW, 11; verbs that take, 16
   NONPAST never used with, 117
   PAST, PRES appear in, 117
   in Portuguese, 30–31
   with SAY, 216–19
   selecting verbs of, 16, 138–41, 148–63, 169, 171–72
   and veridicality, 39–43, 63, 188
   WANT verbs and, 194–95
   *See also* modality; mood; subjunctive
inertia, 79
infinitive
   bouletics select, 194, 199
   (*for*) *to* (English), 197–98, 199
   in French, 227
   Greek lacks, 17, 68, 227
   with implicatives, 260–71
   in Italian, 68, 207–8, 202
   subjunctive and, 10, 226–28, 260–70
information states, 59, 65
intentionality, 257. *See also* choices
*irrealis*, and untruth, 2. See also *realis*

Japanese, 302

Kartunnen, L., 72–73
Korean, 229, 302
Kratzer, A., theory of modality, 22, 40, 66, 67, 80

licensing, 8–9, 15
   of indicative, 63, 193, 221, 313
   of NONPAST, 120
   of NPIs, 9, 53–54, 283
   of subjunctive, 25–27, 43–44, 71, 168, 169–70, 182, 193, 221, 313

metaevaluation, 82–84
   and nonveridical equilibrium, 99
metaevaluation function, 51, 81–86, 91, 105
   empty, 84, 85
modal concord ("harmony"), 90, 91, 101
modality
   always subjective, 237
   ambiguity of, 29, 67
   dynamic, 197, 228
   goal-oriented, 125, 239, 247, 254; WANT verbs and, 202–3
   linguistic vs. aletheic, 66
   and ordering source, 82–86
   *See also* indicative; modals; mood; subjunctive
modal logic, 22, 66, 228
modal operators, and subjunctive of possibility, 66–71
modal particle P, 118
modal space
   epistemic vs. doxastic, 164–65
   partitioned vs. homogeneous, 320
   and veridicality/nonveridicality/antiveridicality, 64–65, 87, 188–89, 220–21, 293, 313, 318
modals
   defined, 66–68
   ABLE: enabling factors and, 229; and implicatives, 225–34; and MUST, 225, 236–39, 240; nonveridicality of, 231, 255–60; temporal vs. atemporal, 243
   adjectives, 67, 154, 159n, 273, 285; with belief statements, 168
   adverbs, 5, 83–84, 320; modal, 3, 51, 66–67, 89–104, 109–10, 125–26;

# Index

possibility, 279, 303; temporal, 3, 56-57, 249, 257
as antiknowledge markers, 22-24
attitudes and, 2-3, 7, 16-22, 45, 183, 312 (*see also* attitudes, propositional)
biased, 53, 55, 87-88, 102
categories of, 66-68
deontic, 19-20, 68-69, 255-58
epistemic, 18-19, 52-53, 68-88, 143, 171-72, 173; MUST, 22-24, 71-92, 94-99, 114-16, 191, 238-39
Greek, 18-20, 24-27, 32-33, 67-69, 83-84, 91-94, 96-97, 102-4
Italian, 20-21, 91-96, 102-3
MANAGE: enabling factors with, 269; as nonveridical, 231-34, 263-64, 269-70; and TRY, 233, 268; and *un*-try + subjunctive, 268, 270n; as veridical, 260
necessity: and bias, 71, 82-86; epistemic, 71-104; nonepistemic, 86; and positive polarity, 89-104
of possibility, 27-28, 31, 53, 66-71, 108-9, 125-26, 142-44, 184
teleological, 19-20
TRY, 233-34, 263-64; no actualization with, 266-68; as nonveridical, 266-67; *un*-TRY, 268, 270n
universal, 100
as weak, 31, 53-55, 65-66, 71-79, 87-88, 92-93
*See also* mood; verbs; *see also under* subjunctive
modal spread, 89-94, 125-26
mood
conditional, 116, 320
grammatical, 10-46
interaction with tense, in complement clauses, 136-38
(non)veridicality theory of, 220-23, 224
selection of, 26-45, 311-12; in French, 11, 36; in Greek, 12-14; in Italian, 12; in Romanian, 26
sentential, 14, 44
and verbs of belief, 30-32 (*see also* attitudes, propositional; belief); in French, 140; in Greek, 5-7, 42-43; in Italian, 136-38; in Portuguese, 31
*See also* indicative; modality; subjunctive
moodP, 110, 118, 137, 145

mood shift/mood flexibility, 24-39, 223-24, 314-15
with assertives, 34, 216-20
with awareness, 290-92
with DENY: in Greek, 216, 34, 218-19; in Italian, 219-20
with HOPE, 32, 204-8
in Italian, 28-30, 36, 163-72
in Italian and Greek, 30-39
with memory verbs, 37-39, 173-75, 297-98
with perception verbs, 178-81, 298-99
with PERSUADE, 33, 211-16
with PROMISE, 32-33, 208-11
with semblance verbs, 175-78
*See also* indicative; modality; subjunctive

necessity, epistemic, 71-88. *See also under* modals
negation
defined, 8
effect on attitude, 170-71
expletive, 301-2, 304, 306, 308
and full commitment, 151
with MUST and adverb, 94-99
scope of, 95-99, 101
negative polarity items (NPIs)
have empty *O*, 99
licensed by emotive, 283
as NONPAST, 120
and nonveridicality, 7-9, 53-54, TRY vs. PROG and, 264
*See also* free choice items (FCIs)
nonveridicality
defined, 4-5
ability and, 228-30
antifactivity entails, 202
with bias, 71-88
and emotiveness, 285-89
mixed, causes subjunctive, 275-76
objective, 8
stance, 43-45, 57, 69, 104, 312
state of, 45, 55, 64-65, 71, 85, 105
subjective, 44-45, 64-66
and subjunctive, 37, 43-46, 51, 66-71, 293, 317
as uncertainty, 22-24, 29-30, 45, 65-66, 99, 104, 210
*See also* antiveridicality; equilibrium, nonveridical; veridicality

Nonveridicality Axiom, 45–46, 182, 211
　doxastics and, 147, 166, 171, 181
　and modals, 66, 69, 71, 104, 228, 270–71
　and propositional attitudes, 221, 313
　and subjunctive, 188–89, 288
　suppositional belief and, 168
　*See also* attitudes, propositional; modals; nonveridicality; subjunctive
normalcy, 82

*O* (metaevaluation position, 82, 110
　manipulated by adverbs, 101–4
optative, 13–14, 111, 118
　and imperative, 48, 121, 201–2, 276, 318
　and subjunctive, 191
ordering source, 80 (*Best*), 90–91
　absence of, 70, 85, 86, 99
　bouletic, 198, 199
　and ideal/nonideal worlds, 82
　*O*, 82–86

particles, subordinating, in Greek
　future, 18, 67, 125, 128–29, 200
　modal, 111, 118, 120, 136–38, 184; *na*, 13–14, 38, 109–11, 125–28, 184; with subjunctive in main clause, 107–11, 125, 130–31, 184, 295
　subordinating: *oti, pu*, 12–13, 21, 36–39, 111, 183, 185–87; presuppositional *pu*, 186, 292–99, 317
　*See also* complementizer (C)
PERSUADE
　mood flexibility of, 33, 192, 211–16
　solipsistic vs. suppositional, 214–15, 222
polarity
　negative: *need* as [NPI], 95; and nonveridicality, 7–9
　positive: of modals, 89–104; *must* and (PPI), 95
　*See also* negative polarity items (NPIs)
Portner, P., 22, 66
Portuguese, doxastic verbs in, 30, 31, 46, 147
possibility, 80, 142–43
　and ability modals, 226, 228, 235
　adverbs and, 83–84, 92; *mipos*, 279–80, 303; *na*, 94, 109–10, 125, 144, 184
　and necessity modal, 18–22, 52–54, 84–85, 87–88, 95
　and nonveridical equilibrium, 54, 85–86, 99–101, 104–5

semantics of, 3, 105, 222, 235, 310
　subjunctive signals, 24, 27, 31–32, 66–71, 108–9
　and veridical equilibrium, 99–101, 319
　*See also* modality
preference
　bouletic, 192, 207; in English, 197–200
　emotions and, 273, 275
　for Ideal$_S$, 84–85
　as irrelevant, 30, 173, 189, 212, 315
　and rationality, 213–16
　for subjunctive, 312–15
projection, nonveridicality, 110n
PROMISE
　modal flexibility of, 32–33, 208–11
　performative vs. nonperformative, 208–11

questions, 53, 54, 86, 318–19
　embedded, 37
　subjunctive in, 24, 27–28, 37, 109, 125, 184
　*See also* equilibrium, nonveridical

ranking, modal, 80, 86–88. *See also* commitment
*realis*, and truth, 2, 5, 162, 163, 309

scope
　narrow, of an indefinite nominal, 26
　wide, of a specific interpretation, 26
sentences
　basic, 40–41
　embedded, 3, 7, 42–44, 58, 90
　*See also* assertion; clauses
settledness, epistemic, 61–62
Spanish, Yucatec, 30, 147, 189
stative verbs. *See under* verbs
stereotypicality, 79–80, 82–83, 85, 100, 169, 199, 238, 294
subjunctive
　bouletics always take, 194–97
　as dependent, 14
　in English, 10, 31
　evaluative, 159n, 277n
　with fear, 300, 304
　in French, 11–12, 35–36, 196–97, 204
　in Greek, 10–20, 22, 32–34, 35–39, 42, 44, 149–50, 170–71, 173, 175, 180, 199, 233–34; with ABLE, 230, 240–42;

# Index

with bouletic, 194–96; in
main/embedded clauses, 107–12
with negation, 24–25; in questions, 184;
in relative clauses, 25–27;
with implicatives, 260–71
in Italian, 11–12, 17–21, 28–30, 32, 34–37,
39, 147–48, 175, 177, 199, 290–91; with
bouletic, 195–96; with doxastic verbs,
165–66; with fear, 302, 305–6
interchangeable with indicative, 163–65,
218 (*see also* mood shift/flexibility)
with lower PAST, 128–31
in main clause, 13, 108–11, 145, 184
mixed (non)veridicality causes, 275–81
with modals, 16–22, 66–71, 105
with negation, 24–25, 170–71
with NONPAST, 116–17, 124–28, 141–44
with nonveridicality, 37, 43–46, 51, 66–71,
317
optional, 24–28
in Portuguese, 30–31
with possibility modal, 27–28, 31–32, 53,
66–71
in questions, 24, 27–28, 37, 109, 125, 184
in relative clauses, 25–26
suppositional belief and, 163–73
verbs that select, 16–22, 141–44, 163–72
*See also* indicative; licensing; modals;
mood; mood shift/mood flexibility;
verbs; WANT

tense
"future perfect," 115–16, 135–36
deictic/nondeictic, 128, 135
with HOPE verbs, 205–6
*imparfait/imperfetto*, 231, 245, 254
interaction with modality, 3, 18, 107–45,
205, 218–19; in Italian, 131–38
morphological, in Greek, 112–18
NONPAST, 18, 19, 118–28, 180–81, 219;
never occurs with indicative, 116–17
(*see also* future)
imperfective vs. perfective, 112–17, 230,
240
nonveridical, 117 (*see also* FUT; future;
subjunctive)
past, 10, 20, 113–14
PAST, 20, 56–57, 112–15, 117–18, 128–31,
135–36, 180–81, 196, 219, 225–26,
240–41

PERF, 122, 135
PRES, 38, 56–57, 89, 96, 112–13, 117, 131,
180–81, 232
present, 4–5, 37, 52–53, 56, 70, 112, 119,
126, 132, 139–40, 205, 215, 310, 316
present perfect, 130; actualistic, 251–52
PROG, 113, 123; as veridical, 264–67
relative, 119, 135, 136, 252
and utterance time, 81–81, 101, 107
veridical, 3, 4–5, 52, 117, 144–45
zero, 227–28, 240–43, 262, 271
*See also* FUT; future; indicative;
subjunctive; time
*that*-selecting attitudes, 197–98
*that* vs. *to* complements, 3, 21, 33, 192,
197–200, 212
time
perspectival, 138
of utterance, 69, 79–81, 100–101, 128,
201, 238, 243, 252, 284
*See also* tense
*to*-selecting attitudes, 197
truth, 66, 147, 209, 309
Aristotle's definition of, 1, 3–4
and commitment, 155
conditions of, 4–9, 42, 43, 62, 63, 70, 79,
80, 84, 96, 98, 248; for believe, 153;
for ABLE, 236, 243, 252–53; and
Boul, 191, 193; and *dox*, 155, 158,
171–72, 183, 189, 192
and emotives, 289; for FIND,
CONSIDER, 159; and knowledge,
151, 309; of MUST, 238; and
presupposition, 220
correspondence theory of, 4
and existence, 5
and objectivity, 40, 47, 52, 56, 188, 312
and veridicality, 3–9, 55, 58, 150, 185, 311
*See also* veridicality
truthfulness, 98, 104, 218, 311

uncertainty, epistemic, triggers subjunctive,
30, 173, 181–82, 188–89, 221
with SAY, 219
with SEEM, 177–78
*See also* nonveridicality; subjunctive
Universal Epistemic Modals (UEMs),
77–78. *See also* modals

verbs

assertive/of saying/asking, 16, 28, 33–35, 138, 140–41; negative, 34, 52, 63, 141, 219–20; vs. presuppositional, 311–12
awareness: Italian and Greek modality differs, 290–92; scale of, 290
belief, 139–40, 147–89; solipsistic, 17–18, 30, 147, 165–66, 168–70, 193, 222; suppositional, 30, 163–171, 222 (*see also* belief; mood)
of certainty, 138–41
consciousness, 138
of denial, 63, 141, 216, 218–20
directive, 142
doxastic, 138–40; flexible, 169–71, 173–83; "pure," 149–51; suppositional, 147–48, 163–73, 176–81; typology of, 171, *172*, 173; as veridical, 147–63
of effort, 142–44
emotive, 273–308; assertion and, 288–89, 294; flexible modality of, 271–84; license NPIs, 282–83; with negativity, 283–84; as nonveridical, 285–86, 287–88; of surprise/nonsurprise, 284 (*see also* verbs: of fear)
evidential, 76–78
factive, 35–37, 117; emotive/epistemic, 35–36, 138, 222, 28–83 (*see also* fact/factive)
of fear: categories of, 300–304; as doxastic, 301–2; and mood choice, 300–4, 306–8; as possibility, 302–4; presupposition of, *305*, 307
fictional/dream, 6–7, 16–18, 28–29, 39–40, 138–39, 160–62, 164
HOPE, 32–33, 204–8, 222
implicative, 142–44, 225–34, 260–70
indicative selecting, 169, 171–72; in Greek, 138–41, 148–63; in Greek and Italian, 16
KNOW: and indicative, 11–13, 16, 22, 36, 42, 118, 138–40, 164–65, 275, 282, 295, 309; and subjunctive, 37
memory, 37–39, 138, 156, 173–75, 295–98; in Italian, 16, 28–29
perception, 16, 37–39, 138, 178–81

permissives, 17, 108, 109, 125, 142, 226–27; *boro* as, 255–56
persuasion, 33, 211–16 (*see also* PERSUADE)
promise, 32–33 (*see also* PROMISE)
of regret, 16, 119; mood choice with, 138, 149, 274, 281–83; with *pu*, 13
reporting conversation, 34, 216–18
SAY, 216–19, 222, *223*
of semblance, 75, 175–78
stative, 93, 195, 226–27, 251; vs. eventive, 132–33, 195–96
subjunctive selecting, 16–22, 141–44, 163–72
volitional (bouletic), 16–18, 48, 142, 222, *223* (*see also* Boul; WANT)
*See also* attitudes, propositional; modals; subjunctive
veridicality, 309–12
defined, 4–5
and commitment, 51–55 (*see also* commitment)
and emotives, 281–84
and indicative, 2, 6, 31, 39–43, 63, 188
and knowledge, 309–12 (*see also under* fact/factive; verbs)
objective, 56–58, 61, 151–52, 282, 309, 312
stance of, 2, 310–12
state of, 22, 40–42, 52, 54–55, 60, 219, 311
subjective, 2–3, 7, 42–43, 150–54, 219, 293–94, 309; defined, 57–63, 150–51; and awareness, 291; and emotives, 277, 282, 288–89, 308
*See also* antiveridicality; nonveridicality

WANT, 194–204
new semantics for, 200–204
subjunctive with (Greek, French, Italian), 18, 196–97
vs. TRY, 266
*See also* attitudes, propositional; Boul
weakening, epistemic, 45, 51, 65, 72
worlds, Ideal, 96–97
MUST and, 79–81, 84–87, 105, 238–39
WANT and, 204

www.ingramcontent.com/pod-product-compliance
Lightning Source LLC
Chambersburg PA
CBHW051349290426
44108CB00015B/1937